Psychology Readings
for the Introductory Student

Edited by

Michael M. Knepp, Diana K. Riser
Michelle A. Patriquin and Robert S. Stephens

Virginia Polytechnic and State University

Custom Publishing

New York   Boston   San Francisco
London   Toronto   Sydney   Tokyo   Singapore   Madrid
Mexico City   Munich   Paris   Cape Town   Hong Kong   Montreal

Pearson
Custom Publishing
is a division of

www.pearsonhighered.com

ISBN 10: 0-558-20785-5
ISBN 13: 978-0-558-20785-4

Copyright Acknowledgments

Grateful acknowledgment is made to the following sources for permission to reprint material copyrighted or controlled by them:

"Research Methods," by Ryan C. Smith. Reprinted by permission of the author.

"Does Server Intervention Training Make a Difference?" by E. Scott Geller, Ph.D., Nason W. Russ, and William A. Delphos, reprinted from *Alcohol & Research World* 11, no. 4 (1987).

"Improving the Accuracy of Self-Reports of Adherence," by Jack W. Finney, Dana E. Putnam, and Christopher M. Boyd, reprinted from *Journal of Applied Behavior Analysis* 31.

"Responses of Infant Titi Monkeys, *Callicebus Moloch*, to Removal of One or Both Parents: Evidence for Paternal Attachment," by Kurt A. Hoffman et al., reprinted from *Developmental Psychobiology* 28, no. 7 (November 1995), John Wiley & Sons, Inc.

"Biological Bases of Behavior," by Lauren L. Golden. Reprinted by permission of the author.

"The Neuropsychology of Depression: A Literature Review and Preliminary Model," by Brian V. Shenal, David W. Harrison, and Heath A. Demaree, reprinted from *Neuropsychology Review* 13, no. 1 (2003), Springer Science+Business Media.

"Impairment of Social and Moral Behavior Related to Early Damage in Human Prefrontal Cortex," by Steven W. Anderson, et al., reprinted from *Nature – Neuroscience* 2, no. 11 (November 1999), Nature Publishing Group.

"Sensation and Perception," by Clinton S. Comer. Reprinted by permission of the author.

"Are We Led by the Nose?" by Terence Monmaney, reprinted from *Discover Syndication* (September 1987), by permission of the author.

"Re-acquisition of Upright Vision while Wearing Visually Left-Right Reversing Goggles," by Hirokazu Yoshimura, reprinted from *Japanese Psychological Research* 44, no. 4 (2002) Blackwell Publishing, Ltd. Copyright © by the Japanese Psychological Association.

"Development," by Conrad Baldner. Reprinted by permission of the author.

"Love in Infant Monkeys," by Harry F. Harlow, reprinted by permission from *Scientific American*, 1959.

"Slow Speech Enhances Younger, but Not Older, Infants' Perception of Vocal Emotion," by Robin Panneton, et al., reprinted from *Research in Human Development* 3, no. 1(2006), by permission of Taylor & Francis, Routledge & Garland Publishing.

"States of Consciousness and Sleep," by Michael Sewell. Reprinted by permission of the author.

"What Dreams Are Made Of," by Barbara Kantrowitz, et al., reprinted by permission from *Newsweek*.

"The Subconscious Mind: Your Unsung Hero," by Kate Douglas, reprinted from *New Scientist*, December 1, 2007.

"Cognition and Memory," by Zhe Wang and Qiong Wu. Reprinted by permission of the authors.

"Searching for Memory: The Brain, the Mind, and the Past," by Daniel L. Schacter, reprinted from *The Norton Psychology Reader*, edited by G. Marcus (2006, 1996), by permission of Perseus Books Group.

"Reconstructing Memory: The Incredible Eyewitness," by Elizabeth F. Lotus, reprinted from *Psychology Today*, December 1974, Sussex Publishers, Inc.

"Learning," by Laura Wilson. Reprinted by permission of the author.

"Evaluation of DRO Schedules to Reduce Disruptive Behavior in a Preschool Classroom," by Carole Conyers, et al., reprinted from *Child & Family Behavior Therapy* 25, no. 3 (2003), reprinted by permission of Haworth Press.

"How to Teach Animals," by B. F. Skinner, reprinted by permission from *Scientific American*, 1951.

"Motivation and Emotion," by Philip L. Klineburger. Reprinted by permission of the author.

"Models of Anger: Contributions from Psychophysiology, Neuropsychology and the Cognitive Behavioral Perspective," by David E. Cox and David W. Harrison, reprinted from *Brain Structure and Function* 212, no. 5 (February 2008), Springer Science+Business Media.

"Where Emotions Come From," by Erica E. Goode, Joannie M. Schrof, and Sarah Burke, reprinted by permission from *U.S. News & World Report*, June 24, 1991.

"Personality," by Nathaniel P. Van Kirk. Reprinted by permission of the author.

"Effortful Control, Surgency, and Reading Skills in Middle Childhood," by Kirby Deater-Deckard, et al., reprinted from *Journal of Reading and Writing* (2009), Springer Science+Business Media.

"Maslow's Puzzle: A Reconfiguration," by Joseph Germana, reprinted from *The Humanistic Psychologist* 35, no. 1 (2007), Erlbaum Taylor & Francis.

"Therapies and Treatment," by Neville Galloway-Williams. Reprinted by permission of the author.

"Social Skills Development in Children with Autism Spectrum Disorders: A Review of the Intervention Research," by Susan Williams White, Kathleen Keonig, and Lawrence Scahill, courtesy of *Journal of Autism & Developmental Disorders* 37 (December 29, 2006), Springer Science+Business Media.

"The Marijuana Check-up: Promoting Change in Ambivalent Marijuana Users," by Robert S. Stephens, et al., reprinted from *Addiction* 102, Blackwell Publishing, Ltd. Copyright © Society for the Study of Addiction.

"Abnormal Behavior," by Sarah Kelleher. Reprinted by permission of the author.

"Fear of the Beast: A Prospective Study on the Effects of Negative Information on Childhood Fear," by Peter Muris, et al., reprinted from *Behaviour Research and Therapy* 41 (2003), by permission of Elsevier Science Ltd.

"Ethnic and Sex Differences in Children's Depressive Symptoms: Mediating Effects of Perceived and Actual Competence," by Janet A. Kistner, Corinne F. David, and Bradley A. White, courtesy of *Journal of Clinical Child and Adolescent Psychology* 32, no. 3 (2003), Erlbaum Taylor & Francis.

"Stress, Health, and Coping," by Greg Longo. Reprinted by permission of the author.

"Hurricane Katrina: Experiences of Psychologists and Implications for Future Disaster Response," by Russell T. Jones, et al., reprinted from *Professional Psychology: Research and Practice* 39, no. 1 (2008), American Psychological Association.

"Forgiveness, Health, and Well-Being: A Review of Evidence for Emotional Versus Decisional Forgiveness, Dispositional Forgivingness, and Reduced Unforgivingness," by Everett L. Worthington, Jr., et al., reprinted from *Journal of Behavioral Medicine* 30 (2007), Springer Science+Business Media.

"Social Psychology," by Christopher O. Downing, Jr. Reprinted by permission of the author.

"Behavioral Study of Obedience," by Stanley Milgram, reprinted from *Journal of Abnormal & Social Psychology* 67, no. 4 (1963), American Psychological Association.

"Effects of Confederate and Subject Gender on Conformity in a Color Classification Task," by Charles A. Collin, Fred Di Sano, and Rajesh Malik, reprinted by permission from *Social Behavior and Personality* 22, no. 4 (1994). Copyright © by the Society for Personality Research, Inc.

"Applied Psychology," by Mark D. Scott. Reprinted by permission of the author.

"Social Influence Principles: Fueling Participation in Occupational Safety," by E. Scott Geller, reprinted from *Professional Safety* 47 (2002).

"Pygmalion Goes to Boot Camp: Expectancy, Leadership, and Trainee Performance," by Dov Eden and Abraham B. Shani, reprinted from *Journal of Applied Psychology* 67, no. 2 (1982), American Psychological Association.

Contents

SECTION 1   Research Methods 1

Article 1   Does Server Intervention Training Make a Difference   7

E. Scott Geller, Nason W. Russ, and William A. Delphos

Discussion Questions   17

Article 2   Improving the Accuracy of Self-Reports of Adherence   19

Jack W Finney, Dana E. Putnam, and Christopher M. Boyd

Discussion Questions   23

Article 3   Responses of Infant Titi Monkeys, *Callicebus Moloch*, to Removal of One or Both Parents: Evidence for Paternal Attachment   25

Kurt A. Hoffman, Sally P. Mendoza, Michael B. Hennessy, and William A. Mason

Discussion Questions   35

SECTION 2   Biological Bases of Behavior   37

Article 1   The Neuropsychology of Depression: A Literature Review and Preliminary Model   43

Brian V. Shenal, David W. Harrison, and Heath A. Demaree

Discussion Questions   57

Article 2   Impairment of Social and Moral Behavior Related to Early Damage in Human Prefrontal Cortex   59

Steven W. Anderson, Antoine Bechara, Hanna Damasio, Daniel Tranel and Antonio R. Damasio

Discussion Questions   73

SECTION 3   Sensation and Perception   75

Article 1   Are We Led by the Nose?   81

Terence Monmaney

Discussion Questions   91

Article 2   Re-acquisition of Upright Vision while Wearing Visually Left-Right Reversing Goggles   93

Hirokazu Yoshimura

Discussion Questions   101

SECTION 4   Development   103

Article 1   Love in Infant Monkeys   107

Harry F. Harlow

Discussion Questions   119

Article 2   Slow Speech Enhances Younger, but Not Older, Infants' Perception of Vocal Emotion   121

Robin Panneton, Christine Kitamura, Karen Mattock, and Denis Burnham

Discussion Questions   133

SECTION 5   States of Consciousness and Sleep   135

Article 1   What Dreams Are Made Of   141

Barbara Kantrowitz and Karen Springen with Pat Wingert and Josh Ulick

Discussion Questions   151

Article 2   The Subconscious Mind: Your Unsung Hero   153

Kate Douglas

Discussion Questions   159

SECTION 6   Cognition and Memory   161

Article 1   From *Searching for Memory: The Brain, the Mind, and the Past*   165

Daniel L. Schacter

Discussion Questions   175

Article 2   Reconstructing Memory: The Incredible Eyewitness   177

Elizabeth F. Loftus

Discussion Questions   183

SECTION 7   Learning   185

Article 1   Evaluation of DRO Schedules to Reduce Disruptive Behavior in a Preschool Classroom   191

Carole Conyers, Raymond Miltenberger, Cathryn Romaniuk, Brandon Kopp, and Michael Himle

Discussion Questions   197

Article 2   How to Teach Animals   199

B. F. Skinner

Discussion Questions   207

SECTION 8   Motivation and Emotion   209

Article 1   Models of Anger: Contributions from Psychophysiology, Neuropsychology, and the Cognitive Behavioral Perspective   215

David E. Cox and David W. Harrison

Discussion Questions   243

Article 2   Where Emotions Come From   245

Erica E. Goode with Joannie M. Schrof and Sarah Burke

Discussion Questions   257

Section 9   Personality   259

Article 1   Effortful Control, Surgency, and Reading Skills in Middle Childhood   263
Kirby Deater-Deckard, Paula Y. Mullineaux, Stephen A. Petrill, and Lee A. Thompson

Discussion Questions   275

Article 2   Maslow's Puzzle: A Reconfiguration   277
Joseph Germana

Discussion Questions   283

SECTION 10   Therapies and Treatment   285

Article 1   Social Skills Development in Children with Autism Spectrum Disorders: A Review of the Intervention Research   289
Susan Williams White, Kathleen Keonig, and Lawrence Scahill

Discussion Questions   309

Article 2   The Marijuana Check-up: Promoting Change in Ambivalent Marijuana Users   311
Robert S. Stephens, Roger A. Roffman, Stephanie A. Fearer, Carl Williams, and Randy S. Burke

Discussion Questions   331

SECTION 11   Abnormal Behavior   333

Article 1   Fear of the Beast: A Prospective Study on the Effects of Negative Information on Childhood Fear   339
Peter Muris, Denise Bodden, Harald Merckelbach, Thomas H. Ollendick, and Neville King

Discussion Questions   357

Article 2   Ethnic and Sex Differences in Children's Depressive Symptoms: Mediating Effects of Perceived and Actual Competence   359
Janet A. Kistner, Corinne F. David, and Bradley A. White

Discussion Questions   379

SECTION 12   Stress, Health, and Coping   381

Article 1   Hurricane Katrina: Experiences of Psychologists and Implications for Future Disaster Response   385

Russell T. Jones, Christopher S. Immel, Rachel M. Moore, and James M. Hadder

Discussion Questions   401

Article 2   Forgiveness, Health, and Well-Being: A Review of Evidence for Emotional Versus Decisional Forgiveness, Dispositional Forgivingness, and Reduced Unforgiveness   403

Everett L. Worthington Jr, Charlotte Van Oyen Witvliet, Pietro Pietrini, and Andrea J. Miller

Discussion Questions   427

SECTION 13   Social Psychology   429

Article 1   Behavioral Study of Obedience   435

Stanley Milgram

Discussion Questions   449

Article 2   Effects of Confederate and Subject Gender on Conformity in a Color Classification Task   451

Charles A. Collin, Fred Di Sano, and Rajesh Malik

Discussion Questions   461

SECTION 14   Applied Psychology   463

Article 1   Social Influence Principles: Fueling Participation in Occupational Safety   467

E. Scott Geller

Discussion Questions   481

Article 2   Pygmalion Goes to Boot Camp: Expectancy, Leadership, and Trainee Performance   483

Dov Eden and Abraham B. Shani

Discussion Questions   493

Section 1
Research Methods

W e are constantly formulating theories about why our friends would act like they did in a given situation, attempting to understand the complexities of our relationship with a significant other, and making an effort to figure out our own thoughts, feelings, and behaviors. In many ways, daily life dictates that we create and act upon our theories about everyone. These conceptions about people often direct our friendships, shape our conversations, and affect the overall behaviors we show different individuals across different situations. Whether or not we are conscious of these conceptions, it is these conceptions that provide us shortcuts and cues for acting in a social context (i.e., act as heuristics). Thus, each of us becomes lay psychologists from a young age. So what then distinguishes psychologists from the rest of the population? The answer lies in the use of scientific investigation and empirical analysis.

Psychology has often been criticized by those outside of the discipline as a "soft" science, nothing more than plain common sense. Pop psychologists dominate bookshelves and television talk shows contributing to the public's misconceptions about the scientific nature of psychology. They often spread ideas that are little more than repackaged old wives tales and glittering generalities about human behavior. Neither these "pop-culture" attempts at psychological dissemination nor our everyday musings about human behavior are entirely useless. In fact, these thoughts and ideas can serve as testable hypotheses that can be confirmed or rejected based on scientific investigation. As you become more familiar with psychology, and the articles in this reader, the difference between legitimate psychological research and pure speculation will become much clearer.

One of the first things you will notice as you are exposed to the science of psychology is that asking questions and formulating theories is not sufficient. Psychology, instead, relies on systematic empiricism. At the root of the term, systematic empiricism means that psychologists rely on observation. The days of pure rationalism and "armchair" psychologists have largely passed where individuals would sit at their desks and only formulate theories about human behavior. Psychology as a science relies on observing human behaviors and collecting data. This data can either be collected by experimentation, where variables are directly manipulated under a controlled setting by the researcher, or through descriptive or correlation research, where the experimenter merely observes a phenomenon without manipulating variables. The collected data is then assessed, often through various statistical procedures, to see whether or not it supports the researcher's theories or hypotheses.

Data collection, and research in general, is highly systematic. While there is value in simple observation, greater gains in knowledge are experienced when research is collected under a set method of operations called research methods, or the scientific method. Not only is the design of this initial research methodology systematic, but also the replication, peer-review, and dissemination of this research are methodical. Through empiricism, the pure speculations that form the basis of many of life's decisions can give way to informed scientific principles of understanding. While the complexity of the human condition makes psychology a challenging discipline, it the scientific approach to psychology that allows us to sort through this complexity and formulate meaningful theories about human behavior.

Article 1: Does Server Intervention Training Make a Difference?

The significant loss and devastation attributable to Driving Under the Influence of alcohol (DUI) has created a need for intervention programs that tackle the problem of alcohol-impaired driving. In this article, Dr. E. Scott Geller studied the efficacy of one such program, "Training for Intervention Procedures by Servers of Alcohol" (TIPS). This program trains alcohol servers on how to effectively intervene with patrons before they reach problematic levels of alcohol consumption. Not only were TIPS trained servers more likely to intervene with the study's pseudopatrons consuming alcohol than untrained servers, but also the pseudopatrons served by TIPS trained servers consumed significantly less alcohol than those served by untrained servers. This research is of particular interest to Virginia Tech students as it was conducted at bars in Blacksburg.

Article 2: Improving the Accuracy of Self-Reports of Adherence

The goal of psychological research is to provide accurate explanations of human behavior. However, the results from a research study can only be as accurate as the data used to draw the conclusions. In an ideal research setting, the researcher collects data by carefully and objectively observing the behaviors of study participants. The nature of the certain types of research often makes such direct observation of participants unfeasible. In these situations, researchers must rely on the self-reports of participants as their source of data. The use of self-report measures has been highly contested in the field of Psychology due to questions about the accuracy of these measures. In this article, Dr. Jack Finney and colleagues seek to better understand the accuracy of self-report measures and potential methodological designs that can maximize the accuracy of self-reports.

Article 3: Responses of Infant Titi Monkeys, *Callicebus Moloch*, to Removal of One or Both Parents: Evidence for Paternal Attachment

Psychologists sometimes use animals instead of humans as research subjects. For ethical, developmental, and various other reasons it is often advantageous to study the behaviors of animals and generalize these observations to theories of human behavior. In this article by Dr. Kurt Hoffman and colleagues, parental separation was studied in titi monkeys. Behavioral observation, blood sampling, and endocrine measures were used to show distinct differences between infant titi monkey's attachment to their mother who nourishes the infant versus father who transports them around. The infant titi monkeys had more adverse negative reactions to separation from their father versus their mother. The infants also maintained overall greater rates of contact with their father. The research demonstrated that the primary attachment figure for titi monkey infants is their father. These findings support attachment related to comfort rather than nourishment.

—*Ryan C. Smith*

Does Server Intervention Training Make a Difference?

An Empirical Field Evaluation

E. Scott Geller
Nason W. Russ
William A. Delphos

Server training as a theoretical and legislative potential for preventing intoxication and impaired driving was examined at length in the Summer 1986 issue of *Alcohol Health & Research World* (Mosher and Colman; Saltz; Vegega; Peters). An evaluation of effectiveness of such training is crucial. So many of the activities in countering impaired driving are based on understandable emotion and a reliance on the purported deterrent effects of punishment. But the truth is that, even with stricter penalties and increased enforcement, alcohol-impaired driving continues as a destructive force in American society. Indeed, 1 million arrests each year in the United States for Driving Under the Influence of alcohol (DUI) have not lowered appreciably the involvement of heavy alcohol use in fatal crashes or those producing injury or property damage (Fell 1983).

An unwillingness by intoxicated people to change their driving plans is consistent with the impairment of judgment expected with heavy alcohol use. It is best, therefore, to intervene with a driver before judgment is seriously impaired. Furthermore, it is optimal to intervene for behavior change at the time when the change is most immediately relevant. Just as point-of-purchase advertising is the most influential marketing strategy, the best time to influence socially responsible drinking is at the place where alcoholic beverages are sold. Server intervention, a prevention strategy that meets this criterion, contrasts with standard educational and awareness messages, which are delivered to a person when sober but have little influence on the behavior of that person when intoxicated.

Although server intervention training has intuitive appeal, its effectiveness must be the ultimate criterion for large-scale application. To that end, two of the authors of this article evaluated the effectiveness of a program entitled "Training for Intervention Procedures by Servers of Alcohol" (TIPS). This program was developed by Morris E. Chafetz, the founding director of the National Institute on Alcohol Abuse and Alcoholism and a member of the Presidential Commission on Drunk Driving. TIPS contains the critical elements for successful server intervention training identified by Mosher (1986) and is representative of server intervention programs in general (see Vegega 1986). The research assessed the potential of server intervention programs such as TIPS to decrease DUI by comparing trained servers with untrained servers in regard to (1) the exit blood alcohol concentration (BAC) levels of their patrons and (2) the amount of gratuities received. A recent report by the National Restaurant Association (Adelman 1985) revealed that the amounts of money restaurant customers leave as gratuities depend on their satisfaction with the service received. Since server intervention requires that servers pay closer attention to their patrons, increased gratuities may result. This, in turn, may influence the servers' motivation to apply their intervention skills.

The TIPS Program and the Study Design

During intervention training in TIPS, servers are given information on the physiological effects of alcohol that can help them identify specific warning signs indicating when a customer is about to overindulge. Next, servers are taught a variety of tactics for dealing with intoxicated customers or those who appear to be approaching their limits. For example, servers learn how to slow a customer's alcohol consumption by delaying drink service, offering food, or serving nonalcoholic beverages. Video vignettes are shown to help servers evaluate customers' behaviors and effective server interventions. Servers also participate in role-play situations that enable them to practice what they have learned and receive feedback regarding their knowledge, skills, and abilities in intervention techniques.

Throughout the training, servers are encouraged to share with the group personal experiences that will make the material more meaningful. At the conclusion of the TIPS training session all servers must answer correctly at least 28 questions on a 40-question written test (i.e., a score of 70 percent) in order to become certified servers.

The server intervention evaluation obtained direct measures of patrons' BAC levels and server gratuities both before and after servers received training in the TIPS program. Seventeen servers of alcohol and 32 research assistants, the latter posing as bar patrons ("pseudopatrons"), participated in the study. The study was conducted during 11 consecutive weeks in 2 bars in a rural university town. The TIPS-trained servers represented 50 percent of the serving staff in each bar.

Throughout the study, the pseudopatrons attempted to drink three alcoholic beverages per hour for 2 hours, an amount sufficient to exceed their legal limit of intoxication—a BAC level of .10 percent in a person weighing 170 pounds or less. The pseudopatrons did not know whether their server had been trained. In the event of server intervention (e.g., verbalizing "slow down" or "eat some food"), the pseudopatrons were instructed to react in their "normal" manner (e.g., "eat only if you are hungry"). Thus, while pseudopatrons entered the bar planning to consume approximately 1 drink every 20 minutes, there existed the possibility that server-intervention strategies would influence the rate at which alcohol actually was consumed.

One objective of the study was to investigate the techniques used by trained servers that resulted in lower BAC's. After all the pseudopatron data was collected, research assistants listened to tapes recorded during server-patron interaction. To analyze a tape, the research assistants tallied signs of alcohol impairment, or "intoxication cues," exhibited by the pseudopatrons. These cues included giggling, excessive loudness, loss of train of thought, and slurred speech. The assistants also categorized active server interventions (e.g., checking driver licenses for age information, offering food, asking who was driving) and more passive interventions (e.g., delaying the serving of a drink, delivering food and drink together instead of serving only an alcoholic beverage). In nine episodes (five during baseline and four during the post-training period), poor sound quality made it impossible for research assistants to score the tape accurately; in these cases, the pseudopatrons scored their own tapes. On the remaining 40 tapes, 2 research assistants independently scored the tapes. The 2 scoring efforts by the research assistants achieved virtually identical results; in survey analysis terms, "intercoder reliability" was 99.5 percent that a particular sign of intoxication appeared during a pseudopatron episode and 98.5 percent that a specific type of intervention was practiced by the server during the episode.

Did Training Result in More Frequent Interventions?

One basic question on the effectiveness of TIPS training was its application to the real world of beverage service: After receiving training, did servers apply the lesson of TIPS to their work by intervening more frequently when patrons ordered an increasing number of drinks? The experience of the pseudopatrons indicates

FIGURE 1   Interventions per number of consecutive drinks.

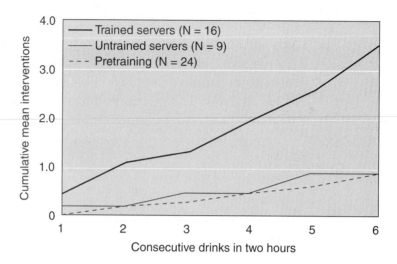

that this was indeed the case in both bars. Figure 1 compares the cumulative mean interventions per drinks consumed for trained servers, the same servers prior to training, and a control group of untrained servers. The figure clearly illustrates that trained servers, on average, attempted a greater frequency of intervention than servers without TIPS training. In statistical terms, the differences are highly significant (p less than .02 for the first drink; all remaining p's less than .007).

The specific types of server interventions typically implemented by each group of servers were quantified, as shown in Table 1. The earliest interventions by trained servers took the form of checking driver licenses and offering food or water. Interventions by trained servers at the fourth, fifth, and sixth drinks consisted largely of continuing to offer food or water, delaying service, and making driving-related comments (e.g., asking who was driving or suggesting that a nondrinking partner drive carefully). Untrained servers demonstrated no pattern in their far less frequent interventions; the incidence of driving-related comments made by servers during the baseline period prior to TIPS training probably reflects their awareness of a police DUI enforcement roadblock operation that was in effect only during the baseline period.

Does Server Intervention Affect Apparent Intoxication?

Figure 2 presents a cumulative record of cues of intoxication during pseudopatron episodes, compared with the number of drinks consumed by the pseudopatrons. Use of the statistical technique known as analysis of variance revealed that differences between the number of intoxication cues displayed by pseudopatrons

TABLE 1   Type and frequency of server interventions for each group by drink.

Intervention	Baseline	Untrained	Trained
Drink #1			
Checked ID	2	1	5
Offered food or water	1	1	3
Delayed service	0	0	2
Explained a house policy	0	0	1
Drink #2			
Checked ID	0	0	1
Offered food or water	0	0	2
Delayed service	0	0	2
Commented on quantity/speed of consumption	1	0	1
Made driving-related comment	1	0	0
Drink #3			
Offered food or water	1	0	1
Delayed service	0	1	1
Commented on quantity/speed of consumption	1	1	1
Drink #4			
Offered food or water	0	0	4
Delayed service	1	0	4
Made driving-related comment	0	0	3
Explained a house policy	1	0	0
Drink #5			
Offered food or water	0	0	4
Delayed service	1	1	1
Commented on quantity/speed of consumption	1	0	2
Made driving-related comment	3	2	4
Drink #6			
Offered food or water	0	0	4
Delayed service	1	0	0
Commented on quantity/speed of consumption	0	0	2
Explained a house policy	0	0	1
Made driving-related comment	3	0	5
Put less alcohol in drink	0	0	1

FIGURE 2   Pseudopatron
intoxication cues per drink.

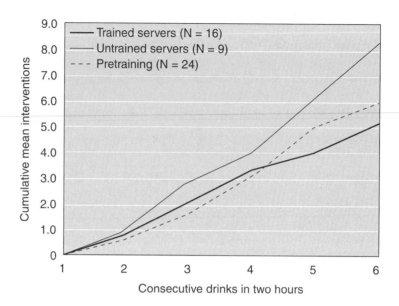

served by untrained servers, servers who would later receive training, and servers who had completed TIPS training failed to achieve statistical significance. On the other hand, the figure shows that, on average, the pseudopatrons of untrained servers displayed more signs of intoxication after the third drink than did pseudopatrons of trained servers. For example, when the sixth drink had been served, the tapes showed that pseudopatrons of untrained servers had already displayed, on average, at least eight intoxication cues; in contrast, pseudopatrons of TIPS trainees had displayed, on average, only five cues.

Does Server Intervention Reduce Blood Alcohol Level?

Prior to TIPS training, 37.5 percent of the pseudopatrons left the bars legally drunk; the remainder left with blood alcohol concentrations in the range of .05 to .099. The average pretraining BAC level of pseudopatrons was 0.096. In contrast, no pseudopatrons served by a TIPS-trained server reached the legal level of intoxication. Slightly over half reached a BAC level of .05. The average BAC of pseudopatrons served by TIPS-certified servers was .059, within the BAC range of reasonable alcohol use.

Because only half of the servers in both bars participated in the training, a number of the pseudopatrons were served in the posttraining phase by servers who were not trained in TIPS. Thus, it was possible to compare the exit BAC levels of pseu-

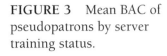

FIGURE 3 Mean BAC of pseudopatrons by server training status.

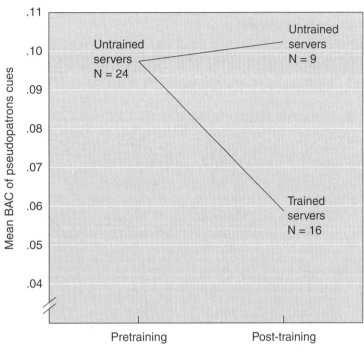

dopatrons who had been served by TIPS-trained and untrained servers after the training period. There were no significant differences between the pretraining exit BAC levels of pseudopatrons and the BAC levels of those served by untrained servers in the posttraining phase. However, the BAC levels of pseudopatrons served by TIPS graduates were significantly lower (p less than .01) than those obtained among pseudopatrons prior to training or served by untrained servers in the posttraining phase. These results are depicted in Figure 3.

Did TIPS Affect Servers' Tips?

Because of the desire for anonymity in the reporting of server gratuities, the results of this analysis were hampered by difficulty in separating trained from untrained servers. In addition, despite the precautions taken to dissociate server names from their gratuity reports, many servers were reluctant to reveal gratuity information.

Analyses conducted on the available data compared the average gratuity reported before and after training in each bar. Because of extreme variation in the size of gratuities observed throughout the study, the differences observed at each bar were not statistically significant. However, there was an increase in the mean dollar

FIGURE 4   Mean server gratuity by training status and bar.

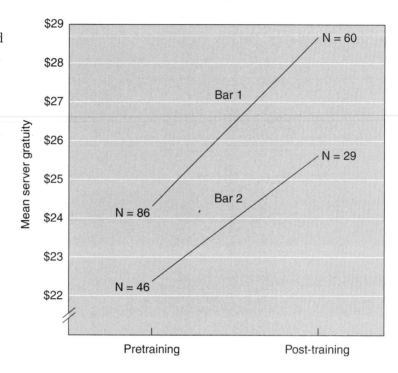

amount of reported gratuities at both locations following the TIPS training. At Bar 1, the average amount increased from a mean of $24.48 per report before training to $28.75; a 14 percent increase. Servers at Bar 2 reported a 12 percent increase in gratuities, from an average of $22.57 before training to $25.62 after training. These results are shown in Figure 4.

Implications of the Evaluation

The evaluation study provided at least preliminary empirical evidence of a beneficial impact of server intervention training. The results showed that pseudopatrons of TIPS-trained servers had significantly lower BAC levels compared with BAC levels of those served by untrained personnel. Moreover, the evaluation indicated that, during the study period, effective server intervention was reflected in the behavior of TIPS-trained personnel on the job.

Despite this apparent success, the researchers advise caution in generalizing to other situations and have suggestions for future evaluation research on server intervention techniques. For example, in this study all servers were initially informed that management had agreed to the study and that they might be serving a pseudopatron. Thus, the willingness of each bar owner to sponsor the training could have motivated the servers to intervene. Focus group study before the development of the TIPS program revealed that servers were reluctant to cut patrons off because they believed that to do so was contrary to management goals. Skills-training programs such as TIPS unite management and servers in achieving a common goal: preventing alcohol abuse. Despite this, the level of server intervention was negligible during the pretraining phase of the study. Likewise, during the post-training phase, untrained servers allowed almost half their pseudopatrons to reach the legal limit of intoxication. This suggests the remarkable DUI-prevention potential of server intervention training.

The application of these pseudopatron results to the general population of "real" patrons must be investigated. While the pseudopatrons were not identified as study participants by the servers, the pseudopatrons may have behaved differently from real patrons (Russ and Geller, in press). Since pseudopatrons were more aware of server intervention than a naive patron, inadvertent positive reaction by pseudopatrons may have encouraged the servers' intervention efforts. In addition, the striking impact of server intervention on reducing patron BAC's may be less dramatic when applied on a larger scale. That is, changes in BAC's may be obscured in a real patron sample as BAC variance increases due to individual differences in alcohol tolerance and rates of alcohol metabolism.

Further investigation should focus on the long-term maintenance of server intervention behaviors. Many of the TIPS-trained servers were university students who moved out of the area soon after the study ended. The current means used by TIPS to address the maintenance concern is to certify servers for 3 years. After this period, a trained server must retake the entire course.

This may not be sufficient to ensure continued use of server intervention skills, however. Servers probably will not practice server intervention unless management and peers support such behavior. Further investigation is needed to define management policies and environmental conditions for motivating long-term use of server intervention skills. The potential for increased gratuities that was suggested by this initial evaluation also may serve as a natural reinforcer for the maintenance of server intervention behaviors and policy.

The results of this study have important implications for large-scale approaches to combat the problem of alcohol-impaired driving. Since server intervention can be tailored to each drinker, it may be more influential than public service announcements directed at larger segments of the population. Also, since server intervention is concerned with drinking immediately preceding a potential DUI situation, such behavior change attempts will be more effective than the standard education and awareness approaches that attempt to modify intentions to behave long before an opportunity to respond is available. Moreover, the cues and events that occur during the drinking situation may negate any beneficial effects of sober driving messages presented outside the drinking situation.

The complexity of skilled server intervention and the emotional nature of the drunk driving issue require strong emphasis on quality control. It is hoped that the evaluation study described here was only the beginning of a series of field investigations relevant to developing an empirical understanding of environmental factors, management policy, serving behaviors, and training practices that reduce the incidence of driving under the influence of alcohol.

References

Full bibliographic references available from your instructor.

Editor's Note

A more technical description of this study is provided in Russ and Geller's "Training Bar Personnel to Prevent Drunken Driving: A Field Evaluation," American Journal of Public Health, *in press.*

E. Scott Geller, Ph.D., is professor of psychology at Virginia Polytechnic Institute and State University.

Nason W. Russ is a Ph.D. candidate at Virginia Polytechnic Institute and State University.

William A. Delphos is past president of Health Communications, Inc., which markets the TIPS program.

Discussion Questions for Article 1

Section 1: Research Methods

Name: _____

PID: _____

Date: __ __ / __ __ / __ __ (MM/DD/YY)

CRN: _____

Recitation Day/Time: _____

Honor Code Signature: _____

1. What are the benefits to intervening on alcohol consumption at the places where alcohol is sold?

2. What are some of the components of the "TIPS" training given to servers?

3. Was the intervention effective? Explain.

4. Discuss possible problems that may arise when implementing this training with bartenders.

Improving the Accuracy of Self-Reports of Adherence

Jack W Finney
Dana E. Putnam
Christopher M. Boyd

Behavioral scientists who study socially important but difficult-to-measure behaviors often rely on self-reports. We evaluated the influence of three experimenter demands—demand for adherence, demand for accurate reports, and demand for accurate reports combined with a prompted recall strategy—on the accuracy of self-reports of adherence to a week-long prescribed regimen of twice-daily telephone calls. Self-reports of adherence were significantly more accurate in the accuracy demand/prompted recall group (p < .05). The analogue study should be replicated with other regimens and populations to determine the most effective strategies for enhancing the accuracy of self-reports.

DESCRIPTORS: adherence, self-reports, measurement, medical regimens

Self-reports of behavior have generated controversy in behavioral research. This controversy has been perpetuated by limited knowledge about how to influence the accuracy of self-reports. For many behaviors of interest to researchers, however, a self-report may be the only possible (e.g., private events) or pragmatic (e.g., sexual behavior) measure available. A self-report is verbal behavior and therefore is subject to stimulus control, reinforcement, punishment, and other contextual influences on behavior (Critchfield, Tucker, & Vuchinich, 1998). Given the importance of addressing socially relevant but difficult-to-measure behaviors, studies of verbal self-reports and strategies for enhancing their accuracy are needed. One area of scientific inquiry that has relied heavily on self-reports of behavior is adherence to prescribed regimens (La Greca & Schuman, 1995), and several studies have shown that patients overreport their medical adherence. However, conditions that influence the accuracy of self-reports of adherence need further study (Babor, Stephens, & Marlatt, 1987). For example, experimenter demand characteristics (e.g., social desirability) are presumed to serve stimulus control functions or alter establishing operations in adherence interviews. We evaluated the influence of three experimenter demands—demand for adherence, demand for accurate reports, and demand for accurate reports combined with a prompted recall strategy—on the accuracy of self-reports of adherence to a week-long prescribed regimen of twice-daily telephone calls.

Method

Participants were 45 undergraduate students (freshmen and sophomores) at a large university who received extra-credit points for an introductory psychology class. They attended a group enrollment session and completed the informed consent form. The experimenter informed participants that the study was about how cognitions influence behavior and, more specifically, whether students' urges to miss class influenced subsequent class attendance. A telephone call regimen was "prescribed" that involved each participant making two telephone calls daily. For the morning call, the participant was to leave a phone message with the participant's code number and a self-report about urge to miss class (on weekdays) or urge to not study (on weekends). For the evening call, the message was to include whether the participant attended classes that day (on weekdays) and whether the participant studied (on weekends). An individual follow-up appointment was scheduled for the 8th day of the regimen. Participants were encouraged to return for the follow-up because reliable and valid results depended on full participation.

Participants were randomly assigned to one of three groups. At the follow-up, each participant met individually with an experimenter. All individuals received much of the same information and instructions, including that (a) a few brief questionnaires would be completed shortly; (b) the phone mail system had malfunctioned and that messages were apparently taped, but were not retrievable; (c) the experimenters therefore had no records of telephone calls and urges and classes missed and attended; and (d) the study information needed to be reported by the participant at this appointment. According to experimental group, the following additional instructions were given by the experimenters, who followed written scripts for each condition.

For the adherence demand group, the experimenter informed each participant that it was important that as many telephone calls as possible had been made and that the study depended on his or her having made the phone calls. For the accuracy demand group, the experimenter informed each participant that while it was obviously important that the participant made the telephone calls during the past 7 days, it was even more important that an accurate self-report be given and that the study's results depended on accurate self-reports. For the accuracy demand/prompted recall group, the experimenter provided the same information as described for the accuracy demand group. In addition, the experimenter helped participants in this group to report more accurately by reviewing events that took place each day of the regimen. The participant was asked to describe his or her telephone adherence in the context of those events. The general procedure was one of improving the accuracy of daily self-report by having the individual recall events that made that day's performance salient.

After questionnaires had been completed, each participant was debriefed about the purposes of the study and informed that the phone mail system had, in fact, worked properly. All subjects' questions about the study were answered. Only 3 participants reported that they suspected that the study was about whether they made the phone calls; none reported that they suspected that the study was about whether they would report accurately about their phone calls.

Two measures were used in the analyses. The number of telephone calls made was determined by listening to messages on phone mail and recording data by the participant's study code number. Two observers retrieved messages simultaneously but independently for 3 days; there was 100% agreement on recorded messages. Self-reports of the number of calls made and missed for the past week were recorded at the individual follow-up sessions.

Results and Discussion

Table 1 shows that all groups on average overreported adherence. The adherence demand group reported they had made 123% of the calls they had actually made; 69% of participants in this group overreported adherence. The accuracy demand group reported they had made 112% of calls made; 53% overreported. The accuracy demand/prompted recall group reported that they had made 107% of their calls; 40% overreported. A Kruskal-Wallis multiple comparison test indicated a significant difference among the groups ($p < .05$). Mann-Whitney U tests showed that accuracy was reliably different between the adherence demand and accuracy demand/prompted recall groups ($p < .05$). Adherence to the telephone-call regimen (i.e., the number of calls made) was not significantly different across the three groups.

Demand characteristics and the prompted recall strategy influenced the accuracy of self-reports of adherence to a prescribed regimen. Although the accuracy demand/prompted recall group had the most accurate average self-report and the largest number of participants reporting accurately, some subjects in each group overreported adherence. Overreporting could be attributable to both experimenter demands and recall errors.

The results of this analogue study, although encouraging, are limited by the small sample size. Systematic replications will provide further knowledge about the use of self-reports for research on adherence and other behaviors that are often measured with self-report methods. Studies of other regimens, participants with

TABLE 1   Self-reported and objective adherence for experimental groups.

	Reported/made = %[a]		
Subject	Adherence demand[b]	Accuracy demand	Accuracy demand/ prompted recall
1	9/5 = 180	11/7 = 157	10/7 = 143
2	9/6 = 150	12/8 = 150	11/8 = 138
3	9/6 = 150	13/11 = 118	10/9 = 111
4	12/9 = 133	8/7 = 114	14/13 = 108
5	10/8 = 125	9/8 = 113	14/13 = 108
6	10/8 = 125	9/8 = 113	14/13 = 108
7	12/10 = 120	13/12 = 108	14/14 = 100
8	12/10 = 120	13/12 = 108	14/14 = 100
9	12/11 = 109	14/14 = 100	13/13 = 100
10	13/13 = 100	14/14 = 100	12/12 = 100
11	12/12 = 100	13/13 = 100	12/12 = 100
12	11/11 = 100	12112 = 100	10/10 = 100
13	12/13 = 92	11/11 = 100	9/9 = 100
14		10/10 = 100	9/9 = 100
15		12/13 = 92	9/9 = 100
Group average	123*	112	107

[a]*Reported* refers to the number of telephone calls that participants reported they had made. *Made* refers to the number of telephone calls that had been made. Percentages greater than 100% indicate overreporting; percentages less than 100% indicate underreporting.

[b]Two subjects in the adherence demand group did not return for the follow-up visit.

*Adherence demand > accuracy demand/prompted recall. $p < .05$.

varying characteristics (e.g., age, educational level, illnesses), and other strategies that influence the accuracy of self-reports (Babor et al., 1987; Critchfield et al., 1998) are needed to improve behavioral scientists' ability to study a range of socially important but difficult-to-measure behaviors.

References

Full bibliographic references available from your instructor.

Editor's Note

Michael Priester, Billy Meyers, and Kirsten Bradbury provided helpful assistance, and Thomas Critchfield provided constructive comments.

Correspondence and requests for the study scripts should be addressed to Jack W. Finney, Department of Psychology, Virginia Polytechnic Institute and State University, Blacksburg, Virginia 24061-0436 (E-mail: finney@vt.edu).

Discussion Questions for Article 2

Section 1: Research Methods

Name: _____

PID: _____

Date: __ __ / __ __ / __ __ (MM/DD/YY)

CRN: _____

Recitation Day/Time: _____

Honor Code Signature: _____

1. Based on these results, do you think self-reports are a legitimate means of collecting scientific data? Explain.

2. In your own words, explain what is meant by the participant's accuracy in this experiment. How did the authors test for this accuracy?

3. Why do you think that participants in all groups overreported their adherence?

4. List some of the practical implications of this study. Does this experiment help to promote the use of self-reports? Why or why not?

Article 3

Responses of Infant Titi Monkeys, *Callicebus Moloch*, to Removal of One or Both Parents: Evidence for Paternal Attachment

Kurt A. Hoffman
Sally P. Mendoza
Michael B. Hennessy
William A. Mason

The response to parental separation in infant titi monkeys was evaluated. Separation from the mother for 1 hr did not elicit an adrenocortical response from the infant unless the father was also removed. Separation from the father elicited a significant elevation in adrenocortical activity even when the mother remained with the infant during the separation period. Infants showed the highest cortisol levels and vocalization rates when both parents were removed and the infant remained alone in the living cage for 1 hr. As in previous research, infants maintained higher levels of contact with the father than with the mother. The results indicate that in this monogamous New World primate, the father is the primary attachment figure for the developing infant.

The long period of infant dependency characteristic of mammals is often associated with the development of a filial bond or emotional attachment with the mother.

Such a bond is manifested in the infant's selective preference for its mother, display of agitation or distress upon maternal separation, and the ability of the mother to attenuate the infant's response to potentially stressful circumstances (Ainsworth, 1972; Bowlby, 1973). For most primate species, the filial bond is reciprocated by an intense attachment of mother to infant (e.g., Mendoza, Coe, Smotherman, Kaplan, & Levine, 1980).

In the absence of the mother, infants will readily redirect their filial attachment to an inanimate or animate mother substitute (Mason, 1971; Mason & Kenney, 1974). As the classic Wisconsin experiments demonstrated with rhesus monkeys, a surrogate mother need not be a source of food, transport, or protection to become the object of a strong filial bond. Instead, it appears that tactile qualities of the attachment figure (i.e., contact comfort) predominate (Harlow & Zimmermann, 1959).

A monogamous South American primate, the titi monkey (*Callicebus moloch*), is particularly interesting in this regard because it represents a rare natural distinction between the parent providing food and the parent contacting the infant most often. The titi monkey infant is nutritionally dependent on the mother for the first 8 to 12 weeks of life; yet, the infant spends 70–90% of its time being transported by the father (Fragaszy, Schwarz, & Shimosaka, 1982; Jantschke, 1992; Meritt, 1980). Moreover, young titi monkeys continue to exhibit a selective preference for their fathers when they are no longer dependent on either parent for food or transport (Mendoza & Mason, 1986b). To date, measures of parental attachment in infant titi monkeys other than preference have not been evaluated.

In contrast to squirrel monkeys in which mothers clearly show a strong adrenocortical response to separation from their infant (Mendoza et al., 1980), studies of attachment in adult titi monkeys indicate that neither parent responds to separation from their dependent offspring (Mendoza & Mason, 1986b). Brief separation from their mate, however, leads to increased heart rate, cortisol levels, and behavioral distress (Cubicciotti & Mason, 1975; Mendoza & Mason, 1986a/1986b). The presence of the mate also decreases adrenocortical responsiveness to novelty or disturbance (Hennessy, Mendoza, Mason, & Moberg, 1995). Finally, in preference-testing situations, both males and females are more strongly attracted to their mate than to their offspring or to unfamiliar adults of either sex (Mason, 1975; Mendoza & Mason, 1986b). Thus, it appears that the relationship between adult titi monkeys resembles the filial bond in other species, but surprisingly, neither parent shows evidence of a comparable bond with their infant (Mendoza & Mason, 1986b).

The present experiment investigated the filial attachment of titi monkeys by examining the infant's behavioral and adrenocortical responses to separation from its parents. Of interest was whether infant titis would respond to separation from their parents as parents respond to separation from each other—with a robust behavioral and adrenocortical reaction, or as parents respond to separation from their infants—with little or no reaction. Further, if infants did respond to separation, would they respond more strongly to separation from their mother, as would be expected based on studies with other primate species or would they respond more strongly to separation from their father, as the preference data predict?

Methods

Subjects and Living Arrangements

The subjects for the experiment were 4 female and 2 male titi monkey infants (*Cullicebus moloch*) living with their parents in six family groups. At the beginning of data collection, the infants were between 3 and 5 months of age. Five family groups also contained two additional offspring, which were between 1 and 3 years older than the subjects. In one family group, the subject had no siblings. Three fathers and 3 mothers were wild-born and imported as adults; the other parents were colony-born and raised in family groups. Parents had been living together for at least 3 years before the study began. All animals except the infants were trained to enter small transport cages; infants generally entered transport cages with a parent.

Living cages measured $1.22 \times 1.22 \times 2.13$ m and were situated such that each family group was visually isolated from others, but auditory and olfactory interactions were possible. All cages were equipped with four horizontal perches, arranged in step-wise fashion. Lighting was maintained on a 12:12 hr light : dark cycle with lights on at 0600 hr. Maintenance procedures followed standard laboratory protocol including daily cleaning and twice daily feeding at 0800 and 1330 hr (commercial monkey chow supplemented with fresh fruits and vegetables).

Procedure

All subjects were tested once in each of five experimental conditions: (a) base, (b) disturbance-control (infant-with-male-and-female), (c) infant-with-male, (d) infant-with-female, and (e) infant-alone.

In the base condition, the infant was captured, manually restrained, and a blood sample (.5 ml) collected as soon as possible for subsequent assay of plasma cortisol levels. In conditions 2 through 5, all family members were caught and placed in separate transport cages, and the infant (plus the mother and/or father as appropriate) was returned to the home cage as quickly as possible. The infant was always the first animal to be returned to the cage and was placed on the top perch; the parents were then released through a small entrance door at the bottom of the cage. Nonparticipating family members were removed from the colony room and housed at a remote location until the test session was complete. After 1 hr, the infant was recaptured and a blood sample was collected.

The order in which conditions were imposed was approximately balanced so that all subjects were exposed to the test conditions in a distinct sequence and at least 1 subject was tested in each condition during each week of testing. At least 5 nontest days intervened between successive conditions for a given subject; testing was completed with a 5-week period. Only one family group was tested in an experimental condition per day. All testing occurred between 1600 and 1730 hr.

Behavioral Observation

At the beginning of testing before any disturbance to the animals, the identity of the family member carrying the infant, if any, was recorded. During experimental conditions, behavioral observations were conducted using the infant as the focal subject. (These observations were not performed during the base condition.) The infant's behavior and interactions with its parents (when present) were recorded for the first 15 min following return of the infant (and parents), and again starting at 45 min following return.

Behaviors were recorded using a time-ruled checklist of predefined behavioral categories. At 15-s intervals, indicated by audible signals from an interval timer, dorsal contact, other contact, tail-twining, and proximity were recorded (on-the-signal). Locomotion, grooming, eating/ drinking, rejection, retrieval, and grabbing/hitting/biting were recorded once if they occurred during a particular 15-s period (1–0). In addition to the checklist behaviors, the total number of vocalizations emitted by the infant and its parent(s) was counted during the 30-min observation period. Instances of eating/drinking, retrieval, and grabbing/hitting/biting occurred too infrequently for data analysis, and will not be discussed further.

All behavioral data were recorded by the same trained observer. Reliability estimates obtained prior to data collection exceeded 85% agreement for all behavioral categories. The criteria used for recording the behaviors were as follows:

1. dorsal contact: infant on parent's back and weight of infant supported by the adult. (Note: Infant titi monkeys are rarely carried ventrally.)

2. other contact: any contact between infant and parent(s) in which the infant was supporting its own weight. This usually involves side-by-side contact.

3. tail-twining: A species-specific form of affiliative contact that occurs when animals are sitting side-by-side and one animal's tail is wrapped around the tail of another. All 3 animals could be tail-twining simultaneously.

4. proximity: within arm's reach of an adult. If the entire triad was positioned closely together, but one adult was located between the infant and the other adult, the infant was considered to be in proximity to the closest parent only.

5. locomotion: independent movement of at least one body length. This was not scored if the infant was being carried.

6. grooming: An individual gently picks through the hair of another individual.

7. rejection: attempts by the adult to remove the infant from the dorsal surface. This is often accompanied by biting the infant's hands or feet, or scraping the infant against the cage. It is also scored when the adult actively resists the infant's attempts to climb onto its back. This measure included unsuccessful rejection attempts, in which the infant remains on the adult's back or successfully climbs onto the back despite resistance.

8. vocalization: any oral sound emitted by the infant or its parents during the observation period.

The procedures for collecting vocalization data were somewhat more complex than those for other behaviors. The majority of vocalizations that are produced during separation conditions are high-pitched distress vocalizations, also called isolation peeps. Because titi monkeys can produce these vocalizations with their mouths closed, and because adults will vocalize when separated from their mates, it is not possible to distinguish infant vocalizations from adult vocalizations. Moreover, it is not always possible to reliably distinguish these vocalizations from other titi vocalizations in type or function. Therefore, the cumulative number of vocalizations emitted by all individuals remaining in the home cage was recorded. A further complication arose from our decision to observe the subjects in the colony room rather than in a separate room isolated from the influence of other monkeys. During some 15-s intervals, loud calls produced by other monkeys in the room made it impossible to determine whether any vocalizations were produced by the animals being observed. When this occurred, "room noise" was marked on the behavioral checklist and no vocalizations were recorded for that 15-s interval. For analysis, vocalizations per minute were calculated for each experimental condition, and included only those 15-s intervals in which room noise did not occur. Room noise occurred in fewer than 10% of the intervals overall and was not different among the various experimental conditions.

Blood Sampling and Endocrine Evaluations

Blood samples were taken by femoral venipuncture while the monkey was manually restrained. The average time between entering the cage and collection of the sample was 2.61 min (range = 1.20 to 4.57 min). Based on studies with laboratory rodents and squirrel monkeys, this was rapid enough to ensure that cortisol levels in the samples collected were not influenced by the blood-sampling procedures (Davidson, Jones, & Levine, 1968; Lyons, Mendoza, & Mason, 1994). Samples were centrifuged, and the plasma fraction was extracted and frozen (–20°C) until assayed. Evaluations of plasma cortisol concentrations were made using commercially prepared kits (Diagnostics Products Corporation). Samples were diluted 1 : 4 prior to assay, and all samples were run in a single assay.

Data Analysis

Infant cortisol levels were analyzed using a one-way repeated measure analysis of variance. Typically, the behavioral measures were either frequently expressed (near or at 100%) or infrequently expressed (near or at 0). In order to avoid ceiling or floor influences in the analysis, all behavioral data were analyzed nonparamerically using Friedman analyses of variance or Wilcoxon signed-ranks tests. The small sample size prevented adjusting p values for the number of tests performed. Preliminary analysis revealed few behavioral changes from the first to the last 15 min of observation and, hence, are not reported. Post-hoc comparisons were performed, where appropriate, using Newman-Keuls (cortisol) or Wilcoxon tests (behavior).

Results

During pretest observations, infants were found to be in dorsal contact on 19 of 30 occasions. Infants were never observed on their mother or siblings and all were carried by their father on at least one occasion. Thus, when infants were not found on their fathers, they were on their own.

In the disturbance-control condition, during which both parents were present, infants spent most of their time in proximity to at least one parent, $M = 86.3\%$ of observations; $r = 65.8–100.0\%$. In this condition, infants were in proximity to their fathers significantly more often than to their mothers, $M = 76.1\%$ and 32.8% of the intervals, respectively; $p < .05$. When in proximity, infants tended to physically contact (dorsal contact, other contact, tail-twine) their fathers more often than their mothers (contact with fathers: 64.9% of observations; contact with mothers: 13.2% of observations; $p < .05$). Much of the contact between infants and fathers was dorsal contact, but this type of contact was rarely observed with the mothers (dorsal contact with fathers: 39.0% of observations; dorsal contact with mothers: 1.0%; $p < .05$).

In the infant-with-male condition, infants maintained high levels of proximity to and contact with their fathers (proximity: 95.8%; contact: 87.9%; dorsal contact: 52.4%). During the infant-with-female condition, infants spent more time in proximity to and contact with their mothers (proximity: 67.6%, $p = .07$; contact: 57.1%, $p < .05$) than they did in the disturbance-control condition. Dorsal contact remained at low levels when only the mother was present (6.9%). In spite of the tendency for infants to spend more time with their mothers during the infant-with-female condition, infants still spent significantly more time with their fathers than with their mothers when only one parent was available (proximity, $p < .05$; contact, $p < .05$; dorsal contact, $p < .05$).

Only one rejection was observed during the disturbance-control condition, when both parents were present. Maternal rejection increased during the infant-with-female condition, $p < .05$, during which the majority of rejections (34 of 41) were observed.

Not all infant–female interactions were negative. Although tail-twine was infrequent, the infants were observed tail-twining with their mothers (55 occasions) as well as with their fathers (113 occasions). Grooming also occurred at least as often between mother and infant (36 instances) as between father and infant (17 instances). Differences between males and females in tail-twining and grooming with their infants were not significant.

Infant activity levels were marginally influenced by experimental conditions. Infants tended to be most active during the infant-alone condition (locomotion was scored during 52.3% of the intervals), somewhat less active in the infant-with-female condition (30.2%) and disturbance-control condition (23.6%), and least active in the infant-with-male condition (12.3%). The difference among conditions in locomotion scores approached significance, $p = .072$.

Vocalization significantly differentiated test conditions, $p < .05$; see Table 1. Post-hoc analyses indicated that the number of vocalizations emitted by the infant and parents (when present) was significantly higher in the infant-alone condition than in the disturbance-control condition and infant-with-male condition, $ps < .05$. Vocalizations also occurred significantly more often in the infant-with-female condition than in the disturbance-control condition, $p < .05$. No other comparisons of conditions were significant.

TABLE 1   Mean number and range of vocalizations detected during the first and last 15 min of each 1-hr test period.

Condition	Mean	Range
Disturbance-Control	23.0	4.8–49.8
Infant-with-Father	78.2	7.8–249.6
Infant-with-Mother	214.1	34.2–727.2
Alone	340.8	37.2–420.0

Analysis of cortisol levels indicated that the experimental conditions significantly altered adrenocortical activity, $F(4,20) = 25.18$, $p < 0.001$; see Figure 1. Infants did not respond to removal of just the mother; cortisol levels when only the mother was removed (infant-with-male condition) did not differ from the disturbance-control or base conditions in which both parents were present. Infants did respond to removal of just the father. Cortisol levels when only the father was removed (infant-with-female condition) were significantly higher than in any of the three conditions in which the father was present (base, disturbance-control, infant-with-male, $ps < .01$). The highest cortisol levels were found in the infant-alone condition; these levels significantly differed from each of the other experimental conditions, $ps < .01$. Each of the 6 subjects showed the same general pattern of response; cortisol levels were always higher in the infant-alone condition than in the infant-with-female condition, and always higher in the infant-with-female condition than in the infant-with-male condition. In sum, cortisol levels show that the infants responded to removal of the father from the living cage, even when the mother was present; whereas infants did not respond to removal of the mother when the father was present. This does not imply that the mother was without effect, however, for the infants responded most vigorously when left entirely alone in the living cage.

Discussion

The behavioral and physiological data clearly indicate that infant titis do respond to separation from their parents. When alone, infants exhibited the highest levels of cortisol and the highest rate of vocalizations, measures which generally indicate stress and agitation. Although it was not possible to count the number of infant vocalizations without also including those produced by the parents, the main result that vocalizations were infrequent when both parents were present and most frequent when the infant was alone is unambiguous.

It is also clear from our data that infants did not respond to separation from their mothers and their fathers equivalently. Separation from the father was a more potent stressor than separation from the mother. Removal of the mother did not lead to increased cortisol levels unless the father was also removed; removal of the father elicited an increase in plasma cortisol levels even when the mother remained with the infant during the separation period.

Capture and handling procedures have been shown to increase adrenocortical activity in adult *Callicebus* (Mendoza, 1991). We presume that in the present study, catching and returning the infant was a stimulus sufficient to increase adrenocortical activity as well. In this context, then, the father seems to completely eliminate the infant's adrenocortical response to experimental disturbance, whereas the mother does not seem capable of doing so.

FIGURE 1 Mean (±*SE*) plasma cortisol levels of infants following no disturbance (base), or 1 hr following disturbance only (dist), removal of the mother (infant-with-father), removal of the father (infant-with-mother), or removal of both parents (alone).

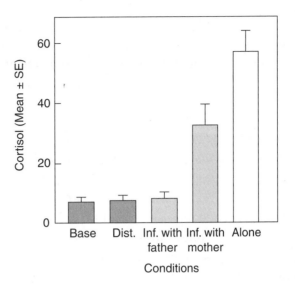

Whether increased secretion of cortisol or other hormones of the hypothalamic–pituitary–adrenal axis in any way affects the attachment process or filial behavior of titi monkeys is unknown. However, results with other species suggest that increased release of corticotropin-releasing factor may play a role in the behavioral responses to separation. This neuropeptide not only stimulates pituitary release of the corticotroph, but also orchestrates various other physiological and behavioral responses to stressors (Dunn & Berridge, 1990), and may modulate or eventually terminate vocalizing and other active behavioral responses to separation (Harvey & Hennessy, in press; Hennessy, Long, Nigh, Williams, & Nolan, in press; Kalin, Shelton, & Barksdale, 1989).

Our behavioral findings replicate previous results indicating that infants, when given the opportunity to be with either parent, prefer to be with their fathers (Mendoza & Mason, 1986b). Even when only one parent was present (infant-with-male and infant-with-female conditions), the infant tended to be in proximity and contact with their fathers more than their mothers. It follows from the patterns of parent–infant contact and the infant's adrenocortical and behavioral responses to separation that the father is the primary filial attachment figure.

This work appears to be the first demonstration in primates of a physiological stress response to brief separation from the father and contrasts with studies of other species in which an infant's response to separation had been observed only when the mother was removed (e.g., Coe, Mendoza, Smotherman, & Levine, 1978; Kaufman & Rosenblum, 1969; Reite, Short, Seiler, & Pauley, 1981; Mendoza, Smotherman, Miner, Kaplan, & Levine, 1978; Vogt & Levine, 1980). We do not know from our findings whether the mother represents a special or distinct social category for the titi monkey infant. That is, it is possible that removal of any familiar social companion would have produced a cortisol elevation comparable to that observed when the mother was removed.

The differential responses displayed by infants to separation from their mothers and fathers could, at least partially, be due to the parental reaction during the separation period. A study by Hinde and Davies (1972) found that the amount of distress behavior displayed by rhesus infants when they were with their mothers depended on how perturbed the mothers were at the time. In our study, the mothers did appear more agitated than the fathers when they were alone with the infant. However, some of the agitation appeared to be due to the mother's attempts to avoid dorsal contact with her infant and, hence, provides further evidence for a weaker bond between mother and infant titi monkeys.

The major implications of this research concern the relationship between parental care, parental contact, and filial attachment. Titi monkeys are one of the few mammalian species in which the infant spends more time with its father than with its mother even though the mother is necessarily the source of food for the first 2–3 months of life. The results from this study indicate that the father, not the mother, is the primary attachment figure for the infant. Thus, the determining factor in the development of attachment in the infant titi is not the source of nourishment, but rather the source of contact.

Notes

This research was supported by Grant RR00169 from the National Institutes of Health and by Grant DIR9113287 from the National Science Foundation. The research was conducted while M.B.H. and S.P.M. were on sabbatical leave at the California Regional Primate Research Center.

References

Full bibliographic references available from your instructor.

Editor's Note

Reprint requests should be sent to Kurt A. Hoffman, California Regional Primate Research Center, University of California–Davis, Davis, CA 95616, U.S.A.

Kurt A. Hoffman and Sally P. Mendoza, Department of Psychology and California Regional Primate Research Center, University of California, Davis, California

Michael B. Hennessy, Department of Psychology Wright State, University of Dayton, Ohio

William A. Mason, Department of Psychology and California Regional Primate Research Center, University of California, Davis, California

Discussion Questions for Article 3

Section 1: Research Methods

Name: _____

PID: _____

Date: __ __ / __ __ / __ __ (MM/DD/YY)

CRN: _____

Recitation Day/Time: _____

Honor Code Signature: _____

1. Why were titi monkeys specifically chosen for this research?

2. Compare and contrast how titi monkeys behaved when their father was removed versus when their mother was removed.

3. How do the results support the hypothesis or research question?

4. What is the strength of using behavioral observations in this study?

Section 2
Biological Bases of Behavior

Alcmaeon of Croton (6 BCE) is credited as one of the first individuals to note the importance of the brain when he discovered a connection between the brain and eyes. Since then, philosophers and physicians such as Plato, Hippocrates, Galen, and Descartes have debated the brain-behavior relationship. Notably, Galen produced the Brain Hypothesis during the 2nd century which suggests that the brain is the source of behavior.

It was not until the late 1800's, when Wilhelm Wundt established the first psychology laboratory in Germany that psychology became a science in its own right. This differentiated psychology from medicine and philosophy. Now, the field of psychology has expanded immensely to include a subfield of biological bases of behavior, in which there are also subfields. These subfields include but are not limited to neuropsychology, psychophysiology, behavioral neuroscience, and biological psychology. Historically, there have been two great debates in psychology related to the biological bases of behavior: the mind–body debate and the localization-holism debate.

The Mind–Body Debate

In 1649, Descartes proposed his idea of dualism. He proposed that the brain was responsible for higher cognitive functions such as intellect and emotion, while a non-material mind (soul) was responsible for thoughts and desires. As a counterpoint, scientists have argued about whether or not Descartes' theory of dualism is accurate or whether the brain acts alone (the theory of monism). The mind–body debate boils down to one question: does the human brain interact with a non-material mind to help us think and make decisions?

Psychologists have not come to a consensus on this debate. One reason this debate has lasted is likely because scientists are unable to prove whether a non-material mind exists. Since the mind is immaterial, it cannot be empirically studied. Without empirical study, the mind can neither be proved nor disproved. The monistic view, however, is generally accepted within the scientific community.

Localization vs. Holism Debate

The foundation of the localization-holism debate existed centuries ago when the ancient Greeks disputed the location of the soul. The Greeks believed the soul was responsible for all of aspects of cognitive function, but were unsure which organ the soul resided in. Galen's research discovered that the brain was the most important part of the nervous system and theorized that it was responsible for thinking, emotion, and sensation.

Between the 2nd and 18th centuries, the debate switched from the location of the soul to whether the cognitive functions of the brain took place in the brain's ventricles or in the brain matter. During this time, the church held a heavy influence on science. The church stated that spirits flowed through the ventricles, which allows us to have thoughts. However, this was questioned throughout the 15th and 16th centuries. Finally in 1664, Willis put an end to the debate with his book, *Cerebri Anatome*, which firmly established his view that cognitive functions take place in the brain matter.

Starting in the 19th century, the localization-holism debate took the shape it resembles today. The debate is concerned with how cognitive functions are organized. The holistic approach (also called the equipotential view) states that each part of the brain plays an equal role in cognitive function. The localized view states that specific cognitive functions are localized to specific brain areas. The work of Gall, Broca, Wernicke, and others helped solidify the localization view. A modern view is a balance between theories explaining that while certain functions are localized, these brain structures do communicate with one another.

Article 1: The Neuropsychology of Depression: A Literature Review and Preliminary Model

Psychological disorders are typically described in terms of their presenting symptoms. Recently, psychologists have noted that different combinations of presenting symptoms can be used to diagnose the same disorder. For example, major depressive disorder (MDD) can be diagnosed when a patient is presenting with symptoms primarily associated with sadness as well as when another person is presenting with symptoms primarily associated with irritability. Due to these inconsistencies, a new perspective on diagnosing MDD is suggested. Shenal et al. present a neuropsychological model that marks neurological patterns associated with diagnosing different presentations of MDD.

Article 2: Impairment of Social and Moral Behavior Related to Early Damage in Human Prefrontal Cortex

The prefrontal cortex is associated with higher cognitive functioning. Previous research has suggested that in adults, damage to the prefrontal cortex results in an impaired ability to plan, make decisions, and moderate socially acceptable behaviors. In this article, Anderson et al. look at two adults who sustained damage to their prefrontal cortices as infants. They found that even though their brains were not fully developed at the time of injury, damage to the participants' prefrontal cortices resulted in deficits in a variety of social-cognitive tasks as adults.

—*Lauren L. Golden*

Article 1

The Neuropsychology of Depression: A Literature Review and Preliminary Model

Brian V. Shenal
David W. Harrison
Heath A. Demaree

Neuropsychological research provides a useful framework to study emotional problems, such as depression, and their correlates. This paper reviews several prominent neuropsychological theories. Functional neuroanatomical systems of emotion and depression are reviewed, including those that describe cerebral asymmetries in emotional processing. Following the review, a model that is composed of three neuroanatomical divisions (left frontal, right frontal, and right posterior) and corresponding neuropsychological emotional sequelae within each quadrant is presented. It is proposed that dysfunction in any of these quadrants could lead to symptomatology consistent with a diagnosis of depression. The proposed model combines theories of arousal, lateralization, and functional cerebral space and lends itself to scientific methods of investigation. Accordingly, research, prevention, and treatment programs in accordance with the proposed model may promote an improved understanding of the neuropsychological mechanisms involved in depression.

Key words: depression; emotion; theory; lateralization; cerebral.

Introduction and Rationale

Depressive disorders present a significant mental health concern to individuals and to our society. According to the *DSM-IV*, the lifetime risk for major depressive disorder (MDO) is between 10% and 25% for women and between 5% and 12% for men (American Psychiatric Association, 1994). Indeed, in an assessment of prospective 1-year prevalence rates, Regier et al. (1993) found that about 5% of Americans aged 18 or older (9.9 million persons) are afflicted with MDD in any given year. Although MDD may develop at any age, the average age of onset is in the 20s (American Psychiatric Association, 1994). The essential feature of depression is either impaired mood or the loss of interest or pleasure. The *DSM-IV* also describes depressed individuals as irritable and/or anxious (American Psychiatric Association, 1994). In addition, other neurologically mediated symptoms—such as insomnia and fatigue—are incorporated in "depression," thereby creating a very heterogeneous construct. Persons -experiencing depression often have significant social and interpersonal difficulties, problems with sexual functioning, and sleep electroencephalogram (EEG) abnormalities. There remains a need for a better understanding of the etiology of this important, yet heterogeneous, construct. Given its broad spectrum of emotional, cognitive, and behavioral sequelae, it should not be surprising that brain dysfunction within disparate regions may produce symptomatology consistent with "depression."

Neuropsychological research provides a useful framework to study emotional disorders, such as depression. Specifically, neuropsychologists have the ability to use instruments that measure mood (such as the Beck Depression Inventory, etc.) as well as a wide variety of cognitive, emotional, perceptual, and expressive abilities. Neuropsychologists are also frequently trained to assess physiological parameters within the central (such as EEG) and autonomic nervous systems [such as heart rate (HR) and systolic and diastolic blood pressures (SBP, DBP)], which are commonly impacted by affective disorders (e.g., Heller and Nitschke, 1997; Musselman, Evans, and Nemeroff, 1998; Robinson and Downhill, 1995). Taken together, these assessment capabilities make it possible to understand how neurological functioning may impact the onset of affective disorders, including depression. For example, largely through neuropsychological investigation, it has been suggested that impaired emotional perception and expression are related to posterior and anterior brain dysfunction, respectively (e.g., Borod, 1992). Accordingly, prominent neuropsychological theories and functional neuroanatomical systems of emotion, with an emphasis on negative emotional processing, are reviewed. Further, neuropsychological theories that describe cerebral asymmetries in the processing of emotion and depression are presented.

The preponderance of research to date has implicated the right cerebrum in the reception, comprehension, expression, and regulation of negative emotions

(Heilman, Bowers, and Valenstein, 1985). Interestingly, recent research has also begun to investigate differential effects of the right-anterior and right-posterior regions of the cerebrum to provide a more accurate representation of emotional processing. Alternate accounts exist, which rely on cerebral balance (e.g., Tucker and Frederick, 1989), or a proportionate degree of processing capability by either cerebrum contingent upon the valence of the emotion (Harrison and Gorelczenko, 1990). For example, Tucker and Frederick (1989) proposed that the left cerebrum differentially processes positive emotions whereas the right cerebrum primarily processes negative emotions. Other researchers have investigated a functional cerebral space model that may aid in the understanding of emotions. The functional cerebral space model provides a useful theory of dynamic cerebral activation. This model accounts for the activation of adjacent cortical regions and is presented along with implications for dual-task priming or interfering effects. A comprehensive review of these neuropsychological literatures is presented to provide a theoretical understanding of emotional processing. This paper asserts that continued neuropsychological research may improve the understanding of the causes and the treatment of negative emotion, and depression in particular.

Neuropsychology of Depression

Early research on the biological substrates of emotion focused on affect and changes within the autonomic nervous system. Subcortical limbic system circuits which mediate specific emotional behaviors were described (e.g., Heilman et al., 1985). As a result of recent research, however, it is clear that the cerebral cortex plays an important role in emotional behavior (see Davidson, 1993, for a review). With an increased focus on the cerebral cortex, researchers have developed numerous neuropsychological models of emotion.

Right-Hemisphere Model of Depression

One neuropsychological theory of emotion proposes that emotions, irrespective of valence, are processed preferentially within the right cerebrum. Past studies of emotional perception have supported the contention that emotion, in general, is differentially controlled by the right cerebrum (Borod, Koff, Lorch, and Nicholas, 1986; Etcoff, 1989). These studies suggest that the right-posterior region of the cerebrum is specialized for the perception of emotional information, regardless of valence.

Heilman (1982) speculated that the right cerebrum may have greater control of the subcortical systems, which are largely responsible for arousal and emotion. Heilman and Van Den Abell (1980) demonstrated the superiority of the right cerebrum for arousal through the facilitation of reaction times following left-visual-field warning lights (right cerebrum). Although left-visual-field warning lights improved reaction times reliably compared with right-visual-field warning lights, improvement occurred at both the left and the right hands. Following these results, researchers suggested that the right cerebrum differentially controls general arousal and attention and may lead to overall cerebral activation (see Tucker and Williamson, 1984, for a review). The concept of overall cerebral activation following arousal will be revisited throughout this paper. Heilman, Bowers, and Valenstein (1993) demonstrated that activation of the posterior cerebral regions, particularly the right-parietal region and the right-temporal region, is likely to result in emotional responses. Further, Heilman et al. (1985) used galvanic skin response (GSR) to demonstrate that right-cerebrum dysfunction yielded altered levels of arousal and reactivity. Lesions within the right cerebrum were found to produce decrements in arousal as measured using GSR in response to provocative stimuli. These findings offered additional support for the right-cerebral mediation of emotion.

Neuropsychological research has investigated the electrodermal activity (EDA) of depressed individuals. These findings are reviewed by Crews and Harrison (1995) and may suggest increased activation of the right hemisphere in depression on the basis of contralateral left hand increased EDA (contralateral processing of EDA is a controversial topic, however). Electroencephalogram studies have examined EEG asymmetries in depressed individuals and found increased right-frontal lobe activation, relative to left-hemisphere activation, in depressed individuals (Kano, Nakamura, Matsuoka, Iida, and Nakajima, 1992; Schaffer, Davidson, and Saron, 1983). For example, Kano et al. (1992) demonstrated decreased and increased activation over right-anterior regions. These results are suggestive of heightened right-frontal activation in depressed individuals and are consistent with past research linking emotion and right-hemisphere functioning (Borod et al., 1986; Etcoff, 1989).

Balance Model of Depression

In contrast to Heilman et al. (1985), Tucker and Frederick (1989) described a balance model of emotion. Heilman et al. (1993) primarily consider the effects of cerebral lesions on emotions, whereas Tucker and Frederick (1989) discuss the effects of relative cerebral activation on emotions. Tucker and Frederick (1989) acknowledge that lesions and activation may relate to each other; however, their perspective differs from the right-hemisphere model of depression. According to the balance model, the left cerebrum primarily processes positive emotions and the right cerebrum primarily processes negative emotions. It was proposed that deactivation of one cerebrum leads to increased relative activation of the opposite cerebrum and, therefore, an increased expression of the dominant cerebrum's primary response pattern. Therefore, deactivation of the left cerebrum may result in an increase of negative emotion whereas deactivation of the right cerebrum may result in an increase of positive emotion. This asymmetry has been noted in other classic studies of emotion as well. For example, Goldstein (1939) reported a high incidence of a "catastrophic reaction" in patients with left-hemisphere lesions. More recently, this "depressive catastrophic reaction" has been characterized by negative affect, fear, pessimism, and crying (Davidson, 1984). These catastrophic and indifference reactions are hypothesized to result from a breakdown of the reciprocal interaction between the damaged and undamaged hemispheres (Crews and Harrison, 1995).

Crews and Harrison (1994a) investigated the influence of depression on the hemispheric processing of emotional faces and found a slower reaction time to affective stimuli in depressed women than that in nondepressed women. Further, the depressed women more often identified neutral faces as angry. The authors suggested relative increased right-hemisphere activation and decreased left-hemisphere activation in the depressed women. Crews and Harrison (1994b) found that women with depressed mood displayed significantly faster reaction times to sad faces presented in the right visual field and happy faces presented in the left visual field. These results provide evidence of differential arousal of both the left- and right-cerebral hemispheres in this sample of anxious–depressed women. This interpretation is supported by arousal theory (Duffy, 1962; Easterbrook, 1959; Harrison and Pavlik, 1983; Hebb, 1955; Lindsley, 1951), which suggests that increased arousal is associated with improved task proficiency up to an optimal level, at which point further increases in arousal may impair performance. Thus, the findings of a significant decrease in reaction time for happy faces presented to the left visual field in depressed women may reflect higher relative arousal within the right cerebrum of depressed versus non-depressed women.

Robinson, Kubos, Starr, Rao, and Price (1984) reported that left-frontal lobe damage resulted in depressive symptomatology, and that patients who developed hostile, manic-like, symptomatology were more likely to have sustained right-hemisphere damage, sparing the left hemisphere. Otto, Yeo, and Dougher (1987) proposed that depression may lead to differential hemispheric activation through either increased right-hemisphere activation or decreased left-hemisphere activation. These results are consistent with the balance model of cerebral lateralization for emotion described by Tucker and Frederick (1989).

In sum, research has supported the findings of heightened right-hemisphere activation relative to the left hemisphere. This may occur as the result of either increased right-hemisphere activation or decreased left-hemisphere activation. However, this conceptualization of depression may be too simplistic. Further, other cerebral activation patterns may also lead to symptoms that may be consistent with the heterogeneous construct known as "depression."

Tucker acknowledged that the brain's processing of emotion is complex and likely involves the interaction of multiple systems that are only partially understood. Tucker cited comparative studies (Ploog, 1981) and human studies (Rinn, 1984) and suggested that emotional processing must integrate reflexive emotional displays that originate in the brain stem with ongoing behaviors. Emerson, Harrison, Everhart, and Williamson (2001) indicated that this may occur by way of corticolimbic mechanisms which integrate ongoing experiences and behavior with reflexive affective representations to recruit emotional significance. A relative weakness of this model, however, is that it does not adequately address resultant behavioral patterns following deactivation of both hemispheres. Moreover, there is no conclusive evidence within the literature that deactivation in one cerebrum necessarily leads to increased activation of the other cerebrum. In fact, it is possible that both the left and right cerebrums may demonstrate concordant deactivation. The following model was developed to provide a better understanding of the complexity of the neuropsychology of depression.

Circumplex Model of Depression

Heller (1993) proposed a model of cerebral activation during emotional processing. Heller's circumplex model divides the brain into four quadrants, defined by the valence axis (pleasant or unpleasant) and the arousal axis (high and low). Most emotions fall within the two anterior and right-posterior quadrants. Further, these dimensions correspond to distinct physiological responses (Heller, Nitschke, and Miller, 1998). For example, HR is related to valence and skin conductance is related to arousal (Fredrickson and Levenson, 1998; Heller, 1993; Lang, Greenwald, Bradley, and Hamm, 1993). These dimensions are characterized by distinct cortical brain activation patterns. Specifically, the valence dimension is associated with the anterior regions of the brain, and the arousal dimension is associated with the right-posterior region. Within the valence axis of this model, increased activation of the right-frontal region relative to the left is differentially related to sadness or depression. Within the arousal axis, decreased activation of the right-parietotemporal regions is also differentially related to depression.

Davidson and Fox (1988) concluded that relative right-frontal activation predisposes participants to experience negative affect. Tucker (1993) hypothesized that EEG desynchrony (increased arousal) in the right-frontal region during a depressed mood state may represent inhibition of the right-posterior region. Accordingly, the right-posterior region's positive emotional processing may suffer following increased right-frontal activation and consequent right-posterior deactivation. Similarly, Tomarken, Davidson, Wheeler, and Doss (1992) found that individuals with extreme left-frontal activation on baseline EEG reported more positive affect and less negative affect than did those who demonstrated right-frontal activation. Davidson (1992a) and Davidson and Tomarken (1989) investigated EEG activation during affective states and suggested that left-frontal activation is associated with positive affect and approach behavior whereas relative right-frontal activation is associated with negative affect and avoidance behavior. Similarly, numerous experiments suggest that depressed individuals evidence right-posterior dysfunction (Heller, 1993; Heller, Etienne, and Miller, 1995) and right hemisphere-related cognitive dysfunction (Sackheim, Decina, and Malitz, 1982). Several other studies have offered support for Heller's model by investigating brain functioning following antidepressive medication treatment. Brumback, Staton, and Wilson (1980), Staton, Wilson, and Brumback (1981), and Wilson and Staton (1984) reported improved performance on neuropsychological measures of right cerebrum and frontal lobe functioning following tricyclic antidepressant treatment with depressed children.

Other EEG studies have uncovered decreased left-frontal activation in depressed individuals relative to non-depressed individuals (Davidson, 1992b; Henriques and Davidson, 1991). These experiments demonstrated that depressed individuals evidenced left-frontal deactivation relative to nondepressed individuals. Demaree, Crews, and Harrison (1995) found supportive evidence of this model, conducting a topographical brain mapping of a depressed woman. Consistent with the described model, this depressed individual demonstrated decreased activation and heightened activation over the left-frontal region relative to the right-frontal region.

In a separate line of research, depressed individual's glucose metabolic rates were investigated using positron emission tomography (PET). Schwartz, Baxter, Mazziotta, Gerner, and Phelps (1987) discussed evidence suggesting that cerebral glucose metabolism for the left-prefrontal cortex in depressed individuals was lower relative to nondepressed individuals, and that depression ratings and the metabolic ratio between left- and right-prefrontal cortices were inversely related.

Finally, single photon emission computed tomography (SPECT) procedures have demonstrated regional cerebral blood flow (rCBF) asymmetries in depressed individuals. Delvenne et al. (1990) and Mathew et al. (1980) demonstrated that depressed individuals evidenced lower cortical blood flow in the left hemisphere relative to nondepressed individuals, suggestive of neural hypoactivation. The circumplex model of emotion, as well as each of the prior models, is useful for the understanding of the neuropsychology of depression. The goal of the present paper is, in part, to synthesize these models into a parsimonious understanding of how very different deficits in cerebral functioning may produce a wide array of sequelae associated with the heterogeneous construct of depression.

Diagnostic Imprecision

Both the right and left hemispheres have been implicated in emotional processing and the experience of depression. Although many researchers consider the right hemisphere as central to negative emotional processing, the physiological mechanisms underlying affect perception and expression are much more complex. However, the "flavor" of the depression—or the criteria met leading to its diagnosis—has been highly variable. For example, patients with right-hemisphere dysfunction may appear indifferent or even euphoric (Heilman et al., 1993). Denny-Brown, Meyer, and Horenstein (1952) echoed the notion that patients with right-hemisphere dysfunction were often inappropriately indifferent. Apparently as a result of this indifference or flat affect, persons with right-hemisphere dysfunction may be diagnosed with depression. A much different "flavor" of depression may result from left-cerebral dysfunction, however. Goldstein (1939) noted that many patients with left-hemisphere dysfunction appeared agitated and sad, which he termed the "catastrophic reaction." Later, Gainotti (1972) confirmed these observations and adopted the same nomenclature. This depressive reaction associated with left-hemisphere dysfunction is usually seen with anterior perisylvian lesions (Heilman et al., 1993). Starkstein, Robinson, and Price (1987) studied the etiology of stroke and depression and found that one third of stroke patients had a major depressive syndrome. They also found dysfunction within the left-frontal and left-caudate regions to be more frequently associated with severe depression.

Not all investigators agree about hemispheric asymmetries and depression. House, Dennis, Warlow, Hawton, and Molyneux (1990), for instance, believed that depression associated with right-hemisphere dysfunction may be underdiagnosed because these patients may have emotional communicative disorders and decreased awareness of their problems. Because patients with right-hemisphere dysfunction may be impaired in emotional expression, they may have reduced feedback and, therefore, appear indifferent (Heilman et al., 1993). Accordingly, patients with right-hemisphere dysfunction may display a reduced awareness of their emotional dysfunction. Depression following right-hemisphere dysfunction, therefore, may be underrepresented in clinical studies.

Even though the neuropsychological models of depression appear to be somewhat inconsistent, this may be due to a lack of precision for the *DSM-IV* diagnostic term "depression" and the initial efforts to interface a neuropsychological theory of emotion with terminology from a non-neuropsychological field. More specifically, "depression" is not a neuropsychological term whereas "agnosia," "aprosodia," and "apraxia" are specific neuropsychological terms that draw from the brain–behavior literature. In fact, it is plausible that many different presentations may be labeled "depression." For example, the *DSM-IV* diagnosis of depression may result from an individual lacking "get-up-and-go" (a motivational quality) and displaying "down-going," or slumped posture (a physical quality). Alternatively, the diagnosis of depression could be made for the labile patient with crying episodes in the presence of normal energy level. The diagnosis might additionally be made for the patient with anosognosia who fails to appreciate his or her deficits and who appears to be "in denial" of their affective symptoms (anosognosia), the patient with a bland affect and emotional bankruptcy (anosodysphoria), or the patient with a failure to appreciate the emotional significance of their problems (anosodiaphoria).

Other researchers have also struggled with this diagnostic issue. Gainotti (1972) attempted to provide a parsimonious understanding of sporadic results by describing different emotional presentations after right- versus left-hemisphere brain damage. For instance, he described patients with left-hemisphere damage as being distressed and tearful. This conceptualization is consistent with Goldstein's description of left-hemisphere damage (Goldstein, 1939) leading to "catastrophic reactions." In contrast, Gainotti (1972) described patients with right-hemisphere damage as displaying a cheerful, euphoric, "indifference reaction," although the emotion may not be congruent with the current situation or condition. Lateralization studies are beginning to be used to classify subtypes of depression. For example, Bruder (1995) distinguished melancholic depression (an inability to experience pleasure) from atypical depression (in which mood can brighten following pleasurable experience) and indicated the former may be related to deficits in right-posterior activation (see Heller et al., 1998, for a review).

Proposed Model of Depression

What follows is the presentation of a new conceptual model that attempts to capture the complexity of the previously reviewed research and that outlines a more comprehensive view on the neuropsychology of depression on the basis of arousal theory and cerebral activation. This model is designed to account for the wide range of cognitive, behavioral, and affective presentations that may be diagnosed as depression. This model is composed of four neuroanatomical divisions (left frontal, right frontal, left posterior, and right posterior), three of which correspond to neuropsychological emotional sequelae that are associated with depression (see Figure 1). Moreover, dysfunction within or among these functional cerebral quadrants may account for variability in symptomatology with more precision than the *DSM-IV* "depression" diagnosis.

FIGURE 1   Proposed model—depressive symptomology may result from dysfunction within three of four neuroanatomical quadrants.

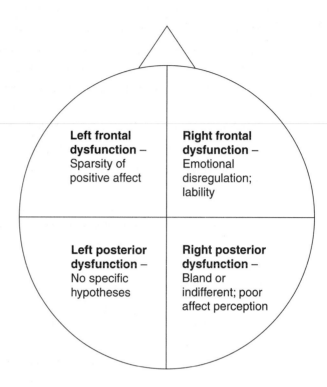

Left-Frontal Dysfunction

Heller et al. (1998) suggested that clinical depression is more common after left-hemisphere damage than after right-hemisphere damage. This relationship between depression and left-hemisphere dysfunction may partially reflect the fact that people may experience a negative emotional reaction to speech difficulties following damage to the left hemisphere. However, neuropsychological studies have directly linked brain activation with emotional experiences (Heller et al., 1998). For example, Davidson (1995) found that when healthy controls experience sadness, they demonstrate decreased left-hemisphere activation and increased right-hemisphere activation. Davidson (1995) suggested that activation of the left-anterior hemisphere is associated with approach behaviors, responses to reward, and increased positive affect. Reductions in left-anterior activation, then, may be expected to lead to a sparsity of these responses.

Heller et al. (1998) indicated that there are stable individual differences in asymmetric brain activation across the life span that predict emotional experience. Fox and Davidson (1988) found that infants who frequently cry following maternal separation evidence less left-anterior activation than do infants who are not distressed during this situation. Further, adults who demonstrate more approach behaviors and positive affect typically display greater left-anterior activation. Studies indicate that patients with left-frontal lesions are significantly more depressed than patients with other lesion sites. For example, Robinson, Starr, Lipsy, Rao, and Price (1985) found that approximately two thirds of their left-frontal lesioned group experienced symptoms consistent with depression and there was a strong positive correlation between the severity of depression symptomatology and the proximity of the lesion to the left-frontal pole. Accordingly, left-frontal dysfunction may account for several symptoms that are consistent with a diagnosis of depression.

It is plausible that an individual with decreased left-frontal activation may have limited positive affect and be consequently diagnosed with depression. Within this quadrant, depressive sequelae include limited positive affect (including deficits in processing and executing sequential positive behaviors), sparsity of speech, difficulty with positive affect initiation, emotional sequencing problems, behavioral slowing, and restricted social approach behaviors. Not surprisingly, then, several studies have noted left-anterior dysfunction associated with depressed mood (Banich, Stolar, Heller, and Goldman, 1992; Debener et al., 2000; Fleminger, 1991; Henriques and Davidson, 1991). For example, Debener et al. (2000) assessed depressed and non-depressed individuals twice (the time between assessments varied from 2 to 4 weeks). Across both assessments, these researchers found decreased left-frontal activation, suggesting that resting left-frontal arousal may be a marker for depression.

Right-Frontal Dysfunction

The right hemisphere has been implicated in the perception and expression of emotion (Borod, Andelman, Obler, Tweedy, and Welkowitz, 1992; Borod et al., 1998; Montreys and Borod, 1998). Considering Davidson's hypothesized model of the anterior regions of the left and right hemispheres (Davidson, 1995) as key components for an affective regulatory system, right-frontal activation can be closely tied to negative emotion. Activation of the right hemisphere is associated with avoidance, withdrawal from aversive stimuli, and the experience of negative affect (Davidson, 1993, 1995, 1998; Davidson, Abercrombie, Nitschke, and Putnam, 1999; Davidson and Irwin, 1999; Heller et al., 1998). Therefore, activation of the anterior right hemisphere could lead to an exacerbation of negative affect and may be diagnosed as depression. Heller et al. (1998) indicated that both depression and anxiety are related to unpleasant valence as well as avoidance behaviors and should be associated with increased activation within the anterior right cerebrum.

Although increased right-frontal activation may lead to an exacerbation of negative affect, dysfunction within this region may also produce depressive symptoms. Decreased right-frontal activation may result in a lack of avoidance and withdrawal from aversive stimuli, which may also be construed as depression and a type of learned helplessness. Patients with right-frontal damage may present with emotional regulation problems and lability for crying (Heilman et al., 1993; Robinson et al., 1993; Wilson, 1924; Woodward, Bisbee, and Bennett, 1984). Consistent with these findings of emotional disregulation, Mayberg and colleagues have presented compelling evidence that right-frontal and anterior-temporal dysfunction is associated with impaired attention/concentration and primary or secondary depressed affect (Liotti and Mayberg, 2001; Mayberg, 2001). Lesser et al. (1994), too, discovered decreased right frontotemporal rCBF in 39 older depressed patients. Multiple patterns of right-cerebrum activation/deactivation may be interpreted as depression, and continued investigations are needed to produce a more specific description of the experienced affect. The term "depression" does not appear to be sufficient to provide a true neuropsychological description of emotional difficulties that may arise following right-frontal dysfunction, which may produce flat affect and difficulty in regulating complex, sequential behaviors related to negative affect expression. These symptoms may be characterized by expressive aprosodia, involuntary and intense emotional expression, difficulty with negative affect inhibition, and the regulation of social behavior.

Left-Posterior Dysfunction

There is a dearth of literature suggesting the involvement of left-posterior regions in depression. As such, no specific predictions regarding its contribution to depression are made in the present model (please see Figure 1).

Right-Posterior Dysfunction

Patients with posterior right-hemisphere lesions have been shown to be impaired in comprehending emotional tone of voice, recognizing facial expressions, and naming emotional scenes relative to left-hemisphere lesion patients (DeKosky, Heilman, Bowers, and Valenstein, 1980; Heller et al., 1998; Tucker, Watson, and Heilman, 1977; see Borod, Haywood, and Koff, 1997, for a review). These results suggest that, across multiple paradigms, right-posterior quadrant may be specialized for emotional information processing. Thus, deficits within this region may produce impaired emotional perception and inappropriate responsiveness (including no response to a context demanding an environmentally appropriate behavior).

Within the posterior right hemisphere, depression is typically associated with decreased arousal and brain activation. Thus, as the right-posterior region becomes less activated, the individual would experience less arousal and a generalized reduction of brain activation. Along with impaired emotional perception and responsiveness, decreased arousal may lead to the diagnosis of a depressive disorder. Similarly, Jorge, Robinson, Starkstein, and Arndt (1993) found that anxious–depressed patients typically display right-hemisphere damage whereas nonanxious–depressed patients tended to display left-hemisphere dysfunction. Recent studies of emotional processing have produced consistent results linking decreased right-posterior activation and depression via a decreased left hemispatial bias (Everhart and Harrison, 1997; Heller et al., 1998) and left-ear advantage (Pine et al., 2000). Many researchers have found impairments in right-posterior visuospatial processing and constructional tasks in depressed individuals and suggested that depression is frequently diagnosed following right-hemisphere stroke (see Crews and Harrison, 1995, for a review).

Within this quadrant, depressive sequelae include bland or "missing" affect perception, and the patient may be characterized as having impaired emotional reception, analysis, and comprehension, poor insight into emotional problems, and an impaired ability to perceive the affective significance of visual, auditory, and somatosensory stimuli.

Conclusions

The proposed model of depression is designed to account for research to date on the neuropsychology of depression. In the existing literature, depression is most frequently related to dysfunction within the left-frontal or right-posterior regions. Although deactivation within any functional quadrant of the proposed model may lead to symptoms consistent with "depression," it is likely that the left-frontal and right-posterior regions may be more frequently related to depression than patterns of right-frontal dysfunction. As the existing literature appears to be somewhat confusing and controversial, an increased precision for the diagnostic term "depression" may afford a better understanding of this emotional construct. Future research projects and innovative neuropsychological models may help to form a better understanding of depression.

Neurocognitive performance has been shown to be related to emotional functioning. For example, studies have found that depressed individuals demonstrate impairments in executive functioning and memory (Crews and Harrison, 1995). An improved understanding of cerebral dysfunction among depressed individuals may yield better predictions of potential cognitive impairments within these patients. As the proposed model suggests that many activation/deactivation patterns may result in depressive symptoms, it is suspected that many different patterns of cognitive impairments may be evidenced in depressed patients. For example, a depressed patient with left-frontal dysfunction, displaying a sparsity of positive affect, may evidence impaired verbal fluency and difficulties planning and sequencing complex information. However, a patient with right-frontal dysfunction, displaying emotional regulation problems and lability for crying, may evidence impaired nonverbal fluency along with ballistic and perseverative responses to cognitive challenges. Therefore, the proposed model affords predictions of different qualities of depressive symptoms as well as different patterns of cognitive impairments corresponding to the specific regions of cerebral dysfunction. Future research is needed to confirm these functional system correlates.

As previously suggested, research has failed to implicate left-posterior dysfunction as an important mediator of depression symptomatology. Because relatively little data measuring functioning within caudal regions of the left hemisphere has been collected, one should not automatically discount this quadrant's potential role in depression. Postcentral functioning may be measured by assessing somatosensory functioning

(Corkin, Milner, and Rasmussen, 1970), tactile form recognition (Benton et al., 1983), contralateral neglect (Schenkenberg, Bradford, and Ajax, 1980), affective memory (Ali and Cimino, 1997), as well as speech and reading comprehension (de Renzi and Faglioni, 1978). Increased use of such measures among both depressed and control populations may suggest that dysfunction within the left-posterior quadrant is associated with depression symptomatology. For example, the finding that mood impacts one's ability to remember affect-consistent information (Ellis and Moore, 1999) in conjunction with Ali and Cimino's conclusion (Ali and Cimino, 1997) that the left- and right-posterior cerebrums are differentially responsible for perceiving and memorizing positive and negative words suggests that depressed individuals may experience left-posterior dysfunction.

Summary

The proposed model is composed of three neuroanatomical divisions within which dysfunction may lead to distinct emotional sequelae, each of which has been associated with "depression." A graphical representation of the model is presented to provide a conceptual framework and visual representation. It should be noted that the present model differs drastically from the diagnosis of depression on the basis of questionnaire measures alone (such as the Beck Depression Inventory, which incorporates questions concerning mood, cognition, and somatic complaints). Depression is a heterogeneous construct, and distinct patterns of brain dysfunction may yield very different clinical pictures of persons diagnosed with "depression." The proposed model combines theories of arousal, lateralization, and functional cerebral space to better understand these distinct clinical pictures, and it should be noted that these regions may be differentially activated following various therapies to depressive symptomatology.

The proposed model lends itself well to scientific methods of investigation. Future research is needed to test the model and to provide nomothetic comparisons of the efficacy of therapeutic interventions between the proposed neuropsychological depressive syndromes. Accordingly, future research, prevention, and treatment programs may be developed and practiced following an increased understanding of the neuropsychological mechanisms involved in depression and the effects of treatment.

References

Full bibliographic references available from your instructor.

Editor's Note

Address correspondence to David W. Harrison, Department of Psychology, Virginia Polytechnic Institute and State University, Derring Hall, Blacksburg, Virginia 24061-0436. E-mail: dwh@vt.edu

Discussion Questions for Article 1

Section 2: Biological Bases of Behavior

Name: _____

PID: _____

Date: __ __ / __ __ / __ __ (MM/DD/YY)

CRN: _____

Recitation Day/Time: _____

Honor Code Signature: _____

1. Why does Heller suggest that depression is more common after damage to the left hemisphere than after damage to the right hemisphere?

2. What are positive depressive symptoms and which hemisphere are they associated with? What are negative depressive symptoms and which hemisphere are they associated with?

3. Depression is most frequently related to dysfunction in which two regions/quadrants of the brain?

4. Why is there no specific hypothesis of left posterior dysfunction and depressive symptoms?

Article 2

Impairment of Social and Moral Behavior Related to Early Damage in Human Prefrontal Cortex

Steven W. Anderson
Antoine Bechara
Hanna Damasio
Daniel Tranel
Antonio R. Damasio

The long-term consequences of early prefrontal cortex lesions occurring before 16 months were investigated in two adults. As is the case when such damage occurs in adulthood, the two early-onset patients had severely impaired social behavior despite normal basic cognitive abilities, and showed insensitivity to future consequences of decisions, defective autonomic responses to punishment contingencies and failure to respond to behavioral interventions. Unlike adult-onset patients, however, the two patients had defective social and moral reasoning, suggesting that the acquisition of complex social conventions and moral rules had been impaired. Thus early-onset prefrontal damage resulted in a syndrome resembling psychopathy.

It is well established that in adults who have had normal development of social behavior, damage to certain sectors of prefrontal cortex produces a severe impairment of decision-making and disrupts social behavior, although the patients so affected preserve intellectual abilities and maintain factual knowledge of social conventions and moral rules[1-6]. Little is known for certain, however, about the consequences of comparable damage occurring before the maturation of the relevant neural and cognitive systems, namely in infancy, because such cases are exceedingly rare. Information about the early onset condition is vital to the elucidation of how social and moral competencies develop from a neurobiological standpoint. A number of questions have arisen in this regard. First, would early-onset lesions lead to the appearance of persistent defects comparable to those seen in adult-onset lesions, or would further development and brain plasticity reduce or cancel the effects of the lesions and prevent the appearance of the defects? Second, assuming early-onset lesions cause a comparable defect, would there be a dissociation between disrupted social behavior and preserved factual social knowledge, as seen in the adult-onset condition, or would the acquisition of social knowledge at factual level be compromised as well? We addressed these questions by investigating two young adults who received focal nonprogressive prefrontal damage before 16 months of age.

Results

The evidence presented here is based on detailed histories obtained from medical and school records, as well as legal documents, extensive interviews with the patients' parents, clinical and experimental cognitive tasks and neuroimaging studies.

Clinical Evidence

The first patient (subject A) was 20 years old at the time of these studies and was ambidextrous. She had been run over by a vehicle at age 15 months. At the time of the accident, she appeared to recover fully within days. No behavioral abnormalities were observed until the age of three years, when she was first noted to be largely unresponsive to verbal or physical punishment. Her behavior became progressively disruptive, so much so that, by age 14, she required placement in the first of several treatment facilities. Her teachers considered her to be intelligent and academically capable, but she routinely failed to complete assigned tasks. Her adolescence was marked by disruptive behavior in school and at home (for example, failure to comply with rules, frequent loud confrontations with peers and adults). She stole from her family and from other children and shoplifted frequently, leading to multiple arrests. She was verbally and physically abusive to others. She lied chronically. Her lack of friends was conspicuous. She ran away from home and from treatment facilities. She exhibited early and risky sexual behavior leading to a pregnancy at age 18. Contingency management in residential treatment facilities and the use of psychotropic medication were of no help. After repeatedly putting herself at physical and financial risk, she became entirely dependent on her parents and on social agencies for financial support and oversight of her personal affairs. She did not formulate any plans for her future and she sought no employment. Whenever employment was arranged, she was unable to hold the job due to lack of dependability and gross infractions of rules. Affect was labile and often poorly matched to the situation, but superficial social behavior was unremarkable. She never expressed guilt or remorse for her misbehavior. There was little or no evidence that she experienced empathy, and her maternal behavior was marked by dangerous insensitivity to the infant's needs. She blamed her misdeeds and social difficulties on other people, and she denied any difficulties with cognition or behavior.

When first seen by us, the second patient (subject B) was 23 years old. He had undergone resection of a right frontal tumor at age three months. He had an excellent recovery and there were no signs of recurrence. Developmental milestones were normal and he was left handed. In early grade school, mild difficulties were noted with behavior control and peer interactions, but he was not especially disruptive in school or at home. By age nine, however, he showed a general lack of motivation, had limited social interactions, usually exhibited a neutral affect and suffered from occasional brief and explosive outbursts of anger. His work habits were poor, and tutoring was recommended. He was able to graduate from high school, but perhaps because of the loss of structure for daily activities, his behavioral problems escalated after graduation. Left to himself, he limited his activities to viewing television and listening to music. His personal hygiene was poor and his living quarters were filthy. He consumed large quantities of foods with high fat and sugar content, and became progressively more obese. He also displayed abnormal food choices, for instance, eating uncooked frozen foods. Given his frequent absences, tardiness and general lack of dependability, he could not hold a job. He showed reckless financial behavior which resulted in large debts, and engaged in poorly planned petty thievery. He frequently threatened others and occasionally engaged in physical assault. He lied frequently, often without apparent motive. He had no lasting friendships and displayed little empathy. His sexual behavior was irresponsible. He fathered a child in a casual relationship, and did not fulfill his paternal obligations. He was dependent on his parents for financial support and legal guardianship. He showed no guilt or remorse for his behavior and could not formulate any realistic plans for his future.

Both patients were raised in stable, middle-class homes by college-educated parents who devoted considerable time and resources to their children. In neither case was there a family history of neurologic or psychiatric disease, and both patients had socially well-adapted siblings whose behavior was normal. The neurological evaluation was normal in both patients, except for their behavioral defects.

Neuropsychological Evidence

Comprehensive neuropsychological evaluations (Table 1) revealed normal performances on measures of intellectual ability (for example, fund of general information, ability to repeat and reverse random sequence of digits, mental arithmetic, verbal reasoning, nonverbal problem solving, verbal and visual anterograde memory, speech

TABLE 1   Standardized neuropsychological test data.

		Subject A	Subject B
WAIS-R			
	Information	37	63
	Digit span	25	37
	Arithmetic	37	63
	Similarities	37	25
	Block design	75	75
	Digit symbol	25	25
RAVLT			
	Trial 5	78	11
	30 min. recall	99	68
JLO		40	57
Complex figure test			
	Copy	21	39
	30 min. recall	32	66
WRAT-R			
	Reading	86	63
	Spelling	81	63
	Arithmetic	32	58
COWA		43	15
WCST			
	Categories	>16	>16
	Persev. errors	1*	88
TOH			
	Trial 1	7*	7*
	Trial 2	1*	51
	Trial 3	1*	1*
	Trial 4	1*	1*
	Trial 5	1*	1*

WAIS-R, Wechsler Adult Intelligence Scale-Revised; RAVLT, Rey Auditory Verbal Learning Test; JLO, Judgment of Line Orientation; WRAT-R, Wide Range Achievement Test-Revised; COWA, Controlled Oral Word Association; WCST, Wisconsin Card Sorting Test; TOH, Tower of Hanoi.

All tests were administered according to standardized procedures[27, 28, 29]. Test performances are represented as percentile scores and impairment is indicated by an asterisk.

and language, visuospatial perception, visuomotor abilities and academic achievement). As in the case of patients with adult-onset lesions, the behavioral inadequacy of the two patients with early-onset lesions cannot be explained by a failure in basic mental abilities.

The patients were asked to perform several cognitive tasks designed to assess their ability to plan and execute multi-step procedures, use contingencies to guide behavior, reason through social dilemmas and generate appropriate responses to social situations. Both patients had significant impairments on these tasks. They failed to show normal learning of rules and strategies from repeated experience and feedback (Wisconsin Card Sorting Test, Subject A; Tower of Hanoi, both subjects). They also had significant impairments of social-moral reasoning and verbal generation of responses to social situations (Figure 1). Moral reasoning was conducted at a very early ('preconventional') stage, in which moral dilemmas were approached largely from the egocentric perspective of avoiding punishment[7]. This stage of moral reasoning is characteristic of 10-year-olds, and is surpassed by most young adolescents. The patients demonstrated limited consideration of the social and emotional implications of decisions, failed to identify the primary issues involved in social dilemmas and generated few response options for interpersonal conflicts. Their performance was in stark contrast to that of patients with adult-onset prefrontal damage, who can access the 'facts' of social knowledge in the format used in the laboratory (verbally packaged, outside of real life and real time[8]).

To explore the decision-making process further, the patients participated in a computerized version of the Gambling Task[9,10]. This task simulates real-life decision-making in the way it factors uncertainty of rewards and punishments associated with various response options. Unlike normal controls, but precisely as patients with adult-onset prefrontal lesions, both patients failed to develop a preference for the advantageous response options. They failed to choose options with low immediate reward but positive long-term gains; rather, they persisted in choosing response options which provided high immediate reward but higher long-term loss (Figure 2).

The electrodermal skin conductance response (SCR) was used as a dependent measure of somatic-state activation, according to methods described elsewhere[11]. After repeated trials, normal controls begin to generate anticipatory SCRs when pondering the selection of a risky response (a response which may lead to long-term punishment). However, both patients failed to acquire these anticipatory SCRs, although they did show normal SCRs to a variety of unconditioned stimuli. Again, these findings were similar to those from patients with adult-onset prefrontal damage[11].

Neuroimaging Evidence

The patients were studied with research-protocol magnetic resonance imaging, which permitted reconstruction of their brains in three dimensions using the

Level 3: Postconventional Stage 6: Personal commitment to universal moral principles. Stage 5: Recognition that moral perspective may conflict with law. Consider rights and welfare of all.	Achieved by a minority of adults One of 6 adult-onset patients at this level.
Level 2: Conventional Stage 4: Recognition of obligations to society. The individual is viewed within the system. Stage 3: Reliance on the Golden Rule. Be a good person in your own eyes and those of others.	Characteristic of most adults and adolescents. Five of 6 adult-onset patients at this level.
Level 1: Preconventional Stage 2: Concrete reasoning that, to serve one's own needs, you must recognize other's rights. Stage 1: Egocentric perspective with decisions based on avoidance of punishment.	Characteristic of most children under age 9. Both early-onset patients at this level.

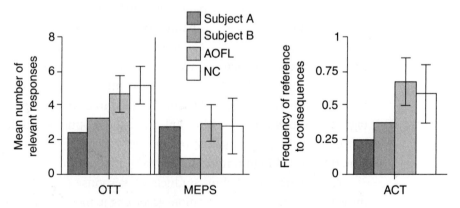

FIGURE 1   Social and moral reasoning. (a) Kohlberg Moral Judgment Task. (b) Social fluency; OTT, optional thinking test; MEPS, means–ends problem solving; ACT, awareness of consequences.

Brainvox technique and subsequent analysis of their anatomical defects. Both patients had focal damage to prefrontal regions, and had no evidence of damage in other brain areas (Figure 3). The lesion in subject A was bilateral and involved the polar and ventromedial prefrontal sectors. The lesion in subject B was unilateral, located in the right prefrontal region, and involved the polar sector, both medially and dorsally. The lesions of both patients were located in sites whose damage

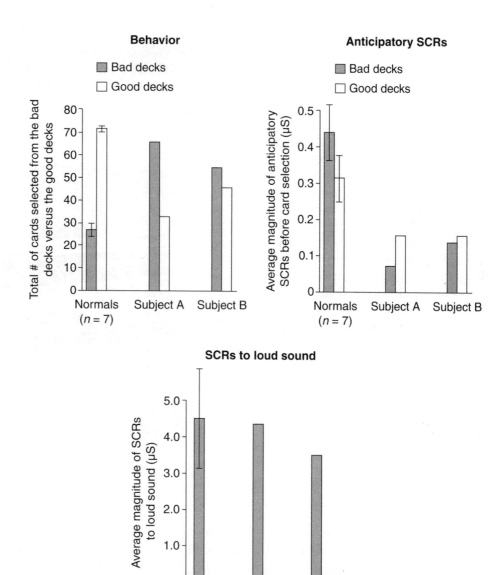

FIGURE 2   Experimental decision-making and psychophysiology. (**a**) Responses on the gambling task. (**b**) Anticipatory skin conductance responses (SCRs). (**c**) SCRs to an unconditioned stimulus (sudden onset of 110-dB noise).

in adults is known to produce the emotional and decision-making defects discussed above[2,3,12]. Most frequently, these defects are caused by ventromedial and bilateral lesions, but the condition also has been noted with exclusively right, medial or lateral prefrontal lesions. The critical issue seems to be dysfunction in the medial prefrontal cortices (which can be caused either by direct cortical damage or white matter undercutting) and the sparing of at least one dorsolateral prefrontal sector.

FIGURE 3   Neuroanatomical analysis.
(**a**) 3-D reconstructed brain of patient 1
(subject A). There was a cystic formation
occupying the polar region of both frontal
lobes. This cyst displaced and compressed
prefrontal regions, especially in the anterior
orbital sector, more so on the left than on the
right. Brodmann areas 11, 10 and 9 bilaterally,
and 46 and 47 on the left, were involved.
Additionally, there was structural damage in
the right mesial orbital sector and the left
polar cortices (Brodmann areas 11, 47 and
10). (**b**) 3-D reconstructed brain of patient 2
(subject B). There was extensive damage to
the right frontal lobe, encompassing prefrontal
cortices in mesial, polar and lateral sectors
(Brodmann areas 10, 9, 46 and 8.) Both the
lateral half of the orbital gyri and the anterior
sector of the cingulate gyrus were damaged.
(Brodmann areas 12, 24 and 32.) The cortex
of the inferior frontal gyrus was intact
(Brodmann areas 44, 45 and 47), but the
underlying white matter was damaged,
especially in the anterior sector.

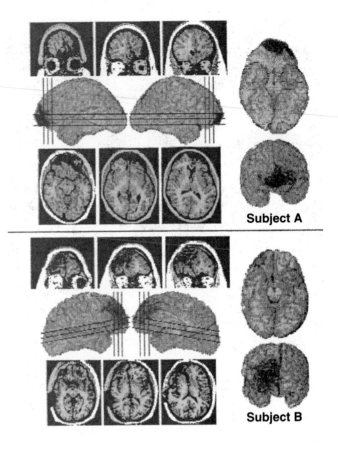

Subject A

Subject B

Discussion

We begin by acknowledging that our sample was small, but our findings accord
with the only two other recorded instances of patients with early onset frontal
lobe damage[13, 14], both with lifelong behavior dysfunction, although in neither case
is there precise neuroanatomical information. (One case, from 1947, predates modern neuropsychological and neuroimaging techniques, and lesions of the other
are not described satisfactorily and may not be confined to the prefrontal region.)
The sample is valuable, nonetheless, because of its rarity, and the evidence is offered
in the hope that it calls attention to other existing cases and facilitates their study
and the extension of the preliminary investigation noted here.

In answer to the first question we posed, the evidence presented above suggests that patients with early-onset prefrontal lesions in bilateral ventromedial or
right sectors resembled patients with comparable adult-onset lesions in a number of ways. In early-onset patients, emotional responses to social situations
and behavior in situations that require knowledge of complex social conventions
and moral rules were inadequate. But whereas the early-onset patients were
comparable, at first glance, to patients with adult-onset prefrontal lesions, a com-

prehensive analysis reveals several distinctive features. First, the inadequate social behaviors were present throughout development and into adulthood; second, those behavioral defects were more severe in early-onset patients; third, the patients could not retrieve complex, socially relevant knowledge at the factual level.

The greater severity of impairment in these two subjects was especially notable. The adult-onset prefrontal-lesion patients we studied ($n > 25$) generally do not show the sort of antisocial behavior noted in the early-onset patients, for example, stealing, violence against persons or property. Beyond the acute period, the disruptive behavior of adult-onset patients tends to be more constrained, although impulsiveness and susceptibility to immediately present environmental cues leave them at risk of violating the rights of others. More often than not, the victims are the adult-onset patients themselves, not others, and their social and moral ineptitude can hardly be described as antisocial.

Patients with impairments of social behavior caused by adult-onset lesions of the prefrontal cortex acquire varied aspects of socially relevant knowledge during normal development, and usually have had decades of appropriate application of such knowledge to social situations before incurring brain damage. As shown here and previously, following lesion onset in adulthood, they can continue to access socially relevant knowledge at the level of declarative facts[5], and they can even solve social problems when presented in a laboratory setting, that is, in a verbal format, outside of real time. This distinction might explain why the two patients described here seemed to show less of a sense of guilt and remorse relative to their conduct than do adult-onset patients. Admittedly, however, this is a clinical impression, and we have no controlled measurement yet to substantiate it.

The mechanisms whereby adult-onset patients fail in social behaviors are still under investigation, but we have suggested that an important mechanism of the defect is the disruption of the systems that hold covert, emotionally related knowledge of social situations[2,9]. Emotionally related knowledge is presumed to bias the reasoning process covertly, namely, by enhancing attention and working memory related to options for action and future consequences of choices, as well as to bias the process overtly, by qualifying options for action or outcomes of actions in emotional terms. When emotionally related knowledge, covert or overt, is no longer available or cannot be retrieved, as shown in experiments involving failure of anticipatory psychophysiological responses[10,11], the declarative recall of socially relevant facts either does not occur or is insufficient to ensure adequate social behavior in real-life and real-time circumstances. Given that early-onset patients failed in both emotionally-related and factual modes of retrieval, it is possible that they never acquired socially relevant knowledge, either in emotional or factual modes, and that their profound behavioral inadequacy is explained by an absence of the diverse knowledge base necessary for social and moral behavior.

The cognitive and behavioral defects present in these patients arose in the context of stable social environments that led to normal and well-adapted social behavior in their siblings. In spite of extensive exposure to appropriate social behavior in their home and school environments, and in spite of the relevant instruction, the patients failed to acquire complex social knowledge during the regular development period. Moreover, they failed to respond to programs aimed at correcting their inappropriate behavior during adolescence and young adulthood. This is an intriguing finding. Although comparison of different complex functions should be cautious, it is noteworthy that patients with early damage to language cortices, including those who undergo ablations of the entire left cerebral cortex at ages comparable to those at which our patients acquired their lesions, emerge into adolescence and adulthood with language defects whose magnitude seems smaller than the defects we encounter in the prefrontal patients described here. That the magnitude of compensation seemed smaller in our patients suggests that neural systems impaired by their lesions were critical for the acquisition of social knowledge, at least in the manner in which that acquisition traditionally occurs. It is possible, for instance, that by destroying a critical cortical control for the punishment and reward system, the acquisition of knowledge that depends on the coordinated contributions of punishment and reward situations becomes severely compromised. Should this be the case, it is possible that other neural systems might be recruited for the learning and processing of social knowledge, provided appropriate behavioral or pharmacological interventions could be developed. For example, cognitive-behavioral strategies that rely on a different balance of punishment and reward contributions might prove successful, and administration of neuromodulators such as serotonin and dopamine might conceivably help those interventions.

The cognitive and behavioral profiles resulting from early prefrontal damage resembled, in several respects, the profiles resulting from adult-onset damage. Unlike adult-onset patients, however, early-onset patients could not retrieve complex social knowledge at the factual level, and may never have acquired such knowledge. Overall, the profiles of early-onset patients bore considerable similarity to those of patients with psychopathy or sociopathy ('Conduct Disorder' or 'Antisocial Personality Disorder', according to DSM-IV nosology[15]), another early onset disorder characterized by a pervasive disregard for social and moral standards, consistent irresponsibility and a lack of remorse. Psychopathy may be associated with dysfunction in prefrontal regions[16–18], especially in persons without predisposing psychosocial risk factors[18]. Also of note, children with antisocial tendencies have deficiencies of moral reasoning relative to age-matched controls[19,20], and abnormal psychophysiological arousal and reactivity are found in adults with antisocial behavior[21]. The behavior of our patients differed from the typical profile of psychopathy in that our patients' patterns of aggression seemed impulsive rather than goal-directed, and also in the highly transparent, almost child-like nature of their transgressions and their attempts to cover them.

In conclusion, early dysfunction in certain sectors of prefrontal cortex seems to cause abnormal development of social and moral behavior, independently of social and psychological factors, which do not seem to have played a role in the condition of our subjects. This suggests that antisocial behavior may depend, at least in part, on the abnormal operation of a multi-component neural system which includes, but is not limited to, sectors of the prefrontal cortex. The causes of that abnormal operation would range from primarily biological (for instance, genetic, acting at the molecular and cellular levels) to environmental. Further clarification of these questions requires not only additional studies in humans, relying on both lesions and functional neuroimaging, but also experimental studies in developing animals, such as those demonstrating defects in social interactions of neonate monkeys with lesions of the amygdala and inferotemporal cortex[22].

Methods

The behavioral histories were based on evidence obtained from medical and school records and legal documents, as well as extensive interviews with the patients' parents. Participants in this research provided informed consent in accord with the policies of the Institutional Review Board of the University of Iowa College of Medicine. Neuroimaging analysis was conducted by an investigator blind to neuropsychological information, on the basis of thin-cut T1 weighted magnetic resonance (MR) images using Brainvox[23,24].

Comprehensive clinical neuropsychological evaluations were conducted according to standardized procedures (Table 1). Assessment of social knowledge and moral reasoning was based on four measures, Standard Issue Moral Judgment (SIMJ)[7], the Optional Thinking Test (OTT)[25], the Awareness of Consequences Test (ACT)[25] and the Means-Ends Problem Solving Procedure (MEPS)[26]. All of these procedures involve standardized verbal presentation to the subject of moral dilemmas or social situations, and require verbal responses.

In the SIMJ task, a subject is presented with a conflict between two moral imperatives (a man must steal a drug in order to save his wife's life). The subject is asked to describe the protagonist's proper actions and their rationale through a series of standard questions (for example, "Should he steal the drug?", "Is it right or wrong for him to steal it?" or "Why do you think that?"). Responses were scored according to explicit criteria to allow staging of specific levels of moral development. The OTT is designed to measure the ability to generate alternative solutions to hypothetical social dilemmas (for instance, two people disagree on what TV channel to watch). A series of probes are used to elicit as many potential solutions as the subject could produce. The number of discrete relevant alternative solutions is scored. The ACT is intended to sample a subject's spontaneous consideration of the consequences of actions. Hypothetical predicaments involving temptation to transgress ordinary rules of social conduct are presented (for instance, receiving too much money in a business transaction through a mistake), and the subject must describe how the scenario evolves, including the protagonist's thoughts prior to the action and the subsequent events. Scoring reflects the frequency with which the likely consequences of response options are considered. The MEPS is intended to measure a subject's ability to conceptualize effective means of achieving social goals. Scoring is based on the number of effective instrumental acts described as methods of achieving goals in hypothetical scenarios (for example, how to meet people in a new neighborhood).

In the Gambling Task, subjects are presented with four decks of cards (named A, B, C and D) and instructed to select cards from the decks in a manner to win as much play money as possible. After each card selection, they are awarded some money, but certain selections are also followed by a loss of money. The magnitude of the yield of each deck and the magnitude and frequency of punishment associated with each deck are controlled such that choosing from the decks with low initial reward turns out to be the most advantageous strategy over a long series of selections[9]. Subjects are required to make a series of 100 card selections, but they are not told in advance how many card selections they will be allowed to make. Cards can be selected one at a time from any deck, and subjects are free to switch from any deck to another at any time and as often as they wish. The decision to select from one deck or another is largely influenced by schedules of rewards and punishment. These schedules are pre-programmed and known to the examiner, but not to the subject. They are arranged in such a way that every time a card is selected from deck A or B, the subject gets $100, and every time a card deck is selected from C or D, the subject gets $50. However, in each of the four decks, subjects encounter unpredictable money loss (punishment). The punishment is set to be higher in the high-paying decks, A and B, and lower in the low-paying decks, C and D. In decks A and B, the subject encounters a total loss of $1,250 in every 10 cards. In decks C and D, the subject encounters a total loss of $250 in every 10 cards. In the longer term, decks A and B are disadvantageous because they cost more (a loss of $250 in every 10 cards). Decks C and D are advantageous because they result in an overall gain in the end (a gain of $250 in every 10 cards[6]).

The methods for the psychophysiological recordings (Figure 2) are described[11]. Response selection in the gambling task was temporally linked by computer to ongoing SCR recordings, and SCRs generated in the four seconds before behavioral response selection were considered to be anticipatory responses. The normal control subjects (three male, four female) were matched to the target subjects for age and education. The control subjects with adult onset prefrontal damage (three male, three female) were selected from our database on the basis of lesion location, in order to provide representation of adult-onset damage to prefrontal areas including, and more

FIGURE 4 Control subjects with adult-onset prefrontal damage. The overlap of lesions in the 6 patients with adult-onset lesions is depicted on a normal reference brain. Lesions of individual subjects were transferred onto the reference brain using MAP-3 (ref. 24). Darker shade indicates a higher number of overlapping subjects. The areas involved include all sectors damaged in the target subjects.

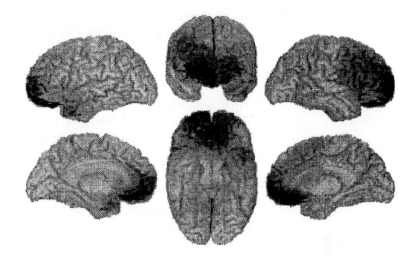

extensive than, the areas of damage in the early-onset cases (Figure 4). Lesions were due to a vascular event ($n = 3$) or resection of a meningioma ($n = 3$). Age of lesion onset ranged from 26 to 51 years, and subjects were studied at least one year following onset.

Acknowledgements

Supported by the National Institute of Neurological Diseases and Stroke Grant PO1 NS19632 and the Mathers Foundation.

1. Damasio, A. R., Tranel, D. & Damasio, H. in *Frontal Lobe Function and Dysfunction* (eds. Levin, H. S., Eisenberg, H. M. & Benton, A. L.) 217–229 (Oxford Univ. Press, New York, 1991).
2. Damasio, A. R. *Descartes' Error.* (Grosset/Putnam, New York, 1994).
3. Damasio, A. R. The somatic marker hypothesis and the possible functions of the prefrontal cortex. *Philos. Trans. R. Soc. Lond. B Biol. Sci.* **351**, 1413–1420 (1996).
4. Grafman, J. in *Structure and Functions of the Human Prefrontal Cortex* (eds. Grafman, J., Holyoak, K. J. & Boller, F.) 337–368 (1995).
5. Shallice, T. & Burgess, P. W. Deficits in strategy application following frontal lobe damage in man. *Brain* **114**, 727–741 (1991).
6. Stuss, D. T. & Benson, D. F. *The Frontal Lobes* (Raven, New York, 1986).
7. Colby, A. & Kohlberg, L. *The Measurement of Moral Judgment* (Cambridge Univ. Press, New York, 1987).
8. Saver, J. & Damasio, A. R. Preserved access and processing of social knowledge in a patient with acquired sociopathy due to ventromedial frontal damage. *Neuropsychologia* **29**, 1241–1249 (1991).
9. Bechara, A., Damasio, A. R., Damasio, H. & Anderson, S. W. Insensitivity to future consequences following damage to human prefrontal cortex. *Cognition* **50**, 7–15 (1994).
10. Bechara, A., Damasio, H., Tranel, D. & Damasio, A. R. Deciding advantageously before knowing the advantageous strategy. *Science* **275**, 1293–1295 (1997).

11. Bechara, A., Tranel, D., Damasio, H. & Damasio, A. R. Failure to respond autonomically to anticipated future outcomes following damage to prefrontal cortex. *Cereb. Cortex* **6**, 215–225 (1996).

12. Damasio, A. R. & Anderson, S. W. in *Clinical Neuropsychology*, 3rd edn. (eds. Heilman, K. M. & Valenstein, E.) 409–460 (Oxford Univ. Press, New York, 1993).

13. Ackerly, S. S. & Benton, A. L. Report of a case of bilateral frontal lobe defect. *Assoc. Res. Nerv. Ment. Dis.* **27**, 479–504 (1947).

14. Price, B. H., Daffner, K. R., Stowe, R. M. & Mesulam, M. M. The comportmental learning disabilities of early frontal lobe damage. *Brain*, **113**, 1383–1393 (1990).

15. American Psychiatric Association. *Diagnostic and Statistical Manual of Mental Disorders* 4th edn. (APA, Washington, District of Columbia, 1994).

16. Deckel, A. W., Hesselbrock, V. & Bauer, L. Antisocial personality disorder, childhood delinquency, and frontal brain functioning: EEG and neuropsychological findings. *J. Clin. Psychol.* **52**, 639–650 (1996).

17. Kuruoglu, A. C. *et al.* Single photon emission computerised tomography in chronic alcoholism. *Br. J. Psychiatry* **169**, 348–354 (1996).

18. Raine, A., Stoddard, J., Bihrle, S. & Buchsbaum, M. Prefrontal glucose deficits in murderers lacking psychosocial deprivation. *Neuropsychiatry Neuropsychol. Behav. Neurol.* **11**, 1–7 (1998).

19. Campagna, A. F. & Harter, S. Moral judgment in sociopathic and normal children. *J. Pers. Soc. Psychol.* **31**, 199–205 (1975).

20. Blair, R. J. R. Moral reasoning and the child with psychopathic tendencies. *Pers. Individ. Diff.* **22**, 731–739 (1997).

21. Scarpa, A. & Raine, A. Psychophysiology of anger and violent behavior. *Psychiatr. Clin. North Am.* **20**, 375–394 (1997).

22. Newman, J. D. & Bachevalier, J. Neonatal ablations of the amygdala and inferior temporal cortex alter the vocal response to social separation in rhesus macaques. *Brain Res.* **758**, 180–186 (1997).

23. Damasio, H. & Frank, R. J. Three-dimensional in vivo mapping of brain lesions in humans. *Arch. Neurol.* **49**, 137–143 (1992).

24. Frank, R. J., Damasio, H. & Grabowski, T. J. Brainvox: An interactive, multimodal visualization and analysis system for neuroanatomical imaging. *Neuroimage* **5**, 13–30 (1997).

25. Platt, J. J. & Spivack, G. *Measures of Interpersonal Problem-Solving for Adults and Adolescents* (Department of Mental Health Sciences, Hahnemann Medical College, Philadelphia, 1977).

26. Platt, J. J. & Spivack, G. *Manual for the Means-Ends Problem Solving Procedure* (Widener University Institute for Graduate Psychology, Chester, Pennsylvania, 1975).

27. Lezak, M. *Neuropsychological Assessment* 3rd edn. (Oxford Univ. Press, New York, 1995).

28. Davis, H. P., Bajsjar, G. M. & Squire, L. R. *Tower of Hanoi Test—Colorado Neuropsychology Tests Version 2.0.* (Western Psychological Services, Los Angeles, 1995).

29. Heaton, R. K. *et al. Wisconsin Card Sorting Test Manual* (Psychological Assessment Resources, Odessa, Florida, 1993).

Editor's Note

Correspondence should be addressed to A.R.D. (antonio-damasio@uiowa.edu)

Discussion Questions for Article 2

Section 2: Biological Bases of Behavior

Name: _____

PID: _____

Date: __ __ / __ __ / __ __ (MM/DD/YY)

CRN: _____

Recitation Day/Time: _____

Honor Code Signature: _____

1. Describe the role of the prefrontal cortex.

2. Compare the long-term effects of brain injury sustained in childhood to the effects of brain injury sustained in adulthood. How are they similar? How are they different?

3. Describe the neuropsychological tests that were used.

4. The two patients in this study displayed socially unacceptable behavior. How do the researchers know that this is not a result of how they were raised?

Sensation and Perception

While sensation and perception are closely related, they play slightly different roles in how we interpret the world around us. Sensation refers to the process of taking in information about our environment through our sensory receptors. The basic five senses of seeing, hearing, tasting, touching, and smelling are all processes of gathering information. This information is then sent to the brain to be interpreted.

Perception is the interpretation of our sensory information and a means of understanding everything around us.

Many researchers in the field of sensation and perception have focused on illusions. This type of research has helped to differentiate between sensation and perception. The illustration above is known as the Hermann Grid, named after L. Herman who first reported this illusion. When examining the matrix of black squares, most see grey spots where the white lines intersect. The same intensity of light is being reflected all along the white spaces within the grid; however lateral inhibition in the light receptors of your eyes causes the intersections to appear grey. You *sense* the same color white yet you *perceive* grey spots in the intersections. This phenomenon is an example of how sensation is different from perception in that what we sense and what we perceive are not always the same.

Although our sensory receptors are somewhat advanced, there are many things around us that we are not able to sense. For example, we don't sense radio waves around us or see the microscopic germs on our skin. Our senses are not designed to detect all of the things in our environment. With any of our senses, there is a minimum amount of stimulation needed for us to be able to sense something, whether it is a sound that is just loud enough for us to hear or a light that is just bright enough for us to see. The point at which a stimulus goes from being undetectable to detectable is known as the absolute threshold.

Just as there are things around us that cannot be sensed, there are also things around us that are sensed but are not perceived. At any given moment, there is a large amount of sensory information being taken in. The human brain is limited in terms of resources and cannot attend to each and every stimulus, only the relevant stimuli are interpreted. For example, we may not always perceive what people are saying in the background. Even though the physical sounds are taken in by our ears, our brain may not process the information if it is focused on another task (such as watching television). When this occurs we fail to perceive the stimulus, thus perception is a subjective experience.

Psychophysics is the study of how sensations are translated into perceptions. Two major process models have been widely accepted: top-down and bottom-up processing. Top-down processing is a way of perceiving things around us by relying on cognitive information. Through this process, perceptions are formed from one's own expectations before the sensory information is carefully examined. With bottom-up processing, perception begins with sensory information. This information works its way from the sensory levels up to the higher cortex areas. In bottom-up processing, perception is determined by how the different sensory stimuli are combined.

Article 1: Are We Led by the Nose?

This article examines our sense of smell, how it differs among people, and how we use odors in everyday life. David Griffin lost his ability to smell as a result of head trauma. Information from David's everyday life without being able to detect odors reveals the importance of this often unappreciated sense. The article moves from this opening story into describing how the sense of smell affects our everyday lives. Although it is historically thought to be a primitive process, studying and understanding olfaction can be rather complicated. The article presents some of the factors that affect our ability to smell odors and ends by suggesting that even though olfaction is not completely understood, it has always been an integral part of neuroscience research.

Article 2: Re-acquisition of Upright Vision while Wearing Visually Left-Right Reversing Goggles

The second article looks at how goggles that induce left-right reversal can also impair our ability to distinguish up from down. When standing upright, the left-right glasses do not affect one's perception of what is up and what is down. However, if using the same left-right glasses while lying on one's side, upright vision suddenly becomes disturbed. In this case, even though touch information is being taken in from the right side of the body lying on the floor, the visual information overpowers and the person feels as if they are lying on their left side. The article concludes by explaining that lying down removes any available symmetry cues. An individual can no longer see his or her body, and this allows the person to be fooled by left-right reversal glasses.

—*Clinton S. Comer*

Article 1

Are We Led by the Nose?

Terence Monmaney

On a rainy October night in Chicago 11 years ago, 33-year-old mathematician David Griffin* stepped off a curb and into the path of a Dodge van. He was on his usual after-dinner walk, although he was perhaps feeling an unusual need for it—the buffet supper of turkey and potatoes and fixings had not fully agreed with him.

Griffin considered himself something of an epicure, with an ability to taste and smell that was the functional equivalent of perfect pitch. Impressed once, for instance, by the exotic flavor of some broiled fish he had eaten in a restaurant in Pisa, he divined the secret recipe and recreated the dish, down to the basting of lime juice, rosemary, and mustard.

The van was moving about five miles an hour when it hit him. He cracked his skull on the pavement. His recovery was good, and during the eight days he spent in the hospital he did not have any remarkable symptoms. True, he noticed that the hospital food was terribly bland and yet very salty, but that was clearly just a sign of his good taste. It appeared he would suffer no deep or lasting injury. The day after returning home he poured his father a snifter of pear brandy—sweet, ethereal, redolent of fruit ripening in a sunwashed orchard—and discovered he could smell absolutely nothing. "I was devastated," he says.

The doctors said that if he still couldn't smell anything after six months to a year, he probably never would. The blow, they explained, apparently tore nerves connecting his brain and nose. Griffin's taste buds worked fine, so at least he sensed

---

*This is not his real name, but all the details of his case are true.

Between your eyes, just below the forebrain, some 20 million olfactory nerves hang from the roof of each nasal cavity, their wispy cilia bathed in mucus, swaying in the currents like sea grass.

the salty, bitter, sour, and sweet ingredients in food. Seven years went by. His condition unchanged, Griffin sued the van's driver and won a modest settlement.

These days—well, he has resigned himself to an odorless existence, rationalizing that it certainly could be worse. Yet he has learned it is a hazardous as well as a hollow way of life.

Shortly after the accident his apartment building caught fire; he awoke to the shouts of neighbors, not to the smell of smoke that might have alerted him sooner. He cannot detect leaking gas. He has been poisoned by spoiled food. But Griffin says he suffers a more profound loss: deprived now of the rush of memory that an odor can let loose, he feels cut off from moments in his own past. "Think about rotting leaves or a campfire or a roast or a Christmas tree—I enjoyed those smells so much. I miss not being able to experience them again and be reminded of other times. A dimension of my life is missing. I feel empty, in a sort of limbo."

Approximately one out of every 15 victims of head trauma wakes up in a permanently odorless world. Accidents are the leading cause of anosmia (loss of smell) in people Griffin's age. Influenza, brain tumors, allergies, and the uncertain effects of old age are other reasons some 2 million people in the United States can't small anything. No surveys have charted what these people miss most, but it's safe to say their lives lack spice

At least three quarters of the flavors in food and drink are not tastes but aromas. The volatile essences of black pepper or blue cheese are breathed into passageways originating at the back of the mouth and delivered to olfactory nerve endings high in the nasal cavities.

Sex without smells is not quite the same either, according to Robert Henkin, former director of the Center for Sensory Disorders, Georgetown University. He says about one in four people with little or no smelling ability loses some sex drive. This is hardly the loss suffered by a male golden hamster with such a disability— remove that part of his brain devoted to olfaction and he'll give up mating entirely. But it suggests how our lives are enriched by olfactory signals, however unconsciously we tune them in.

The mysterious way smells refresh memories fascinates novelists as well as neuroscientists. Proust said the aroma of lime-flower tea and madeleines launched his monumental *Remembrances of Things Past*. Kipling, in his poem "Lichtenberg," wrote that the pungence of rainsoaked acacia meant home. That smell should be the most nostalgic sense seems logical. Compared with sights, sounds, and touch, odors are messages that last; the smell of burned gunpowder lingers long after the firecracker has sparkled and popped.

Unlike some other animals, we don't much rely on our noses to get around anymore, although some curious new experiments suggest we could if we were so inclined. Researchers at the Monell Chemical Senses Center in Philadelphia have shown that humans can smell the difference between two mice that are identical except for a small set of genes on one chromosome. People can in fact distinguish the urine of these two mice. If we close our eyes and lower our noses, we might not only find the urine-marked trails mice leave but tell one mouse's route from another's.

But we don't often track odors—we just keep track of them. The close tie between odors and memory is more than happy coincidence; without it, odors would be meaningless. You can't identify an odor you've never experienced any more than you can recognize a face you've never seen.

The most primitive and evocative of the senses, smell is also the most intimate. Odors give you away. Everyone knows you can't hide alcohol on the breath. The urine of children with the genetic disease phenylketonuria is mousy. Intimate, too, is the very act of smelling. You have to inhale the stimulus, bring it inside, before you know what to make of it. "Touch seems to reside in the object touched . . ." Helen Keller wrote, "and odor seems to reside not in the object smelt, but in the organ."

The smelling organ turns out to be a lot more complicated than scientists imagined it would be: Chemicals flowing into some hollow tubes and reacting with a bunch of nerves—what could be simpler? But there are two strange things about olfactory nerves. For one, they constantly replace themselves, the only nerves we have capable of rebirth. One by one they die after a month or so, and new nerves sprout from cells in the nasal lining, growing thin filaments that seek the brain like seedlings pushing toward sunlight.

The reason olfactory nerves probably need to renew themselves is the other strange thing. Protected merely by a film of mucus, they are the only nerve endings out in the open. In the nose, in other words, the brain directly confronts and tries to sort out the world.

Michael Shipley, a neurobiologist at the University of Cincinnati College of Medicine, is one of the new breed of olfaction researchers trying to get to the brain through the nose. "I've got a hunch if we can come close to understanding how the brain keeps track of odors," he says, "we'll be a long way toward understanding how it processes other kinds of information."

Between your eyes, just below the forebrain, some 20 million olfactory nerves hang from the roof of each nasal cavity, their wispy cilia bathed in mucus, swaying in the currents like sea grass. Just here, where olfactory nerves greet odorants dissolved in mucus, researchers have for decades drawn a blank. What nobody understands is what everybody wants to know: Why do things smell the way they do?

Solving the problem would be easier if all odors could be broken down into a few elements, as visible light can be separated into its spectral colors. The retina can faithfully reproduce a scene, in color, by means of a few sensory cell types, such as those dedicated to picking up red, green, or blue. But there is no odor spectrum. Olfactory nerves must recognize each odorant individually.

Many scientists imagine that olfactory receptors work like other receptors—like, say, the specialized protein on a muscle cell that receives the hormone insulin in the way a lock admits a key, and passes along insulin's message to break down more glucose. One problem with this idea, though, is that it doesn't account for the smell of a new car. While it's conceivable that olfactory nerves have evolved receptors for natural odorants, surely humans haven't had time to evolve receptors devoted specifically to smelling the vinyl odors in a new car's interior. Around 10,500 chemical compounds are invented or discovered each week, and many are smelly.

Another idea, publicized by physician-essayist Lewis Thomas a decade ago, suggests that the immune and smelling systems, both dedicated to recognizing new, foreign substances, perform that task in much the same way. Recently, researchers at the Johns Hopkins Medical School offered some support for the theory. They discovered a protein in the nasal linings of cows that binds specifically to six different types of smelly chemicals, including pyrazines, which give scent to bell peppers. This pyrazine-binding protein, they say, looks and behaves somewhat like

Boys and girls both start smelling right away. We're generally outfitted to smell days before birth, so it is possible we get a whiff of the world in the womb. Perhaps from spicy amniotic fluid we might begin to acquire a taste for garlic.

a disease-fighting antibody protein. From this bit of evidence it would appear that our smelling and immune systems literally come to grips with the outside by tailoring a protein to fit new materials encountered.

This theory of made-to-odor receptors represents a promising new approach, but it probably won't tell the whole story even if it holds up. Neurobiologist Robert Gesteland of the University of Cincinnati College of Medicine says, "Since these nerve cells are sitting out there in the fluid, accessible to the world—anything that gets into the fluid in your nose is certainly going to get to those cells—probably a few different receptor mechanisms have evolved. And no experiment so far favors one mechanism over another."

Seeing, touching, hearing—the neurons controlling these senses are relatively "hard wired," a fact of life the brain seems to have taken advantage of. It keeps track of stimuli by sending them down dedicated circuits. A dot of light on the retina, for instance, sets off an impulse through the optic nerve that activates brain cells corresponding to just that point on the retina.

Gordon Shepherd, a Yale University neuroscientist, believes olfaction works in a manner something like that of the other senses, despite its obvious differences. In his view, an odorant first stimulates particular receptors, which then transmit a signal to neurons dedicated to that odor in the olfactory bulbs, two matchstick-size brain structures above the nasal cavities. Those cells relay the news to brain centers involved, ultimately, in behavior appropriate to that odor. When researchers in Shepherd's lab analyzed the olfactory bulbs of newborn rats, they found that certain odors—especially those associated with the mother rat's nipples—were processed by a particular patch of cells on the bulbs, the makings of a kind of olfactory circuit. One stimulus, one circuit, one response—presented with the odor, the newborn suckles.

Walter Freeman, a neurophysiologist at the University of California, Berkeley, doesn't believe in olfactory circuits. He measures brain waves emanating from the olfactory bulb of a rabbit while it sniffs an odor. When a rabbit is presented with an odor for the first time, according to Freeman's studies, its olfactory bulbs give off brain waves in fairly disordered fashion. After several exposures to an odor, a pattern emerges, and thereafter that odor prompts that pattern of neuronal activity—the sign of recognition.

The essence of Freeman's view is that olfactory neurons—and perhaps all neurons devoted to the senses—are not hard wired to perform single tasks but are creative; given a stimulus, they improvise a song of brain waves to go with it, and later sing the theme whenever cued. When Freeman speaks of neurons in action, he refers not to circuits but to ensembles.

Freeman's and Shepherd's views of olfactory-signal processing may simply be different versions of the same reality. It is too early to tell. But it's important to know, because the stakes are high: an understanding of the means by which the brain turns stimulus into sensation. Many olfaction researchers believe that even those who study vision and hearing (the so-called higher senses) and touch will have to turn to olfaction for inspiration. Ultimately, sensory biologists are in pursuit of the answer to the same question: How does a particular clump of neurons in the brain generate the awareness of an F-sharp, say, or a 1983 chardonnay?

Richard Doty is in a glistening steel room showing off his olfactometer. Fluorescent lights shine through chrome grids in the ceiling, and the walls and floors are paneled with stainless steel. The room, in a University of Pennsylvania hospital, is as odor proof as can be.

The olfactometer is a closet-size machine connected by steel piping to a thing on a table that looks like a glass octopus with 11 tentacles. You put your nostril over the tip of a tentacle and the machine serves up a precisely measured wisp of, say, phenylethyl alcohol, an essence of rose. Then you indicate whether or not you detect it. In this way Doty measures smelling thresholds.

From the looks of this room you might get the idea that olfaction research is so advanced that the only task remaining is to add more decimal places to existing data. Yet smelling isn't such a precise experience. Your sensitivity to phenylethyl alcohols depends on your health, your allergies, whether you're tired or rested, whether you smelled it an hour ago, the humidity, the elevation above sea level, your age, and your sex.

So, the exquisite high-tech instruments so impressive to funding agencies won't necessarily solve the mysteries of human smelling. Consider Doty's low-tech success. He recently settled two much-debated questions—does smelling ability decline with age, and are men or women better smellers?—using a $20 scratch-and-sniff test.

It comes in a letter-size envelope and consists of 40 scratch-and-sniff patches: bubble gum, paint thinner, menthol, cherry, leather, skunk, pizza. Next to each patch are the words, "This odor smells most like," followed by four choices. One is correct. At his lawyer's request, David Griffin, the mathematician struck by a van, took the test twice, and the scores helped convince the judge of Griffin's anosmia. He scored 9 and 8 out of 40. A score of 35 or better is considered normal. By now the researchers have administered the University of Pennsylvania Smell Identification Test to more than 5,000 people—males and females, white and black Americans, Korean-Americans, native Japanese (they had trouble recognizing cherry), some 50 five-year-olds, and many over 90.

Doty and his coworkers discovered that smelling power does fade late in life and that the sense is sharpest around middle age: The average score for 20- to 50-year-olds was 37. The average for 75-year-olds was 30. What's more, a quarter of the people between 65 and 80, and half of those over 80, appear anosmic. As the researchers concluded, "it is not surprising that many elderly persons complain that food lacks flavor and that the elderly account for a disproportionate number of accidental gas poisoning cases each year."

In a study published last May, these investigators showed that patients with Alzheimer's disease are unusually likely to have smelling deficits. Of 25 men and women diagnosed with Alzheimer's, all but 2 scored lower on the test than age-matched control subjects without the degenerative disease. "It's interesting that in a disease like Alzheimer's where memory loss is a major dysfunction there is also a problem with olfaction," Doty says. Researchers at Stanford and other universities have also demonstrated that memory and smelling often fade together in Alzheimer patients. Olfaction may even sometimes disappear before other problems become evident, Doty says. Scratching and sniffing could turn out to be an effective and inexpensive screening tool for the disease.

Digging deeper into the test results, Doty found that at every age, women scored better on the smelling test than men, in all ethnic groups tested so far. At peak performance, by those subjects around middle age, the differences were slight—a point or less, on average. At the extremes it was more dramatic. Five-year-old boys scored an average of 27, while girls of the same age scored 34. At the other end, 65-year-old men averaged 33, compared with the 36 scored by 65-year-old women.

Doty can't explain the sex differences, but he may have ruled out one popular theory. Researchers who previously said women are superior smellers often gave credit to ovarian hormones like estrogen. After all, pregnant women, who are besieged by hormones, are considered especially acute smellers. But, Doty asks, if ovarian hormones are the key, why are five-year-old girls, years shy of puberty, better smellers than five-year-old boys?

Whatever their differences, boys and girls both start smelling right away. We're born with a set of olfactory nerves and bulbs already in working order. We're generally outfitted to smell days before birth, so it is possible we get a whiff of the world in the womb. Researchers have even suggested, and not entirely in jest, that from spicy amniotic fluid we might begin to acquire a taste for garlic, or cigarettes.

Rats, anyway, learn a thing or two about their mothers in utero, according to experiments done at Johns Hopkins by psychologists Elliot Blass and Patricia Pedersen, who now works in Shepherd's lab at Yale. A rat pup, born deaf and blind, smells the way to its mother's nipples, homing in on the already familiar odor of amniotic fluid on her underside. They found that if they injected a pregnant rat with citral, a lemon scent, a few days before she gave birth, the pups would prefer citral-rinsed nipples to their own mother's.

Blass and psychologist Thomas Fillion, of Yale, completed further experiments showing how odors shape behavior. Again the experiments were done on rats, and again the researchers can't say what the findings mean for the rest of us. But you have to wonder. They say odors that rats experience while suckling can be a sexual turn-on later in life.

Each experiment began with a litter of pups that were suckled by mothers whose nipples and genitals were painted with citral. After weaning, the male pups were isolated from both citral odors and females until they reached sexual maturity, at about 100 days. Then the rats were introduced to a female in heat—either a normal female or one with citral-scented genitals.

Blass and Fillion found that males exposed to citral while suckling were more eager to mate with citral-scented females and finished mating more quickly—an average of five minutes, or 30 percent, faster than when mating with normal females. "These findings," the researchers concluded, "suggest that, at least for this mammal, the degree to which a feminine feature is sexually arousing to adult males can be established in the context of suckling."

What's exciting to the male rat, apparently, is not any particular odor—fragrance of lemon furniture polish will do—but the sensation associated with it. "There's a learning process going on," Fillion says. "My intuition is that suckling is such a powerful experience, and the arousal provided by it is so powerful, it's an ideal time and place for any mammal to learn an important sensory cue." Far from coldly objectifying rat sex, Blass and Fillion have revealed its poignance, showing it is in part a rat's pursuit of infantile satisfactions.

No equivalent studies have been done on humans, but research does show that babies experience and recognize maternal odors while suckling. The first such study was done a decade ago at the University of California, San Francisco, by Michael Russell, then a graduate student. A two-day-old infant, he showed, would not respond to a cotton pad worn for three hours in its mother's bra. Yet most six-week-olds tested did begin suckling if they smelled a cotton pad worn by their mothers, although they didn't respond to a pad worn in the bra of an unfamiliar lactating woman. Writing in *Nature*, Russell also noted that most infants were obviously attracted to their mother's scent and often repulsed by a stranger's. Russell concluded: "The existence of olfactory maternal attraction suggests that humans have a pheromonal system and that it operates at a very early age."

A pheromone is a substance that is produced by an organism and that elicits a specific and unlearned response in another member of the same species. At least that's how researchers defined it in 1959, after collecting several examples of chemicals that insects use to communicate—ant trail markers, queen-bee anointments, and so forth. By the mid-1970s there was an increased interest in human pheromones, and Russell's study was considered by many as support for the substances' existence.

But critics say Russell never ruled out the possibility that the infants were merely recognizing ordinary odors, even traces of their own saliva. What Russell called "olfactory maternal attraction," they said, was simply the infant's recognition, after learning, of their mothers' body odor.

The strongest case for a human pheromone involves menstrual synchrony. Psychologist Martha McClintock wasn't the first to notice that when women live together in close quarters for months at a time, their menstrual cycles begin to coincide. But her 1970 study of women in a college dormitory documented synchrony so thoroughly that the phenomenon is now widely known as the McClintock effect. And she made the crucial observation that many of the dormitory residents adopted the rhythms of a certain few women—perhaps, she said, because they broadcast a chemical signal, a pheromone, that the other women heeded.

Skeptics have said women achieve menstrual synchrony because they eat, study, wash, vacation, talk, and stay up all night together; shared stresses and joys regulate their cycles, not chemical messages. Still, late last year, researchers at the Monell Chemical Senses Center and the University of Pennsylvania offered the firmest evidence yet that pheromones mediate the McClintock effect. George Preti and Winnifred Culter exposed 10 women with no normal cycles to underarm sweat from other women. The subjects were daubed under the nose every few days with the female sweat. After three months, the subject's cycles began to coincide with sweat-donors' cycles—evidence, the researchers say, that a pheromone in sweat mediates menstrual synchrony (other women, controls, were daubed with alcohol and showed no significant change). "Pheromone effects are real in human beings," Preti grandly told the *Washington Post*, "and the anec-

Researchers at the Monell Chemical Senses Center have shown that humans can smell the difference between two mice that are identical except for a small set of genes on one chromosome.

dotal evidence suggests they even occur here in the United States, where we're all deodorized and perfumized."

Maybe so. But Doty doesn't believe that humans, like moths, have automatic or built-in responses to certain odors or pheromones; instead, he says, we interpret odors much as we do visual or auditory signals: "If I'm walking down the street and see a woman with beautiful blond hair and I get sort of excited—you don't say blond hair is a *visualmone*. Our idea of what is attractive depends on styles we grow up with, what we see on TV, what society values. In some cultures blond hair is unattractive. The same thing occurs in the sense of smell. Smelling is just a way of extracting information from chemicals in the environment. The *meaning* that information may have is affected by locale and learning and memory, by the context of the experience."

That is partly what makes the smell of smoke pleasant at a barbecue, not so welcome in a movie theater. Even a rat can learn that an odor's message depends on the context. Trained to anticipate a rewarding sip of water after smelling the banana odor of amyl acetate, a rat will quickly learn to avoid amyl acetate if the "reward" is changed to an electric shock. A silkworm moth is less flexible. It is difficult to imagine training the moth not to respond to bombykol, a mating pheromone secreted by females that males can detect from miles away.

Psychologist William Cain's experiments at the Pierce Foundation at Yale spell out how important the context is. Cain asked a dozen undergraduates to identify by smell alone 80 familiar things, such as baby powder, burned toast, shoe polish, and popcorn. The samples were kept in opaque jars and the students, eyes closed, sniffed them through cloth. They could identify fewer than half. "They knew the smell was familiar," says Cain. "They just couldn't always name it."

It happens all the time. You've smelled it before, you like it—but what is the spice in that dish, what is it about that perfume? Cain, Shipley, and others believe odors often leave us dumb because brain centers concerned with language are not richly connected to the olfactory cortex.

For most of us, as Cain's study suggests, smelling is somehow remote from the higher cognitive functions. You cannot really conjure up an odor in the way you can imagine a face or voice. Nor can you manipulate that image as you can rotate an imaginary cube, for example, or put words in someone's mouth. And while odors evoke memories, the opposite is not generally true.

That's because there are different brain structures for detecting and remembering odors, according to Gary Lynch, a neurobiologist at the University of California, Irvine. After the olfactory bulbs receive and sort a signal, they relay it to several places—to the olfactory cortex (to make you aware you smell something), and from there to centers involved in memory (most importantly the hippocampus, which connects to higher visual centers). Although information flows from olfactory bulbs to hippocampus to visual cortex, prompting a memory, visual information can't make it back to odor-sensing areas of the olfactory cortex.

Kipling saw this memory lane as a one-way street in "Lichtenberg." After reaching town and its smell of wattle, or acacia, a cascade of memories—"the picnics and brass-bands"—is let loose, courtesy of hippocampal connection:

> "It all came over me in one act
> Quick as a shot through the brain—
> With the smell of the wattle round Lichtenberg,
> Riding in, in the rain."

Lynch believes that the kind of memory we use to store facts began to emerge in some primitive mammal 100 million years ago, as a means of keeping track of odors. It was only a matter of time before a more advanced smeller made a breakthrough, rousing the image corresponding to an odor—"mother," say—without actually smelling her. In this evolutionary view, the collections of neurons originally designed to process olfactory information gave rise to higher forms of memory and cognition; the human forebrain, seat of art making and history writing and joke telling, is basically a souped-up smelling machine.

You can take this as an insult to your intelligence or a celebration of your nose. But the more neuroscientists learn about smelling, the more it looks right for this sophisticated new role. Olfactory nerves in flux, receptors arising to each smelly occasion, bulbs creating patterns of neuronal activity for each odorant, memory linking the sensation of odor with whatever happens to be around—you'd expect this sort of creativity of the sense that introduced learning and memory into the world.

Brainy snobs, our noses up in the air, we don't follow odor trails anymore. We work in skyscrapers where the windows don't open, drive around in climate-controlled cars, hide behind "five-day deodorant protection," gobble up processed cheese. We are starting to act like birds, too high up and fast-moving to heed earthly chemical signals.

Even as our lives become more rarefied, the orphan sense, as Lynch calls it, is turning into one of the premier problems in biology. "Olfaction has always been in the back shed of neuroscience," Walter Freeman says. "The reason is largely emotional, I think. It has always been thought of as primitive. It's not glamorous. Olfaction is—it's *smells*."

Editor's Note

Terence Monmaney writes about health for Newsweek.

Discussion Questions for Article 1

Section 3: Sensation and Perception

Name: _____

PID: _____

Date: __ __ / __ __ / __ __ (MM/DD/YY)

CRN: _____

Recitation Day/Time: _____

Honor Code Signature: _____

1. How was David Griffin's life affected by anosmia?

2. How are odors and memories related?

3. What differences exist between the neurons involved in smell and the neurons involved with our other senses?

4. If you had to chose one of your senses to live without, what would it be and why?

Article 2

Re-acquisition of Upright Vision while Wearing Visually Left-Right Reversing Goggles

Hirokazu Yoshimura

Abstract: The present research aimed to identify the important factor that makes it difficult to re-acquire upright vision when wearing visually trans-posed goggles. The author wore left-right reversing goggles and up-down reversing goggles each for 14 days in 1986 and in 1990, respectively. When lying on one side with the left-right reversing goggles on, the observer could get upside-down vision, which made it possible to compare the difficulty of attaining upright vision when wearing up-down reversing goggles. The only difference between the two situations is the dimension of the body image to be exchanged: The observer had to exchange the left and right halves of his body in the former situation and had to exchange along the top-bottom axis of body in the latter situation. Introspective data revealed that attaining an upright sense is easier in the former situation; this means that the asym-metrical structure of our body in the top-bottom dimension is an important factor in the difficulty of re-acquiring upright vision.

Key words: upright vision, visual transposition, perceptual adaptation, left-right reversal, up-down reversal.

The problem of upright vision has been explored only through visual up-down reversal or inversion (180-degree rotation) experiments that contain the visual reversal of the up-down dimension. The present research, however, demonstrates that left-right reversal vision experiments are effective when the observer lies on his side. The left-right reversing goggles do not reverse up and down along the vertical body axis; thus, we may think the goggles do not affect the upright vision. This notion, however, is true only when the observer is standing upright. When the observer lies down, the situation changes drastically. In that condition, the left-right reversing goggles transpose vision in the up-down (ceiling-floor) dimension, thus producing upside-down vision. The upside-down impression when lying on one's side in the left-right reversal experiments is common to the impression when standing in the up-down reversal experiments in the sense that the visual information of ceiling and floor contradicts the gravity information. In this article, "upright vision" indicates that the observer sees the ceiling upward and the floor downward in space, resulting in perception consistent with body orientation.

Generally speaking, it takes a long time to re-acquire upright vision when wearing up-down reversing or inverting goggles. Since Stratton's (1897) experiment, researchers in this field have recognized that upright vision could be re-acquired by unifying the seen and felt sense of the body. In their experiments, the observers barely achieved unstable upright vision after wearing inverting or up-down reversing goggles for a long time: Stratton (1897) wearing for 8 days, Peterson and Peterson (1938) for 14 days, Snyder and Pronko (1952) for 30 days, and Dolezal (1982) for 14 days.

There are three factors that may explain the reason for the difficulty in unifying the seen and felt sense of the body in visual up-down reversal experiments. First, the ceiling (sky)—floor (ground) axis, which defines the up-down dimension of space, has a very distinguishable meaning; therefore, "up" and "down" should not be exchangeable (compared to the similarity of the left and right sides). Second, the information from gravity disturbs the exchange. Third, the asymmetrical structure of our body in the top–bottom axis, as compared to the highly symmetrical structure in the left-right axis, should make it more difficult to reverse the up-down body axis.

When the observer wearing the left-right reversing goggles lies down on either side, the first two factors are preserved but the condition for the last factor changes drastically. When the observer lies down, he should visually reverse the left-right halves of the body, but not the asymmetrical upper-lower parts. The purpose of the present research was to estimate the importance of the last factor for unifying the seen and felt sense of the body. This can be realized by comparing the difficulty of re-acquiring upright vision between the two kinds of visual reversal experiments.

Method

Subject

The observer was the author, who wore the left-right reversing goggles for 14 days (from Day 1 to Day 15) in 1986, and the up-down reversing goggles for the same period in 1990.

Goggles

Both the left-right reversing and up-down reversing goggles were hand-made with two acrylic right-angle prisms, 60 mm hypotenuse face $\times$ 43 mm lateral face $\times$ 40 mm length. In order to reverse the vision, a pair of the right-angle prisms was set immediately in front of each eye. The prisms were mounted on a light wood frame and fixed to the head by a cloth band. The binocular visual field of the left-right reversing goggles was set at about 75 degrees horizontally and 55 degrees vertically, overlapping at the center by about 15 degrees; the up-down reversing goggles were set at about 80 degrees horizontally and 44 degrees vertically, overlapping at the center by about 12 degrees. The total weight for each was about 160 g.

Procedure

During the time of the experiments, the observer wore the prism goggles continually, except when sleeping or taking a bath; then he wore a sleeping-mask to exclude visual stimuli. The observer spent most of his time in or near his house, and at the university, where he was taken by car. The results of several different tests done periodically during the wearing time are reported in other articles (Yoshimura, 1996, 1999).

The present article focuses on the introspective data concerning the re-acquisition of upright vision reported by the observer. The observer carried a portable tape recorder throughout the experiments and recorded his perceptual impressions, including the behavioral strategies he employed.

Results and Discussion

Introspection Reported in the Experiment Using Up-Down Reversing Goggles

On the first day, the observer perceived himself to be standing upright and the scene to be upside down. In spite of the prolonged wearing time, this impression essentially did not change, as the following introspection points out.

Day 10. When walking under the room light facing forward, I felt as if my body would have touched the light suspended from the ceiling. Still, I am standing upright and the scene was upside down.

The sense of being upright was limited to the specific situation and it was unstable, as suggested from the following introspection.

Day 13. I'm now lying on my stomach and looking forward. The field of vision is mostly occupied by the images of the closest parts of the tatami. Then, I look at my four-year-old son who is sitting at his low desk. He looks normal in the right side up position, not upside down. I think he looks upright for two reasons. First, most of the field of vision is occupied by tatami mats, which indicate the ground of space; in turn, these become the frame of reference for perceiving the orientation of the desk, chair, and the child's body. Second, the lying-down position should be advantageous for unifying the seen and felt sense of the body because the two are much closer to each other when in that position than when standing upright.

Under this situation, the observer need not exchange asymmetrical upper and lower parts of the body to unify the seen and felt sense. The unification of the body sense was limited to this situation in the present experiment.

In other research that used the prism- or lens-type goggles, the observer remained in the same unstable adaptation stage, where they perceived a strange sense of the body experiencing partial upright vision. For example, as the subject of his own experiment, Dolezal (1982) wrote, "The top of the head was judged to be closer to the ground than any other part of the head. The visually perceived location of my head was variable, though my effective point of observation was mostly judged to be just inches above the ground" (p. 205). The observers would represent such a strange body image because of the difficulty to reverse the upper and lower parts of the body completely. Including my experiment, reports indicate that it is not easy to re-acquire secure and stable upright vision in the up-down visual reversal experiments. The only exception is Kohler's (1964) experiment, in which the subject M wore a mirror-type up-down reversing goggles for 10 days and reported the re-acquisition of stable upright vision. Kohler, however, did not refer to the unification of the seen and felt sense of the body, although it should be critical for upright vision. Dolezal (1982) criticized the verbal ambiguity in Kohler's experiment and concluded that Kohler's data cannot be interpreted (p. 270).

Introspection Reported during the Experiment Wearing Left-Right Reversing Goggles

Four years before the above experiment, I myself wore the left-right reversing goggles for 14 days. On the 13th day of the experiment, the observer had a critical experience with the upright vision. He then lived in the world of perfectly left-right reversed mental maps in contrast to the before-wearing, normal vision world. Suppose he was facing the door and there was a window to his right and the next room to his left. On Day 13, he perceived the opposite: In his mental map, the window would be to his left and the next room to his right. When he was lying on tatami mats (see Figure 1), he experienced a curious but valuable event.

> *Day 13. I'm now lying on my back with my legs to the entrance of the tatami room. Then I perceive that the window is to my left and the next room is to my right. I clearly visualize this and cannot imagine it otherwise. When I change my position to lying on my actual right, the window comes into the field of vision. Now, in spite of lying on my right side, I perceive as if I were lying on my left side. It is reasonable to think that it would be difficult to misperceive the side of the body touching the tatami when lying on either side because of the correct proprioceptive information received from touching one's face and body to the tatami mat. However, my vivid mental map, which informs me that the window should be to my left, leads to the misperception that I'm lying on my left side. When lying on my left side and facing to the window, do I see the image upside down? No, tatami mats are perceived as lower than the window. They are seen to be right side up.*

In Figure 2, the disappearance of upside down impressions is demonstrated. Physically, the observer is lying on his right side and gets the image of the parts of the window and tatami mats shown in the balloon of Figure 2 ("physical arrangement"). In his field of vision, the window image is seen near to his right ear and that of tatami mats is seen near to his left. But subjectively, he perceives he is lying on his left side as shown in Figure 2 ("subjective arrangement"). The relationships

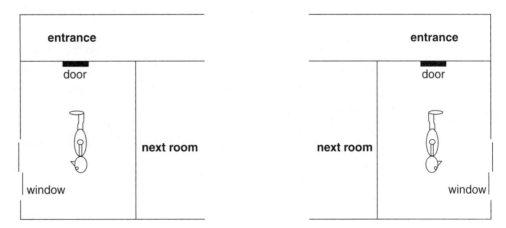

FIGURE 1   The room arrangements in which the observer is lying on his side facing the window.

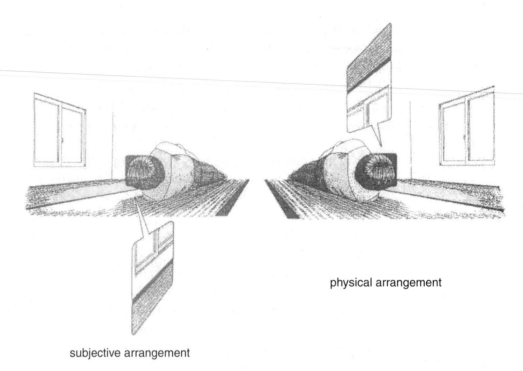

physical arrangement

subjective arrangement

FIGURE 2   Demonstration of disappearance of the upside-down impression.

of the images of the window and tatami mats to the head (to the left-right ears) are common to the physical and subjective situations. Now, he perceives lying on his left side and sees the tatami mat leftward in the field, which, in turn, means that tatami mats are downward and that the window is upward. There is no contradiction, and the upside down impression has disappeared. While he was living in the left-right reversed mental map with the left-right reversed body image, he re-acquired upright vision. In this article, "mental map" represents the environmental arrangements around the observer and "body image" indicates the observer's own representation of his own posture.

Until the 13th day the observer had not perceived the upright vision when lying on tatami mats. Instead, he had repeatedly experienced the confusion of the body image with the left-right reversed mental map from the second day of the experiment as shown in the following.

> Day 12. Now I'm watching television lying down in the tatami room. As the TV display is seen near to my feet, I try to move my body to catch it in front of the face. But I can't do it. I lose my sense of direction in the room.

The critical point in realizing upright vision is how to get the body image to be lying on the left side although the observer is lying on his actual right side. On Day 13, the observer used a smart strategy to facilitate the unification of the seen and felt sense of the body. At this time, the observer's mental map was perfectly left-right reversed. By lying on his back and turning the whole body repeatedly from his right side to his left side and passing through the lying-on-his-back position, he could unify the two sense of the body. Mediated by the dynamic visual information in the field of vision, such as visual-flow direction and the occlusion-disocclusion relationship contingent on the body's turning, the observer easily achieved unification.

Why Is It Difficult to Re-Acquire Upright Vision when Wearing Visually Up-Down Reversing Goggles?

Supported by the strategy unifying the seen and felt sense of the body, the observer wearing left-right reversing goggles could re-acquire upright vision within 2 weeks. In contrast, when wearing up-down reversing goggles, the same observer could not get secure upright vision within the 2-week prism wearing period. What is the factor that differentiates between the two visual transpositions?

In the Introduction, I pointed out three factors that might make it difficult to unify the body sense: distinctive meaning of ceiling (sky)—floor (ground), competition of the information from gravity, and the asymmetrical structure of the human body. The third factor would be nullified when the observer lies on his side wearing left-right reversing goggles, leaving the other two factors intact. In this situation, the observer re-acquired clear upright vision.

The present research indicates that the re-acquisition of upright vision would be facilitated by the mental map that represents the surroundings left-right reversed from actual arrangements. As shown in Figure 1, the observer facing the window represented the posture holding the left-right reversed mental map in mind. Without the reversed map, he should have perceived the actual side when lying down, based on the strong proprioceptive information given from the face and body touching to the tatami mats, which, in turn, should have resulted in the persistence of the upside-down impression.

This notion, induced from the introspection, can also be deduced from theoretical considerations. Upright vision should coincide with the representation of the observer's seen and felt bodies. Harris (1965, 1980), for example, speculates that adaptation to the visually transposed world can be achieved by changing the proprioception to the positions that coincide with vision. The lack of symmetry of the upper and lower parts of the body makes it difficult to exchange them when wearing up-down reversing goggles. However, it becomes much easier when the observer lies on his side wearing left-right reversing goggles. Harris (1965), indeed, insisted his proprioceptive change hypothesis by using the left-right visual reversal experiments, not the up-down reversal experiments.

The finding of the present research should be valuable because it was revealed by comparing the two experiments imposed on the same observer for the same goggles-on period in similar situations. The observer experienced only a partial and unstable upright impression in the up-down reversal experiment. In the left-right reversal experiment, he got a clear upright impression, even though it was limited to the situation of lying on tatami mats.

In conclusion, the symmetrical structure of our body in the left-right dimension is a facilitating factor to unify the seen and felt sense of the body which, in turn, would lead to upright vision in the visually transposed world.

References

Dolezal, H. (1982). Living in a world transformed: *Perceptual and performatory adaptation to visual distortion.* New York: Academic Press.

Harris, C. S. (1965). Perceptual adaptation to inverted, reversed, and displaced vision. *Psychological Review, 72,* 419–444.

Harris, C. S. (1980). Insight or out of sight?: Two examples of perceptual plasticity in the human adult. In C. S. Harris (Ed.) *Visual coding and adaptability* (pp. 95–149). Hillsdale, NJ: Lawrence Erlbaum Associates.

Kohler, I. (1964). The formation and transformation of the perceptual world. *Psychological Issues, 3,* 1–173.

Peterson, J., & Peterson, J. K. (1938). Does practice with inverting lenses make vision normal? *Psychological Monographs, 50,* 12–37.

Snyder, F. W., & Pronko, N. H. (1952). *Vision with spatial inversion.* Wichita: University of Wichita Press.

Stratton, G. M. (1897). Vision without inversion of the retinal image. *Psychological Review, 4,* 341–360, 463–481.

Yoshimura, H. (1996). A historical review of long-term visual-transportation research in Japan. *Psychological Research, 59,* 16–32.

Yoshimura, H. (1999). Qualitative analysis of critical aspects in the adaptation process to the visually left-right reversed world. *Japanese Psychological Research, 41,* 143–151.

Editor's Note

Preparation of this article was supported by the Japanese Ministry of Education, Science, and Culture Grant-in-Aid for General Scientific Research Grant no. 09610074 allocated to Hirokazu Yoshimura.

I wish to thank Dr R Dyck of Capital University and Dr D Erickson of Ohio State University for their polite and careful proofing of my English manuscript.

Correspondence concerning this article should be sent to: Professor Yoshimura Hirokazu, Department of Psychology, Meisei University, Hodokubo 2-1-1, Hino-shi, Tokyo 191-8506, Japan (Email: yoshimura@psy.meisei-u.ac.jp).

Discussion Questions for Article 2

Section 3: Sensation and Perception

Name: _____

PID: _____

Date: __ __ / __ __ / __ __ (MM/DD/YY)

CRN: _____

Recitation Day/Time: _____

Honor Code Signature: _____

1. What are the three factors that help us make sense of an up-down reversed environment? How does each one affect perception of the environment?

2. The author mentioned that we are able to adapt to up-down reversed environments with enough exposure. What do you think this says about how the brain processes visual information?

3. During the author's experiment, what strategy did he develop in order to overcome his left-right reversed environment while lying down?

4. Describe an experience where you felt a visual distortion in your life. How did it impact you?

Section 4
Development

People change significantly over time. A child will walk and talk early in life, enter school at four to 5 years old, and go through puberty during the teenage years. Eventually that child will become a mature adult. We call this "life-span development," and even though some life periods are studied more than others—particularly childhood and older adulthood—people have novel experiences throughout their life. The field of development would not seem very useful, however, if this was all developmental psychology told us. Fortunately, humans never stop developing physically, socially, or emotionally. Developmentalists desire the knowledge of why and how people change, not simply what happens to people as they age.

If you've heard of the "nature vs. nurture" debate, then you already know a little about developmental psychology. The core of the nature-nurture debate asks if it our experiences or genes that determine what kind of people we turn out to be. Over time it has become not just a question of one or the other but how nature and the environment interact. This question can be applied to physical as well as social and emotional development. For instance, is growing up in an academically enriched home a greater contributor to school achievement than basic overall IQ scores? Are children of strict parents more or less likely to have social adaptation issues when they enter school? Further, will these children grow up to be strict parents to their own children?

Other developmentalists are concerned with why certain common developmental processes—the ones we "all" experience—*do not* occur in some people. Why do certain people appear to skip phases of development? Much of this research occurs with young children. If we are able to assist with these developmental problems at a young age, these children might have an easier time adjusting to adult society.

Developmental Psychology is a broad field. Current research includes, but is not limited to, the development of physical abilities (how they are initially developed and how they are lost), cognitive abilities (the role of intelligence, and the developmental of linguistic, literacy, and mathematics skills), and socioemotional skills (how parenting, peers, and neighborhoods teach emotion and social skills). There are even lines of developmental research determining how children develop in different cultures across continents and how something as benign as language can impact a person's development.

Article 1: Love in Infant Monkeys

Do infants actually love their mothers, or do they use them solely for the fulfillment of biological needs (i.e., hunger)? As love is a complex issue and infants difficult to work with (particularly with movement and ethical issues), Harry Harlow looked at this question with an inventive design. Harlow used infant rhesus monkeys instead of human infants, as they both went through similar developmental processes. Harlow separated the infant rhesus monkeys from their mothers, and placed them in cages with both a wire mesh monkey and a terrycloth monkey. The wire mesh monkey included a feeding bottle, and represented the idea that monkeys use their mothers for food. Further, the cloth monkey offered no sustenance, but provided the comfort that an actual mother would. Harlow observed the amount of time the monkey spent with the surrogate mothers in several conditions, including when a scary object was added to the cage. He discovered that comfort not nourishment was a driving force behind attachment.

Article 2: Slow Speech Enhances Younger, but Not Older, Infants' Perception of Vocal Emotion

Why do people always talk to babies with that "baby talk"? Wouldn't babies prefer normal adult tones, which they will have to become accustomed to eventually? Actually, previous research has suggested the opposite. While babies seem to prefer and attend more to speech which is infant-directed and speech high in positive emotion, little research has been conducted on how duration of speech affects babies' attention to speech. Is speech that is more drawn out likely to be attended to more than faster speech? The authors also examined how emotionality affects the various types of speech that infants hear. While the slower speech enhances younger infants, it does not enhance the abilities of older infants to perceive emotion in voice.

—*Conrad Baldner*

Love in Infant Monkeys

Harry F. Harlow

Affection in infants was long thought to be generated by the satisfactions of feeding. Studies of young rhesus monkeys now indicate that love derives mainly from close bodily contact.

The first love of the human infant is for his mother. The tender intimacy of this attachment is such that it is sometimes regarded as a sacred or mystical force, an instinct incapable of analysis. No doubt such compunctions, along with the obvious obstacles in the way of objective study, have hampered experimental observation of the bonds between child and mother.

Though the data are thin, the theoretical literature on the subject is rich. Psychologists, sociologists and anthropologists commonly hold that the infant's love is learned through the association of the mother's face, body and other physical characteristics with the alleviation of internal biological tensions, particularly hunger and thirst. Traditional psychoanalysts have tended to emphasize the role of attaining and sucking at the breast as the basis for affectional development. Recently a number of child psychiatrists have questioned such simple explanations. Some argue that affectionate handling in the act of nursing is a variable of importance, whereas a few workers suggest that the composite activities of nursing, contact, clinging and even seeing and hearing work together to elicit the infant's love for his mother.

Now it is difficult, if not impossible, to use human infants as subjects for the studies necessary to break through the present speculative impasse. At birth the infant is so immature that he has little or no control over any motor system other than that involved in sucking. Furthermore, his physical maturation is so slow that

FIGURE 1 Cloth and wire mother-surrogates were used to test the preferences of infant monkeys. The infants spent most of their time clinging to the soft cloth "mother," (*foreground*) even when nursing bottles were attached to the wire mother (*background*).

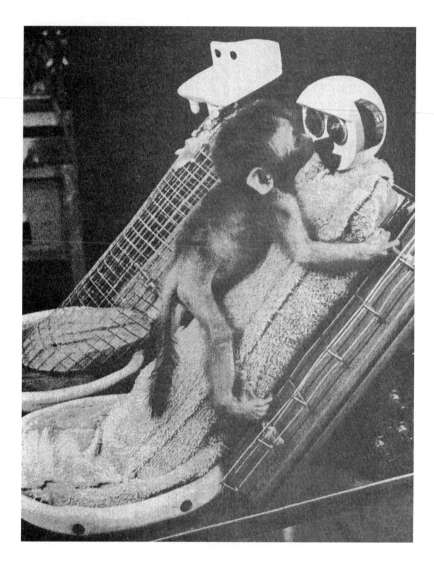

by the time he can achieve precise, coordinated, measurable responses of his head, hands, feet and body, the nature and sequence of development have been hopelessly confounded and obscured. Clearly research into the infant-mother relationship has need of a more suitable laboratory animal. We believe we have found it in the infant monkey. For the past several years our group at the Primate Laboratory of the University of Wisconsin has been employing baby rhesus monkeys in a study that we believe has begun to yield significant insights into the origin of the infant's love for his mother.

Baby monkeys are far better coordinated at birth than human infants. Their responses can be observed and evaluated with confidence at an age of 10 days or even earlier. Though they mature much more rapidly than their human contemporaries, infants of both species follow much the same general pattern of development.

Our interest in infant-monkey love grew out of a research program that involved the separation of monkeys from their mothers a few hours after birth. Employing techniques developed by Gertrude van Wagenen of Yale University, we had been rearing infant monkeys on the bottle with a mortality far less than that among monkeys nursed by their mothers. We were particularly careful to provide the infant monkeys with a folded gauze diaper on the floor of their cages, in accord with Dr. van Wagenen's observation that they would tend to maintain intimate contact with such soft, pliant surfaces, especially during nursing. We were impressed by the deep personal attachments that the monkeys formed for these diaper pads, and by the distress that they exhibited when the pads were briefly removed once a day for purposes of sanitation. The behavior of the infant monkeys was reminiscent of the human infant's attachment to its blankets, pillows, rag dolls or cuddly teddy bears.

These observations suggested the series of experiments in which we have sought to compare the importance of nursing and all associated activities with that of simple bodily contact in engendering the infant monkeys' attachment to its mother. For this purpose we contrived two surrogate mother monkeys. One is a bare welded-wire cylindrical form surmounted by a wooden head with a crude face. In the other the welded wire is cushioned by a sheathing of terry cloth. We placed eight new-born monkeys in individual cages, each with equal access to a cloth and a wire mother [see illustration]. Four of the infants received their milk from one mother and four from the other, the milk being furnished in each case by a nursing bottle, with its nipple protruding from the mother's "breast."

The two mothers quickly proved to be physiologically equivalent. The monkeys in the two groups drank the same amount of milk and gained weight at the same rate. But the two mothers proved to be by no means psychologically equivalent. Records made automatically showed that both groups of infants spent far more time climbing and clinging on their cloth-covered mothers than they did on their wire mothers. During the infants' first 14 days of life the floors of the cages were warmed by an electric heating pad, but most of the infants left the pad as soon as they could climb on the unheated cloth mother. Moreover, as the monkeys grew older, they tended to spend an increasing amount of time clinging and cuddling on the pliant terry-cloth surface. Those that secured their nourishment from the wire mother showed no tendency to spend more time on her than feeding required, contradicting the idea that affection is a response that is learned or derived in association with the reduction of hunger or thirst.

These results attest the importance—possibly the overwhelming importance—of bodily contact and the immediate comfort it supplies in forming the infant's attachment for its mother. All our experience, in fact, indicates that our cloth-covered mother surrogate is an eminently satisfactory mother. She is available 24 hours a day to satisfy her infant's overwhelming compulsion to seek bodily

FIGURE 2   Strong preference for cloth mother was shown by all infant monkeys. Infants reared with access to both mothers from birth (*top chart*) spent far more time on the cloth mother (*gray curves*) than on the wire mother (*black curves*). This was true regardless of whether they had been fed on the cloth (*solid lines*) or on the wire mother (*broken lines*). Infants that had known no mother during their first eight months (*bottom chart*) soon came to prefer the cloth mother, but spent less time on her than the other infants.

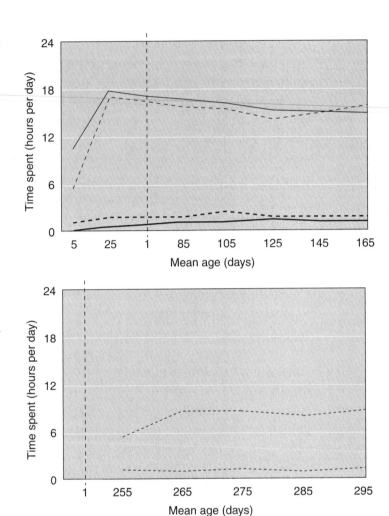

FIGURE 3   Results of "fear test" showed that infants confronted by a strange object quickly learned to seek reassurance from the cloth mother (*gray curves*) rather than from the wire mother (*black curves*). Again infants fed on the wire mother (*broken lines*) behaved much like those fed on the cloth mother (*solid lines*).

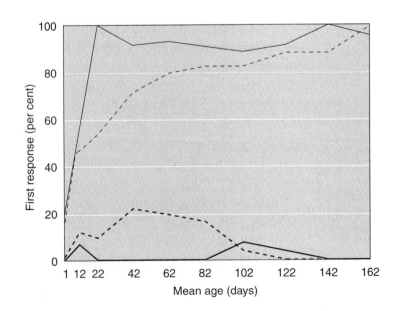

contact; she possesses infinite patience, never scolding her baby or biting it in anger. In these respects we regard her as superior to a living monkey mother, though monkey fathers would probably not endorse this opinion.

Of course this does not mean that nursing has no psychological importance. No act so effectively guarantees intimate bodily contact between mother and child. Furthermore, the mother who finds nursing a pleasant experience will probably be temperamentally inclined to give her infant plenty of handling and fondling. The real-life attachment of the infant to its mother is doubtless influenced by subtle multiple variables, contributed in part by the mother and in part by the child. We make no claim to having unraveled these in only two years of investigation. But no matter what evidence the future may disclose, our first experiments have shown that contact comfort is a decisive variable in this relationship.

Such generalization is powerfully supported by the results of the next phase of our investigation. The time that the infant monkeys spent cuddling on their surrogate mothers was a strong but perhaps not conclusive index of emotional attachment. Would they also seek the inanimate mother for comfort and security when they were subjected to emotional stress? With this question in mind we exposed our monkey infants to the stress of fear by presenting them with strange objects, for example a mechanical teddy bear which moved forward, beating a drum. Whether the infants had nursed from the wire or the cloth mother, they overwhelmingly sought succor from the cloth one; this differential in behavior was enhanced with the passage of time and the accrual of experience. Early in this series of experiments the terrified infant might rush blindly to the wire mother, but even if it did so it would soon abandon her for the cloth mother. The infant would cling to its cloth mother, rubbing its body against hers. Then, with its fears assuaged through intimate contact with the mother, it would turn to look at the previously terrifying bear without the slightest sign of alarm. Indeed, the infant would sometimes even leave the protection of the mother and approach the object that a few minutes before had reduced it to abject terror.

The analogy with the behavior of human infants requires no elaboration. We found that the analogy extends even to less obviously stressful situations. When a child is taken to a strange place, he usually remains composed and happy so long as his mother is nearby. If the mother gets out of sight, however, the child is often seized with fear and distress. We developed the same response in our infant monkeys when we exposed them to a room that was far larger than the cages to which they were accustomed. In the room we had placed a number of unfamiliar objects such as a small artificial tree, a crumpled piece of paper, a folded gauze diaper, a wooden block and a doorknob [*a similar experiment is depicted in the illustrations on page 112*]. If the cloth mother was in the room, the infant would rush wildly to her, climb upon her, rub against her and cling to her tightly. As in the

FIGURE 4   Frightening objects such as a mechanical teddy bear caused almost all infant monkeys to flee blindly to the cloth mother, as in the top photograph. Once reassured by pressing and rubbing against her, they would then look at the strange object (*bottom*).

FIGURE 5   "Open field test" involved placing a monkey in a room far larger than its accustomed cage; unfamiliar objects added an additional disturbing element. If no mother was present, the infant would typically huddle in a corner (*left*). The wire mother did not alter this pattern of fearful behavior, but the cloth mother provided quick reassurance. The infant would first cling to her (*center*) and then set out to explore the room and play with the objects (*right*), returning from time to time for more reassurance.

previous experiment, its fear then sharply diminished or vanished. The infant would begin to climb over the mother's body and to explore and manipulate her face. Soon it would leave the mother to investigate the new world, and the unfamiliar objects would become playthings. In a typical behavior sequence, the infant might manipulate the tree, return to the mother, crumple the wad of paper, bring it to the mother, explore the block, explore the doorknob, play with the paper and return to the mother. So long as the mother provided a psychological "base of operations" the infants were unafraid and their behavior remained positive, exploratory and playful.

If the cloth mother was absent, however, the infants would rush across the test room and throw themselves facedown on the floor, clutching their heads and bodies and screaming their distress. Records kept by two independent observers—scoring for such "fear indices" as crying, crouching, rocking and thumb and toe-sucking—showed that the emotionality scores of the infants nearly tripled. But no quantitative measurement can convey the contrast between the positive, outgoing activities in the presence of the cloth mother and the stereotyped withdrawn and disturbed behavior in the motherless situation.

The bare wire mother provided no more reassurance in this "open field" test than no mother at all. Control tests on monkeys that from birth had known only the wire mother revealed that even these infants showed no affection for her and obtained no comfort from her presence. Indeed, this group of animals exhibited the highest emotionality scores of all. Typically they would run to some wall or corner of the room, clasp their heads and bodies and rock convulsively back and forth. Such activities closely resemble the autistic behavior seen frequently among neglected children in and out of institutions.

In a final comparison of the cloth and wire mothers, we adapted an experiment originally devised by Robert A. Butler at the Primate Laboratory. Butler had found that monkeys enclosed in a dimly lighted box would press a lever to open and reopen a window for hours on end for no reward other than the chance to look out. The rate of lever-pressing depended on what the monkeys saw through the opened window; the sight of another monkey elicited far more activity than that of a bowl of fruit or an empty room [see "Curiosity in Monkeys," by Robert A. Butler; SCIENTIFIC AMERICAN, February, 1954]. We now know that this "curiosity response" is innate. Three-day-old monkeys, barely able to walk, will crawl across the floor of the box to reach a lever which briefly opens the window; some press the lever hundreds of times within a few hours.

When we tested our monkey infants in the "Butler box," we found that those reared with both cloth and wire mothers showed as high a response to the cloth mother as to another monkey, but displayed no more interest in the wire mother than in an empty room. In this test, as in all the others, the monkeys fed on the wire mother behaved the same as those fed on the cloth mother. A control group raised with no mothers at all found the cloth mother no more interesting than the wire mother and neither as interesting as another monkey.

Thus all the objective tests we have been able to devise agree in showing that the infant monkeys' relationship to its surrogate mother is a full one. Comparison with the behavior of infant monkeys raised by their real mothers confirms this view. Like our experimental monkeys, these infants spend many hours a day clinging to their mothers, and run to them for comfort or reassurance when they are frightened. The deep and abiding bond between mother and child appears to be essentially the same, whether the mother is real or a cloth surrogate.

While bodily contact clearly plays the prime role in developing infantile affection, other types of stimulation presumably supplement its effects. We have therefore embarked on a search for these other factors. The activity of a live monkey mother, for example, provides her infant with frequent motion stimulation. In many human cultures mothers bind their babies to them when they go about their daily chores; in our own culture parents know very well that rocking a baby or walking with him somehow promotes his psychological and physiological well-being. Accordingly we compared the responsiveness of infant monkeys to two cloth mothers, one stationary and one rocking. All of them preferred the rocking mother, though the degree of preference varied considerably from day to day and from monkey to monkey. An experiment with a rocking crib and a stationary one gave similar results. Motion does appear to enhance affection, albeit far less significantly than simple contact.

The act of clinging, in itself, also seems to have a role in promoting psychological and physiological well-being. Even before we began our studies of affection, we noticed that a newborn monkey raised in a bare wire cage survived with difficulty unless we provided it with a cone to which it could cling. Recently we have raised two groups of monkeys, one with a padded crib instead of a mother and the other with a cloth mother as well as a crib. Infants in the latter group actually spend more time on the crib than on the mother, probably because the steep incline of the mother's cloth surface makes her a less satisfactory sleeping platform. In the open field test, the infants raised with a crib but no mother clearly derived some emotional support from the presence of the crib. But those raised with both showed an unequivocal preference for the mother they could cling to, and they evidenced the benefit of the superior emotional succor they gained from her.

Still other elements in the relationship remain to be investigated systematically. Common sense would suggest that the warmth of the mother's body plays its part in strengthening the infant's ties to her. Our own observations have not yet confirmed this hypothesis. Heating a cloth mother does not seem to increase her attractiveness to the infant monkey, and infants readily abandon a heating pad for an unheated mother surrogate. However, our laboratory is kept comfortably warm at all times; experiments in a chilly environment might well yield quite different results.

Visual stimulation may forge an additional link. When they are about three months old, the monkeys begin to observe and manipulate the head, face and eyes of their mother surrogates; human infants show the same sort of delayed responsiveness to visual stimuli. Such stimuli are known to have marked effects on the behavior of many young animals. The Austrian zoologist Konrad Lorenz has demonstrated a process called "imprinting"; he has shown that the young of some species of birds become attached to the first moving object they perceive, normally their mothers [see " 'Imprinting' in animals," by Eckhard H. Hess; SCIENTIFIC AMERICAN, March, 1958]. It is also possible that particular sounds and even odors may play some role in the normal development of responses or attention.

The depth and persistence of attachment to the mother depend not only on the kind of stimuli that the young animal receives but also on when it receives them. Experiments with ducks show that imprinting is most effective during a critical period soon after hatching; beyond a certain age it cannot take place at all. Clinical experience with human beings indicates that people who have been deprived of affection in infancy may have difficulty forming affectional ties in later life. From preliminary experiments with our monkeys we have found that their affectional responses develop, or fail to develop, according to a similar pattern.

Early in our investigation we had segregated four infant monkeys as a general control group, denying them physical contact either with a mother surrogate or with other monkeys. After about eight months we placed them in cages with access to both cloth and wire mothers. At first they were afraid of both surrogates,

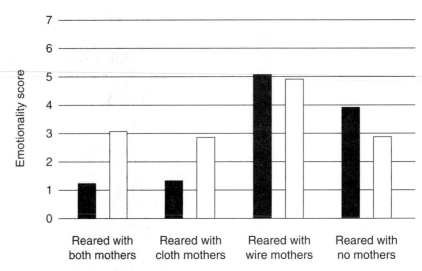

FIGURE 6   Scores in open field test show that all infant monkeys familiar with the cloth mother were much less disturbed when she was present (*black*) than when no mother was present (*white*); scores under 2 indicate unfrightened behavior. Infants that had known only the wire mother were greatly disturbed whether she was present (*black*) or not (*white*).

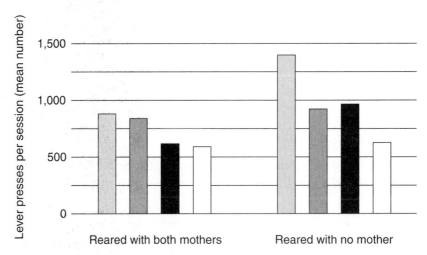

FIGURE 7   "Curiosity test" showed that monkeys reared with both mothers displayed as much interest in the cloth mother (*solid gray*) as in another monkey (*hatched*); the wire mother (*black*) was no more interesting than an empty chamber (*white*). Monkeys reared with no mother found the cloth and wire mother less interesting than another monkey.

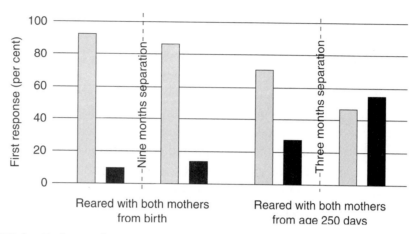

FIGURE 8   Early "mothering" produced a strong and unchanging preference for the cloth mother (*gray*) over the wire mother (*black*). Monkeys deprived of early mothering showed less marked preferences before separation and no significant preference

but within a few days they began to respond in much the same way as the other infants. Soon they were spending less than an hour a day with the wire mother and eight to 10 hours with the cloth mother. Significantly, however, they spent little more than half as much time with the cloth mother as did infants raised with her from birth.

In the open-field test these "orphan" monkeys derived far less reassurance from the cloth mothers than did the other infants. The deprivation of physical contact during their first eight months had plainly affected the capacity of these infants to develop the full and normal pattern of affection. We found a further indication of the psychological damage wrought by early lack of mothering when we tested the degree to which infant monkeys retained their attachments to their mothers. Infants raised with a cloth mother from birth and separated from her at about five and a half months showed little or no loss of responsiveness even after 18 months of separation. In some cases it seemed that absence had made the heart grow fonder. The monkeys that had known a mother surrogate only after the age of eight months, however, rapidly lost whatever responsiveness they had acquired. The long period of maternal deprivation had evidently left them incapable of forming a lasting affectional tie.

The effects of maternal separation and deprivation in the human infant have scarcely been investigated, in spite of their implications concerning child-rearing practices. The long period of infant-maternal dependency in the monkey provides a real opportunity for investigating persisting disturbances produced by inconsistent or punishing mother surrogates.

Above and beyond demonstration of the surprising importance of contact comfort as a prime requisite in the formation of an infant's love for its mother—and the discovery of the unimportant or nonexistent role of the breast and act of nursing—our investigations have established a secure experimental approach to this realm of dramatic and subtle emotional relationships. The further exploitation of the broad field of research that now opens up depends merely upon the availability of infant monkeys. We expect to extend our researches by undertaking the study of the mother's (and even the father's!) love for the infant, using real monkey infants or infant surrogates. Finally, with such techniques established, there appears to be no reason why we cannot at some future time investigate the fundamental neurophysiological and biochemical variables underlying affection and love.

Discussion Questions for Article 1

Section 4: Development

Name: _____

PID: _____

Date: __ __ / __ __ / __ __ (MM/DD/YY)

CRN: _____

Recitation Day/Time: _____

Honor Code Signature: _____

1. List some of the reasons Harlow suggests that the infant monkey preferred the cloth "mother" to the wire "mother." What do you think of these reasons?

2. Even though Harlow found results with the rhesus monkey sample, would you expect human infants to act in the same way? Why or why not?

3. Were you convinced by Harlow's results? What problems do you see in his study?

4. Why is this type of experiment possible with infant monkeys but not with human infants?

Slow Speech Enhances Younger, but Not Older, Infants' Perception of Vocal Emotion

Robin Panneton
Christine Kitamura
Karen Mattock
Denis Burnham

Infants attend more to infant-directed speech (IDS) than to adult-directed speech (ADS) but infants also prefer speech judged to be high in positive emotion over less emotional speech, regardless of whether it is IDS or ADS. Emotion in voices is often conveyed by absolute pitch, pitch contours, and tempo (or duration). The purpose of our study was to explore how perceived emotion in speech is enhanced or attenuated by duration. Eighteen- and 32-week-old infants were tested for attention to IDS that was either high or low in emotion (as judged by adults) and at two different durations (normal vs. slow). The results showed that 18-week-olds attended more to slow IDS (with affect constant), attended more to high affect (with duration constant), and showed equal attention when affect and duration were juxtaposed. In contrast, 32-week-olds showed greater attention to normal IDS regardless of its emotional level. Slower IDS may enhance younger infants' perception of vocal emotion, but does not increase attention in older infants perhaps because they no longer rely on this acoustic cue for emotion. Future studies are suggested to help tease apart these interpretations.

As all of the articles in this issue make clear, the communication of emotion plays a significant role in intra- and interpersonal relations throughout the human lifespan, including infancy. In fact, it is during infancy that the foundation for emotion regulation is laid, primarily via the interactive dynamics between caretakers and infants. This dynamic is complex in that it involves the ability of each partner to transmit as well as receive information across a variety of sensory channels, and to adjust patterns of behavior in ways that promote positive emotion regulation in the self as well as the other (Fogel & Thelen, 1987). Clearly, one important aspect of this mutual regulatory process for many infants is emotion conveyed in voices (Fernald, 1992).

Human infants are sensitive to acoustic features of adults' communicative signals, and infant-directed speech (IDS) across many of the world's cultures contains *exaggerated prosody*, such as longer pauses, slower speaking duration, more repetition, higher pitch (F_0), greater F_0 modulation and F_0 width, and increased hyperarticulation compared to adult directed speech (ADS) (Burnham, Kitamura & Vollmer Conna, 2002; Fernald, Taeschner, Dunn, Papousek, Boysson-Bardies, & Fukui, 1989; Kuhl, Andruski, Chistovich, & Chistovich, 1997). The perceptual salience of IDS for infants is clear in that infants of different ages and in various contexts show more attention to IDS than ADS (e.g., Panneton-Cooper & Aslin, 1990; Pegg, Werker, & McLeod, 1992). However, it has recently been suggested that infants' greater attention to IDS is attributable more to its heightened emotion rather than the fact that it is being spoken to an infant (Singh, Morgan, & Best, 2002). These authors found that infants attended more to 'happy' than 'sad' speech, regardless of whether the speaker was addressing an infant or an adult.

It makes good sense that infants should be responsive to the affective characteristics of ID speech because of the universal involvement of prosody in the communication of emotion and attitudes (Bolinger, 1989). Essentially emotion in speech is transmitted using variations in the acoustic correlates of prosody: F_0 (perceived as pitch and intonation), intensity (perceived as loudness) and duration (perceived as tempo or rhythm) (Katz, Cohn, & Moore, 1996; Scherer, 1986). In adults, high F_0 and expanded F_0 range often signal positive emotion in conversation, and this might also be the case for infants. Interestingly, 6-month-olds prefer high-affect IDS to low-affect IDS (as rated by adults), even when the F_0 height and variation are matched (Kitamura & Burnham, 1998), implying that vocal emotion extends beyond exaggerated F_0 patterns (see also Singh, Morgan, & Best, 2002). Even so, 'vocal emotion' is based on a listener's interpretation of the psychoacoustics carried in a speaker's voice, so infants must be attending to one or more characteristics (other than pitch) that correlate with emotion. In addition to pitch information, vocal emotion is also conveyed by timing, voice quality (spectral richness), amplitude patterns, and formant structure (Banse & Scherer, 1996; Murray & Arnott,

1993). These correlates have yet to be examined with respect to infants' perception of vocal emotion.

One possibly potent correlate for infants is longer utterance duration (i.e., slower speech), which appears to distinguish between 'love' and 'comfort' utterances in IDS and ADS (Trainor, Austin, & Desjardins, 2000). There is evidence that at both 1.5- and 4-month-olds attend more to slow IDS than normal duration IDS, even though their pitch characteristics were equivalent (Panneton, McIlreavy, Cooper, Ostroff, & Aslin, 2005). However, in this same study, 8-month-olds showed no differential attention to normal or slow versions of the same IDS utterances. Thus, even though infants consistently prefer IDS, the aspects of IDS to which they attend may change with age and experience, i.e., emotional tone in early infancy, and other affective information as they approach meaningful productions of their own.

Such changes in infants' perception could be related to changes in caretakers' styles of interaction over age. For example, Kitamura and Burnham (2003) found that emotional intent used by mothers to *convey affection*, *comfort and soothe*, *direct infant behavior*, and *attract attention* changes across age. The distinct patterns of communicative intent, accompanied by modifications to mean F_0 and F_0 range, suggest that mothers are responsive to the developmental needs of the infant and modify their speech accordingly. These authors found that in the first few months, mothers tend to use a comforting voice, around 6 months of age more affection is expressed, and later in the first year mothers' speech register is aimed at attracting infant attention and directing infant behavior, rather than conveying affection. However, developmental changes in infants' *perception* of IDS requires further empirical attention. That is, we do not yet know how infants' attention to various aspects of vocal emotion changes across this same developmental timeframe.

This study investigates younger (18-week-olds) and older (32-week-olds) infants' attention to speech that is rated as high or low in positive emotion when duration is also varied (either normal or slow IDS). Variations in effect were produced by selecting natural vocalizations of mothers talking to their infants and rated by adults to be either high or low in *positive emotional expressiveness*. Although it is possible to also produce utterances that are high in *negative* emotional expressiveness (e.g., extreme anger or fear), no such utterances were found in the maternal recordings. Also, the emotional valence of the utterances that we used were rated by adults listening to filtered versions so that their emotional ratings were based on prosody, and not on lexical content (given that we do not expect infants at the ages tested here to process the utterances semantically). These recordings were further manipulated to produce slow versions of both High Affect and Low Affect IDS. Thus, we were able to assess developmental similarities and/or dissimilarities in infants' attention to vocal emotion, and whether utterance duration acts to enhance infants' attention to speech within the emotion context.

General Method

Separate groups of 18- and 32-week-old full-term infants with no known hearing difficulties were recruited from monolingual English, predominantly Caucasian, middle income families. Testing for all experiments was conducted at MARCS Auditory Laboratories, Sydney, Australia. Sixteen IDS utterances varying in apparent emotional expressiveness were selected from an Australian IDS corpus. Slow (double duration) versions of these utterances were produced using STRAIGHT software (Kawahara, 1999 #300). The resulting 16 normal and 16 slow utterances were low-pass filtered at 400Hz to remove word content, and were (a) rated by adults for their degree of positive emotion expression, and (b) assigned (by adult listeners) to one of three categories: approving/loving, comforting/soothing, or disapproving. The four utterances with the highest and the four with the lowest affect ratings were used in the experiments (again, 'low affect' in this context does not mean negative affect). Mean affective ratings and category assignments for both the normal and slow versions of the High and Low Affect utterances are presented in Table 1, along with their mean pitch, pitch range, and durations.

Apparatus

The infant was seated on his/her parent's lap in a sound-attenuated room. Directly in front of the infant was an attention-getting light display. Two 51 cm television monitors (Sony S/KVG21S2) were positioned 40cm to either side of the flashing lights and each monitor was also connected to a VCR (Sony SLV-777) in the control room. A single sidelight and loudspeaker were positioned below each television monitor. A Panasonic NV-M40 video camera connected to a Panasonic NV-200 VCR in the control room was used to videotape and time infants' fixations to each video display.

In the control room was a computer, toggle switch, two foot pedals, two cassette players (Sony TC-K390), one stereo amplifier (JVC AX-22), two VCRs; and for response monitoring/recording: a television monitor (Panasonic TC-14S10A), and a video recorder (Panasonic NV-200). A customized computer program controlled the experiment. The foot pedals were used to signal the start of the experiment or the start of each trial in the test phase, only after the infant's gaze was centered to the flashing lights.

Procedure

Each parent held their infant on their lap at midline, approximately 1.5 meters from the monitors, and wore headphones with masking speech. Sessions began with two 10-second familiarization trials, during which the appropriate speech type for each side was played. Trials started when the infant attended to the central flashing lights, whereupon the visual target (a colored bull's-eye, 20.5 cm in diameter, which subtended a visual angle of 8°) and its paired speech type and side-light were activated. Side of presentation was counterbalanced so that half the infants heard one speech type on the right and half heard that same speech type on the left. Six 20-second test trials followed familiarization. When the infant's gaze was centered, both television monitors displayed the bull's-eye continuously. Visual fixation of the target on one side turned on one of the speech types, and likewise for the other side. The speech type played until the infant looked away. Each trial continued until at least 20 sec total fixation (accumulated over both sides). Infants' data were included in the final analyses only if the total duration of fixation to both targets was at least 40% of the 120 sec of presentation time. Inter-observer reliabilities were calculated across all 3 experiments, with approximately 25% of each experiment's sample of infants being re-coded offline, resulting in correlations between observers of $r = .95$ (Experiment 1), $r = .98$ (Experiment 2), and $r = .97$ (Experiment 3).

Experiment 1: High Affect/Slow IDS vs. High Affect/Normal IDS

In the first experiment, infants were presented with High Affect/Normal and High Affect/Slow IDS (see Table 1). It was predicted that the 18-week-olds would attend more to High Affect/Slow speech (if slow speech enhances emotional perception), and although it was unclear how the 32-week-olds should respond, it is reasonable to expect that they would show no looking time differences given that Panneton et al. (2005) found that attention to slowed speech decreased across age.

Participants: 24 18-week-old infants, 12 boys/12 girls (range: 16–20 wks) and 24 32-week-olds, 12 boys/12 girls (range: 30–34 wks) were tested. Data from nine additional infants were not included in the analyses because they failed to reach the looking time criterion due to inattentiveness (n = 8), or crying (n = 1).

Results and Discussion: The dependent variable was the mean looking time across trials to the two screens as a function of speech type. Preliminary analyses found no significant main effect for side of presentation in this and the subsequent experiments, so further analyses were collapsed across this variable.

Mean fixation durations are shown in Figure 1a. A 2 × (2) mixed analysis of variance (ANOVA) with age (18 weeks, 32 weeks) as the between-subjects factor and duration (Normal, Slow) as the within-subject factor revealed no significant main effects for age or duration, but a significant age × duration interaction ($F(1, 46) = 13.4, p < .001$). The 18-week-olds looked longer to High Affect/Slow IDS ($M = 9.9$ sec, $SD = 3.2$) compared to High Affect/Normal IDS ($M = 7.1$ sec, $SD = 2.9$; $t(23) = 2.44, p < .03$), whereas 32-week-olds looked longer to High

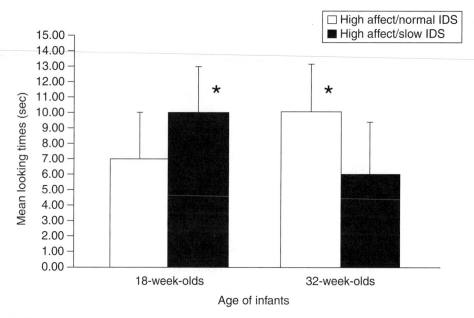

FIGURE 1A   Mean looking times (sec) for the 18- and 32-week-old infants (*n* = 24 in each age group) for High Affect/Normal vs. High Affect/Slow IDS. Standard deviations are also shown for each measurement.

Affect/Normal IDS (*M* High Affect/Normal = 9.6 sec, *SD* = 3.8; *M* High Affect/ Slow = 6.5 sec, *SD* = 2.7; *t* (23) = 2.73, *p* < .02).

The 18-week-olds attended more to IDS slow than IDS normal even though they were both high affect (4.23 and 4.29, respectively; see Table 1). Nonetheless, these High Affect utterances were more often categorized (by adult judges) as 'approving/loving' when they were slow (46%) compared to when they were normal (24%) in duration (i.e., they shifted away from the category 'comforting/ soothing'; only 1 High Affect utterance was ever judged as being 'disapproving'). If infants attend more to utterances judged to be approving/loving in their intent, then it follows that the 18-week-olds would prefer the High Affect/Slow speech. Although there is little evidence that this preference for affective category exists, at least one study did find that infants preferred a rising pitch contour (more characteristic of approval bids) to a falling contour (more characteristic of soothing bids; Papousek, Papousek, & Symmes, 1991). Also, both 4- and 6-month-olds discriminate changes in intentional categories when listening to filtered IDS utterances (Spence & Moore, 2003) so we know that they are sensitive to acoustic correlates of speaker intent. However, it is also possible that younger infants attend more to slow speech because it is easier to process, independent of its affective intensity. In this case, infants would always attend more to slower speech.

This was clearly not the case, however, in the 32-week-olds who attended more to High Affect/normal than High Affect/slow speech. If older infants did not perceive slower speech as being higher in affect, then these two speech types should be attended to equally (i.e., both have the same level of affect which was high). Given that the 32-week-olds attended more to the normal duration utterances, some additional explanation is needed. One possibility is that older infants attend more to speech that best matches the characteristics of that which they hear from caretakers and others. In other words, older infants have become attuned to a normalized range of speaking rates, of which the High Affect/slow IDS fell outside. Thus, High Affect/normal speech would be more familiar to them. We addressed this issue in the next experiment by exposing 18- and 32-week-olds to High Affect/Slow vs. Low Affect/Slow IDS.

Experiment 2: High Affect/Slow IDS vs. Low Affect/Slow IDS

Participants: 24 18-week-old infants, 12 boys/12 girls (range: 16–20 wks) and 24 32-week-olds, 12 boys/12 girls (range: 31–34 wks) from English-speaking families. The data of nine further infants was not used because of failure to reach criterion due to inattentiveness (n = 7) or crying (n = 2).

Results and Discussion: Mean fixations are shown in Figure 1b. A 2 × (2) mixed ANOVA with age (18 weeks, 32 weeks) as the between subjects factor and emotion (High Affect, Low Affect) as the within subject factor revealed a significant main effect of emotion ($F(1, 46) = 7.83$, $p < .02$), as well as a significant emotion × age interaction ($F(1, 46) = 3.93$, $p = .05$). The 18-week-olds looked longer to High Affect/Slow ($M = 9.8$ sec, $SD = 3.5$) compared to Low Affect/Slow IDS ($M = 6.2$ sec, $SD =2.6$; $t (23) = 3.02$, $p < .01$), whereas 32-week-olds did not look significantly longer to either side (M High Affect/Normal = 7.6 sec, $SD = 2.9$; M High Affect/Slow = 7 sec, $SD = 2.2$; $t (23) = .67$, $p >.05$).

The 18-week-olds' greater attention to the High Affect/Slow IDS complements Kitamura and Burnham (1998) who found that 6-month-olds prefer high over low affect speech with F_0 equated. In the current study, duration was equated but average pitch and pitch range were allowed to vary, and were actually higher in High Affect/Slow IDS than Low Affect/Slow IDS (see Table 1). Thus, it is unclear whether the 18-week-olds' preference is due to differential pitch or affect level (or their combined effect). Nevertheless the younger infants show a preference for speech with high positive affect even though both speech types were IDS (also consistent with Singh et al., 2002), unlike the older group of 32-week-olds, who showed no differential attention to either speech type. It is possible that slowing IDS in both speech samples effectively neutralizes the perception of affect for the older

TABLE 1 Average acoustic features, adults' emotion ratings (*n* = 16), and adults' affective categorizations (*n* = 33) for normal and slow High and Low Affect utterances.

	Mean F_0 (Hz)	F_0 Range (max–min)	Duration (sec)	Mean Emotion Rating 1 = Low; 5 = High	Affective Category (%)		
					App/ Lov	Com/ Sooth	Disapp.
Normal Duration							
High 1	260.27	387.10	1.87	4.44	.09	.91	0
High 2	332.07	302.70	1.84	3.94	.61	.39	0
High 3	246.35	348.93	1.58	4.33	.06	.94	0
High 4	291.72	210.02	3.59	4.44	.21	.79	0
Mean	**282.60**	**312.19**	**2.22**	**4.29**	**.24**	**.76**	**0**
Slow Duration							
High 1	235.92	342.73	3.23	4.44	.24	.73	.03
High 2	291.73	292.01	3.44	4.17	.70	.30	0
High 3	261.69	312.11	3.15	4.44	.64	.36	0
High 4	340.30	209.01	7.15	3.88	.24	.76	0
Mean	**282.41**	**288.96**	**4.24**	**4.23**	**.46**	**.54**	**0**
Normal Duration							
Low 1	184.66	157.09	1.28	1.77	.27	.27	.45
Low 2	225.32	204.20	1.66	2.33	.30	.12	.56
Low 3	177.02	286.00	2.23	1.77	.27	.27	.45
Low 4	191.56	227.03	2.60	1.88	.27	.09	.67
Mean	**194.64**	**218.58**	**1.94**	**1.94**	**.27**	**.19**	**.54**
Slow Duration							
Low 1	208.54	142.87	2.13	2.83	.30	.06	.64
Low 2	195.45	206.95	3.35	2.77	.64	.21	.15
Low 3	189.08	212.75	4.39	2.78	.58	.15	.27
Low 4	217.16	215.67	5.00	2.50	.55	.12	.33
Mean	**202.55**	**194.56**	**3.72**	**2.72**	**.52**	**.13**	**.35**

infants. That is, the exaggerated durations of both speech types interfere with the older infants' perception of affect because they are discordant with the normal range of speech durations to which they are exposed. If this interpretation is valid, then placing affect and duration in competition with one another will neutralize younger infants' attention to both speech types, but promote more attention in older infants to the IDS with normal duration.

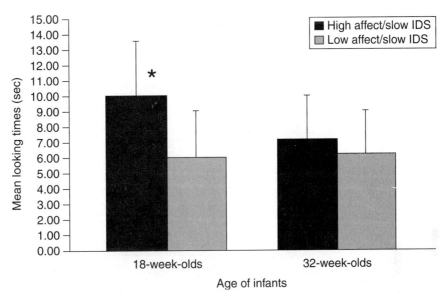

FIGURE 1B   Mean looking times (sec) for the 18- and 32-week-old infants ($n = 24$ in each age group) for High Affect/Slow vs. Low Affect/Slow IDS. Standard deviations are also shown for each measurement.

Experiment 3: High Affect/Normal IDS vs. Low Affect/Slow IDS

Participants: Twenty-three 18-week-olds, 12 boys/11 girls (range: 16–19 wks) and 24 32-week-olds, 12 boys/12 girls were tested (range: 30–34 wks). Data from an additional five infants were eliminated because of infant inattentiveness (n = 3) or crying (n = 2).

Results and Discussion: Mean looking times durations are shown in Figure 1c. A $2 \times (2)$ mixed ANOVA with age (18 wks, 32 wks) as the between-subjects factor and rate (High Affect/Normal, Low Affect/Slow) as the within-subject factor revealed a significant main effect of emotion/duration ($F(1, 43) = 5.7$, $p < .03$), but no other significant main effects or interactions. Infants attended more to High Affect/Normal IDS ($M = 8.9$ s, $SD = 3.5$) compared to Low Affect/Slow IDS ($M = 6.9$ s, $SD = 2.7$). While the age $\times$ emotion/duration interaction was not statistically significant, mean looking times for High Affect/Normal vs. Low Affect/Slow differed for 32-week-olds ($M_{\text{High Affect/Normal}} = 9.0$ s, $SD = 3.2$; $M_{\text{Low Affect/Slow}} = 6.2$, $SD = 2.4$; $t(23) = 2.68$, $p < .02$), but not for the 18-week-olds ($M_{\text{High Affect/Normal}} = 8.7$ s, $SD = 3.9$; $M_{\text{Low Affect/Slow}} = 7.6$, $SD = 2.81$; $t(22) = .88$, $p > .05$).

Older infants paid more attention to High Affect/Normal than Low Affect/Slow IDS either because two features that guide attention at this age were present: higher affect and normal duration (as opposed to slower duration), or solely due to normal

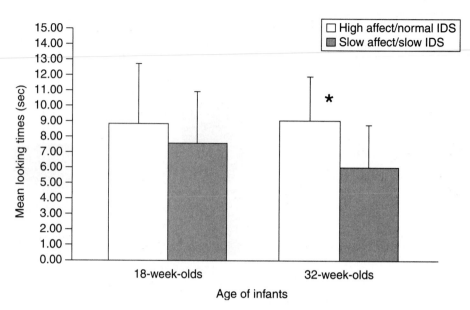

FIGURE 1C   Mean looking times (sec) for the 18- (*n* = 23) and 32-week-old (*n* = 24) infants for High Affect/Normal vs. Low Affect/Slow IDS. Standard deviations are also shown for each measurement.

speaking duration. In contrast, looking times did not differ significantly to the two speech types in the 18-week-olds, possibly because the two features that influence their perception of emotion (High Affect, Slow Duration) were juxtaposed, effectively neutralizing their attention to both.

General Discussion

The results show that younger infants attend more to slow over normal duration IDS when the positive affect in both speech samples is high (Experiment 1), and attend more to IDS with higher affect when both speech samples were slow (Experiment 2). Thus, for younger infants, vocal emotion is influenced by various acoustic cues including (but not limited to) utterance duration. When High Affect and Slow Duration were placed in competition, younger infants attended equally to both IDS types (Experiment 3). Vocal emotion and duration can enhance younger infants' attention independently, but also appear to work best when they co-occur in speech. That is, average looking times in 18-week-olds was highest when listening to High Affect/Slow IDS. Putting vocal emotion and utterance duration in competition may have neutralized 18-week-olds' attention because they perceive these speech types as equal in affect, or because each enhances attention for slightly different reasons: High Affect/normal speech because it sounds more emotionally positive, and Low Affect/slow speech because it is easier to process. One way to tease these possibilities apart is to test 18-week-olds with affectively neutral utterances (e.g., flat intonation contours) at normal and slowed rates to see if infants attend more to slower speech that is devoid of emotion. It seems likely that slower IDS was perceived as more affectively positive by younger infants insofar as adult judges categorized the same utterances differently depending on their duration (more High *and* Low Affect utterances were judged as approving/loving when they were slow, compared to comforting/soothing or disapproving when they were normal duration; see Table 1). Also, Low Affect utterances were given higher overall emotion ratings when they were slow.

This potential relationship between slower speaking rate and higher positive emotion is partially supported by acoustic analyses of emotion in adult vocal expressions (Banse & Scherer, 1996; Breitenstein, van Lancker, Daum, & Waters, 2001) in that slower voiced speech segments are sometimes associated with happiness and elation. However, the ability of speaking rate to convey vocal emotion is also highly influenced by pitch; low pitch, slow speech is perceived most often as sad (or bored), whereas high pitch, slow speech is more often perceived as happy/joyful (Banse & Scherer, 1996). Thus, the perception of positive vocal emotion requires the consideration of the perceptual 'package', with different combinations of acoustic parameters such as pitch (contour, width, variability), vocal duration, and intensity correlated with different valences. In the case of our younger infants, high variable pitch and slow duration were potent indicators of positive emotion.

A different pattern emerged for older infants—they attended more to normal IDS in Experiment 1 and 3, and showed no differential attention in Experiment 2 during which they heard slow High and Low Affect IDS. This replicates the finding that 8-month-olds do not attend more to slow speech (Panneton et al., 2005). It could be that 32-week-olds attend more to high affect speech only with normal durations, or they simply attend more to normal duration independent of vocal emotion. To test this idea, 32-week-olds could be given High Affect/slow vs. Low Affect/normal utterances (the inverse of Experiment 3). If vocal emotion enhances attention, these infants should attend more to High Affect IDS; but if only utterance duration matters, infants should attend more to Low Affect IDS.

In sum, we found that positive emotion increases young infants' attention to speech, and that slower duration is a naturally occurring prosodic feature of IDS that appears to augment infants' perception of vocal affect. In older infants, attention to emotional prosody attenuates as they focus on other levels of information in the speech stream (Burnham, Kitamura & Lancuba, 1999; Morgan & Saffran, 1995). Interestingly, Smith, Calkins, and Keane (this issue) found that 2-year-olds rely less on their mothers for regulatory cues during situations that evoked positive emotion, but significantly more on their mothers' regulatory strategies when experiencing negative emotion. This raises the possibility that during infancy, positive emotion regulation becomes internalized sooner than that involving negative emotion regulation, allowing toddlers to better manage themselves in situations that do not evoke anger, frustration, and/or fear.

Several other questions arise from these data for future work: (i) we contrasted infants' attention to high- (positive) vs. low-affect IDS, so it is unknown whether infants would attend more to high- (negative) vs. low-affect IDS; (ii) although we found that slow duration augments positive vocal emotion in both high- and low-affect IDS, it is unclear whether slow duration would render negative vocal emotion more positive (perhaps neutralizing), or more negative (e.g., an angry utterance sounds even more angry when slow); (iii) because emotional perception/regulation are multisensory processes, it is important to explore how infants' perception of vocal emotion intersects with facial emotion, which has a powerful influence over behavioral regulation as infants become toddlers (e.g., joint attention; social referencing), and (iv) because emotion communication differs across contexts, it is important to compare infants with other experiential histories (e.g., hearing-impaired infants; infants from cultures that deemphasize vocal emotion) and at different points in development to more fully understand the emotion regulation process (Burnham & Sekiyama, 2005).

References

Full bibliographic references available from your instructor.

Editor's Note

Robin Panneton, Department of Psychology, Virginia Polytechnic Institute and State University, Christine Kitamura, MARCS Auditory Laboratories, University of Western Sydney, Karen Mattock, MARCS Auditory Laboratories, University of Western Sydney, and Denis Burnham, MARCS Auditory Laboratories, University of Western Sydney.

This study was funded in part by an International Visiting Fellow grant for Robin Panneton, from the University of Western Sydney to D. Burnham and C. Kitamura.

Correspondence concerning this article should be addressed to Robin Panneton, Department of Psychology (0436), Virginia Tech, Blacksburg, VA 24061. E-mail: panneton@vt.edu.

Discussion Questions for Article 2

Section 4: Development

Name: _____

PID: _____

Date: __ __ / __ __ / __ __ (MM/DD/YY)

CRN: _____

Recitation Day/Time: _____

Honor Code Signature: _____

1. List some of the explanations given for why infants prefer infant-directed speech (IDS) as compared to adult-directed speech (ADS). What do you think of these explanations?

2. How does mother's use of emotional intent change across the infant's development?

3. Why might infants attend more to slow speech? Was this effect found in this study?

4. What were the hypotheses of these experiments? Were they confirmed or refuted?

States of Consciousness and Sleep

The term subconsciousness was first coined by Pierre Marie Félix Janet, a French philosopher who is considered by some to be the true founder of psychoanalytic theory. But it was Sigmund Freud who popularized the idea of a part of the mind not accessible to our conscious. His theories regarding the subconscious have greatly impacted psychology as a science and planted Freud as arguably the most influential psychologist of all time. Even though Freud's psychoanalytic theory is not widely accepted today, it is still relevant for its impact and ground breaking ideas.

In Freud's psychoanalytic theory there are three levels of consciousness: the conscious, unconscious, and preconscious. The unconscious by definition is the area of the mind that is unreachable by the consciousness. By contrast, the preconscious is accessible with minimal effort. According to Freud, the unconscious is a very powerful force that manipulates most of human behavior. Freud believed the unconscious to be more influential than even a person's environment.

From Freud's study of the interaction between conscious and unconscious, he further theorized on three psychic structures that account for the dynamic complexity of human and emotional processes. The id is the first psychic force to develop after birth. The id is an irrational and amoral drive that is hedonistic and focuses on being pleasured. Its primary goal is to reduce tension and satisfy drives by any means necessary. An example of the id would be a baby's demand to be fed immediately when hungry. Satisfaction of the id can also be accomplished through "wish fulfillment" or fantasizing.

The ego develops second after birth. Its purpose is to assist the id in reducing tension, but does so in a more sophisticated way. The ego has been called the reality check. It listens to the demands of the id and seeks to rectify those needs by interacting with the real world. Where the id may fantasize to reduce a drive, the ego problem solves and uses real world objects. Freud related the relationship between the id and ego to a man riding a horse. The man must control the superior strength of the horse with his own lesser strength (Freud, 1961). The id is the source of power which the ego must control.

The superego is the structure that develops last and is commonly called the conscience (not to be confused with conscious). The superego is the summation of the processes in which we choose morality or social norms over our primal desires. This is the structure that is capable of guilt and can view our actions as right and wrong. The superego is learned through various social interactions and cultural values. It holds our morals and checks our actions against these social values. It is through the interaction of the id, ego, and superego that human behavior and motivation are explained by Freud.

Freud considered his book *The Interpretation of Dreams* one of his greatest achievements (Gay, 1989). The primary focus of the book is on the psychoanalytic approach to interpreting dreams. In this theory, Freud theorized that dreams are an expression of unconscious desires. These desires can be seen in two forms: the manifest content and latent meaning. Manifest content is the meaning of the dream on a surface level. Latent meaning is the complicated, real meaning of a dream. It is not obvious like the manifest content, but is instead interpreted through symbolism and associations inside the dream. Freud felt that children's dreams are more superficial than adults. He rationalized that children's dreams are primarily wish fulfillment that is seen in the manifest content. Understanding Freud's groundbreaking perspective on the states of consciousness can help us appreciate where current theories are and can aid in their understanding.

Article 1: What Dreams Are Made Of

The historical views on dreams are fascinating and enchanting. Cultures have viewed dreams as being messages from the gods or ways to be healed. In Psychology, Sigmund Freud was once considered the expert on dreams. Until the 1970s, Freud's psychoanalysis perspective, introduced in *The Interpretation of Dreams*, dominated psychology's view on dreaming. This theory was supplanted by Hobson's beliefs that dreams are randomly formed by nerve signals sent from an area of the brain called the pons.

With newer technology, such as the electroencephalograph, newer scientific views on sleep are made possible that agree and conflict with Hobson. Among these is the discovery of the REM stage. This stage of sleep is characterized by rapid movement of the eyes. Use of PET and fMRI technology has also given newer perspectives. Lower activity in the prefrontal cortex has been demonstrated to occur during sleep. This would account for the illogical associations that make up dreaming.

Article 2: The Subconscious Mind: Your Unsung Hero

The subconscious may be more important than many people think. It may be one of the mental facilities that make humans unique from animals. Even though it is a powerful and important aspect of the human mind, there is no reliable way to distinguish the subconscious from the conscious. There have been studies that can point to its evidence, but substantial proof is still elusive. Abstract measures of the subconscious have shown that our brain is aware of our environment even when our conscious is not. Some argue that the subconscious and conscious should be considered two parts of the same system. This conclusion seems logical because of evidence that the subconscious scans the environment to see what is relevant to the conscious. It is not our conscious thought which causes our "eureka!" moments, but our unconscious mind's work. It is unclear how this happens, but it is evidenced throughout many learning studies.

—*Michael Sewell*

Article 1

What Dreams Are Made Of

Barbara Kantrowitz
Karen Springen
Pat Wingert
Josh Ulick

*New technology is helping brain scientists unravel the mysteries of the night.
Their work could show us all how to make the most of our time in bed.*

In the middle of the night, we are all Fellini—the creator of a parade of fleeting images intended for an audience of one. At times, it's an action flick, with a chase scene that seems endless . . . until it dissolves and we're falling, falling, falling into . . . is it a field of flowers? And who is the gardener waving at us over there? Could it be our old high-school English teacher? No, it's Jon Stewart. He wants us to sit on the couch right next to him. Are those TV cameras? And what happened to our clothes? In the morning, when the alarm rudely arouses us, we might remember none of this—or maybe only a fraction, perhaps the feeling of lying naked in a bed of daisies or an inexplicable urge to watch "The Daily Show."

This, then, is the essence of dreaming—reality and unreality in a nonsensical, often mundane but sometimes bizarre mix. Dreams have captivated thinkers since ancient times, but their mystery is now closer than ever to resolution, thanks to new technology that allows scientists to watch the sleeping brain at work. Although there are still many more questions than answers, researchers are now able to see how different parts of the brain work at night, and they're figuring out how that division of labor influences our dreams. In one sense, it's the closest we've come to recording the soul. "If you're going to understand human behavior," says Rosalind

Cartwright, a chairman of psychology at Rush University Medical Center in Chicago, "here's a big piece of it. Dreaming is our own storytelling time—to help us know who we are, where we're going and how we're going to get there."

The long-range goal of dream research is a comprehensive explanation of the connections between sleeping and waking, a multidimensional picture of consciousness and thought 24 hours a day. In the meantime, dream science is helping us understand and treat depression, posttraumatic stress, anxiety and a whole range of other problems. Neuroscientists are gleaning insights into how we learn by studying the physiology of dreaming in adults and children. Psychologists are also studying dreams to learn how both ordinary people and great artists resolve problems in their life and work by "sleeping on it." For many of these researchers, accounts of ordinary dreams are a rich resource. Psychologist G. William Domhoff and his colleagues at the University of California, Santa Cruz, have meticulously cataloged and posted more than 17,000 dreams. That database (dreambank.net) is the source of the dreams printed here.

1. History of Dream Research

I am with an older, "lecherous-looking" Freudian analyst who wants me to lie on the couch and recall the moment of my birth while he counts 1, 2, 3. I pretend and then tell him the truth. Then he gets undressed and wants to make love to me but just then Mother looks in by the door! And I lie very still; she closes the door. I awaken. (Then I remember wishing that I was still with my analyst.)

Thousands of years ago, dreams were seen as messages from the gods, and in many cultures, they are still considered prophetic. In ancient Greece, sick people slept at the temples of Asclepius, the god of medicine, in order to receive dreams that would heal them. Modem dream science really begins at the end of the 19th century with Sigmund Freud, who theorized that dreams were the expression of unconscious desires often stemming from childhood. He believed that exploring these hidden emotions through analysis could help cure mental illness. The Freudian model of psychoanalysis dominated until the 1970s, when new research into the chemistry of the brain showed that emotional problems could have biological or chemical roots, as well as environmental ones. In other words, we weren't sick just because of something our mothers did (or didn't do), but because of some imbalance that might be cured with medication.

After Freud, the most important event in dream science was the discovery in the early 1950s of a phase of sleep characterized by intense brain activity and rapid eye movement (REM). People awakened in the midst of REM sleep reported vivid dreams, which led researchers to conclude that most dreaming took place during REM. Using the electroencephalograph (EEG), researchers could see

TABLE 1   Top Dreams by Gender: Women dream more often about friends, family and domestic settings. Men are more likely to dream about sex and violence.

% WHO HAVE HAD THESE DREAMS		
	Men	Women
1. Chased or pursued, not injured	78%	83%
2. Sexual experiences	85	73
3. Falling	73	74
4. School, teachers, studying	57	71
5. Arriving too late, e.g., for a train	55	62
6. On the verge of falling	53	60
7. Trying to do something repeatedly	55	53
8. A person living as dead	43	59
9. Flying or soaring through the air	58	44
10. Sensing a presence vividly	44	50
11. Failing an examination	37	48
12. Being physically attacked	40	44
13. Being frozen with fright	32	44
14. A person now dead as living	37	39
15. Being a child again	33	38

Source: Dreaming journal

that brain activity during REM resembled that of the waking brain. That told them that a lot more was going on at night than anyone had suspected. But what, exactly?

Scientists still don't know for sure, although they have lots of theories. On one side are scientists like Harvard's Allan Hobson, who believes that dreams are essentially random. In the 1970s, Hobson and his colleague Robert McCarley proposed what they called the "activation-synthesis hypothesis," which describes how dreams are formed by nerve signals sent out during REM sleep from a small area at the base of the brain called the pons. These signals, the researchers said, activate the images that we call dreams. That put a crimp in dream research; if dreams were meaningless nocturnal firings, what was the point of studying them? More recently, new theories have made some scientists take dreams more seriously. In 1997, Mark Solms of the University of Cape Town in South Africa published the results of his study of people with damage to different parts of the brain; he found that there was more than one mechanism in the brain for activating dreams. Since then, Solms has argued that technology like functional magnetic resonance imaging (fMRI) and positron emission tomography (PET) might actually lend new weight to Freud's ideas because the parts of the brain that are most active during dreaming control emotion, the core of Freud's dream theory. Today, many therapists have a looser view of Freud, accepting that dreams may express unconscious thoughts, although not necessarily childhood conflicts.

Many others think the answer ultimately lies in a reconciliation of the different disciplines that study dreaming: neurobiology and psychology. "Both are useful, but they're different," says Glen Gabbard, professor of psychoanalysis and psychiatry at Baylor College of Medicine in Houston. "To have a truly comprehensive understanding of dreams, you have to be bilingual. You have to speak the language of the mind and the language of the brain."

2. The Biology of Dreaming

Doctors are on the roof talking to people, saying they shouldn't be up there because it's dangerous. One doctor gives shots to immobilize the brain, rather than fixing ailments. I say if I fall to fix me up but leave my brain so I can dream.

Adult humans spend about a quarter of their sleep time in REM, much of it dreaming. During that time, the body is essentially paralyzed but the brain is buzzing. Scientists using PET and fMRI technology to watch the dreaming brain have found that one of the most active areas during REM is the limbic system, which controls our emotions. Much less active is the prefrontal cortex, which is associated with logical thinking. That could explain why dreams in REM sleep often lack a coherent story line. (Some researchers have also found that people dream in non-REM sleep as well, although those dreams generally are less vivid.) Another active part of the brain in REM sleep is the anterior cingulate cortex, which detects discrepancies. Eric Nofzinger, director of the Sleep Neuroimaging Program at the University of Pittsburgh Medical Center, thinks that could be why people often figure out thorny problems in their dreams. "It's as if the brain surveys the internal milieu and tries to figure out what it should be doing, and whether our actions conflict with who we are," he says.

These may seem like vital mental functions, but no one has yet been able to say that REM sleep or dreaming is essential to life or even sanity. MAO inhibitors, an older class of antidepressants, essentially block REM sleep without any detectable effects, although people do get a "REM rebound"—extra REM—if they stop the medication. That's also true of selective serotonin reuptake inhibitors (SSRIs) like Prozac, which reduce dreaming by a third to a half. Even permanently

TABLE 2   Dreams: A Forgotten World: Adults dream at least four to six times a night but often don't remember. Children recall dreams less frequently.

RECALL	FREQUENCY*
Every night	14%
Frequently	23
Occasionally	33
Rarely	24
Never	6

* For Adults. Source: Inge Strauch, Ph.D., University of Zurich

losing the ability to dream doesn't have to be disabling. Israeli researcher Peretz Lavie has been observing a patient named Yuval Chamtzani, who was injured by a fragment of shrapnel that penetrated his brain when he was 19. As a result, he gets no REM sleep and doesn't remember any dreams. But Lavie says that Chamtzani, now 55, "is probably the most normal person I know and one of the most successful ones." (He's a lawyer, a painter and the editor of a puzzle column in a popular Israeli newspaper.)

The mystery of REM sleep is that even though it may not be essential, it is ubiquitous—at least in mammals and birds. But that doesn't mean all mammals and birds dream (or if they do, they're certainly not—talking about it). Some researchers think REM may have evolved for physiological reasons. "One thing that's unique about mammals and birds is that they regulate body temperature," says neuroscientist Jerry Siegel, director of UCLA's Center for Sleep Research. "There's no good evidence that any cold-blooded animal has REM sleep." REM sleep heats up the brain and non-REM cools it off, Siegel says, and that could mean that the changing sleep cycles allow the brain to repair itself. "It seems likely that REM sleep is filling a basic physiological function and that dreams are a kind of epiphenomenon," Siegel says—an extraneous byproduct, like foam on beer.

But dreaming may also fulfill many functions that we don't yet understand. Allan Rechtschaffen, a longtime sleep researcher and professor emeritus at the University of Chicago, compares dreaming to breathing. "We need to breathe to get oxygen," he says. "That's a physiological must. That's why the breathing apparatus evolved. But once it evolved, you can put it to other uses, like for speech or laughing or playing the saxophone." Perhaps dreaming, too, adapted to other uses. "There's no reason dreams have to be any one thing," he says. "Is our waking consciousness any one thing?"

3. Different Dreamers: Age and Gender

All night long, Jared is drunk and talking in his incoherent mumbly monotone. Finally, I have enough and tell him off. I call him a boring bastard. Then I notice a baby girl standing inside a flaming fireplace. I go up to her and say sympathetically, "You must be very hot and uncomfortable." She agrees. I pick her up and I hold her, taking her away from the fire.

We're born to be dreamers—although it apparently takes a while to get all the equipment working. While parents-to-be fantasize about their babies, fetuses probably aren't dreaming about Mom and Dad. "Almost the entire state of being before we're born is REM sleep," says Mark Mahowald, director of the Minnesota Regional Sleep Disorders Center in Minneapolis. "I can't imagine that there's a lot of conflict resolution going on in utero." Young children get a lot of REM sleep as well, which scientists think is probably stimulation for brain growth, not real dreaming. Researchers believe children have to reach a certain level of intellectual maturity, around the age of 8 or 9, before their dreams resemble adults'.

Inge Strauch, a psychology professor at the University of Zurich, has collected 550 dreams from a group of twenty-four 9- to 15-year-olds she studied in her lab over a period of two years. She found that children dreamed about animals more often than adults and were more likely to report being victims than aggressors. They were also more likely to have "fantastic" dreams, while adults' dreams tend to contain more elements of reality. A typical fantastic dream from a 10-year-old Strauch studied included a cat asking for directions to the "cat bathroom." Similarly, an 11-year-old boy dreamed that a snake wanted to go up a ski lift.

Gender differences in dream content show up in studies of adults as well. The biggest myth? That adult dreams are "full of sex," says Domhoff, author of "The Scientific Study of Dreams." When they do have dreams that include sex, they're often about someone they're not really attracted to or some conflict, he says. "They are not often joyful occasions." In fact, about two thirds of the characters in men's dreams are men; gender is more evenly divided in women's dreams. These differences appear to be true in many different cultures. Men's dreams also involve more physical aggression than women's dreams; they're more likely to be about chasing, punching, breaking, stealing or killing, Domhoff says. A more typical expression of aggression in women's dreams would be rejection or an insult ("That dress makes you look fat").

A favorite topic for women: weddings. But they're not always happily-ever-after dreams. "Something always goes wrong," Domhoff says. "It's the wrong dress, the wrong guy, the wrong church." In one recorded on dreambank.net, a woman is about to get married and doesn't have anything to wear. "I ended up wearing a genie outfit, genie pants, a gauze orange top, slippers, a belt with belts on it, lots of jewelry and my hair in a ponytail," she wrote. "I remember reassuring myself by thinking it was close to Halloween."

YOUR DREAMING BRAIN: Scientists are using brain scans to uncover the physiological basics of dreams.

VISUAL IMAGES: Areas that generate internal imagery are active, providing visual detail, even though regions receiving signals from the eyes are shut down.

LOGIC & EMOTION: Emotional centers rev up, while areas involved in judgment wind down, perhaps giving free rein to unconscious feelings and drives, as Freud theorized.

MEMORY: Regions responsible for short-term memory become inactive, so the dreamer forgets what just happened and accepts rapidly shifting scenes or characters.

Sources: Allen Braun, M.D., NIDCD, National Institutes of Health; Thomas Balkin, Ph.D., Walter Reed Army Institute of Research

Not surprisingly, new mothers frequently dream about their babies, says Tore Nielsen, associate professor of psychiatry at the University of Montreal, who has analyzed the content of 20,000 dreams collected over the Web. In a separate study of 220 new mothers' dreams, he found that "a lot of bad things happen to their infants—the cat eating them, or they're suddenly lost, or they left them in the care of a relative who left them in a shopping center."

4. How We Use Dreams

There is a man talking calmly on a pay phone. He is a gunman. He talks casually as he blasts a machine gun up the stairs next to the pay phone, killing people. When he is out of bullets, he casually alters his weapon to use shotgun shells. He is poised, cold like steel, calm, and he kills.

People who don't remember their dreams can learn to recall them. In general, more introverted, psychologically oriented people naturally remember their dreams. Practical, concrete thinkers probably won't. It also helps to get enough sleep so you have time to dream. If you want to remember more, try to keep the REM state going by lying still and keeping your eyes closed while you repeat the dream scenario in your head to solidify it in your memory. Cartwright even suggests giving it a title, like "My Date with Brad Pitt." Keep a notebook by your bed and write down what's in your head as soon as you wake up.

A LOOK BACK AT DREAMS: Once seen as divine inspiration, the meaning of dreams has evolved over the ages.

EGYPT: As in other ancient civilizations, Egyptians viewed dreams as messages from the gods, building special temples dedicated to them.

THE BIBLE: Prophetic dreams figure throughout. Joseph won his freedom by accurately interpreting Pharaoh's visions.

ANCIENT GREECE: Aristotle was among the first to suggest dreams were products of the mind, not the gods. Hippocrates thought dreams could be used to diagnose illness.

MIDDLE AGES: Hoping to monopolize contact with the divine, the church downplayed dreams as messages from God. Instead they were blamed on the workings of the Devil.

PSYCHOANALYSIS: Sigmund Freud thought our hidden drives, repressed during waking life, bubble up to surface in dreams. Carl Jung thought symbols in dreams are shared and understood by all humanity.

MODERN STUDIES: In 1953 scientists discovered REM, intervals in sleep when people dream vividly. The finding provided a starting point for the biological study of dreams.

Source: "Our Dreaming Mind" by Robert Van de Castle

Why should you care what happens in your head at night? Although there's lots of disagreement about the psychological function of dreams, researchers in recent years have come up with some tantalizing theories. One possibility is that dreaming helps the mind run tests of its Emergency Broadcast System, a way to prepare for potential disaster. So, for example, when new mothers dream about losing their babies, they may actually be rehearsing what they would do or how they would react if their worst fears were realized. There's also evidence that dreaming helps certain kinds of learning. Some researchers have found that dreaming about physical tasks, like a gymnast's floor routine, enhances performance. Dreaming can also help people find solutions to elusive problems. "Anything that is very visual may get extra help from dreams," says Deirdre Barrett, assistant professor at Harvard Medical School and editor of the journal Dreaming. In her book "The Committee of Sleep," she describes how artists like Jasper Johns and Salvador Dali found inspiration in their dreams. In her own research on problem solving through dreams, Barrett has found that even ordinary people can solve simple problems in their lives (like how to fit old furniture into a new apartment) if they focus on the dilemma before they fall asleep.

Whatever the function of dreams at night, they clearly can play a role in therapy during the day. The University of Maryland's Clara Hill, who has studied the use of dreams in therapy, says that dreams are a "back door" into a patient's thinking. "Dreams reveal stuff about you that you didn't know was there," she says. The therapists she trains to work with patients' dreams are, in essence, heirs to Freud, using dream imagery to uncover hidden emotions and feelings. Dreams provide clues to the nature of more serious mental illness. Schizophrenics, for example, have poor-quality dreams, usually about objects rather than people. Cartwright has been studying depression in divorced men and women, and she is finding that "good dreamers," people who have vivid dreams with strong story lines, are less likely to remain depressed. She thinks that dreaming helps diffuse strong emotions. "Dreaming is a mental-health activity," she says.

People often deal with traumatic events through dreams. Tufts University psychiatrist Ernest Hartmann, author of "Dreams and Nightmares," analyzed dreams from the same group of people before and after September 11 (none of them lived in New York). He found that the later dreams were not necessarily more negative, but they were more intense. "The intensity is a measure of emotional arousal," he says. For people suffering from posttraumatic stress disorder (PTSD), dream content can be a marker of the level of distress, says psychiatrist Thomas Mellman of the Howard University School of Medicine, who studies PTSD. Dreams that mimic the real-life trauma indicate that the patient may be "stuck" in the experience. He thinks one way to help people move past the memory is through an "injury rehearsal," where they imagine a more positive scenario.

All this has led to a rethinking of Freud's great insight, that dreams are a "royal road" to the unconscious. Mapping that royal road is a daunting task for scientists who are using sophisticated imaging techniques and psychological studies in an attempt to synthesize what we know about the inner workings of the mind and the brain. Dreaming, like thinking, is what makes us human—whether we're evoking old terrors or imagining new pleasures. "We dream about unfinished business," says Domhoff. And, if we're lucky, we wake up with a little more insight to carry the day.

Discussion Questions for Article 1

Section 5: States of Consciousness and Sleep

Name: _____

PID: _____

Date: __ __ / __ __ / __ __ (MM/DD/YY)

CRN: _____

Recitation Day/Time: _____

Honor Code Signature: _____

1. How are men and women's dreams different and why do you think this is?

2. What do you think the reason/purpose of dreams is?

3. How are dreams associated with psychological disorders?

4. Can you relate any of your recent dreams to recent experiences? Explain your answer.

The Subconscious Mind: Your Unsung Hero

Kate Douglas

Earlier this year I found myself thinking about thinking. Specifically, what is it that makes the human mind so special? Like many people, I have always believed that the answer lies in our capacity for conscious thought. But listening to speakers at a recent Ernst Strungmann Forum in Frankfurt, Germany, I began to wonder if there might be more to it than that.

It was a discussion entitled "Better than conscious" that had me intrigued. The more I listened to what the assembled scientists had to say and talked to them about their work, the more it seemed that our higher consciousness alone is not what sets us apart from other animals. In fact, far from playing second fiddle to the conscious mind, subconscious thought processes may play a crucial role in many of the mental facilities we prize as uniquely human, including creativity, memory, learning and language.

Modern notions of the subconscious were invented by Sigmund Freud as part of his now-discredited theory of psychoanalysis. These days the subconscious is on a firmer scientific footing—although many neurobiologists avoid the word "subconscious", preferring "non-conscious", "pre-conscious" or "unconscious" to describe thought processes that happen outside consciousness. Where Freud and his followers saw the subconscious as little more than an emotional and impulsive force in a constant tug of war with the more logical and detached conscious mind, we now know that this view is too simplistic. Our subconscious is not an unthinking autopilot that needs to be subjugated by rationality, but a purposeful, active and independent guide to behaviour.

Some scientists go so far as to believe that it is responsible for the vast majority of our day-to-day activity and that we are nothing more than "zombies" guided by our subconscious. This is an extreme point of view, but in the past few years, researchers trying to understand the nature of human consciousness and how it differs from the subconscious have made some surprising discoveries. Put the findings of many studies together and another picture emerges. There is more to being human than consciousness.

To get to this new view of the subconscious, neuroscientists and psychologists have had to fight hard to overcome a major barrier. So far, there is no reliable way to distinguish between conscious and subconscious thought processes. They can be described easily enough—psychologists use terms such as explicit/implicit, procedural/declarative or automatic/controlled to distinguish between the thought process. Explicit, declarative—or conscious—thoughts are those that can easily be expressed in words, for example, whereas subconscious ones are hard to articulate. Conscious thought processes are disrupted if you are forced to direct your attention elsewhere. Subconscious ones are not. But as yet you cannot simply look at an image of the brain and say what kind of thought process is being used.

Yet there are several ways to investigate the conscious/subconscious divide, as Stanislas Dehaene, director of the Cognitive Neuroimaging Unit at INSERM, the French equivalent of the US National Institutes of Health, points out. One is to study people with brain damage who have conditions such as blindsight—where they are unable to see visual stimuli on one side following an injury or stroke. While they may be unaware of seeing an action or an object, if forced to guess what was in that visual field they perform far better than would be expected by chance. This suggests that while they may not consciously see a stimulus, they are able to subconsciously process what they have seen and respond appropriately.

Another approach, which Dehaene uses in his lab, is called masking. Here volunteers are shown a word for just a few tens of milliseconds, followed by another image, the mask, which prevents the subject consciously noticing the word. By gradually increasing the delay between the word and mask, awareness of the word moves from the subconscious into the conscious mind. You can measure when this happens by asking subjects to say when they first notice the flashed word or, more objectively, by asking the volunteers questions about the target word—for example, asking them to decide whether it is a natural or artificial item. Using brain scans you can also look for differences in brain activity during subconscious and conscious perceptions of the word (*PLoS Biology,* vol 5, e260).

These methods show the masked word "popping" into consciousness when the interval between the two images is around 50 milliseconds—less if the word has emotional significance, which makes it more attention-grabbing. Dehaene's neuroimaging experiments, using both functional MRI and EEG, seem to reflect this, revealing widespread brain activity once the word is consciously perceived. He believes that two things are required for conscious processing: the stimulus has to be strong enough, and we have to focus our attention on it. Once this happens many areas of the brain, including working memory, have access to the word.

Sit Up and Take Notice

So much for conscious perception. What does work like this tell us about the other side of the coin? Dehaene's masking experiments suggest that the subconscious is far from being a closed box. He has found that even when a word flashes up for less than 50 milliseconds and people are not aware of having seen it, they could still guess whether the word described a natural or artificial item more often than by chance.

What this suggests is that our brains constantly monitor our internal and external environment such that when the input becomes important enough, the subconscious decides to engage the conscious and we become aware of what is there. This is certainly what neurobiologist Michael Shadlen from the University of Washington in Seattle believes. "We suspect that the normal unconscious brain monitors the environment for cues that prompt it to decide whether to awaken and engage . . . The decision to engage at all is, in effect, an unconscious decision to be conscious."

This idea that consciousness is orchestrated by the subconscious brain finds support in the recent dramatic "awakening" of a man who had spent six years in a minimally conscious state. Nicholas Schiff of the Weill Cornell Medical College in New York and his team stimulated a part of the man's brain called the thalamus, which lies between the brainstem and the cerebral hemispheres and forms connections to the cortex (New Scientist, 4 August, p 14). A special class of neurons within the thalamus, the calbindinpositive cells, have long been thought to play a role in arousal by stimulating the cortex. Sure enough, following stimulation of the thalamus, the man was suddenly able to open his eyes, speak and feed himself. In a commentary on the work, Shadlen and his colleague Roozbeh Kiani argue that this is the network through which the subconscious brain makes its decision to generate consciousness (*Nature*, vol 448, p 539).

Crucially, Shadlen sees the subconscious and conscious as two parts of the same system, rather than two separate thought processors working in the same machine. However, while Shadlen argues for a unified model of mental processing, others want to further subdivide conscious and subconscious thought and have come up with alternative descriptions to replace the old two-part model. Peter Dayan, a theoretical neuroscientist at University College London, and colleagues Nathaniel Daw and Yael Niv, see the mind as comprising four systems (see Diagram) that work together to control our decisionmaking and behaviour (*Nature Neuroscience*, vol 8, p 1704).

First is the Pavlovian controller—the brain's autopilot, programmed by evolution to perform routine and instinctive behaviours such as fleeing from danger. Working primarily at the subconscious level, the Pavlovian controller is fast and efficient, if inflexible.

The other three control systems combine both conscious and subconscious thought to achieve the best possible outcome depending on the level of uncertainty about the situation you are in. The goal-directed controller corresponds most closely to popular notions of "rational thought". It allows you to optimise your choices by evaluating all the available information. When information is scarce, however—in unfamiliar situations or the very early stages of learning—another system, the episodic controller, takes charge. Instead of making complex calculations, it simply recommends adopting behaviours that have proved successful in similar situations in the past. Both rely heavily on conscious reasoning, and require you to focus on the problem at hand.

Once you achieve expertise in a skill such as driving, typing or playing golf, the fourth system, the habitual controller, comes into its own. Although we consciously learn to do these things, with experience they become second nature and we can do them automatically—in fact, once this happens, conscious analysis actually inhibits performance (*Journal of Experimental Psychology*, vol 8, p 6).

In this model, subconscious/implicit thought processes and conscious/explicit ones are more like equal partners than competitors. The two work together in the goal-directed controller, for example, to evaluate all the available information whether consciously or subconsciously perceived. So, for example, your decision to buy a certain product may be influenced by both explicit factors such as price and quality and implicit ones such as your mood, or an advert that you have seen but not necessarily noticed.

Dayan says that our behaviour is often driven by more than one of the four controllers—the various types of explicit and implicit thought process may be actively integrated, and this is especially true when we are learning something new where the balance between ignorance and experience changes. Importantly, the subconscious isn't the dumb cousin of the conscious, but rather a cousin with different skills.

Out of the Blue

What's more, non-conscious thinking may actually work best in some cases where you might imagine rational, conscious thought is the best tool for the job. In situations where people have to make difficult choices based on large amounts of hard-to-assess information, psychologist Ap Dijksterhuis at the University of

Amsterdam in the Netherlands has found that they are happier with their decision when acting on gut instinct than when forced to try to think the choice through rationally (*New Scientist*, 5 May 2007, p 35). Dijksterhuis is convinced that subconscious thought processes are superior in many situations—including most social interactions—because they allow us to integrate complex information in a more holistic way than can be managed by rational thought processes.

Something similar sometimes happens in problem solving, according to Jonathan Schooler from the University of British Columbia in Vancouver. By asking subjects to explain their reasoning as they go, he has found that verbalising what they are doing has no effect on people's ability to solve analytical, mathematical or logic problems but actually hinders performance on insight problems, such as solving a riddle—those for which the solution seems to pop out of the blue in an aha! moment. Remember that subconscious thought processes differ from conscious ones in that we are unable to articulate the former. So here, it seems, is experimental evidence for something we all instinctively know: that subconscious thinking is the source of our inspiration—it is central to creativity.

A classic study into the neural basis of creativity suggests that it depends on an ability to shift gear between subconscious and conscious processing. Three decades ago, Colin Martindale of the University of Maine in Orono charted what is happening in the creative mind using EEG. He asked people to invent stories and found two distinct stages of brain activity. During the initial "inspiration" stage, their brains were remarkably quiet. Any activity was dominated by alpha waves, which indicates very low cortical arousal as though the conscious mind was quiescent while the subconscious worked behind the scenes. Intriguingly, you find a similar pattern during dream sleep and relaxation, two mental states also associated with high creativity. This "inspiration" stage was followed by a second stage, "elaboration", characterised by far more activity especially in the cortex, and probably associated with the conscious analysis and evaluation of ideas. People with the greatest difference in brain activity between these two stages were the most creative. More recently, Jordan Peterson at the University of Toronto, Canada, has argued that in highly creative people subconscious information is more likely to overspill into consciousness, giving them richer mental resources from which to make creative connections (*New Scientist*, 29 October 2005, p 39).

It'll Come to Me

The sort of inspiration that comes in a flash is not just about creativity, however. Elke Weber from Columbia University, New York, points out that it is important for memory too. For example, when we are having difficulty remembering someone's name we often consign the problem to our subconscious in the knowledge that it will probably pop into our minds when we are no longer actively thinking about it. How this works is a mystery but, Weber argues, it surely belies the idea of the subconscious mind as inflexible and constrained.

So does all of this mean that the subconscious is as important an aspect of our humanity as the conscious mind? Ours is a species distinguished by its superior ability to learn new tricks, so maybe the subconscious—perhaps in the form of the habitual controller—took a crucial role in the evolution of our ancestors from bipedal apes to highly skilled tool-makers, hunters and craftspeople. Studies on rats and monkeys indicate that they too consign skills to subconscious control once they become expert. "Still, we may have a greater capacity for this," says Dayan, "since we have the huge advantage of being able to use language to boost our goal-directed control and so provide a much richer substrate for acquiring habitual skills."

The subconscious mind may even have a hand in our unique talent for language. Often we are only consciously aware of words as we speak them. So does that make language the mouthpiece of the non-conscious mind? And what about the process of learning to speak? Infants do not need tutoring to acquire their native language; they pick it up subconsciously. What's more they do this with remarkably little linguistic data—what the Harvard University linguist Noam Chomsky has called the "poverty of stimulus"—suggesting that this subconscious learning allows youngsters to use information very efficiently. Perhaps this also explains why new languages are more difficult to acquire after about the age of 8—if we then gradually lose that subconscious ability and so have to learn language in a more formal, didactic and conscious way. These questions remain unanswered, and perhaps that is not surprising. As Dayan points out, we still have a long way to go before we fully understand the various components of subconscious thought. "The aspects of learning that lead us to acquire a language may have nothing whatsoever in common with other non-conscious facets," he says.

It is intriguing to wonder whether the human subconscious mind is different from that of other animals. Is there a human "higher subconscious" on a par with our "higher consciousness"? Given the difficulties of even pinning down the nature of consciousness, it is far too early to start elevating the subconscious to such heights. Still, if there is one thing everyone in Frankfurt agreed on, it is that our non-conscious thought processes are a lot cleverer than we once realised.

Discussion Questions for Article 2

Section 5: States of Consciousness and Sleep

Name: _____

PID: _____

Date: __ __ / __ __ / __ __ (MM/DD/YY)

CRN: _____

Recitation Day/Time: _____

Honor Code Signature: _____

1. How is the modern view of the subconscious different from Sigmund Freud's view?

2. How does the subconscious affect creativity?

3. If you were to design a simple study to test for evidence of the subconscious, what would it be?

4. Describe an incident in which you answered a problem by "not thinking" about it and allowed your subconscious to work it out.

Section 6
Cognition and Memory

What did you wear yesterday? What was the television program you watched last Saturday? How much did you borrow from your friend last month? When your brain begins to process these items, cognition is inevitably started. Cognition can be broadly defined as the mental activity in the brain. Therefore, it is not a difficult stretch to understand that memory has a rather close relationship with cognition.

Cognitive psychology is the study of perception, learning, memory and thought. Psychologists have long been fascinated by how we insert the sensory information all around us into the iconic memory and eventually store it in the long-term memory. Later, an individual can use this information to induce and deduce about the world, solve problems and make decisions. Cognitive processes are not only used in everyday life, but also they are used in the psychotherapy to diagnose mental problems of patients and treat the psychological illness. Moreover, since certain cognitive processes are closely associated with human being's IQ ability, many studies in psychology involve researching in how to develop a person's intelligence from an early age.

Memory is a facet of cognition which has received lots of attention from psychologists. There has been the early discovery of forgetting curve by *Ebbinghaus* followed by the classical experiments done by Sperling that demonstrated the existence of a subtype of sensory memory—iconic memory. More recently there has been the work of Elizabeth Loftus, who showed us how malleable our memory is.

Currently, limitations of individual cognition have been noticed a lot by cognitive psychologists spanning many realms of psychology. These limitations include the fundamental attribution error in the realm of social cognition. Memory serves as a good example of this current tendency of research in cognitive psychology. Loftus and her colleagues have done numerous experiments in eyewitness testimonies through which it has been demonstrated how inventive and fragile memory can be. One should also be warned to take caution when using the therapeutic techniques such as regression because the clinicians' suggestions might play a role in distortion of the clients' memory.

Article 1: Searching for Memory: The Brain, the Mind, and the Past

In this section of the reader, Dr. Daniel L. Schacter discusses many fascinating and uncanny idiosyncrasies associated with cognition from our past experiences. The highlights of this writing include a kind of memory that exists, yet we cannot reflect on it. We never know when implicit memory may imbed automatically in our brain. Moreover, Dr. Schacter's research about amnesic patients also provides us interesting examples to deeply understand what the implication is for implicit memory and how we can retrieve important information from it.

Article 2: Reconstructing Memory: The Incredible Eyewitness

Eyewitness testimony is one of the most important resources that juries can rely on when making a judgment. Yet, is this resource as reliable as once thought? According to this article and a series of experiments, Loftus tells us that the answer is most likely no. Our memory can change drastically from the points of witnessing and recalling an event. Instead of simple retrieval, it is possible to reconstruct the event, using information other than what was acquired during the actual event. Even a non-descriptive word such as *a* or *the* in the leading questions can change the eyewitness account. As you read this article, you would learn the why and how of poor eyewitness testimony and what effect it can have in a court of law.

—*Zhe Wang and Qiong Wu*

From *Searching for Memory: The Brain, the Mind, and the Past*

Daniel L. Schacter

December afternoons darken early in Boston. For most people, this is one of the more depressing features of the New England winter. I don't mind it much, because the early evenings allow me to enjoy the sunset from the windows of my office near the northern fringe of the Harvard campus. The stunning view of the entire Boston skyline is especially lovely in the fading light of dusk on a winter afternoon. At the close of one such afternoon in December 1993, I took a much-needed break and gazed out the windows. But my pleasant reverie was interrupted by the ring of a telephone.

The caller introduced himself as Rowan Wilson, an attorney with the prestigious New York firm of Cravath, Swaine, and Moore. His firm had been representing the computer giant IBM in a major lawsuit in which questions about memory seemed likely to play a role. I agreed to hear about the case and to consider becoming involved in it.

Wilson's first question struck an immediate chord: Is it possible, he wanted to know, for a person to retrieve information from a past experience without being aware that he is relying on memory? Most of my scientific efforts for the past decade had been directed toward precisely that issue. I had been conducting experiments investigating what my colleagues and I call *implicit memory:* when people are influenced by a past experience without any awareness that they are remembering. Yes, I responded, a person most definitely can make use of memory for a past experience without any awareness of remembering. But why on earth would an attorney have any interest in knowing that?

This one had excellent reasons: parts of his case hinged on the viability of the idea that memory can be manifested without awareness of remembering. Wilson's case entailed a dispute over intellectual property: Who owns the rights to the ideas and knowledge that an employee develops in the course of performing his duties? Much depended on the status of technical knowledge residing in the head of an electrical engineer who had once worked at IBM, Peter Bonyhard. Beginning in 1984, Bonyhard played a key role in IBM's development of a revolutionary new technology for reading information from a computer disk. He had helped to develop what is known in the industry as an MR (magneto-resistive) head. This almost unimaginably tiny, paper-thin device uses a magnetically based method for decoding information stored on a disk that allows computer manufacturers to pack much more information onto the disk than they could with previous technology. The technical and financial implications of MR head technology are enormous, and Bonyhard was a valued IBM employee. But his services were also coveted by others. In 1991 Bonyhard left IBM to join a rival company, Seagate, that specializes in manufacturing disk drives and heads.

IBM objected to the fact that Bonyhard was allowed to work on MR heads at Seagate. While at IBM, he had been exposed to a large amount of confidential, trade-secret information about the manufacture and function of MR heads, information he had promised not to disclose. IBM contended that because he was deeply involved in Seagate's attempt to develop its own MR head, it would be virtually impossible—despite his best intentions—for Bonyhard not to disclose trade-secret information. This was the heart of Rowan Wilson's case and the reason he was consulting me: he suspected that Bonyhard might unknowingly divulge trade-secret information in his new job.

Although I never had the opportunity to address the issues—IBM and Seagate settled their dispute and Bonyhard could no longer work directly on the development of MR heads—the case raises questions that are central to understanding memory's fragile power: To what extent can people show memory for previous experiences even when they are not aware of remembering them? What is the evidence for such implicit memories, and how do they influence what we do and what we think in our day-to-day lives? What does the existence of implicit memory tell us about the nature and organization of memory in mind and brain?

During the past fifteen years, psychology and neuroscience have made immense progress toward answering those questions. It is no exaggeration to say that research on implicit memory has revolutionized how we measure the effects of past experiences and how we think about the nature of memory. The path that led to implicit memory—both for me personally and for the field as a whole—can be traced back to events that unfolded some two decades earlier in the ancient town of Oxford.

Why Do Amnesic Patients Learn?

When I arrived in Oxford just after the New Year in 1978, it was the first time I had ever been to England. I was captivated immediately by the impressive towers and intricate spires of All Soul's College, the golden brown stones of the magnificent Bodleian library, and the narrow stone paths that lead to centuries-old stores and pubs. Enrolled as a graduate student at the University of Toronto, I had been blessed with a stroke of good fortune: my supervisor, Endel Tulving, had been awarded a visiting chair at Oxford for a year and I would be spending most of that year with him.

Tulving had arranged for me to meet weekly with Professor Lawrence Weiskrantz, one of the world's authorities on how the brain accomplishes perception and memory. Weiskrantz and his colleague, the London neuropsychologist Elizabeth Warrington, had recently published several articles about amnesic patients that intrigued and puzzled memory researchers. In their experiments, amnesics and a group of normal volunteers studied a list of common words, such as *table* or *garden*. When shown some of these words several minutes later, together with words that were not on the list, amnesic patients had great difficulty remembering which had been on the list and which hadn't. No surprise here: previous studies had already shown that amnesics have problems recognizing words from a recently presented study list. But Warrington and Weiskrantz gave another kind of memory test. They provided the first three letters of a word, such as tab__ __ or gar__ __, and asked people to supply the remaining letters. On this test, amnesic patients wrote down more words from the study list than would be expected if they were guessing randomly. Even more impressively, in some experiments they wrote down as many words as did people who had no memory problems. How is it possible to explain such a curious pattern?

Warrington and Weiskrantz suggested one reason why the three-letter cues might have been especially useful to amnesic patients: they help patients avoid being confused by irrelevant memories that ordinarily spring to mind and interfere with their recall of the correct answer. But something else was noteworthy about the amnesic patients' performance: they did not appear to be aware that they were recalling words from the study list when they provided them in response to the three-letter test cues. Instead, they often behaved as if they were in a guessing game. They were showing memory for the studied words, but they were not "remembering" in the ordinary sense of the term.

Weiskrantz noticed something even more extraordinary about a different type of brain-damaged patient. He started to study a man who had lost much of his vision as a result of damage to the occipital lobes, the structures in the rear of our brains that are necessary to perceive the external world around us. When a light was flashed in the part of visual space affected by his brain damage, the patient typically claimed to see nothing. But when asked to "guess" the location of the flash, he performed extremely accurately! The patient seemed capable of some form of unconscious perception. Weiskrantz called this remarkable ability *blindsight,* and suggested that it might be related in some way to memory without awareness in amnesic patients.

I was excited by these observations, which dovetailed with pioneering studies in the 1960s by Brenda Milner and her colleagues showing that the profoundly amnesic patient HM could learn new motor skills. When HM practiced tracking a moving target, his performance—just like that of people with intact memories—became increasingly accurate. HM, however, was not aware that he had ever performed the task before.

When first confronted with this surprising finding, memory researchers did not show much interest in it. The standard interpretation held that HM could learn new motor skills because motor learning is a special kind of memory that does not depend on the hippocampus and the other medial temporal lobe structures that were removed from HM's brain. Most memory researchers conceded that motor learning is different from other kinds of memory and pursued the matter no further. Yet Warrington and Weiskrantz's findings with amnesic patients, together with the demonstration of blindsight in vision, suggested that preserved motor learning in HM might have much broader implications. To me, these counterintuitive observations intimated the existence of a subterranean world of nonconscious memory and perception, normally concealed from the conscious mind.

Philosophers, physicians, and psychiatrists had already made sporadic observations about this intriguing hidden world. I was well aware that Freud and other psychoanalysts had theorized for decades about an unconscious mind that is a repository of repressed wishes, fantasies, and fears. But, as far as I could tell, retention without awareness in amnesic patients or perception without awareness in blindsight had nothing to do with repressed urges and desires. And there had been scant scientific progress in investigating or understanding the Freudian notion of the unconscious. Even before Freud, the British physician Robert Dunn reported in 1845 that a woman who had been rescued from a near-drowning incident seemed incapable of remembering anything (probably because of oxygen loss to the brain). Dunn wrote with some amazement how she learned to be a skilled dressmaker—even though she couldn't remember making any of the dresses! In 1911, the great French philosopher Henri Bergson distinguished conscious remembering of the past from learned habits that influence our behavior unconsciously. Bergson argued with great eloquence that the past survives in two fundamentally different forms, conscious and unconscious. It was exciting for me to contemplate using scientific techniques to study what Bergson and others had theorized about or observed in the clinic.

After returning to Toronto, I witnessed firsthand the peculiar kind of memory that others had described in amnesic patients. During the summer of 1980, Dr. Paul Wang, a clinical psychologist, invited me to test a patient who had sustained a serious head injury in an accident. The patient, whom I refer to as Mickey, remembered little or nothing of his recent experiences. I sat across a testing table from him and told him that I was going to try to teach him some interesting bits of trivia. I asked him about obscure facts that I had dredged up by rummaging through encyclopedias and similar sources, such as "Where was the first game of baseball played?" (Hoboken) and "Who holds the world's record for shaking hands?" (Theodore Roosevelt). When Mickey did not know the correct answer—and he almost never did—I told it to him. He was intrigued by these tidbits and enjoyed our trivia game. After I left the testing room and returned twenty minutes later, Mickey maintained only a dim memory that I had tested him. He did not recollect that I had mentioned any items of trivia. But when I asked him where the first game of baseball was played, he confidently answered "Hoboken," and when I inquired about the world's record for shaking hands, he felt certain that it was Theodore Roosevelt. He generally said that he had no idea how he had acquired this knowledge—the answer just "seemed reasonable"—although sometimes he proffered that he might have heard about it from his sister.

My encounter with Mickey dramatically confirmed what I had discussed with Professor Weiskrantz and read about in medical journals: amnesic patients could indeed be influenced by recent experiences that they fail to recollect consciously. At the same time, Tulving and I continued to mull over the Warrington and Weiskrantz experiments. Why did amnesic patients do so well when given letter cues as hints for recently studied words? If these cues tapped into some sort of nonconscious memory that is preserved in amnesic patients, shouldn't it be possible to uncover something similar in people without amnesia?

We designed an experiment to find out. Our reasoning was simple: if letter cues tap into a form of memory that is spared in amnesic patients, then we might be able to elicit such memory in healthy volunteers by giving them letters from a previously studied word and asking them to try to guess the answer. Weiskrantz had observed that amnesic patients treat the letter cue test as a guessing game. If young adults could also be induced to treat the test as a guessing game, we reasoned, then they might rely on the same kind of memory that Warrington and Weiskrantz had observed in amnesics.

We carried out our experiment in the summer of 1980. For you to get a feel for our procedure, you should study each of the following words carefully for five seconds: *assassin, octopus, avocado, mystery, sheriff,* and *climate*. Now imagine that you go about your business for an hour and then return to take a couple of tests. First I show you a series of words and ask whether you remember seeing any of them on the earlier list: *twilight, assassin, dinosaur,* and *mystery*. Presumably you had little difficulty here. Next I tell you that I am going to show you some words with missing letters. Your job is to fill in the blanks as best you can: ch_ _ _ _ _nk, o_t_ _us, _og_y_ _ _, _l_m_te. You probably had a hard time coming up with a correct answer for two of the word fragments (*chipmunk* and *bogeyman*). But with the other two fragments, the correct answers probably jumped out at you. The reason these fragments are so easy to complete, of course, is that you just saw the words *octopus* and *climate* in our study list. This kind of memory is called *priming:* seeing the words on the list seems to prime your ability to come up with the correct solution when you try to complete a word fragment.

We tested people either one hour or one week after they studied the list. Conscious memory was, of course, much less accurate after a week than after an hour, but there was just as much priming on the word fragment-completion test after a week as there was after an hour. The implication of this finding is fascinating: something other than a conscious memory of seeing the word is responsible for priming on the word fragment-completion test. Equally intriguing, priming occurred even when people said they did not remember seeing a word during the study phase; in fact, the priming effect was just as strong for words that people did not remember seeing earlier as for words they did remember seeing. The results pushed us toward a strong, seemingly unavoidable conclusion: priming occurs independent of conscious memory.

These findings hit us with the force of an avalanche. We believed that we had been able to get a handle on the peculiar kind of memory that Warrington and Weiskrantz had documented in amnesic patients with the letter cueing task. This "other" kind of memory seemed to be lurking in the minds of healthy adults, and could be tapped by giving the word fragment completion test. We felt a bit like astronomers must feel when discovering a new star or an entire galaxy whose existence had been only suspected: a whole new world of possibilities is suddenly open for exploration.

I also started to notice manifestations of priming in everyday life. It is likely involved in instances of unintentional plagiarism. Probably the best known case in recent decades involved the former Beatle George Harrison and his 1970s hit "My Sweet Lord." Unfortunately for Harrison, his melody nearly duplicated the tune of a 1962 classic by The Chiffons, "He's So Fine." When a lawsuit was brought against him, Harrison conceded that he had heard "He's So Fine" prior to writing "My Sweet Lord," but denied that he had intentionally borrowed from the earlier song. Reasoning that the resemblance between the two was simply too strong to be the product of coincidence, the trial judge "held that Harrison's work did infringe through what the courts felt must have been unintentional copying of what was in Harrison's subconscious memory."

You may have encountered instances of this kind of priming, too. You propose an idea to a fellow employee or a friend, who seems unimpressed by it or even rejects it altogether. Weeks or months later, that person excitedly relates your idea as if he had just come up with it. When you draw this inconvenient fact to his attention—with an edge in your voice betraying exasperation—you may be faced with either heated denial or a sheepish apology born of a sudden dose of explicit memory. An incident from Sigmund Freud's life clearly illustrates this. Freud had maintained for years an intense and tumultuous friendship with the Berlin physician Wilhelm Fliess. He frequently confided his latest ideas and insights to Fliess, and was emotionally dependent on his approval of them. When Freud announced to Fliess a momentous new insight—that every person is fundamentally bisexual—he fully expected Fliess to be amazed by the idea. Instead, Fliess responded by reminding Freud that he himself had made exactly the same discovery two years earlier and told Freud all about it, and that Freud had rejected the idea. Freud eventually explicitly remembered the earlier incident, commenting that "[i]t is painful to have to surrender ones originality this way." Inspired by such observations, psychologists have recently been able to demonstrate a kind of unintentional plagiarism in the laboratory and tie it directly to priming.

Research into priming exploded during the early 1980s, as provocative new articles appeared in scientific journals. Priming occurred on a variety of tests in which people were instructed to identify a briefly flashed word or object, or guess an answer, rather than try explicitly to remember a word or an object from a list they had studied earlier. For example, Larry Jacoby and Mark Dallas found similar amounts of priming after deep encoding (focusing on a word's meanings and associations) and shallow encoding (focusing on the individual letters in the word)—a remarkable result, since deep encoding yields much higher levels of explicit memory than shallow encoding. Yet the priming effect could be easily eliminated. If people heard the target words on an audiotape during the study task but did not see a printed version of them, little or no priming was observed on a later visual test. Something about perceiving the actual word form was crucial for priming to occur.

Considered together with the results of our word fragment-completion experiment, these findings indicated that the new and mysterious phenomenon of priming obeys different rules than the kind of memory that researchers had been investigating for years. It became increasingly clear that part of the mystery could be traced to the instructions people are given when their memories are tested. For example, when amnesic patients are given word beginnings or other cues, and are instructed to think back to the study list to try to remember target words, they perform quite poorly. But when given the same test cues with instructions to guess or to provide the first word that pops to mind, they do just as well as people without memory problems. Likewise, depth of encoding influences later retention when normal volunteers try to remember the target items, yet has little effect when they respond with the first word that comes to mind.

Scientists love a good mystery, and many researchers tried to figure out what priming effects might mean. Tulving and I had already staked out a position: because priming seemed unrelated to conscious recollection, we reasoned that it does not depend on the episodic memory system that allows us to recollect specific incidents from the past. That system plays a key role in much of what I have discussed in the book so far: remembering what happened at last year's Thanksgiving dinner, remembering where you hit a tee shot during a round of golf, or remembering that you saw the word *octopus* in a study list. Amnesic patients have little or no episodic memory, but they often show normal priming. We concluded that the source of priming must lie outside the episodic system. But where?

Semantic memory—the intricate network of concepts, associations, and facts that constitutes our general knowledge of the world—seemed a reasonable place to look. When an amnesic patient such as Mickey learns that the first game of baseball was played in Hoboken but does not remember the episode in which he acquired that fact, semantic memory may be responsible. Likewise, in a priming experiment, exposure to a word such as *octopus* might result in a jolt to semantic memory, a kind of power surge that excites or activates the semantic representation of *octopus*. Perhaps amnesic patients benefit from such a jolt to semantic memory, even though their defective episodic memory prevents them from consciously recalling that they saw the word *octopus* during a recent study episode. The idea is reasonable enough, but we could see that it had problems. If priming depends on semantic memory, why doesn't deep, semantic processing of a word during the study task lead to more priming than shallow, nonsemantic processing? Why does priming depend on actually seeing the word during the study task? And since priming can be quite long-lasting, and we are constantly encountering words in our everyday lives, shouldn't just about all entries in semantic memory be chronically primed? We speculated that priming reflects "the operation of some other, as yet little understood, memory system."

We had postulated the existence of a new memory system, even though we didn't yet know what it was. The idea that the mind contains more than a single memory system had been around for a while. Bergson had come to this conclusion in 1911 when he distinguished conscious memory from habit, and other philosophers had made similar distinctions. In fact, during the early nineteenth century, a little-known French philosopher, Maine de Biran, had argued that memory can be subdivided into three different systems for ideas, feelings, and habits. But many experimental psychologists were reluctant to part with the idea of one all-purpose memory system. It is simpler and more parsimonious to assume a single memory system until and unless the evidence forces one to postulate multiple memory systems. During the 1960s and 1970s, they had fought a great battle about whether short-term memory (now called working memory) depends on a different system than long-term memory. I earlier mentioned evidence that it does, but not everyone was convinced. Tulving introduced the distinction between episodic and semantic memory in 1972, and some psychologists resisted this division of long-term memory into two further systems. Now we were proposing the addition of a third system—and this was simply unacceptable to some. Priming, these researchers believed, occurs within a single, undifferentiated memory system that can be investigated in different ways. Appealing to the operation of different memory systems seemed unparsimonious and just plain wrong.

A lively debate surrounded these questions. To fuel the fires, new evidence showed that amnesic patients could learn perceptual skills without remembering when and where they learned them. Neal Cohen and Larry Squire studied amnesic patients and healthy volunteers who read mirror-image versions of common words. Everyone has difficulty reading such images at first, but with practice people typically read them faster and faster. Amnesic patients showed a normal benefit of practice, yet they had problems consciously remembering which words they had read. The researchers suggested that such skill learning depends on a "procedural" memory system that is spared in amnesia. This system is selectively involved in "knowing how" to do things: ride a bicycle, type words on a keyboard, solve a jig-saw puzzle, or read words in mirror-image form. Could the procedural memory system also be involved in priming? Or does procedural memory constitute a fourth memory system, in addition to episodic memory, semantic memory, and the memory system Tulving and I had alluded to?

By the mid-1980s, the controversy over multiple memory systems had become so intense that it was difficult to talk about priming and skill learning without committing to one side of the quarrel or the other. The field needed terms that allowed researchers to talk about the exhilarating new phenomena of priming and learning without remembering, yet did not force them to side with one or the other warring faction in the memory systems debate. I decided to face this problem squarely in 1984, when my colleague Peter Graf and I were writing up the results of some new priming experiments. We recognized that new vocabulary was needed to talk about what we and others had been observing in our experiments.

We worked through several possibilities before settling on the contrast that seemed best to capture the distinction we wished to draw: *implicit* memory versus *explicit* memory. When amnesic patients showed priming or learned a skill, they were implicitly remembering some aspect of a recent experience, even though they had no explicit recollection of it. When a college student completed the fragment o__t__ __us with *octopus*, yet said that she did not remember seeing *octopus* on the list, she was showing the implicit influence of an experience she did not explicitly remember.

Soon I began to see that implicit memory might play a more prominent role in our everyday lives than anyone had suspected. For example, social psychologists who sought to understand why people prefer some things more than others had shown that a brief glimpse of a drawing—so brief that it was hardly possible to see it—led participants in an experiment later to say that they liked the flashed drawing more than one they had not seen. Yet people could not explicitly remember which drawings had been presented. These findings smacked of subliminal perception, illustrated by the apocryphal story about a sinister 1950s advertising ploy in which the words *Coca-Cola* and *popcorn* were flashed on a movie screen so briefly that nobody in the theater could see them. Supposedly, there would be a sudden mad dash to the concession stand to purchase these products. Although the effect turned out to be part of a publicity hoax, implicit memory was held to be reflected by an unexplained desire to drink Coke and eat popcorn.

By the mid-1980s a number of well-controlled studies had shown that preferences and feelings can be shaped by specific encounters and experiences that people do not remember explicitly. For instance, exposure to negative words that were flashed too quickly to register in conscious perception caused people later to feel hostility toward a fictional person. Some form of memory was responsible for their hostility, but participants had no idea that they were "remembering" any negative information. Likewise, studies of amnesic patients revealed implicit memory for emotional experiences they could not remember explicitly. For instance, the encephalitic patient Boswell, whose severe amnesia I mentioned in the previous chapter, took part in an experiment in which one researcher was designated a "good guy" (he gave Boswell special treats), another was designated a "bad guy" (he denied requests for treats), and a third behaved neutrally. Later, Boswell had no explicit memory for, or any sense of familiarity with, any of these people. Yet when pictures of them were each paired with pictures of unfamiliar people, and Boswell was asked to choose which one of the two he liked best, he selected the "good guy" most often and the "bad guy" least often.

There were also intriguing reports about people who had been given general anesthesia during surgical procedures. Received wisdom holds that patients cannot perceive or attend to anything that is said or done when they are unconscious during an operation. But in an experiment conducted during the 1960s, surgeons staged a mock crisis during surgery that included dire statements to the effect that the operation was in trouble and the patient might not pull through. Some of the patients who had been exposed to the mock crisis subsequently became extremely agitated when asked about it later, suggesting that they formed some sort of implicit memory while lying unconscious on the operating table.

On a more positive note, later studies showed that anesthetized patients who were given suggestions that they would make a quick recovery spent less time in the hospital postoperatively than patients who were not given any such suggestions. Yet none of the patients explicitly remembered the suggestions. My colleagues and I later demonstrated that patients who heard a list of spoken words during surgery showed priming for those words when tested during postoperative recovery. Not surprisingly, they had no explicit memory for the words.

Implicit memory may also be related to some of the memory distortions I considered earlier. When we forget the source of retrieved information—who said what, whether an incident actually occurred or was merely imagined—we may generate an inaccurate source and hence become prone to false recollections. Implicit memory, by definition, does not involve recollection of source information. Thus, we may generate plausible but incorrect sources in attempting to make sense of why a particular idea pops to mind or why we feel a certain emotion.

Discussion Questions for Article 1

Section 6: Cognition and Memory

Name: _____

PID: _____

Date: __ __ / __ __ / __ __ (MM/DD/YY)

CRN: _____

Recitation Day/Time: _____

Honor Code Signature: _____

1. What is the difference between implicit memory and explicit memory? Can you use some examples to explain it?

2. What is a third memory system that some researchers advocate to be added?

3. What is priming? Why is it important to the study of implicit memory?

4. Have you ever had an experience similar to Sigmund Freud's where you thought you had come up with an original idea only to discover you subconsciously borrowed it from someone else? If yes, explain. If not, do you think it is possible that you may have borrowed someone else's idea but you don't remember? Why or why not?

Reconstructing Memory: The Incredible Eyewitness

Elizabeth F. Loftus

"I saw it with my own eyes." That statement has ended many an argument, since for most people seeing is believing. But it shouldn't be. Between the time you first witness an event and the time you recount it to someone else, your memory of the event may change drastically. Many factors can affect the accuracy of your report. I have found that the questions asked about an event influence the way a witness "remembers" what he saw. Changing even one word in a single question can systematically alter an eyewitness account.

Most previous research on this topic has been directed toward demonstrating how poor eyewitness testimony is, without exploring why people make the errors they do. One favorite method of study has been to stage an incident, then interrogate all the witnesses about what happened. Typically, everyone tells a different story.

In a study conducted at Dartmouth in the 1930s, some students unknowingly became subjects in such an experiment. While a class was in session, a man dressed in workman's overalls entered the room, made some remarks about the heat, tinkered with the radiator for a minute or two, and left. About two weeks later he returned with five other men of similar appearance, and the students were asked to pick him out from a lineup of all six individuals. Seventeen percent of the students chose the wrong man.

Another group of students, who had not witnessed the event but who were told they had seen it, also had to make a selection. Seventy percent of these subjects reported (correctly) that they could not recall the incident, but 29 percent did point to one of the men. That is, they "identified" a man they had never seen.

In a more recent study by Robert Buckhout and his colleagues at California State University, Hayward, 141 students witnessed a staged assault on a professor.

Seven weeks later they were asked to pick out the assailant from a group of six photographs. Although the episode had been a dramatic one that could hardly have gone unnoticed, 60 percent of the witnesses, including the professor who had been attacked, chose the wrong man. Twenty-five percent selected an individual who had been at the scene of the crime, but as an innocent bystander.

Tragic Mistakes

This kind of demonstration is rather entertaining, but when something similar happens in real life, the results can be serious. A few months ago, the *Los Angeles Times* reported the erroneous conviction of a man whom seven witnesses had identified as the robber of a bank. In a similar case last year, 17 witnesses identified a man charged with shooting a police officer; later it turned out the man had not even been in the vicinity of the crime while it was going on. Innocent people have sat in prison for years on the strength of eyewitness testimony. The witnesses in these cases probably were all honest people, but they were tragically wrong.

Yet, despite the poor performance of eyewitnesses, judges and juries continue to place great faith in them. My colleagues and I recently studied the influence a single eyewitness can have in the courtroom. We simulated a criminal trial, using 150 students as jurors. The students received a written description of a grocery store robbery in which the owner and his granddaughter were killed. They also received a summary of the evidence and arguments presented at the defendant's trial. Each juror had to arrive at a verdict, guilty or not guilty.

We told some of the jurors that there had been no eyewitnesses to the crime. We told others that a store clerk testified he saw the defendant shoot the two victims, although the defense attorney claimed he was mistaken. Finally, we told a third group of students that the store clerk had testified to seeing the shootings, but the defense attorney had discredited him. The attorney claimed the witness had not been wearing his glasses on the day of the robbery, and since he had vision poorer than 20/400 he could not possibly have seen the face of the robber from where he stood.

That's the Man

When we analyzed our results, we found that 82 percent of the jurors who had not heard about an eyewitness voted for acquittal, while 72 percent of those who thought there was a credible witness voted guilty. Most important, 68 percent of the jurors who had heard about the discredited witness still voted for conviction, in spite of the defense attorney's remarks. It seems that people are convinced by a witness who declares with conviction, "That's the man."

Percentage of Guilty Verdicts		
No Eyewitness	Eyewitness	Discredited Eyewitness
18%	72%	68%

Since eyewitness testimony carries so much weight, it is important to find out why distortion occurs in a witness' memory. I would like to know what goes on in a person's mind when he is trying to make a truthful report but makes a false one. To find the answer, one must consider the nature of human memory.

Studies of memory for sentences and pictures indicate that when we experience an event, we do not simply file a memory, then on some later occasion retrieve it and read off what we've stored. Rather, at the time of recall or recognition, we reconstruct the event, using information from many sources. These include both the original perception of the event and inferences drawn later, after the fact. Over a period of time, information from these sources may integrate, so that a witness becomes unable to say how he knows a specific detail. He has only a single, unified memory.

I studied the way leading questions can introduce new information that alters one's memory of an event. A leading question is one that by its form or content suggests to a witness the answer he should give, as in the classic "When did you stop beating your wife?" We all probably ask leading questions without realizing we are doing so. Lawyers, though, have long recognized the usefulness of deliberately asking such questions. They know that by the time the opposing lawyer objects and the judge rules the question improper, a suggestion may already have taken hold in the minds of the jurors.

Police undoubtedly use leading questions too, when they are interrogating witnesses to a crime. If they influence a witness to make a false statement (and that can happen easily, even with well-intentioned police officers), chances are good he will repeat the error later when a trial lawyer asks him to "tell in your own words what happened."

A famous example of police suggestion occurred in the 1921 case of Nicola Sacco and Bartolomeo Vanzetti, two Italian anarchists tried for murder and robbery in Massachusetts, at the height of nationwide hysteria over radicalism. Five prosecution witnesses identified Sacco at the trial, yet most of these witnesses had originally told police they could not identify anyone. Four witnesses identified Vanzetti, although one of them had earlier told police he had been unable to get a good look at the robbers. This same witness stated at the trial that he had had a very good look, after all. In fact, he was able to recall that the gunman had a dark complexion, high cheek bones, red cheeks, short hair, a trimmed mustache, a high forehead, and a hard, broad face. Sacco and Vanzetti were convicted of the crime, and eventually executed. A later investigation of the identification techniques used in this case indicated that witnesses had been subject to enormous suggestion from the police.

Traffic Accidents

Such cases, while instructive, do not prove conclusively that leading questions affect testimony. In order to examine more carefully the influence of the interrogator's language on an eyewitness, I took the problem into the laboratory. My assistants and I conducted several experiments, using students as eyewitnesses, and films of automobile accidents as the events they had to remember and report. Since we had a permanent record of each event, and we asked specially constructed questions, we were able to pinpoint the sources and types of inaccuracies.

In our first study, we showed 100 students a short film segment depicting a multiple-car accident. In the film, a car makes a right-hand turn into the main stream of traffic. The turn causes oncoming cars to stop suddenly, and there is a five-car, bumper-to-bumper collision. After our subjects viewed this film, they filled out a 22-item questionnaire containing 16 fillers and six critical questions. Three of the key questions asked about items that had appeared in the film, while three others asked about items that had not actually been present. For half the subjects, the critical questions began with the words *Did you see a*, as in "Did you see a broken headlight?" For the rest, the critical questions began with the words *Did you see the*, as in "Did you see the broken headlight?" Thus the sentences differed only in the form of the article, *the* or *a*.

We had a good reason to look at this contrast. A speaker uses *the* when he assumes the object referred to exists and may be familiar to the listener. An investigator who asks, "Did you see the broken headlight?" essentially says, "There was a broken headlight. Did you happen to see it?" His assumption may influence the witness. But *a* requires no such assumption.

When we tabulated the percentage of "yes," "no," and "don't know" responses, we found that witnesses who received questions with *the* were much more likely to report having seen something that had not really appeared in the film; 15 percent in the *the* group said "yes" when asked about a nonexistent item; while only seven percent in the *a* group made that error. On the other hand, witnesses who received questions with *a* were more likely to respond "don't know," both when the object had been present and when it had not. We see, then, that even this subtle change in wording can influence eyewitness reports.

Percentage of "Don't Know" Responses to Questions With "A" Or "The"			
Item Present		Item Not Present	
the	a	the	a
23%	51%	13%	38%

Some Got Smashed

We also wanted to know whether the substitution of one word for another could affect quantitative judgments, *e.g.*, judgments of speed. We showed 45 subjects seven films of traffic accidents, again varying the form of the questions we asked after the film. For some of our subject-witnesses, the critical question was "About how fast were the cars going when they hit each other?" For others we replaced the verb *hit* with *smashed, collided, bumped* or *contacted*. Although these words all refer to the coming together of two objects, they differ in what they imply about speed and force of impact. We wondered if these differences would affect judgments about velocity.

They did. Our subjects' estimates varied considerably, depending on which question they had to answer. Those questioned with *contacted* gave the lowest speed estimates, while those questioned with *smashed* gave the highest.

Average Speed Estimates for Different Verbs	
smashed	40.8 mph
collided	39.3 mph
bumped	38.1 mph
hit	34.0 mph
contacted	31.8 mph

Four of our films involved staged crashes, and we knew exactly how fast the cars had been traveling: one 20 mph, another 30 mph, and two others 40 mph. The average estimates for these collisions were 37.7, 35.2, 39.7 and 36.1 mph, respectively. These figures bear out previous findings that people are not very good at judging the speed of a vehicle, and increase our confidence that our results were due to the way our questions were worded.

The studies I've described so far do not tell us why people are influenced by leading questions. Perhaps they are merely biased by the form of the question to give one answer instead of another. For example, a witness might be uncertain whether to say 30 mph or 40 mph, but the verb *smashed* could sway him toward the higher estimate. In that case, we could not say that his memory of the event had changed, only that his answer had.

To find out if our subjects were really misremembering, we ran one more experiment. Again, we showed subjects a short film of a traffic accident. A third of them answered the question, "About how fast were the cars going when they smashed into each other?" Another third answered the same question with *hit* instead of *smashed.* The remaining third, which acted as a control group, did not get a question about automobile speed. As in our previous study, witnesses who saw *smashed* gave higher estimates than those who saw *hit.*

A week later our subjects returned. Without viewing the film again, they answered a new series of questions about it. This time, the critical question asked whether the witness had seen any broken glass, although, in fact, there had been none in the film. If *smashed* really influenced subjects to remember the accident as more severe than it had been, they might also "remember" details that were not shown but were commensurate with an accident occurring at high speed—like broken glass.

Our analysis showed that more than twice as many subjects queried with *smashed* reported seeing the nonexistent glass as those queried with *hit.* This result is consistent with our interpretation that memory itself undergoes a change as a result of the type of question asked.

Murder or Self-Defense?

Eyewitnesses are inaccurate in estimating not only speed, but also time and distance. Yet in courts of law they must make quantitative judgments all the time. Last year I worked with the Seattle Public Defender's office on a case involving a young woman who had killed her boy friend. The prosecutor called it first-degree murder, but her lawyer claimed she had acted in self-defense. What was clear was that during an argument, the defendant ran to the bedroom, grabbed a gun, and shot her boy friend six times. At the trial, a dispute arose about the time that had elapsed between the grabbing of the gun and the first shot. The defendant and her sister said two seconds, while another witness said five minutes. The exact amount of elapsed time made all the difference in the world to the defense, which insisted the killing had occurred suddenly, in fear, and without a moment's hesitation. In the end the jury must have believed the defendant; it acquitted her.

I do not know whether leading questions played a role in this case, but I am sure they have in others. Accident investigators, police officers, lawyers, reporters and others who must interrogate eyewitnesses would do well to keep in mind the subtle suggestibility that words carry with them. When you question an eyewitness, what he saw may not be what you get.

Editor's Note

Dr. Elizabeth F. Loftus is Assistant Professor of Psychology at the University of Washington.

Discussion Questions for Article 2

Section 6: Cognition and Memory

Name: _____

PID: _____

Date: __ __ / __ __ / __ __ (MM/DD/YY)

CRN: _____

Recitation Day/Time: _____

Honor Code Signature: _____

1. According to this article, when people try to recall an event that they have experienced, what is the actual cognitive process involved?

2. According to the experiments done by Loftus and her colleagues, what kind of factors in leading questions can influence testimony?

3. How can various kinds of people, such as police officers, lawyers and reporters influence others with leading questions?

4. Describe an example of memory reconstruction from your own life. When have you recalled events differently than had actually occurred?

Learning

At times, it can be difficult to appreciate how research conducted by Ivan Pavlov in the late 1800's examining the behaviors of salivating dogs relates to the interplay between the cognitions, emotions, and environmental cues in the lives of humans. Yet, learning processes have compelling implications for understanding human and animal behavior. For example, aspects of various learning theories have been applied to areas such as aversion therapy for phobias, dieting and weight loss, even advertising through product placement. Thus, a deeper examination of how our past experiences shape our future responses is vital for not only understanding the effects of learning on daily behaviors, but also for applied implications, such as treatment strategies for psychiatric disorders.

Classical conditioning, a model of learning first demonstrated by Ivan Pavlov, details how a previously neutral stimulus gradually acquires the ability to elicit a particular response through repeated associations with an unconditioned stimulus (one that innately triggers the response). For example, in John Watson's Little Albert study, when a child was shown a white rat, a loud noise was also presented. Eventually, Albert began to demonstrate signs of distress at the presentation of the rat, in addition to other white objects.

Another form of learning, operant conditioning, postulates that the occurrence and/or form of behaviors can be altered based on consequences. Through his observations of cats attempting to escape from puzzle boxes, Edward Thorndike found that as time progressed, cats began to either repeat or discontinue specific behavioral responses based on the effectiveness of those behaviors. Successful behaviors by the cats were reinforced by their ability to escape, leading the cats to escape more quickly in the future. Thus, rather than trial and error, the cats had developed a trial and success model. Substantial research has examined variations of operant conditioning, such as the effects of different schedules of reinforcement, and its real-world implications (i.e., classroom management).

The acquisition of new behaviors can be achieved through exposure to other individuals' behaviors and the consequences they experience, known as observational learning. In the 1960s, the Bobo doll experiments conducted by Bandura and colleagues demonstrated that children were more likely to take aggressive actions towards an inflated Bobo doll after observing an adult perform such behaviors. Understandably, the Bobo doll experiments led to substantial debate regarding the impact of television on children.

Like the lever-pressing rats of classical psychology experiments, much of our everyday behaviors are influenced by processes related to learning theory. Although there are a plethora of theories, each one offers a unique perspective on factors that influence human and animal behaviors. Based on the Premack Principle of learning, reading this chapter (i.e., low probability behavior) to further examine the processes of learning will allow you to achieve a more desired behavior of succeeding on the learning portion of your Introductory Psychology class (i.e., high probability behavior).

Article 1: Evaluation of DRO Schedules to Reduce Disruptive Behavior in a Preschool Classroom

As previously discussed, operant conditioning has numerous real world applications, such as classroom management. In this article, Conyers and colleagues examined the effectiveness of several reinforcement schedules in reducing disruptive behaviors in a pre-school classroom. To do so, they examine whether it was more effective to deliver reinforcement when a target behavior had been absent for the entirety of the specified interval or when the target behavior was absent at conclusion of said interval. In addition, they examined differential outcomes related to tangible (toys) and edible reinforcements. As you read this article, consider additional reinforcement schedules and techniques that you have learned about that may prove useful in a classroom setting.

Article 2: How to Teach Animals

Since the processes of animal learning were first examined in the laboratory, humans have been amazed by the behaviors animals can be trained to perform. Keller and Marian Breland, two of Skinner's students, opened the IQ Zoo which featured animal acts such as a rabbit that rides a fire engine and raccoons that play basketball. In the article *How to Teach Animals*, B.F. Skinner discusses the learning techniques used to train animals to perform complex behaviors. The article includes the necessary components of learning as well as important steps to follow. While reading this article, consider ways you could implement these training techniques to influence the behaviors of your family, friends, and possibly even your professors.

—*Laura Wilson*

Evaluation of DRO Schedules to Reduce Disruptive Behavior in a Preschool Classroom

Carole Conyers
Raymond Miltenberger
Cathryn Romaniuk
Brandon Kopp
Michael Himle

Abstract. This study examined the effectiveness of momentary DRO (mDRO) and whole interval DRO (wDRO) schedules on high rates of disruptive behavior in a classroom of 22 children. In both procedures, children earned tokens for the absence of disruptive behavior and exchanged tokens for tangible or edible reinforcers. mDRO and wDRO, with tangible reinforcement, produced modest decreases in disruptive behavior (36%–44% decrease from baseline). However, wDRO with edible reinforcement produced larger decreases in disruptive behavior (66–81% decrease from baseline).

Keywords. DRO schedules, disruptive behavior, preschool classroom

Differential reinforcement of other behaviors (DRO) is a procedure in which reinforcement is delivered contingent on the absence of a target behavior. In whole-interval DRO (wDRO), a reinforcer is given if the target behavior has been absent throughout the entire interval, whereas in momentary DRO (mDRO), a reinforcer is delivered if the target behavior is absent at the instant the interval ends. (e.g., Repp, Barton, & Brulle, 1983). A small number of studies has investigated the effectiveness of mDRO and wDRO schedules in supressing problem behaviors exhibited by children and adults with developmental disabilities (Barton, Brulle, & Repp, 1986; Derwas & Jones, 1993; Kahng, Abt, & Schonbachler, 2001; Miller & Jones, 1997; Repp et al., 1983). Overall, these studies have produced mixed results. Barton et al. (1986) and Repp et al. (1983) found that mDRO was only modestly effective at reducing inappropriate behavior. However, Kahng et al. (2001) found mDRO to be effective and Derwas and Jones (1993) and Miller and Jones (1997) found mDRO to be more effective than wDRO for some subjects. The purpose of this study was to extend previous research by examining the effectivness of mDRO and wDRO schedules and assessing their ability to suppress inappropriate behaviors within a classroom of young children.

Method

Participants and Setting

The participants included eight girls and 14 boys, two to three years of age, who exhibited a high level of disruptive behaviors. The study was conducted in a 20 m by 20 m preschool classroom for typically developing children. During each session, three to four teachers were present and the children engaged in a variety of activities including playing with toys, listening to stories read by a teacher, and engaging in group activities such as art projects around tables located in the room.

Target Behaviors and Measurement

Disruptive behavior was defined as screaming, crying, throwing oneself on the floor, hitting, kicking, property destruction, throwing objects or using them as weapons, and refusing, ignoring, or resisting a staff member's request. The number of children exhibiting target behaviors during each observation interval was recorded using a 10-s partial interval procedure (8-s observe, 2-s record). An additional observer was present during 48% of the sessions to conduct interobserver agreement assessments. Interobserver agreement was calculated by dividing the number of intervals of agreement by the total number of intervals and multiplying by 100%. The mean percentage of agreement was 94.2% (range: 90–98%).

Procedure

A reversal design with multiple treatment conditions was used. Sessions occurred on three separate days each week over the course of an eight-month period.

Baseline. During baseline no formal contingencies were in effect for either inappropriate or appropriate behaviors, and the staff interacted with the children in their usual manner. Disruptive behaviors typically resulted in a verbal reprimand. Each baseline session lasted 30 min.

DRO. DRO sessions lasted from 15 to 40 minutes depending on the condition. During *mDRO-2* a board listing every child's name was set up against a wall in the classroom. At the beginning of each session, the children were told that those who were not engaging in a disruptive behavior when the timer rang would receive a star beside their name. Next, disruptive behaviors were defined and the children were told how many stars were required to choose a prize at the end of the session. The timer was set to a randomly chosen number between 1 min 30-s and 2 min 30-s (mean, 2 min), and at the moment the timer rang, the children who were not engaging in disruptive behavior received a star and praise. No feedback was given to those who did not earn a star. At the end of a session, the children who had earned at least 8 out of 10 stars were allowed to choose a small toy from a box containing an assortment of small tangible items (e.g., toy car, bead necklace, stickers). In *mDRO-1* the timer was set to a number between 30-s and 1 min 30-s (mean, 1 min) and the children had to earn at least 13 out of 15 stars to choose a tangible item at the end of a session. In *wDRO-1* the children were told that in order to receive a star, they could not engage in any disruptive behaviors throughout the entire interval. The timer was set to a randomly chosen number between 30-s and 1 min 30-s (mean, 1 min). They needed 13 out of 15 stars to choose a tangible item at the end of the session. In *wDRO'-1* the children who had earned at least 13 out of 15 stars received a 'surprise' edible reinforcer (e.g., jelly beans, chocolates, lollipops). In *wDRO'-2* the timer was set to a number between 1 min 30-s and 2 min 30-s (mean, 2 min) and the children were told that they had to earn at least 8 out of 10 stars in order to obtain an edible. In *wDRO'-3* the timer was set to a number between 2 min 30-s and 3 min 30-s (mean, 3 min) and the children had to earn 8 out of 10 stars to obtain an edible. In *wDRO'-4* the timer was set to a number between 3 min 30-s and 4 min 30-s (mean, 4 min) and the children had to earn 8 out of 10 stars to obtain an edible.

Results

The top panel of Figure 1 shows the percentage of intervals with disruptive behaviors. During baseline, disruptive behavior occurred in a mean of 64% of intervals. Disruptive behavior occurred in 36% of intervals with mDRO-2, 41% of intervals with mDRO-1, and 38% of intervals with wDRO-1. The use of wDRO with edibles (wDRO'-1) decreased disruptive behavior to lower levels (mean = 22%). Disruptive behavior then increased to 70% of intervals in the second baseline phase and decreased to 14% of intervals in the second wDRO'-1 phase. In the following phases, during which the wDRO interval was increased from 1 to 4 min, disruptive behavior remained low (means = 14%, 13%, and 12%, respectively).

The bottom panel of Figure 1 depicts the mean number of disruptive children per scored interval. This number was calculated by dividing the number of scored intervals (intervals with disruptive behavior) by the total number of children engaging in disruptive behavior in those intervals. During baseline the number of children engaging in disruptive behavior per interval ranged from 1 to 4.7, with a mean

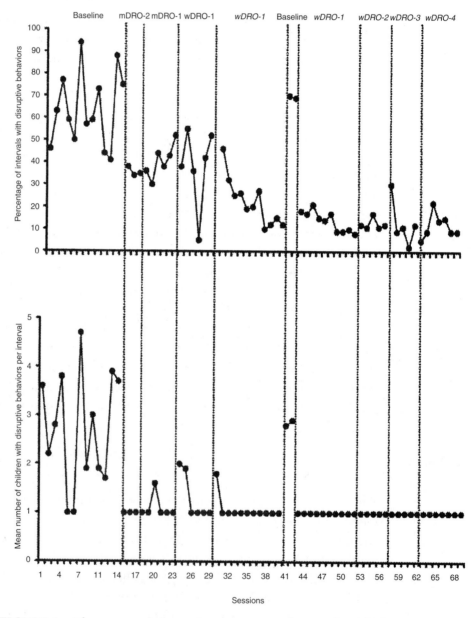

FIGURE 1   The top panel shows the percentage of intervals with disruptive behavior. The bottom panel shows the mean number of children engaging in disruptive behavior per scored interval.

of 2.8. In the first mDRO phase, there was just 1 disruptive child per interval. With few exceptions, the number of disruptive children per interval remained at 1 in the mDRO-1 and wDRO-1 phases using tangible reinforcers, and the wDRO-1' phase using edible reinforcers. Furthermore, there was just 1 child engaging in disruptive behavior per interval as the DRO interval was increased from 1 to 4 min.

Discussion

Overall, the mDRO and wDRO schedules were moderately effective in reducing the percentage of intervals of disruptive behaviors when tangible reinforcers were used. However, when edible reinforcers were used with mDRO schedules, the percentage of intervals of disruptive behavior decreased significantly. Interestingly, the number of children engaging in disruptive behavior per interval decreased markedly from baseline with the first mDRO phase, but did not change substantially across the different mDRO and wDRO phases. Across momentary and whole DRO using tangible and edible reinforcers, when disruptive behavior occurred in an interval, there was typically just one child engaging in the disruptive behavior compared to almost 3 children per interval on average during baseline.

This study replicates prior research by Barton et al. (1986) and Repp et al. (1983) in showing the modest effect of mDRO schedules and extends prior research as it shows that wDRO schedules can be effective with large numbers of young children in a classroom setting. This is the first evaluation of DRO schedules on a class-wide basis and shows that DRO can be effective in a class of 22 preschool children.

The relative superiority of edible reinforcers over tangible reinforcers in the wDRO phases highlights the importance of identifying the most effective reinforcers for use in DRO schedules.

There are two limitations in the present study that warrant comment. First, it is not clear whether mDRO would have been more effective initially had edible reinforcers been used. Because we compared mDRO and wDRO with tangible reinforcers but not with edible reinforcers, we do not know whether mDRO with edibles would have been equally as effective as wDRO with edibles. Future research should investigate this issue.

Second, the DRO interval was increased to only 4 min. To enhance the practicality of this procedure, the interval would need to be increased to 10–15 min so that teachers can implement the procedure in the classroom without too much disruption of ongoing activities. Unfortunately, the school year ended and we were unable to increase the interval further. Further research should evaluate the effectiveness of longer, more practical DRO intervals in class-wide applications of DRO.

References

Barton, L. E., Brulle, A. R., & Repp, A. C. (1986). Maintenance of therapeutic change by momentary DRO. *Journal of Applied Behavior Analysis, 19,* 277–282.

Derwas, H., & Jones, R. (1993). Reducing stereotyped behavior using momentary DRO: An experimental analysis. *Behavioral Residential Treatment, 8,* 45–53.

Kahng, S., Abt, K., & Schonbachler, H. (2001). Assessment and treatment of low-rate high-intensity problem behavior. *Journal of Applied Behavior Analysis, 34,* 225–228.

Miller, B., & Jones, R. (1997). Reducing stereotyped behaviour: A comparison of two methods of programming differential reinforcement. *British Journal of Clinical Psychology, 36,* 297–302.

Repp, A. C., Barton, L. E., & Brulle, A. R. (1983). A comparison of two procedures for programming the differential reinforcement of other behaviors. *Journal of Applied Behavior Analysis, 16,* 435–445.

Editor's Note

Carole Conyers, MS, Raymond Miltenberger, PhD, Cathryn Romaniuk, MS, Brandon Kopp, BS, and Michael Himle, MS, are affiliated with the North Dakota State University.

Address correspondence to: Raymond G. Miltenberger, Department of Psychology, North Dakota State University, Fargo,ND58105 (E-mail: ray.miltenberger@ndsu.nodak.edu).

The authors thank the staff, parents, and children at the Fraser Daycare Center for their support and cooperation.

Discussion Questions for Article 1

Section 7: Learning

Name: _____

PID: _____

Date: __ __ / __ __ / __ __ (MM/DD/YY)

CRN: _____

Recitation Day/Time: _____

Honor Code Signature: _____

1. What is the difference between momentary differential reinforcement of other behaviors and whole-interval differential reinforcement of other behaviors? Provide an example of each.

2. What were the two major limitations of the study identified by the researchers?

3. Explain what Figure 1 depicts in regards to the major findings of the current study.

4. What reinforcers did your parents use when you were a child? Which one do you think worked best and why?

How to Teach Animals

B. F. Skinner

Some simple techniques of the psychological laboratory can also be used in the home. They can train a dog to dance, a pigeon to play a toy piano and will illuminate the learning process in man.

Teaching, it is often said, is an art, but we have increasing reason to hope that it may eventually become a science. We have already discovered enough about the nature of learning to devise training techniques which are much more effective and give more reliable results than the rule-of-thumb methods of the past. Tested on animals, the new techniques have proved superior to traditional methods of professional animal trainers; they yield more remarkable results with much less effort.

It takes rather subtle laboratory conditions to test an animal's full learning capacity, but the reader will be surprised at how much he can accomplish even under informal circumstances at home. Since nearly everyone at some time or other has tried, or wished he knew how, to train a dog, a cat or some other animal, perhaps the most useful way to explain the learning process is to describe some simple experiments which the reader can perform himself.

"Catch your rabbit" is the first item in a well-known recipe for rabbit stew. Your first move, of course, is to choose an experimental subject. Any available animal—a cat, a dog, a pigeon, a mouse, a parrot, a chicken, a pig—will do. (Children or other members of your family may also be available, but it is suggested that you save them until you have had practice with less valuable material.) Suppose you choose a dog.

The second thing you will need is something your subject wants, say food. This serves as a reward or—to use a term which is less likely to be misunderstood—a "reinforcement" for the desired behavior. Many things besides food are reinforcing—for example, simply letting the dog out for a run—but food is usually the easiest to administer in the kind of experiment to be described here. If you use food, you must of course perform the experiment when the dog is hungry, perhaps just before his dinnertime.

The reinforcement gives you a means of control over the behavior of the animal. It rests on the simple principle that whenever something reinforces a particular activity of an organism, it increases the chances that the organism will repeat that behavior. This makes it possible to shape an animal's behavior almost as a sculptor shapes a lump of clay. There is, of course, nothing new in this principle. What is new is a better understanding of the conditions under which reinforcement works best.

To be effective a reinforcement must be given almost simultaneously with the desired behavior; a delay of even one second destroys much of the effect. This means that the offer of food in the usual way is likely to be ineffective; it is not fast enough. The best way to reinforce the behavior with the necessary speed is to use a "conditioned" reinforcer. This is a signal which the animal is conditioned to associate with food. The animal is always given food immediately after the signal, and the signal itself then becomes the reinforcer. The better the association between the two events, the better the result.

For the conditioned reinforcer you need a clear signal which can be given instantly and to which the subject is sure to respond. It may be a noise or a flash of light. A whistle is not effective because of the time it takes to draw a breath before blowing it. A visual signal like a wave of the arm may not always be seen by the animal. A convenient signal is a rap on a table with a small hard object or the noise of a high-pitched device such as a "cricket."

You are now ready to start the experiment with your dog. Work in a convenient place as free as possible from distraction. Let us say that you have chosen a "cricket" as your conditioned reinforcer. To build up the effect of the reinforcer begin by tossing a few scraps of food, one at a time and not oftener than once or twice a minute, where the dog may eat them. Use scraps of food so small that 30 or 40 will not greatly reduce the animal's hunger. As soon as the dog eats each scrap readily and without delay, begin to pair the cricket with the food. Sound the cricket and then toss a piece of food. Wait half a minute or so and repeat. Sound the cricket suddenly, without any preparatory movements such as reaching for food.

At this stage your subject will probably show well-marked begging behavior. It may watch you intently, perhaps jump on you, and so on. You must break up this behavior, because it will interfere with other parts of the experiment. Never sound the cricket or give food when the dog is close to you or facing you. Wait until it turns away, then reinforce. Your conditioned reinforcer is working properly when your subject turns immediately and approaches the spot where it receives food. Test this several times. Wait until the dog is in a fairly unusual position, then sound the signal. Time spent in making sure the dog immediately approaches the food will later be saved manyfold.

Now, having established the noise as the reinforcer, you may begin teaching the dog. To get the feel of the technique start with some simple task, such as getting the dog to approach the handle on a low cupboard door and touch it with its nose. At first you reinforce any activity which would be part of the final completed act of approaching and touching the handle of the cupboard. The only permissible contact between you and the dog is *via* the cricket and the food. Do not touch the dog, talk to it, coax it, "draw its attention" or interfere in any other way with the experiment. If your subject just sits, you may have to begin by reinforcing any movement, however slight. As soon as the dog moves, sound the cricket and give food. Remember that your reaction time is important. Try to reinforce as nearly simultaneously with the movement as possible.

After your subject is moving freely about, reinforce any turn toward the cupboard. Almost immediately you will notice a change in its behavior. It will begin to face toward the cupboard most of the time. Then begin to reinforce only when the dog moves nearer the cupboard. (If you withhold reinforcement too long at this stage, you may lose the facing response. If so, go back and pick it up.) In a very short time—perhaps a minute or two—you should have the dog standing close to

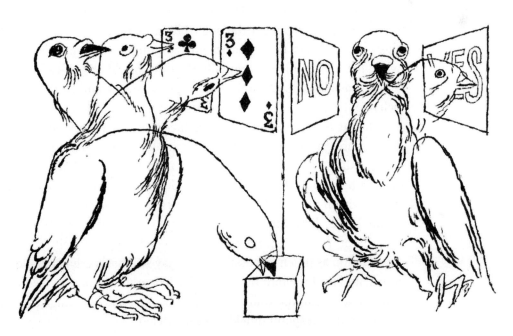

FIGURE 1 Pigeon can be taught to choose one card rather than another and even apparently to read. This is done by "reinforcing" the animal when it pecks the right card and turning out the light when it pecks the wrong one.

the cupboard. Now begin to pay attention to its head. Reinforce any movement that brings the nose close to the handle. You will have to make special efforts now to reduce the time between the movement and the reinforcement to the very minimum. Presently the dog will touch the handle with its nose, and after reinforcement it will repeat this behavior so long as it remains hungry.

Usually it takes no more than five minutes, even for a beginner, to teach a dog this behavior. Moreover, the dog does not have to be particularly smart to learn it; contrary to the usual view, all normal dogs will learn with about equal facility by this conditioning technique.

Before going on with other experiments test the effect of your conditioned reinforcer again two or three times. If the dog responds quickly and eats without delay you may safely continue. You should "extinguish" the response the dog has already learned, however, before teaching it another. Stop reinforcing the act of touching the cupboard handle until the dog abandons this activity.

As a second test, let us say, you want to teach the dog to lift its head in the air and turn around to the right. The general procedure is the same, but you may need some help in sharpening your observation of the behavior to be reinforced. As a guide to the height to which the dog's head is to be raised, sight some horizontal line on the wall across the room. Whenever the dog, in its random movements, lifts its head above this line, reinforce immediately. You will soon see the head rising above the line more and more frequently. Now raise your sights slightly and reinforce only when the dog's head rises above the new level. By a series of gradual steps you can get the dog to hold its head much higher than usual. After this you can begin to emphasize any running movement in a clockwise direction while the head is high. Eventually the dog should execute a kind of dance step. If you use available food carefully, a single session should suffice for setting up this behavior.

Having tested your ability to produce these simple responses, you may feel confident enough to approach a more complex assignment. This time suppose you try working with a pigeon. Pigeons do not tame easily. You will probably want a cage to help control the bird, and for this you can rig up a large cardboard carton with a screen or lattice top and windows cut in the side for observing the bird. It is much less disturbing to the bird if you watch it from below its line of vision than if you peer at it from above. In general keep yourself out of the experimental situation as much as possible. You may still use a cricket as a conditioned reinforcer, and feed the bird by dropping a few grains of pigeon feed in to a small dish through a hole in the wall. It may take several daily feedings to get the bird to eat readily and to respond quickly to the cricket.

Your assignment is to teach the pigeon to identify the visual patterns on playing cards. To begin with, hang a single card on a nail on the wall of the cage a few inches above the floor so that the pigeon can easily peck it. After you have trained the bird to peck the card by reinforcing the movements that lead to that end, change the card and again reinforce the peck. If you shuffle the cards and present them at random, the pigeon will learn to peck any card offered.

Now begin to teach it to discriminate among the cards. Let us say you are using diamonds and clubs (excluding face cards and aces) and want the bird to select diamonds. Reinforce only when the card presented is a diamond, never when it is a club. Almost immediately the bird will begin to show a preference for diamonds. You can speed up its progress toward complete rejection of clubs by discontinuing the experiment for a moment (a mild form of punishment) whenever it pecks a club. A good conditioned punishment is simply to turn off the light or cover or remove the card. After half a minute replace the card or turn on the light and continue the experiment. Under these conditions the response which is positively reinforced with food remains part of the repertoire of the bird, while the response that leads to a blackout quickly disappears.

There is an amusing variation of this experiment by which you can make it appear that a pigeon can be taught to read. You simply use two printed cards bearing the words PECK and DON'T PECK, respectively. Be reinforcing responses to PECK and blacking out when the bird pecks DON'T PECK, it is quite easy to train the bird to obey the commands on the cards.

The pigeon can also be taught the somewhat more "intellectual" performance of matching a sample object. Let us say the sample to be matched is a certain card. Fasten three cards to a board, with one above and the two others side by side just below it. The board is placed so that the bird can reach all the cards through windows cut in the side of the cage. After training the bird to peck a card of any kind impartially in all three positions, present the three chosen cards. The sample to be matched, say the three of diamonds, is at the top, and below it put a three of diamonds and a three of clubs. If the bird pecks the sample three of diamonds at the top, do nothing; if it pecks the matching three of diamonds below, reinforce it; if it pecks the three of clubs, black out. After each correct response and reinforcement, switch the positions of the two lower cards. The pigeon should soon match the sample each time. Conversely, it can also be taught to select the card that does not match the sample. It is important to reinforce correct choices immediately. Your own behavior must be letter-perfect if you are to expect perfection from your subject. The task can be made easier if the pigeon is conditioned to peck the sample card before you begin to train it to match the sample.

In a more elaborate variation of this experiment we have found it possible to make a pigeon choose among four words so that it appears to "name the suit" of the sample card. You prepare four cards about the size of small calling cards, each bearing in block letters the name of a suit: SPADES, HEARTS, DIAMONDS and CLUBS. Fasten these side by side in a row and teach the pigeon to peck them by reinforcing in the usual way. Now arrange a sample playing card just above them. Cover the name cards and reinforce the pigeon a few times for pecking the sample. Now present, say, the three of diamonds as the sample. When the pigeon pecks it, immediately uncover the name cards. If the pigeon pecks DIAMONDS, reinforce instantly, If it pecks a wrong name instead, black out for half a minute and then resume the experiment with the three of diamonds still in place and the name cards covered. After a correct choice, change the sample card to a different suit while the pigeon is eating. Always keep the names covered until the sample card has been pecked. Within a short time you should have the bird following the full sequence of pecking the sample and then the appropriate name card. As time passes the correct name will be pecked more and more frequently and, if you do not too often reinforce wrong responses or neglect to reinforce right ones, the pigeon should soon become letter-perfect.

A toy piano offers interesting possibilities for performances of a more artistic nature. Reinforce any movement of the pigeon that leads toward its pressing a key. Then, by using reinforcements and blackouts appropriately, narrow the response to a given key. Then build up a two-note sequence by reinforcing only when the sequence has been completed and by blacking out when any other combination of keys is struck. The two-note sequence will quickly emerge. Other notes may then be added. Pigeons, chickens, small dogs and cats have been taught in this way to play tunes of four or five notes. The situation soon becomes too complicated, however, for the casual experimenter. You will find it difficult to control the tempo, and the reinforcing contingencies become very complex. The limit of such an experiment is determined as much by the experimenter's skill as by that of the animal. In the laboratory we have been able to provide assistance to the experimenter by setting up complicated devices which always reinforce consistently and avoid exhaustion of the experimenter's patience.

The increased precision of the laboratory also makes it possible to guarantee performance up to the point of almost complete certainty. When relevant conditions have been controlled, the behavior of the organism is fully determined. Behavior may be sustained in full strength for many hours by utilizing different schedules of reinforcement. Some of these correspond to the contingencies established in industry in daily wages or in piece-work pay; others resemhle the subtle but powerful contingencies of gambling devices, which are notorious for their ability to command sustained behavior.

The human baby is an excellent subject in experiments of the kind described here. You will not need to interfere with feeding schedules or create any other state of deprivation, because the human infant can be reinforced by very trivial environmental events; it does not need such a reward as food. Almost any "feedback" from the environment is reinforcing if it is not too intense. A crumpled newspaper, a pan and a spoon, or any convenient noisemaker quickly generates appropriate behavior, often amusing in its violence. The baby's rattle is based upon this principle.

FIGURE 2   Dog can easily be trained to touch its nose to the handle of a cupboard with the aid of a mechanical "cricket." The experimenter holds the cricket in one hand and a bit of food in the other. When the dog makes any movement toward the handle, the experimenter sounds the cricket and tosses the food. Babies are just as smart as dogs in learning such tricks. At right a baby is taught to lift its arms when a lamp is turned off and on.

One reinforcer to which babies often respond is the flashing on and off of a table lamp. Select some arbitrary response—for example, lifting the hand. Whenever the baby lifts its hand, flash the light, in a short time a well-defined response will be generated. (Human babies are just as "smart" as dogs or pigeons in this respect.) Incidentally, the baby will enjoy the experiment.

The some principle is at work in the behavior of older children and adults. Important among human reinforcements are those aspects of the behavior of others, often very subtle, that we call "attention," "approval" and "affection." Behavior which is successful in achieving these reinforcements may come to dominate the repertoire of the individual.

All this may be easily used—and just as easily misused—in our relations with other people. To the reader who is anxious to advance to the human subject a word of caution is in order. Reinforcement is only one of the procedures through which we alter behavior. To use it, we must build up some degree of deprivation or at least permit a deprivation to prevail which it is within our power to reduce. We must embark upon a program in which we sometimes apply relevant reinforcement and sometimes withhold it. In doing this, we are quite likely to generate emotional effects. Unfortunately the science of behavior is not yet as successful in controlling emotion as it is in shaping practical behavior.

A scientific analysis can, however, bring about a better understanding of personal relations. We are almost always reinforcing the behavior of others, whether we mean to or not. A familiar problem is that of the child who seems to take an almost pathological delight in annoying its parents. In many cases this is the result of conditioning which is very similar to the animal training we have discussed. The attention, approval and affection that a mother gives a child are all extremely powerful reinforcements. Any behavior of the child that produces these consequences is likely to be strengthened. The mother may unwittingly promote the very behavior she does not want. For example, when she is busy she is likely not to respond to a call or request made in a quiet tone of voice. She may answer the child only when it raises its voice. The average intensity of the child's vocal behavior therefore moves up to another level—precisely as the head of the dog in our experiment was raised to a new height. Eventually the mother gets used to this level and again reinforces only louder instances. This vicious circle brings about louder and louder behavior. The child's voice may also vary in intonation, and any change in the direction of unpleasantness is more likely to get the attention of the mother and is therefore strengthened. One might even say that "annoying" behavior is just that behavior which is especially effective in arousing another person to action. The mother behaves, in fact, as if she had been given the assignment to teach the child to be annoying! The remedy in such a case is simply for the mother to make sure that she responds with attention and affection to most if not all the responses of the child which are of acceptable intensity and tone of voice and that she never reinforces the annoying forms of behavior.

Discussion Questions for Article 2

Section 7: Learning

Name: _____

PID: _____

Date: __ __ / __ __ / __ __ (MM/DD/YY)

CRN: _____

Recitation Day/Time: _____

Honor Code Signature: _____

1. What are the steps posed by Skinner to begin teaching an animal?

2. What must you do if the animal exhibits begging behaviors during the conditioning phase and why must you do it?

3. How does the learning model discussed by Skinner relate to the reinforcement of disruptive behaviors in children?

4. Skinner teaches us how to reinforce desired behaviors. Do we ever reinforce undesired behaviors? What are some examples, and how do we reinforce them?

Section 8
Motivation and Emotion

"Music is the shorthand of emotion"

—*Leo Nikolaevich Tolstoy*

A	lthough the question of "what are emotions" sounds like a straightforward question, the answer is not a clear one. There have been many variable definitions throughout the subsciences of psychology. One commonality is that due to the inherent difficulty in sufficiently explaining or describing the experiencing of an emotion with words, it seems as though emotions are a form of language all their own. We move them out into our environment via a facial display such as a smile or frown, body posture, and/or language. Emotions also exist on a cognitive level.

A few theories have set out to explain emotions. William James is responsible for one of the better-known theories, the James-Lange theory of emotion in 1884. While psychology was in its infancy he published an article entitled "What is an emotion?" He proposed that first physiological changes (including increased respiration, heart rate, etc.) in response to a stimulus occur and are subsequently interpreted and perceived by the individual. This perception of these corporeal reactions is what we call emotion and may have some support from research involving the brain and physiology. The brainstem in this case is responsible for almost reflexive like physiological changes, especially the "fight or flight" response that would most likely occur first, only to be followed by an interpretation by the limbic system. Later, the analytical, reasoning speaking brain called the cortex consciously perceived and fit the sensations with an appropriate label or "emotion". A near accident on the interstate happens so fast that it may seem as though your body responds first (increased heart rate, respiration rate, increased arousal), followed by your intense feeling of fear and possibly even anger.

The Cannon-Bard theory flips the cause and effect around: the emotional interpretation of a stimulus happens first which then causes a bodily reaction. For instance, this theory suggests that if you are afraid of heights and are traveling to the top of a tall building or are on the roof, you are likely to experience the emotion of fear and subsequently your body will respond with increased heart rate. What can be thought of as a compromise between the two previous theories is the Two-factor theory of emotion. This theory suggests that emotional experience is the result of a two-step, self-perception process in which people first experience physiological arousal and then seek an appropriate explanation for it. If an individual attributes the arousal to an emotional source, they experience that emotion. The common thread among theories of emotion is that arousal and cognition are essential elements.

Motivation, on the other hand, can be thought of as goal-oriented behavior in which desire is the driving force behind action. In one case, you eat if you are hungry. Biological needs prompt behavior and goal-seeking activities every day from when you make breakfast to going to sleep when tired. The Drive-Reduction theory of motivation suggests that we behave as if a thermostat regulates us. For example, in the case of hunger, as time goes by, the desire to eat grows until we eat. The action of eating then reduces the drive to eat, much like a thermostat is prompted to turn off the heat when the temperature reaches a certain point. But there is a much larger picture including the question about what motivates you to ignore biological motives (staying awake to complete an assignment despite exhaustion).

Article 1: Models of Anger: Contributions from Psychophysiology, Neuropsychology, and the Cognitive Behavioral Perspective

This article is a review and integration of the psychophysiological, neuropsychological, and cognitive-behavioral aspects of hostility and anger. The bulk of the studies included not only represents the current knowledge of anger but also demonstrates that these broad literatures can converge in order to further our understanding of anger. The article delineates anger and hostility and the cognitive and emotional experience of anger. Drs. Cox and Harrison aim at fostering new research questions from an integrated theoretical standpoint. This aim is in addition to being beneficial to applied psychology as it may provide a more complete conceptualization of anger. Finally, it provides therapists with a method of systematically approaching the clinical manifestation of anger.

Article 2: Where Emotions Come From

This article explains the biology behind emotions. First, this article explores the amygdala, a subcortical brain structure that sits at the front of the limbic system behind the frontal lobes is considered to be a central player in emotional experience. This article describes the specific neural pathways between the amygdala and other brain regions responsible for emotion development and expression. This article proceeds to describe how the two brain hemispheres are differentially involved the experiencing of positive and negative emotions. Specifically, the right brain is more active during negative emotions such as fear and disgust, in particular, the right frontal lobe. In contrast, the left hemisphere is relatively more active during positive emotions such as happiness and amusement. Finally, a condition where one is unable to recognize faces, prosopagnosia, is discussed. This condition is interesting in that although one is unable to recognize faces, the ability to distinguish emotions remains. This intriguing condition demonstrates that, in the brain, facial recognition and the understanding of emotions may be separate.

—*Philip L. Klineburger*

Models of Anger: Contributions from Psychophysiology, Neuropsychology and the Cognitive Behavioral Perspective

David E. Cox

David W. Harrison

The current review examined the research and current models of anger from three distinct literatures: psychophysiology, neuropsychology and the cognitive-behavioral perspective. Two primary conceptual difficulties are addressed in this review. First, the debate over how and when to differentiate between anger and hostility is discussed. Second, the issue regarding cognitive or emotional dominance or primacy in the experience of anger is considered. Once the conceptual ambiguity is addressed, data from the cognitive-behavioral, psychophysiological and neuropsychological literatures are reviewed with a focus on issues of laterality. Particular attention is given to research of appraisal theory from the cognitive literature, cortical arousal and related cerebral models from the psychophysiological literature, and functional cerebral systems from the neuropsychological literature. Despite significant differences appearing both within and between the bodies of literature, when viewed without the traditional ambiguity surrounding this topic, there appears to be a great deal of overlap which may be conducive to the construction of a unified theoretical model. Such a model is proposed in the final section of this paper.

Introduction

Although anger is not a defined clinical syndrome (Fava et al. 1990), it is commonly treated in clinical settings and has been shown to be present in many of the disorders described in the Diagnostic and Statistics Manual of Mental Disorders (American Psychiatric Association 1994). It has been suggested that anger and its behavioral sequelae, aggression, are associated with an increased risk of criminality and represent one of the most costly problems in modern society (Hare 1999). Despite the prevalence of anger in psychopathology and the associated societal cost, the construct continues to be inconsistently defined by many researchers, leading to incongruent findings in the literature and incomplete theoretical models (Eckhardt et al. 2004).

While a substantial portion of the confusion surrounding anger results from semantic issues and differing theoretical orientations among researchers, there are very tangible difficulties in teasing apart the highly correlated cognitive, affective and behavioral dimensions of the construct (Biaggio et al. 1981). While some researchers referred to these different dimensions interchangeably (e.g., Siegel 1985; Siegman and Snow 1997; Wingrove and Bond 2005), other researchers believe that despite the relationship between these dimensions, the conceptual and practical differences are sufficient to warrant their consideration as separate constructs (Berkowitz 1993; Eckhardt and Deffenbacher 1995; Spielberger et al. 1983). Although the theoretical rationale for separating these dimensions for clarification seems logical, there is very little empirical data to support the notion of distinct constructs (Eckhardt et al. 2004). Such inconsistencies in theoretical underpinnings and operational definitions of the construct and its dimensions may provide difficulties in the interpretation and application of research conducted on anger (Eckhardt et al. 1997). The current review will attempt to disambiguate the definitional and theoretical elements of anger in order to facilitate a clearer evaluation of research findings.

The second goal of the current review will be to examine the research in the area of anger that may serve to provide a better understanding of the construct and its related factors. Cognitive psychologists, neuropsychologists, and psychophysiologists have provided some very important data relevant to the study of anger. This review will examine the extant literature surrounding anger from the cognitive, psychophysiological, and neuropsychological perspectives and evaluate how the research from these three distinct bodies of research can be utilized in synchrony to inform an integrative model of anger and hostility. Finally, an integrative model, as mentioned above, will be proposed, along with some suggestions for future research that may be used to evaluate the proposed model.

Defining Anger

The construct of anger is considered to be multidimensional with distinct affective, behavioral, and cognitive dimensions and distinct physiological elements that contribute to both the experience and expression of the emotion (Spielberger et al. 1983). The affective dimension of anger refers to the emotional experience and is what is generally referred to as anger. The behavioral dimension of anger, most frequently referred to as aggression, represents a set of behaviors that are aimed at causing harm to another or achieving retaliation for a perceived wrong (Williams et al. 1982). The cognitive dimension of anger, which will be discussed later in detail, refers to a set of cognitive appraisals, which guide the valence of perceived emotion (Hollon and Kendall 1980). While there are multiple manifestations of aggression, the primary component is that of doing harm.

The Affective Dimension of Anger

The term anger serves a dual role in the multidimensional conceptualization in that it refers to both the overarching construct as well as the affective dimension. The operational definition most frequently ascribed to the affective dimension of anger is that of a subjective, negatively felt state associated with cognitive deficits and distortions as well as physiological correlates that occur in response to a stimulus that is perceived as negative and may result in maladaptive patterns of behavior (Kassinove and Suckhodolsky 1995). While this definition provides some clarification of how the affective dimension of anger is associated with the overarching construct, further elaboration is necessary in order to capture how this emotion occurs as an emotive state. In order to evaluate anger in this manner, the stability, frequency and intensity with which this emotion is experienced as well as how the experience and expression of this emotion differ must be addressed (Deffenbacher et al. 1996).

To capture the construct as an emotive state, anger is further defined in terms of state, trait, anger in and anger out. Trait anger refers to the overarching construct of anger and is defined as anger-proneness or a relatively stable predisposition to react to stimuli perceived as negative in an angry manner (Spielberger et al. 1995). Conversely, state anger refers to the affective dimension and is defined as an emotional response to an immediate stressor that may vary in both intensity and duration (Spielberger et al. 1995). Furthermore, Spielberger and his colleagues also address the expression of anger in terms of "anger in" or "anger out", referring to whether individuals suppress angry responses (anger in) or overtly express their anger (anger out). These elaborative points, when used in conjunction with the aforementioned description of the affective dimension of anger provide an adequate description of anger both as an entity and as an affective element.

The Behavioral Dimension of Anger

It has been suggested that all observable behaviors are influenced by an integration of emotions and cognitions (Lemerise and Arsenio 2000). Therefore, the behavioral dimension of anger, most frequently referred to as aggression, may arise from the cognitive and affective dimensions (Weiner 1995). Although there has been considerable debate regarding fear induced aggression or aggression as a "defensive" act (Graham and Hoehn 1995), and these behaviors may be shown to meet the physical dimension of aggression (e.g., causing harm), they lack the cognitive intent of maliciousness (Lemerise and Arsenio 2000). Thus, it is inappropriate to conceptualize this factor as an independent construct as the cognitive, affective and behavioral dimensions of anger are highly interrelated and interdependent (Loeber and Coie 2001). Furthermore, negative emotions may decrease the occurrence of appropriate behavioral responses and limit the cognitive capacity to engage in successful problem solving (Pakaslahti 2000). Although there is a substantial body that has investigated this behavioral domain independently of its associated dimensions, as a distinct construct known as aggression, this distinction provides further ambiguity.

The Cognitive Dimension of Anger

The cognitive dimension of anger, often referred to as hostility in the literature, has most frequently been defined as a cognitive phenomenon of an attitudinal nature that subserves the emotional process, but is not an emotion per se (Smith 1994). Buss (1961), who is most frequently credited with the definition of hostility, suggested that hostility is defined by negative cognitive appraisals of circumstances and individuals, and represents a construct independent of the experience and expression of anger. Consistent with this definition, many researchers have developed models attempting to separate the cognitive dimension from the overarching construct of anger to create an independent construct of hostility.

One of the most prevalent models of hostility as an independent construct is the transactional model, which describes hostility as possessing its own, unique affective, behavioral and cognitive dimensions that contribute to an emotional outcome (Deffenbacher 1994). Mistrust, denigration and cynicism are the cognitions that are proposed to be central to the transactional model of hostility (Miller et al. 1996; Suls and Bunde 2005). Each of these cognitive factors of this model addresses some element of interpersonal interaction, suggesting that hostility is both a product of and reaction to interpersonal environmental factors. That is to say that hostility is an attitude that may be derived from negative interpersonal experiences and may also predict negative responses to future interpersonal interactions (Berkowitz 1993). Proponents of this conceptualization of hostility suggest that these hostile cognitions cause hostile individuals to experience and create more interpersonal stressors (Smith and Pope 1990), creating a reciprocal state in which the experience of hostile thoughts is confirmed and perpetuated through negative, hostile interpersonal interactions (Allred and Smith 1991). However, models of hostility have not been shown to support affective or behavioral dimensions that are distinct from anger and aggression.

The strength of the theoretical argument that hostility represents an independent construct rather than a dimension of anger is drawn from the fact that certain measures of the constructs have demonstrated significant psychometric evidence of distinction (Smith et al. 2004). However, the empirical support has not been overwhelming and a factor analysis of 24 different self-report measures of anger and related constructs revealed that although three distinct domains may be discerned, there is substantial overlap between hostility and anger that cannot be accounted for by measurement similarities alone (Martin et al. 2000). Thus, the terms anger, hostility and aggression may merely serve as convenient, heuristic labels to differentiate between the affective, behavioral and cognitive components of a single construct (LeDoux 1994). The current review will attempt to discuss the relevant literature in terms of the overarching concept of anger with distinctions between the cognitive, affective, and behavioral domains as necessitated by the study under consideration.

The Cognitive-Behavioral Perspective

While there are numerous theories of anger within the cognitive-behavioral literature, appraisal theory, in one form or another, dominates the current cognitive-behavioral literature (e.g., Deffenbacher et al. 2003; Scherer et al. 2003; Jones and Trower 2004; Kassinove and Suckhodolsky 1995). There is a lengthy history of debate regarding the association between cognition and emotion that is integrally related to the development of cognitive theories of anger. While a comprehensive review of this debate is not possible here, it is important to note that the controversy involves what level of cognition is considered part of the process of emotion (Frijda 1986). Although many appraisal models maintain that cognitive processes such as sensory perception provide evidence for the dominance of appraisal in emotion, other theorists indicate that appraisal processes occur following perception and represent a separate cognitive process (Izard 1993). While there is little debate that perception is a necessary part of any sensory experience, there is substantial debate as to whether perceptual processes are the foundation of cognitive models of emotion or if these emotions are concerned with higher order cognitive appraisals that assign meaning and valence (Eckhardt et al. 2004).

Despite these general controversies, most cognitive models of anger indicate that the experience of anger depends on the higher order appraisal of events. Under this appraisal framework, cognitive processes determine whether or not an event will lead to the experience of anger based on the individual's appraisal of the situation, the interactions between eliciting events, and the individual's mental state or traits (Deffenbacher 1994; Frijda 1986; Lazarus and Smith 1988). These theories suggest that, since it is at the level of the appraisal process at which the individual's attitude becomes involved in determining the subjective experience of anger, higher order cognition is the causal factor in the experience of anger. Under this cognitive framework, appraisal is both sufficient and necessary for the experience of anger.

In an attempt to account for the mechanisms by which these cognitive processes direct anger, elements of generalized arousal (Schachter and Singer 1962) and cognitive appraisals (Lazarus 1991; Roseman 1991) have been integrated into current models of anger. Similar to the general model upon which they are based, these models of anger maintain that sensory perception stimulates a generalized arousal of psychological and physiological systems, including the autonomic nervous system (ANS; Lazarus 1991). This generalized arousal then triggers the appraisal process (Frijda 2005; Lazarus 1984; Snyder et al. 1997). The appraisal process is then directed by automatic thoughts, which are shaped by the individual's previous experiences, self-valuation and other situational and trait factors (e.g., negative self-evaluation, negative perception of others). These automatic thoughts may lead to cognitive misperceptions regarding the environment and/or situation (Fernandez and Beck 2001; Lazarus 1984). The connotative meaning that the individual attaches to the stimuli is then directed into the subjective emotional experience. The intuitive appeal of this model and incidental role ascribed to the physiological elements have been embraced by clinical psychologists and serve as the cornerstone for even the most recent incarnations of cognitive-behavioral therapy (e.g., Beck et al. 1996; Lazarus 1982). The generalized arousal model's appeal for those interested in measuring and treating anger-related disorders may be associated with the congruence between cognitive appraisals and the psychometric methods (Lang 1994).

Limitations of the Cognitive Model

The primary limitation to such appraisal models is the suggestion that specific patterns of physiological changes may be observed in anger occurrence after the subjective experience of anger. Research in psychophysiology has not supported these cognition first models and has, in fact, demonstrated an affect first effect in which emotion specific patterns of physiological arousal precede cognitive processes (Zajonc 1980). In regard to anger, experiments which have demonstrated that participants reported increased feelings of anger after viewing visual images of angry faces, presented below the threshold of cognitive awareness (Kunst-Wilson and Zajonc 1981). Similarly, patterns of physiological arousal, specific to the experience of anger have been recorded from individuals performing a list-learning task that included angry or hostile words (Mollet 2004). Furthermore, the bulk of contemporary research has indicated that, while there are many commonalities in the physiological patterns displayed across different emotions, it is possible to identify discrete emotions based on the differences in associated physiological phenomena. In particular, anger has shown distinct patterns of cerebral activation (e.g., Davidson 2000; Heilman 1997; LeDoux 1994; Tomarken et al. 1990), cardiovascular reactivity (Demaree 2000; Demaree and Harrison 1997), and motor function (Demaree et al. 2002). Therefore, the cognitive model does not account for the full range of experience and expression of anger in terms of physiological and behavioral elements. Omissions such as these begin to limit the understanding of the construct and lead to interpretations that have not been consistently supported through empirical investigation (Martin et al. 2000).

The Psychophysiology of Anger

Results from psychophysiological research on the experience and expression of emotion have shown significant changes in numerous physiological variables such as electrocortical arousal patterns (e.g., Demaree et al. 2005; Harmon-Jones 2003; Tomarken et al. 1992), cardiovascular functions (e.g., Porges 1991; Thayer et al. 1996; Thayer and Lane 2000), and skin conductance (e.g., Buck 1977; Critchley et al. 2000; Kettunen et al. 2000). Additionally, several lines of research have shown coherence across multiple physiological systems in terms of emotional responses (e.g., Christie and Friedman 2003; Damasio 1989; Levenson 1988; Mauss et al. 2005). These general findings have been extended to illuminate the role of physiological processes in anger. The resulting physiological models of anger are couched in overarching physiological models of emotion. The current review will provide a very brief description of the general models before detailing the anger component.

Cerebral Models of Anger

The most widely acknowledged cerebral models of emotion are based on hemispheric laterality associated with emotional valence (e.g., Schwartz et al. 1975) or motivational direction (e.g., Davidson 1995; Gray 1982). These models have been derived from studies of patterns of EEG of patient populations, case studies of individuals with focal brain lesions, and experiments designed to evoke particular emotions while participants undergo EEG analyses. The models reviewed here include the right hemisphere model (Borod et al. 1983; Heilman and Bowers 1990), the valence model (Ehrlichman and Barrett 1983), the approach/avoidance (appetitive/aversive) model (Davidson 1998) and the behavioral inhibition–behavioral activation (BIS/BAS) model (Gray 1990).

The Right Hemisphere Model   The fundamental tenet of the right hemisphere model is that all emotion is processed in the right hemisphere, regardless of emotional valence (Tucker 1981). This model arose intuitively from years of accumulated observations of affective changes associated with right hemisphere damage (e.g., Mills 1912). Specifically, the right hemisphere model proposes that perception of emotion results in cortical activation of the right temporal region and subsequent expression or inhibition of expression of emotion is demonstrated by increased right frontal activation (Heilman and Bowers 1990). Empirical support for this model comes from electroencephalography and neuroimaging studies which have demonstrated greater activation of the right temporal region during presentation of emotionally valenced stimuli (e.g., Davidson and Schwartz 1977), perception of emotional faces (Tabert et al. 2001; Vanderploeg et al. 1987), generation of negative facial affect (Kestenbaum and Nelson 1992), and recognition of affective prosody (Demaree et al. 2004).

In regard to anger, some studies have demonstrated a right hemisphere specificity for processing anger related stimuli. For example, individuals instructed to remember an event that made them angry demonstrated significant relative right hemispheric activation during the anger recollection (Narumoto et al. 2001). Similarly, Foster and Harrison (2002) had individuals recall a recent memory that had made them angry while concurrent electroencephalography was conducted. Participants were then asked to rate the subjective level of anger produced by the event on a 7-point scale. Results from this study indicated that the subjective ratings correlated significantly with relative right frontal and temporal activation. These findings may suggest that the subjective experience of anger, without behavioral expression may result in relative activation of the right anterior region. However, findings in regard to the right hemisphere dominance for anger are equivocal, with some studies demonstrating more symmetrical patterns (e.g., Waldstein et al. 2000), or left hemisphere asymmetry (Cole and Ray 1985; Harmon-Jones 2003; Tomarken et al. 1990, 1992; Tucker and Dawson 1984). A meta-analytic review of neuroimaging studies failed to demonstrate any support for the right hemisphere model (Barrett and Wager 2006).

The Valence Model   Valence models propose that emotion is a property of bilateral regions and which hemisphere is involved is determined by the emotional valence of the emotion (Ehrlichman and Barrett 1983; Tucker and Williamson

1984). The most common iteration of the valence model posits that emotions are processed by the anterior region with the right anterior region facilitating negative emotional experience and positive emotions being facilitated by the left anterior region (Davidson and Fox 1982; Eckman and Davidson 1993; Ehrlichman and Barrett 1983; Tucker 1981). Support for this model has come from clinical evidence regarding the affective changes in patients who differed depending on the hemisphere that was damaged (e.g., Robinson and Manes 2000) and EEG studies. For example, it has been demonstrated that infants show relative right hemispheric activation when presented with pictures of "sad" faces and relative left hemispheric activation when shown pictures of "happy" faces (Davidson and Fox 1982). Likewise, it has been shown that individuals demonstrate relative activation of the right anterior region while viewing negatively valenced video and relative activation of the left anterior region when viewing a positively valenced video (Davidson and Schwartz 1977).

Anger has proved to be the most problematic emotion for the valence model. Despite the implementation of multiple novel research paradigms and large numbers of replication studies, not all researchers have produced results supportive of this model in regard to anger (Cole and Ray 1985; Tucker and Dawson 1984). Although anger is viewed as a negative emotion, it has been shown to produce relative activation of the left anterior region (e.g., Davidson 1995; Harmon-Jones and Allen 1998), contrary to the predictions made by this model. Additionally, a comprehensive review of neuroimaging studies revealed no distinct patterns of activation congruent with a valence hypothesis (Wager et al. 2003). Based on these neuroimaging data and the poor fit of the valence model on the construct of anger, researchers began to investigate emotions in terms of their motivational direction, rather than valence.

Approach-Withdrawal Model   The approach-withdrawal model draws on the same theoretical foundation as the valence model in terms of frontal asymmetries being the fundamental element of interest. However, rather than examining behaviors in terms of positive and negative valence, the determination of emotionality is made based on whether the emotion tends to provoke approach behaviors or withdrawal behaviors. This model proposes that emotions that tend to provoke withdrawal behaviors are associated with relative activation of the right hemisphere while emotions associated with approach behaviors are associated with relative left hemisphere activation (Davidson 1995). Support for this model comes from multiple electroencephalograph studies of clinical populations. Such studies have shown that among depressed patients, relative right activation or left deactivation is associated with degree of depressive symptom exhibition, particularly withdrawal type behaviors (Heller et al. 1998; Henriques and Davidson 1991; Robinson and Downhill 1995). Similar results have been obtained in numerous experiments with adults (Davidson 1992, 1993, 1995; Davidson et al. 1999).

In terms of anger, the Harmon Jones laboratory (Harmon-Jones and Allen 1998; Harmon-Jones et al. 2003, 2004) has provided impressive support for the approach-withdrawal model. Utilizing novel research methods, these researchers have demonstrated that anger produces relative activation of the left anterior region consistent with approach behavior rather than negative valence dimensions. For example, a series of experiments demonstrated increased relative activation of the left anterior region in response to an immediate stressor (insult) as a measure of state anger (Harmon-Jones et al. 2004) and that resting relative activation of the left anterior region predicted increased anger response to a stressor, as a measure of trait anger (Harmon-Jones and Allen 1998). This group has also produced evidence that individuals who believe that they will have the opportunity to engage in angry response to an elicitor demonstrate greater relative activation of the left anterior region, compared to individuals who believe that they will not have the opportunity to respond to the same stressor (Harmon-Jones et al. 2003). Although neuroimaging studies have demonstrated equivocal support for a motivational model, through demonstration of lateralized activation of subcortical systems (Killgore and Yurgelun-Todd 2001), meta-analytic review of the evidence argues against specific patterns of activation in the frontal regions (Phan et al. 2004).

The BIS/BAS Model   The inconsistent and negative neuroimaging findings associated with the approach-withdrawal model may be partially accounted for the BIS/BAS model. It has been suggested that data from investigations of emotional states map onto the BIS/BAS model with greater precision and trait data tend to fit the approach-withdrawal model better (Demaree et al. 2005). A more incidental point of divergence for these two models is the pathways underlying emotional experience. While the approach-withdrawal model proposes different neural systems or pathways for approach and withdrawal behaviors (Davidson 1994), the BIS/BAS model proposes that the BAS system may subserve both approach and withdrawal behaviors (Gray 1982). In this model, BIS represents a disruption (or passive avoidance) and extinction (McNaughton and Gray 2000). Under this framework, active inhibition (i.e., anger control) would represent behavioral activation, whereas passive avoidance would be behavioral inhibition (Hewig et al. 2004). This would be consistent with findings from neuroimaging studies that show distinct subcortical systems involved in specific emotional experiences, based on motivation (Demaree et al 2005).

Research in support of the BIS/BAS predictions that anger is lateralized primarily to the left hemisphere has grown with an increased number of studies indicating relative activation of the left hemisphere in response to anger provocation (Lane et al. 1997). For example, Wacker et al. (2003) demonstrated that relative activation patterns of the left anterior region in response to imagining a past event that elicited anger were strongly correlated with scores on measures of BAS. Building from the evidence produced by Harmon-Jones and Allen (1998) regarding the utility of resting anterior cortical activation to predict trait anger, researchers have shown that resting relative activation of the left anterior region is associated with measures of BAS and trait anger (Hewig et al. 2004). However, it has been proposed that there is a relationship between BAS and positive affect, causing some researchers to question whether the observed patterns of anterior cortical activation are due to the BAS system or positive affect (Carver and White 1994). Neuroimaging studies have indicated that such inconsistent findings may emerge from the failure to look at both BIS and BAS systems as on a continuum and relative deactivation of BIS or activation of BAS might be equally involved in aggressive behavior (Beauchaine 2001; Fowles 1998).

Summary

The research reviewed here represents a very small segment of the summary findings for each of the models and provides a complex web of support for certain aspects of each model. A recent meta-analysis of the research surrounding these models offered some clarification to the seemingly conflicting results. Murphy et al. (2003) examined 106 studies on functional neurosystems underlying emotional experience resulting in some interesting patterns of results. The results of this meta-analysis did not support the predictions of right hemisphere dominant processing for all emotions. Furthermore, these results indicated that activation of the posterior regions were equivalent in the left and right hemisphere for the reception of emotions. Although the examination of the valence model suggested symmetrical activation in the experience of both positive and negatively valenced emotions, there was some evidence that resting asymmetries may reflect some degree of trait anger. Results from a very thorough meta-analytic study of neuroimaging data show no direct support for either the right hemisphere or valence models (Phan et al. 2004). Motivational models received moderate support for patterns of activation based on the appetitive-aversive continuum, but not on BIS/BAS distinctions from both electrophysiological studies and some neuroimaging results.

Despite the complexity of this line of research, the results of the experiments investigating each model, as well as the meta-analytic results can be used to draw some useful distinctions regarding cortical activation in the perception and experience of anger. First, the evidence does not appear to support clear patterns of asymmetry in the perception of emotion. However, there is significant evidence that emotional perception may occur preferentially in the posterior regions (Adolphs et al. 1996; Borod et al. 1998; Heller et al. 1998; Murphy et al. 2003). There has been equivocal support for preferential relative left anterior cortical activation associated with anger in line with the predictions made by motivational models (Davidson 1998; Henriques and Davidson 2000; Murphy et al. 2003), although alternative models have received some empirical support. There appears to be at least marginal support for the suggestion that resting right hemisphere asymmetry may be associated with trait anger (Davidson 1998; Lane et al. 1997; Hagemann et al. 2001). Finally, neuroimaging data clearly indicate that anger, as a multifaceted construct, is subserved by a very complex system of subcortical and cortical systems, which may only be evident when investigated as a functional system. Perhaps the most important contribution of this literature is its support of the utility of investigating the patterns of cortical activation in relation to discrete emotional states and traits.

The Neuropsychology of Anger

While neuropsychological assessment provides greatest utility in the area of assessing functional impairments in brain function (e.g., aphasia, dysgraphia, dyslexia, agnosia, delirium, and dementia), when coupled with the substantial evidence from the cortical activation literature, the tools of neuropsychology may prove to be extremely useful in the investigation of other psychological phenomena. The idea of functional "space" holds that tasks involving competing systems may provide interference for one another (Kinsbourne 1978, 1985). This idea of competing systems has provided the platform for the investigation of the neuropsychology of emotion and functional mapping of proposed functional systems of emotion (e.g., Everhart et al. 2005; Foster et al. 2005; Snyder and Harrison 1997; Demaree et al. 2002). The following sections will discuss the effects of negative affectivity, in general, and specifically anger on neuropsychological measures of cognitive function.

The impact of affect on cognitive performance is well documented in the literature with negative affect generally associated with poorer performance on neuropsychological measures and positive affect associated with optimal performance (Lezak 1983). To understand the potential impact that emotion may have on specific cognitive functions, it is necessary to describe the functional systems proposed to subserve particular cognitive functions. Although the subject of functional lateralization is much more complex than presented in early descriptions (e.g., left hemisphere subserves verbal functions and right hemisphere subserves visuospatial processes), certain processes can provide discrimination between hemispheres (Kandel et al. 2000). A brief description of neuropsychological tasks associated with the functional systems outlined in the cortical activation models is presented below to provide the basic framework for discussing these systems in terms of their involvement in the perception, experience and expression of anger.

Functional Systems

The right hemisphere is generally associated with motor control of the contralateral (left) side of the body, global visuospatial processes, perception of distance between objects and spatial measurement (Max 2004). In particular design fluency tasks are primarily associated with the right frontal region (Ruff et al. 1987), as is the left hand grip strength (Demaree et al. 2002), map making, and facial affect recognition (Suberi and McKeever 1977). The right posterior region is associated with visuospatial praxis (Rao 2000), visuospatial memory (Hellige et al. 1979), verbal prosody (Ross 2000), and facial recognition (Ekman and Friesen 1971). Conversely, the left hemisphere is typically associated with verbal fluency, speech production and reception (Damasio and Damasio 2000), and verbal memory (Max 2004). Specifically, verbal fluency is viewed as a property of the left frontal region (Block et al. 1999) while receptive and generative speech, as well as verbal memory is associated with left posterior regions (Damasio and Damasio 2000).

The key to the neuropsychological investigation of emotional states and traits lies in Luria's functional cerebral systems model (Mollet 2006). The functional cerebral systems model proposes that there are specific coordinated regions of the brain that are utilized to complete certain tasks. While the original model as proposed by Luria (1973) is far too complex to thoroughly explain in this brief review, the most important feature of this model is that it moves away from the notion of strict localization and toward a more systemic view of cerebral systems. The functional systems model proposes that multiple regions in different parts of the brain may be involved in similar tasks, so while there may be evidence of diffuse activation in a given process (e.g., expressive speech), the activation patterns will be consistent for that particular activity across individuals (Luria 1973). The following sections will discuss the effects of anger on functional cerebral systems across the visual, auditory, and motor modalities.

Visual Modality

Research has demonstrated that anger can be shown to impact visual system functioning in both reactive (state) and predictive (trait) paradigms. For example, research has shown the induction of anger can negatively impact latency and accuracy on measures of facial affect recognition (Harrison and Gorelczenko 1990; McKeever and Dixon 1981; Reuter-Lorenz et al. 1983; Suberi and McKeever 1977). Extending this line of research, Herridge et al. (2004) found that these latency and accuracy effects can be shown to be greater for individuals scoring higher on the Cook–Medley Hostility Inventory (CMHI; Cook and Medley 1954) than those scoring in the lower range. Utilizing a go/no go paradigm, Maxwell et al. (2005) examined the effects of emotionally valenced faces on inhibitory processes. The results of this experiment indicated that presentation of angry faces as distractors led to increased inhibitory errors compared to happy or neutral face presentation.

Auditory Modality

Although there is limited investigation on the effect of anger on auditory processes, there have been some experimental investigations. For example, it has been shown that individuals reporting high levels of cognitive anger demonstrate a left ear (right hemisphere) advantage on a dichotic listening task while individuals reporting lower levels of cognitive anger demonstrate a relative right ear (left hemisphere) advantage on dichotic listening tasks (Demaree and Harrison 1997). Although numerous studies utilizing the affective auditory verbal learning test (AAVL; Snyder and Harrison 1997) have demonstrated interesting effects in terms of cortical activation and cardiovascular effects, these studies have failed to demonstrate any consistent patterns related to the affective verbal learning component in the auditory modality (Everhart et al. 2005).

Motor Modality

Experiments looking at the effects of anger on gross motor function have shown significant evidence of emotional effects. For example, Demaree et al. (2002) found increased grip strength at the left hand (right hemisphere) and increased grip strength at the right hand (left hemisphere) among individuals reporting higher levels of cognitive anger. Other experiments have demonstrated that a higher reported level of cognitive anger is associated with reduced performance on reaction time tasks (Bolmont et al. 2000), increased muscle tonus at the shoulder (Rugieri and Giustini 1991), and increased activity of the corrugator muscle (Vigne et al. 1988).

Summary

Although functional neuropsychological systems have become much more complicated than early localizationalists indicated, research in this area has yielded some very important findings regarding the manner in which the brain directs certain types of behavior. For example, the lateralization of verbal and visuospatial processes, although not without its detractors, has received substantial support in the literature and is frequently used to index hemispheric function (Kandel et al. 2000). Likewise, the importance of the posterior regions to perceptual processes (Maitlin 1998) and the anterior regions in planning and sequencing (Stuss 1992) are well supported and widely utilized within the field of neuropsychology. In regard to the current review of the effects of anger on functional systems, there appears to be substantial evidence for preferential impairment of right hemisphere processes across the visual auditory and motor sensory modalities associated with higher reported levels of cognitive anger. Systematic investigations of the impact of anger on left hemisphere systems have been less conclusive, perhaps due to the difficulty of separating the prosodic components of speech from basic verbal processes.

An Integrative Model Informed by Multiple Perspectives

Each of the literatures reviewed in the preceding sections reflect many years of intense study as well as theoretical and methodological evolution. As new information and technologies are introduced, previous theories are expanded upon and refined to incorporate new findings. Inherent to this process is the existence of tremendous variability in the theoretical interpretations of the empirical results. The greatest difficulty in merging diverse literatures is in determining which theoretical models maintain viability in the face of the rigorous challenges brought about under the scientific method. When attempting to merge the research and models presented in the current review, certain elements seem to be of limited utility in designing an integrative model. For example, the definitional difficulties surrounding anger and its related constructs create tremendous ambiguity in the literature and have been shown to provide marginal heuristic value (Martin et al. 2000; LeDoux 1994). The model proposed here will not refer to anger, hostility and aggression as separate constructs due to the inconsistency with which they have been used historically, and the fact that they appear to represent factors of a single construct rather than distinct constructs (Martin et al. 2000). Rather, the current model will refer to anger as the construct of interest and will delineate its affective, behavioral, and cognitive elements as necessary.

Likewise, the concept of "generalized arousal" does not appear to offer any utility in the study of emotion and, in fact, this concept has been mostly abandoned in the psychophysiological literature since the early 1970's (Lang 1994). Under the current model, arousal will refer to specific patterns of relative cortical activation and specific patterns of activity in the autonomic nervous system. The concept of strict localization of complex functions in the brain does not appear to reflect the manner in which these complex processes, such as cognition and emotion, occur in the brain. Although these elements have a long history within this area of study, they seem to be of limited utility and add to the somewhat cumbersome verbiage surrounding this literature.

Elements such as those listed above highlight the fact that few, if any, of the models from the cognitive, psychophysiological or neuropsychological literatures can be shown to have unequivocal support. However, each of these models may be shown to contain some element that is supported by multiple empirical data sources and may contribute to the overall understanding of the construct of anger. Examination of these models with a systems perspective may allow for greater integration across the cognitive, psychophysiological and neuropsychological perspectives and may allow for a better understanding of the nature of anger. The following section will attempt facilitate this goal by extracting the most clearly supported elements from the models reviewed here in order to form an integrative model that may generate further research and provide some applied utility.

Structure

As psychology moves away from the ideas of "black boxes" and isolated causal elements, there is greater awareness of how multiple factors are required to explain even the simplest of behaviors. Therefore, cerebral models that focus on certain regions of the brain as responsible for the entire process (perception, experience and expression) of anger seem to be somewhat outdated and inefficient. The current model proposes that, in order to fully represent the affective, behavioral, and cognitive elements of anger, multiple regions of the brain are involved in various associated processes. While the current model assigns particular function to these various regions of the brain, it is important to note that these assignments are within a functional cerebral system for anger and do not ascribe responsibility for anger to any single region of the brain. Structurally, the implications of this proposal dictate that all the four divisions of the brain are involved in some part of the perception, experience and expression of anger. This model appears to bear the closest resemblance to the multidimensional model proposed by Heilman (2000), in that it stresses the involvement of all regions of the cerebral cortex. Additionally, this model attempts to integrate the subcortical structures that are involved in the process.

Posterior Regions

The structural design proposes a sequential functional system for anger that begins, necessarily, with the perception of emotion valence. This part of the model is not specific for anger, as it accounts for emotional perception in general. Consistent with Heilman's (2000) model and meta-analytic findings (Murphy et al. 2003), it is proposed that these initial perceptual processes occur within bilateral posterior cerebral systems. In particular, it is proposed that initial perception of valence is subsumed by the right posterior region, as directly evidenced in the results from previous experiments (e.g., Demaree 2000; Everhart and Harrison 1995, 2000; Heilman 2000; Heller 1993; Kimbrell et al. 1999; Schutter et al. 2004) and consistent with research that has identified underlying mechanisms of sensory registration (Zajonc 1984), and the involvement of the amygdale in response to perceived threat (Adolphs et al. 1999). The current model proposes that the left posterior region may become involved in the perception of emotion through the initiation of cognitive appraisals. The mechanisms by which it is proposed to occur have a substantial empirical support. It is proposed that memory and language play a part in the cognitive appraisal process and account for the left posterior activation.

Virtually in every explanation of cognitive appraisals there is an element of applying a personal world view or attitude to the interpretation of stimuli that is inherently linked to the language and memory at some level, suggesting that appraisals are necessarily associated with significant memory processes and some verbal or subverbal process (Snyder et al. 1997). Meta analyses of neuroimaging studies have provided clear evidence of left temporal activation in response to emotional material, associated with increased hippocampal involvement in the emotion-memory circuit (Phan et al. 2004). As previously discussed, neuropsychological evidence has consistently shown that language processes are largely subsumed by the left hemisphere (Max 2004). The combination of this neuropsychological evidence and neuroimaging data provide an empirical basis for the hypothesized relationship between left posterior activation and appraisal processes. Furthermore, this hypothesis proposes a network that would account for the bilateral activation that has been demonstrated in numerous studies.

Anterior Regions

The model proposed here suggests that the anterior regions are associated with the activation or inhibition of the behavioral outcome of anger. This regulatory role of the frontal lobes, and the medial prefrontal cortex in particular, is consistent with evidence from neuroimaging studies (e.g., Beauregard et al. 2001) and the neuroanatomical pathways in which primary projections of the amygdale, via the basal ganglia, interface with the frontal lobes (Wager et al. 2007). In terms of cortical activation, it has been shown that expression of anger results in relative activation of the left anterior regions, while inhibition of experienced anger leads to relative activation of the right anterior region (Harmon-Jones 2003). However, it is important to note that relative activation does not mean that the basal ganglia projections are lateralized. The model maintains that the frontal systems are not lateralized; rather the system remains intact but differentially activated under the different expression conditions. Similar to the BIS/BAS model (McNaughton and Gray 2000), this model suggests that relative activation of the right anterior region may occur as the result of inhibition of emotional expression or active avoidance of emotional experience, which could explain different patterns of activation found across studies.

Summary

By examining the subcortical components of the separate, yet interacting functional systems underlying the perception and expression of anger, this model provides a method for explaining and integrating the somewhat conflicting findings produced from different investigators examining patterns of cortical activation. The proposed model provides a pattern of activation that is more consistent with the underlying neuroanatomy than previous models that have proposed distinct systems with little attention paid to the implications of relative activation. The proposed model addresses the components of anger in such a manner that the summation of these components may be examined as a unitary construct, while allowing investigation of their discrete properties in terms of associated functional cerebral systems. Finally, the structure of this current model provides an empirical rationale for considering a functional cerebral system (memory and language) that accounts for cognitive appraisals in association with anger.

Function

As the goal of the current model is to provide a high degree of integration of the structure and functional elements of anger, there remains little to discuss here other than the functional implications of the current model. Under the model proposed here, functional manifestations of anger may be clearly linked to underlying cerebral systems in which anger "disorders" could be a result of dysregulation of any of the proposed systems or combination of systems. Dysfunction in the perceptual system may increase an individual's receptivity for anger-provoking material or the interpretation of material as negative, thus increasing the possibility that they may experience anger. Behaviorally, this constellation may manifest itself in overt aggression, diminished self-esteem, or persecutory delusions. The exact nature of the difficulties caused by perceptual dysfunction is somewhat dependent on the expression system, as it will determine whether the anger will be self or other directed. Dysfunction in the expression system may lead to an inability to regulate expression of anger and increase the occurrence of angry response, or chronic repression of anger expression, leading to various psychiatric difficulties.

It is important to note that although this model is primarily concerned with the cortical representation of anger, the proposed patterns are consistent with subcortical and neuroanatomical models of anger (Heilman 2000). In fact, it is the subcortical pathways (e.g., the basal ganglia, amygdale, and hippocampus) that direct this model and account for the patterns of cortical activation.

There are numerous functional changes that may occur associated with dysregulation of the functional cerebral systems proposed by this model. Changes in the autonomic nervous system such as cardiovascular function and skin conductance have been shown to be associated with activation of the frontal regions (Gläscher and Adolphs 2003; Wittling 1995). Likewise, changes in neuropsychological performance have been shown to be associated with different patterns of cortical arousal (Foster et al. 2005). The current model could serve to generate numerous testable hypotheses, based on these observations, which could advance both the model and associated areas of investigation. For example, investigating the various hypotheses related to sympathetic and parasympathetic contributions to cardiovascular functions in relation to anger or utilizing double-dissociation paradigms in neuropsychological assessment could provide valuable data regarding functional neural systems involved in the experience and expression of anger.

One of the important functional implications of this model is the manner in which therapeutic interventions for anger related disorders are treated within applied clinical psychology. Evidence regarding the effectiveness of traditional cognitive behavioral therapies in anger disorders has been equivocal (Andrews and Bonta 2003) and, in some cases, shown to have deleterious effects in terms of rehabilitation (Day and Howells 2002). It is possible that some of the difficulties in treating these disorders may be associated with competition within a functional cerebral system. Traditional cognitive-behavioral therapies have utilized therapeutic options that are heavily dependent on verbal processes, aimed at changing cognitive appraisals (Kassinove and Tafrate 2002). However, under the current model, cognitive appraisals follow perceptual processes carried out by the right posterior region, which is largely not concerned with verbal processes. Therefore, a therapeutic environment may be created which is very likely to fail, as environmental stimuli may trigger appraisal processes and make it less likely that the individual will be able to actively attend to the therapist's verbal instructions. Under the current model, therapeutic environments that are likely to reduce relative activation of the right posterior region (e.g. ambient lighting, musical tones, and positive verbal prosody) may reduce the perception of anger-provocation and the resulting appraisal processes. These contextual therapies may enable the therapist to reduce arousal of the functional cerebral system from the point of origin and make it more likely that attempts to address other elements in the system will be more successful.

Summary and Conclusions

The current review has attempted to briefly describe and integrate three very broad and distinct literatures as related to a solitary emotional construct and provide a conceptual model of how these literatures can advance our understanding of anger. While the above review is almost certain to have failed to provide an exhaustive evaluation of the literature, it is believed that the bulk of the studies that best represent the current knowledge of anger are thoroughly covered. In general, the literatures appear to demonstrate considerable potential for convergence, with only minimal distinctions inhibiting their integration. It is the goal of this review to initiate further discussion and research on how cognition and psychophysiological variables work together to produce the subjective experience and objective response to anger. The possible functional implications of this model may be of tremendous utility in the area of applied psychology as it may allow for a more complete conceptualization of anger and provide therapists a method of systematically addressing the clinical manifestations of anger. Further discourse on this topic is needed to examine potential methods to investigate the elements of the proposed model.

References

Adolphs R, Damasio H, Tranel D (1996) Cortical systems for the recognition of emotion in facial expressions. *J Neurosci* 16:7678–7687

Adolphs R, Tranel D, Hamann S, Young AW, Calder AJ, Phelps E, Anderson A, Lee AR, Damasio AR (1999) Recognition of facial emotion in nine individuals with bilateral amygdale damage. *Neuropsychologia* 37:1111–1117

Allred KD, Smith TW (1991) Social cognition in cynical hostility. *Cognit Ther Res* 15:399–412

American Psychiatric Association (1994) *The Diagnostic and statistic manual of mental disorders* (4th edn). APA Publishers, Washington DC

Andrews DA, Bonta J (2003) *Psychology of criminal conduct.* Anderson Press, Cincinnati, pp 277–299

Barrett LF, Wager TD (2006) The structure of emotion: Evidence from neuroimaging studies. *Curr Dir Psychol Sci* 15:70–83

Beauchaine D (2001) Vagal tone, development, and Gray's motivational theory: toward an integrated model of autonomic nervous system functioning in psychopathology. *Dev Psychopathol* 13:183–214

Beauregard M, Levesque J, Bourgouin P (2001) Neural correlates of conscious self-regulation of emotion. *J Neurosci* 21:165

Beck AT, Emery G, Greenberg RL (1996) Cognitive therapy for evaluation anxieties. In: Lindemann CG (eds) *Handbook of the treatment of the anxiety disorders.* Jason Aronson, Inc, Lanham, pp 26–54

Beck AT, Epstein N, Harrison R (1983) Cognitions, attitudes and personality dimensions in depression. *Br J Cognit Psychother* 1:1–16

Beck R, Fernandez E (1998) Cognitive-behavioral self-regulation of the frequency, duration, and intensity of anger. *J Psychopathol Behav Assess* 20:217–229

Berkowitz L (1993) *Aggression: its causes, consequences, and control.* McGraw-Hill, New York

Biaggio MK, Supplee K, Curtis N (1981) Reliability and validity of 4 anger scales. *Pers Assess* 45:639–648

Block GW, Nanson JL, Lowry NJ (1999) Attention, memory and language after pediatric ischemic stroke. *Child Neuropsychol* 5:81–91

Bolmont B, Thullier F, Abraini JH (2000) Relationships between mood states and performances in reaction time, psychomotor ability and mental efficiency during a 31-day gradual decompression in a hypobaric chamber from sea level to 8848 m equivalent altitude. *Physiol Behav* 71:469–476

Borod JC, Cicero BA, Obler LK (1998) Right hemisphere emotional perception: Evidence across multiple channels. *Neuropsychology* 12:446–458

Borod JC, Koff E, White B (1983) Facial asymmetry in posed and spontaneous expressions of emotion. *Brain Cogn* 2:165–175

Buck R (1977) Nonverbal communication of affect in preschool children: relationships with personality and skin conductance. *J Pers Soc Psychol* 35:225–236

Buss AH (1961) *The psychology of aggression.* Wiley, Oxford

Carver CS, White TL (1994) Behavioral inhibition, behavioral activation, and affective responses to impending reward and punishment: The BIS/BAS Scales. *J Pers Soc Psychol* 67:279–301

Christie IC, Friedman BH (2003) Autonomic specificity of discrete emotion and dimensions of affective space: A multivariate approach. *Int J Psychophysiol* 51:143–153

Cole HW, Ray WJ (1985) EEG correlates of emotional tasks related to attentional demands. *Int J Psychophysiol* 3:33–41

Cook WW, Medley DM (1954) Proposed hostility and Pharisaic-virtue scales for the MMPI. *J Appl Psychol* 38:414–418

Critchley HD, Elliot R, Mathias CJ, Dolan RJ (2000) Neural activity relating to the generation and representation of galvanic skin conductance responses: a functional magnetic resonance imaging study. *J Neurosci* 20:3033–3040

Damasio AR (1989) Time-locked multiregional retroactivation: A systems-level proposal for the neural substrates of recall and recognition. *Cognition* 33:25–62

Damasio H, Damasio AR (2000) Emotion, decision making and the orbitofrontal cortex. *Cereb Cortex* 10:295–307

Davidson RJ (2000) Affective style, psychopathology, and resilience: brain mechanisms and plasticity. *Am Psychol* 55:1196–1214

Davidson RJ (1998) Affective style and affective disorders: Perspectives from affective neuroscience. *Cogn Emot* 12:307–330

Davidson RJ (1995) Cerebral asymmetry, emotion, and affective style. In: Davidson RJ, Hugdahl K (eds) *Brain asymmetry.* The MIT Press, Cambridge, pp 127–143

Davidson RJ (1994) Asymmetric brain function, affective style, and psychopathology: the role of early experience and plasticity. *Dev Psychopathol* 6:741–758

Davidson RJ (1993) Cerebral asymmetry and emotion: conceptual and methodological conundrums. *Cogn Emot* 7:115–138

Davidson RJ (1992) Anterior cerebral asymmetry and the nature of emotion. *Brain Cogn* 20:125–151

Davidson RJ, Abercrombie H, Nitschke JB, Putnam K (1999) Regional brain function, emotion and disorders of emotion. *Curr Opin Neurobiol* 9:228–234

Davidson RJ, Ekman P, Saron CD, Senulis A, Friesen BR (1990) Approach/withdrawal and cerebral asymmetry: emotional expression and brain physiology. *J Pers Soc Psychol* 58:330–341

Davidson RJ, Fox NA (1982) Asymmetrical brain activity discriminates between positive and negative affective stimuli in human infants. *Science* 218:235–1237

Davidson RJ, Schwartz GE (1977) Brain mechanisms subserving self-generated imagery: electrophysiological specificity and patterning. *Psychophysiology* 14:598–602

Day A, Howells K (2002) Psychological treatments for rehabilitating offenders: evidence-based practice comes of age. *Aust Psychol* 37:39–47

Deffenbacher JL (1994) Anger reduction: issues, assessment, and intervention strategies. In: Siegman AW, Smith TW (eds) *Anger, hostility, and the heart.* Erlbaum, Hillsdale, pp 319–337

Deffenbacher JL, Oetting ER, Huff ME (1996) Evaluation of two cognitive-behavioral approaches to general anger reduction. *Cogn Ther Res* 20:551–573

Deffenbacher JL, Petrilli RT, Lynch RS, Oetting PD, Swain C (2003) The Driver's angry thoughts questionnaire: a measure of angry cognitions when driving. *Cognit Ther Res* 27:383–402

Demaree HA (2000) Analysis of quantitative electroencephalographic and cardiovascular responses to stress among low- and high-hostiles. *Diss Abstr Int B Sci Eng* 61(1-B):526

Demaree HA, Everhart ED, Youngstrom EA, Harrison DW (2005) Brain lateralization of emotional processing: historical roots and a future incorporating 'dominance'. *Behav Cogn Neurosci Rev* 4:3–20

Demaree HA, Harrison DW (1997) Physiological and neuropsychological correlates of hostility. *Neuropsychologia* 35:1405–1411

Demaree HA, Higgins DA, Williamson J, Harrison DW (2002) Asymmetry in hand grip strength and fatigue in low- and high-hostile men. *Int J Neurosci* 112:415–428

Demaree HA, Robinson JL, Everhart DE, Schmeichel BJ (2004) Resting RSA is associated with natural and self-regulated responses to negative emotional stimuli. *Brain Cogn* 56:14–23

Eckhardt CI, Barbour KA, Stuart GL (1997) Anger and hostility in martially violent men: conceptual distinctions, measurement issues, and literature review. *Clin Psychol Rev* 17:333–358

Eckhardt CI, Deffenbacher J (1995) Diagnosis of anger disorders. In: Kassinove H (eds) *Anger disorders: definition, diagnosis and treatment.* Taylor & Francis, Washington DC

Eckhardt CI, Kassinove H (1998) Articulated cognitive distortions and cognitive deficiencies in maritally violent men. *J Cognit Psychother* 12:231–250

Eckhardt CI, Norlander B, Deffenbacher J (2004) The assessment of anger and hostility: a critical review. *Aggress Violent Behav* 9:17–43

Ehrlichman H, Barrett J (1983) Right hemispheric specialization for mental imagery: a review of the evidence. *Brain Cogn* 2:55–76

Ekman P, Davidson RJ (1993) Voluntary smiling changes regional brain activity. *Psychol Sci* 4:342–345

Ekman PJ, Davidson RJ, Friesen WV (1990) The Duchenne smile: emotional expression and brain physiology. *J Pers Soc Psychol* 58:342–353

Ekman P, Friesen WV (1971) Constants across cultures in the face and emotion. *J Pers Soc Psychol* 17:124–129

Ekman PJ, Levenson RW, Friesen WV (1983) Autonomic nervous system activity distinguishes among emotions. *Science* 221:1208–1210

Everhart DE, Demaree H, Harrison DW (2005) The Merging of cognitive and affective neuroscience: studies of the affective auditory verbal learning test. In: Clark AV (ed) *Causes, role and influence of mood states.* Nova Biomedical Books, Hauppauge

Everhart DE, Harrison DW (1995) Hostility following right CVA: support for right orbital frontal deactivation and right temporal activation. *J Neurother* 1:55–59

Everhart DE, Harrison DW (2000) Facial affect perception in anxious and nonanxious men. *Psychobiology* 28:90–98

Everhart DE, Harrison DW, Shenal BV, Williamson J, Wuensch KL (2002) Grip-strength, fatigue, and motor perseveration in anxious men without depression. *Neuropsychiatry Neuropsychol Behav Neurol* 15:133–142

Fava M, Anderson K, Rosenbaum JF (1990) Anger attacks: possible variants of panic and major depressive disorder. *Am J Psychiatry* 147:867–870

Fernandez E, Beck AT (2001) Cognitive-behavioral self-intervention versus self-monitoring of anger: effects on anger frequency, duration and intensity. *Behav Cogn Psychother* 29:345–356

Foster PS, Harrison DW (2002) The relationship between magnitude of cerebral activation and intensity of emotional arousal. *Int J Neurosci* 112:1463–1477

Foster PS, Williamson JB, Harrison DW (2005) The Ruff Figural Fluency Test: heightened right frontal lobe delta activity as a function of performance. *Arch Clin Neuropsychol* 20:427–434

Fowles DC (1998) Biological variables in psychopathology: a biological perspective. In: Sutker PB, Adams HE (eds) *Comprehensive book of psychopathology,* 2nd edn. Plenum Press, New York, pp 157–182

Frijda NH (1986) Passions: Emotion and socially consequential behavior. In: Kavanaugh RD, Zimmerberg B, Fein S (eds) *Emotion: interdisciplinary perspectives.* Lawrence Erlbaum Associates, Inc, Hillsdale

Frijda NH (2005) Emotion experience. *Cogn Emot* 19:473–497

Gläscher J, Adolphs R (2003) Processing of the arousal of subliminal and supraliminal emotional stimuli by the human amygdala. *J Neurosci* 23:10274–10282

Graham S, Hoehn S (1995) Children's understanding of aggression and withdrawal as social stigmas: an attributional analysis. *Child Dev* 66:1143–1161

Gray JA (1982) *The neuropsychology of anxiety: an enquiry into the functions of the septo-hippocampal system.* Clarendon Press/Oxford University Press, New York

Gray JA (1990) Brain systems that mediate both emotion and cognition. *Cogn Emot* 4:69–288

Hagemann D, Naumann E, Thayer JF (2001) The quest for the EEG reference revisited: a glance from brain asymmetry research. *Psychophysiology* 38:847–857

Hare RD (1999) Psychopathy as a risk factor for violence. *Psychiatr Q* 70:181–197

Harmon-Jones E (2003) Clarifying the emotive functions of asymmetrical frontal cortical activity. *Psychophysiology* 40:838–848

Harmon-Jones E, Allen JHB (1998) Anger and frontal brain activity: EEG asymmetry consistent with approach motivation despite negative affective valence. *J Pers Soc Psychol* 74:1310–1316

Harmon-Jones E, Sigelman JD, Bohlig A, Harmon-Jones C (2003) Anger, coping, and frontal cortical activity: the effect of coping potential on anger-induced left frontal activity. *Cogn Emot* 17:1–24

Harmon-Jones E, Vaughn-Scott K, Mohr S, Sigelman J, Harmon-Jones C (2004) The effect of manipulated sympathy and anger on left and right frontal cortical activity. *Emotion* 4:95–101

Harrison DW, Gorelczenko PM (1990) Functional asymmetry for facial affect perception in high and low hostile men and women. *Int J Neurosci* 55:89–97

Heilman K (1997) The neurobiology of emotional experience. *J Neuropsychiatry Clin Neurosci* 9:439–448

Heilman KM (2000) Emotional experience: a neurological model. In: Lane RD, Nadel L (eds) *Cognitive neuroscience of emotion.* Oxford University Press, New York

Heilman KM, Bowers D (1990) Neuropsychological studies of emotional changes induced by right and left hemispheric lesions. In: Stein NL, Nancy B. Leventhal, Trabasso T (eds) *Psychological and biological approaches to emotion.* Lawrence Erlbaum Associates, Inc, Hillsdale

Heller W (1993) Neuropsychological mechanisms of individual differences in emotion, personality, and arousal. *Neuropsychology* 7:476–489

Heller W, Nitschke JB (1997) Regional brain activity in emotion: A framework for understanding cognition in depression. *Cogn Emot* 11:637–661

Heller W, Nitschke JB, Miller GA (1998) Lateralization in emotion and emotional disorders. *Curr Dir Psychol Sci* 7:26–32

Hellige JB, Cox PJ, Litvac L (1979) Information processing in the cerebral hemispheres: Selective hemispheric activation and capacity limitations. *J Exp Psychol Gen* 10:251–279

Henriques JB, Davidson RJ (1991) Left frontal hypoactivation in depression. *J Abnorm Psychol* 100:535–545

Herridge ML, Harrison DW, Mollet GA, Shenal B (2004) Hostility and facial affect recognition: Effects of a cold pressor stressor on accuracy and cardiovascular reactivity. *Brain Cogn* 55:564–571

Hewig J, Hagemann D, Seifert J, Naumann E, Batussek B (2004) On the selective relation of frontal cortical asymmetry and anger-out versus anger-control. *J Pers Soc Psychol* 87:926–939

Hollon SD, Kendall PC (1980) Cognitive self-statements in depression: development of an automatic thoughts questionnaire. *Cognit Ther Res* 4:383–395

Izard CE (1993) Organizational and motivational functions of discrete emotions. In: Lewis M, Haviland JM (eds) *Handbook of emotions.* Guilford Press, New York

Jones J, Trower P (2004) Irrational and evaluative beliefs in individuals with anger disorders. *J Ration Emot Cogn Behav Ther* 22:153–169

Kandel ER, Schwartz JH, Jessell TM (2000) *Principles of neural science* (4th ed). McGraw-Hill Publishers, New York

Kassinove H, Suckhodolsky DG (1995) Anger disorders: basic science and practice issues. *Issues Compr Pediatr Nurs* 18:173–205

Kassinove H, Tafrate RC (2002) *Anger management: The complete treatment guidebook.* Impact Publishers, Atascadero

Kestenbaum R, Nelson CA (1992) Neural and behavioral correlates of emotion recognition in children and adults. *J Exp Child Psychol* 54:1–18

Kettunen J, Ravaja N, Keltikangas-Jarvinen L, Näätänen P (2000) The relationship of respiratory sinus arrhythmia to the co-activation of autonomic and facial responses during the Rorschach test. *Psychophysiology* 37:242–250

Killgore WD, Yurgelun-Todd DA (2001) Sex differences in amygdala activation during the perception of facial affect. *Neuroreport* 12:2543–2547

Kimbrell TA, George M, Parekh PI (1999) Regional brain activity during transient self-induced anxiety and anger in healthy adults. *Biol Psychiatry* 46:454–465

Kinsbourne M (1978) *Asymmetrical function of the brain.* Cambridge University Press, Oxford

Kinsbourne M (1985) Deviant development of lateralization and cerebral function. *Psychiatr Ann* 15:439–444

Kunst-Wilson WR, Zajonc RB (1981) Affective discrimination of stimuli that cannot be recognized. *Science* 207:557–558

Lane RD, Fink GR, Chau PM (1997) Neural activation during selective attention to subjective emotional responses. *Neuroreport* 8:3969–3972

Lang PJ (1994) The varieties of emotional experience: A meditation on James-Lange theory. *Psychol Rev* 101:211–221

Lazarus RS (1982) Thoughts on the relations between emotion and cognition. *Am Psychol* 37:1019–1024

Lazarus RS (1984) On the primacy of cognition. *Am Psychol* 39:124–129

Lazarus RS (1991) *Emotion and adaptation.* Oxford, New York

Lazarus RS, Smith CA (1988) Knowledge and appraisal in the cognition-emotion relationship. *Cogn Emot* 2:281–300

LeDoux JD (1994) Cognitive-emotional interactions in the brain. In: Eckman P, Davidson RJ (eds) *The nature of emotion.* Oxford University Press, New York

Lemerise EA, Arsenio WF (2000) An integrated model of emotion processes and cognition in social information processing. *Child Dev* 71:107–118

Levenson RW (1988) Emotion and the autonomic nervous system: a prospectus for research on autonomic specificity. In: Wagner HL (eds) *Social psychophysiology and emotion: theory and clinical applications.* Wiley, Oxford

Lezak MD (1983) *Neuropsychological assessment,* 2nd edn. Oxford University Press, New York

Loeber R, Coie J (2001) Continuities and discontinuities of development, with particular emphasis on emotional and cognitive components of disruptive behaviour. In: Hill J, Maughan B (eds) *Conduct disorders in childhood and adolescence.* Oxford University Press, New York

Luria AR (1973) The frontal lobes and the regulation of behavior. In: Pribram KH, Luria AR (eds) *Psychophysiology of the frontal lobes.* Academic Press, Oxford

Maitlin MW (1998) *Cognition.* 4th edn. Harcourt Brace, NY

Martin R, Wan C, David JP, Wegner E, Olson BD, Watson D (2000) Style of anger expression: relation to expressivity, personality, and health. *Pers Soc Psychol Bull* 25:1196–1207

Mauss IB, Levenson RW, McCarter L, Wilhelm FH, Gross JJ (2005) The tie that binds? Coherence among emotion experience, behavior, and physiology. *Emotion* 5:175–190

Max JE (2004) Effect of side of lesion on neuropsychological performance in childhood stroke. *J Int Neuropsychol Soc* 10:698–708

Maxwell JS, Shackman AJ, Davidson RJ (2005) Unattended facial expressions asymmetrically bias the concurrent processing of nonemotional information. *J Cogn Neurosci* 17:1386–1395

McKeever WF, Dixon MS (1981) Right-hemisphere superiority for discriminating memorized from nonmemorized faces: Affective imagery, sex, and perceived emotionality effects. *Brain Lang* 12:246–260

McNaughton N, Gray JA (2000) Anxiolytic action on the behavioural inhibition system implies multiple types of arousal contribute to anxiety. *J Affect Disord* 61:161–176

Miller TQ, Smith TW, Turner CW, Guijarro ML, Hallet AJ (1996) A meta-analytic review of research on hostility and physical health. *Psychol Bull* 119:322–348

Mills CK (1912) Preliminary note on a new symptom complex due to lesion of the cerebellum and cerebello-rubro-thalamic system, etc. *J Nerv Ment Dis* 39:73–76

Mollet GA (2004) Hostility and negative emotion induction: implications for verbal learning and cardiovascular regulation. Unpublished Master's Thesis. Virginia Polytechnic Institute and State University, Blacksburg, VA

Mollet G (2006) Emotion and pain: a functional cerebral systems integration. Unpublished Doctoral Dissertation. Virginia Polytechnic Institute and State University, Blacksburg, VA

Murphy FC, Nimmo-Smith I, Lawrence AD (2003) Functional neuroanatomy of emotions: a meta-analysis. *Cogn Affect Behav Neurosci* 3:207–233

Narumoto J, Okada T, Sadato N, Fukui K, Yonekura Y (2001) Attention to emotion modulates fMRI activity in human right superior temporal sulcus. *Cogn Brain Res* 12:225–231

Pakaslahti L (2000) Children's and adolescents' aggressive behavior in context: The development and application of aggressive problem-solving strategies. *Aggress Violent Behav* 5:467–490

Phan KL, Wager TD, Taylor SF, Liberzon I (2004) Functional imaging studies of human emotions. *CNS Spectr* 9:258–266

Porges SW (1991) Vagal mediation of respiratory sinus arrhythmia: Implications for drug delivery. In: Hrushesky WJ, Langer R, Theeuwes F (eds) *Temporal control of drug delivery*. New York Academy of Sciences, New York

Rao SM (2000) Neuropsychological evaluation. In: Fogel BS, Schiffer RB, Rao SM (eds) *Synopsis of neuropsychiatry*. Lippincott, Williams & Wilkins Publishers, Philadelphia

Reuter-Lorenz PA, Givis RP, Moscovitch M (1983) Hemispheric specialization and the perception of emotion: Evidence from right-handers and from inverted and noninverted left-handers. *Neuropsychologia* 21:687–692

Robinson RG, Downhill JE (1995) Lateralization of psychopathology in response to focal brain injury. In: Davidson RJ, Hugdahl K (eds) *Brain asymmetry*. The MIT Press, Cambridge, MA

Robinson RG, Manes F (2000) Elation, mania, and mood disorders: evidence from neurological disease. In: Borod JC (ed) *The neuropsychology of emotion.* Oxford University Press, New York

Roseman IJ (1991) Appraisal determinants of discrete emotions. *Cogn Emot* 5:161–200

Ross P (2000) Electrophysiology of working memory: Task modality and load effects. *Diss Abstr Int B Sci Eng* 61:3319

Ruff RM, Light RH, Evans RW (1987) The Ruff Figural Fluency Test: a normative study with adults. *Dev Neuropsychol* 3:37–51

Schachter S, Singer J (1962) Cognitive, social, and physiological determinants of emotional state. *Psychol Rev* 69:379–399

Scherer KR, Ellsworth PC, Forgas JP (2003) Part V: Cognitive components of emotion. In: Davidson RJ, Scherer KR, Goldsmith HH (eds) *Handbook of affective sciences.* Oxford University Press, New York

Schutter DJG, deHaan EHV, van Honk J (2004) Functionally dissociated aspects in anterior and posterior electrocortical processing of facial threat. *Int J Psychophysiol* 53:29–36

Schwartz GE, Davidson RJ, Maer F (1975) Right hemisphere lateralization for emotion in the human brain: interactions with cognition. *Science* 190:286–288

Siegel JM (1985) Anger and cardiovascular risk in adolescents. *Health Psychol* 3:293–313

Siegman AW, Snow SC (1997) The outward expression of anger, the inward experience of anger and CVR: the role of vocal expression. *J Behav Med* 20:29–45

Smith TW (1994) Concepts and methods in the study of anger, hostility and health. In: Siegman AW, Smith TW (eds) *Anger, hostility and the heart.* Erlbaum, Hillsdale

Smith TW, Galzer K, Ruiz JM, Gallo LC (2004) Hostility, anger, and aggressiveness and coronary heart disease: an interpersonal perspective on emotion and health. *J Pers* 72:1217–1270

Smith TW, Pope MK (1990) Cynical hostility as a health risk: current status and future directions. *J Soc Behav Pers* 5:77–88

Snyder CR, Crowson JJ, Houston BK, Kurylo M, Poirier J (1997) Assessing hostile automatic thoughts: development and validation of the HAT Scale. *Cognit Ther Res* 21:477–492

Snyder KA, Harrison DW (1997) The affective auditory verbal learning test. *Arch Clin Neuropsychol* 12:477–482

Spielberger CD, Johnson EH, Russell SF, Crane RS, Jacobs G, Worden TJ (1983) Assessment of anger: the state-trait scale. In: Butcher JN, Spielberger CD (eds) *Advances in personality assessment,* 2. Erlbaum, Hillside

Spielberger CD, Reheiser EC, Sydeman SJ (1995) Measuring the experience, expression, and control of anger. *Issues Compr Pediatr Nurs* 18:207–232

Stuss DT (1992) Biological and psychological development of executive functions. *Brain Cogn* 20:8–23

Suberi M, McKeever WF (1977) Differential right hemispheric memory storage of emotional and non-emotional faces. *Neuropsychologia* 15:757–768

Suls J, Bunde J (2005) Anger, anxiety, and depression as risk factors for cardiovascular disease: the problems and implications of overlapping affective dispositions. *Psychol Bull* 131:260–300

Tabert M, Borod JC, Tang CY, Lange G, Wei T, Johnson R, Nusbaum A, Bushbaum M (2001) Differential amygdala activation during emotional decision and recognition memory tasks using unpleasant words: an fMRI study. *Neuropsychologia* 39:556–573

Thayer JF, Friedman BH, Borkovec TD (1996) Autonomic characteristics of generalized anxiety disorder and worry. *Biol Psychiatry* 39:255–266

Thayer JF, Lane BH (2000) Phasic heart period reactions to cued threat and nonthreat stimuli in generalized anxiety disorder. *Psychophysiology* 37:361–368

Tomarken AJ, Davidson RJ, Henriques JB (1990) Resting frontal brain asymmetry predicts affective responses to films. *J Pers Soc Psychol* 59:791–801

Tomarken AJ, Davidson RJ, Wheeler RE, Doss E (1992) Psychometric properties of resting anterior EEG asymmetry: temporal stability and internal consistency. *Psychophysiology* 29:576–592

Tucker DM (1981) Lateral brain function, emotion, and conceptualization. *Psychol Bull* 89:19–46

Tucker DM, Dawson SL (1984) Asymmetric EEG changes as method actors generated emotions. *Biol Psychol* 19:63–75

Tucker DM, Williamson PA (1984) Asymmetric neural control systems in human self-regulation. *Psychol Rev* 91:185–215

Vanderploeg RD, Brown WS, Marsh JT (1987) Judgments of emotion in words and faces: ERP correlates. *Int J Psychophysiol* 5:193–205

Vigne JJ, Dale JA, Klions HL (1988) Facial electromyogram and heart-rate correlates of a paradoxical attitude change to antinuclear war information. *Percept Mot Skills* 67:755–762

Wacker J, Heldmann M, Stemmler G (2003) Separating emotion and motivational direction in fear and anger: Effects on frontal asymmetry. *Emotion* 3:167–193

Wager TD, Barrett LF, Bliss-Moreau E, Lindquist K, Duncan S, Kober H, Joseph J, Davidson M, Mize J (2007) The neuroimaging of emotion. In: Lewis M (ed) *Handbook of Emotion* (3rd edn). Guilford Press, New York (in Press)

Wager TD, Phan KL, Liberzon I, Taylor SF (2003) Valence, gender, and lateralization of functional brain anatomy in emotion: a meta-analysis of findings from neuroimaging. *Neuroimage* 19:513–531

Waldstein SR, Kop WJ, Schmidt LA, Haufler AJ, Krantz DS, Fox NA (2000) Frontal electrocortical and cardiovascular reactivity during happiness and anger. *Biol Psychol* 55:3–23

Weiner B (1995) Inferences of responsibility and social motivation. In: Zanna MP (ed) *Advances in experimental social psychology*. Academic Press, San Diego

Williams TM, Zabrack ML, Joy LA (1982) The portrayal of aggression on North American television. *J Appl Soc Psychol* 1:360–380

Wingrove J, Bond AJ (2005) Correlates between trait hostility and faster reading times for sentences describing angry reactions to ambiguous situations. *Cogn Emot* 19:463–472

Wittling W (1995) Brain asymmetry in the control of autonomic-physiologic activity. In: Davidson RJ, Hugdahl K (eds) *Brain asymmetry*. The MIT Press, Cambridge

Zajonc RB (1980) Feeling and thinking: preferences need no inferences. *Am Psychol* 35:151–175

Zajonc RB (1984) On the primacy of affect. *Am Psychol* 29:117–123

Discussion Questions for Article 1

Section 8: Motivation and Emotion

Name: _____

PID: _____

Date: __ __ / __ __ / __ __ (MM/DD/YY)

CRN: _____

Recitation Day/Time: _____

Honor Code Signature: _____

1. What is hostility and how does it relate to anger?

2. Describe the right hemisphere model of anger. Why is it or is it not a valid model?

3. In the functional systems model, what tasks are generally regulated by the right frontal lobe?

4. How can anger impact the processing of visual and auditory information?

Article 2

Where Emotions Come From

Joy and disgust. Sorrow and shame. Science is plumbing the passions that make us human.

Erica E. Goode
Joannie M. Schrof
Sarah Burke

"We humans are full of unpredictable emotions that logic cannot solve."

—*Capt. James Kirk,* Star Trek

Pop singer Morris Albert crooned about them. Wives complained that their husbands wouldn't discuss them. And by the 1970s, an entire generation of Americans had learned to "get in touch" with their feelings. Scientists, however, were preoccupied with thinking, not emotion. Rational thought, after all, was the faculty deemed by the English philosopher Francis Bacon "the last creature of God." Leagues of researchers devoted their attention to how people solved problems, made decisions, formed opinions and learned skills. Fear and joy, anger and disgust were seen as peripheral, of interest mostly when they interfered with thought or became deviant or extreme, as in mental illness.

It was, in the words of psychologist Silvan Tomkins, an "overly imperialistic cognitive theory." Tomkins, who died last week at age 80, published two thick volumes in the early 1960s arguing that emotions were a crucial component of evolutionary design, even more important than basic drives such as hunger and sex. Anxiety, he pointed out, could drive a man from the bedroom. Fear could pre-empt appetite. Despair could lead to a fatal flirtation with a razor blade.

Tomkins was a lone voice, and he was almost entirely ignored by mainstream psychology. Yet there was a very small core of scientists who took his work seriously, and, building upon it, began to pioneer a new field of emotion research. Today, in disciplines ranging from psychology to neuroscience, from semiotics to genetics and anthropology, emotions have moved center stage. What was once a trickle of journal articles has become a publishing torrent. Researchers have developed methods for mapping the face and measuring emotional responses. They are studying the development of emotions in infants. Their work meshes with the efforts of biologists and neuroscientists who, using increasingly sophisticated technologies, were beginning to trace the "pathways" of emotion in the brain. Cognitive scientists, too, are talking about "hot" cognition, realizing that emotions and moods influence memory, judgment and learning.

It is not that there are, as yet, any solid answers. Even the most elemental question posed by turn-of-the-century psychologist William James—"What is an emotion?"—remains controversial. But researchers are beginning to untangle the first threads of an enormously complex tapestry, finding clues not only to normal emotions but also to how feelings go awry, fear turning to phobia, sadness to debilitating depression.

In the process, they are rejecting the notion of man as simply a "thinking machine," seeing human beings instead as biological organisms whose survival depends upon constant interaction with the environment. In this interplay, evolved over countless centuries and through dozens of steps on the evolutionary ladder, emotions have a critical role. Far from being "trivial," they contain, as one expert put it, "the wisdom of the ages"—warning us of danger, guiding us toward what is good and satisfying, signaling our intentions and our reactions to others. Emotions are the most familiar—and the most intimate aspect of human experience, and they are gradually yielding their secrets.

Brain researchers, like other scientists, have spent much of the 20th century engrossed in the study of thinking and memory. But earlier investigators took some first steps toward tracing the biological underpinnings of emotion. In the late 1800s, for example, physiologists discovered that surgically removing a dog's cerebral cortex—the brain's thin outer layer of gray matter—did not prevent it from displaying primitive rage responses. By the late 1950s, researchers were identifying specific brain regions that seemed to play a central role in emotion. But only in the last few years have high-tech brain scanners, new methods of staining cells, powerful computers and other developments allowed scientists to begin systematically mapping the highways and traffic patterns of the emotional brain.

Neural Pathways

While earlier investigators probed the emotional roles played by specific brain regions, scientists now put more emphasis upon the complex circuitry that interconnects them. Until recently, the limbic system, a loose network of brain structures beneath the cortex, was thought to do the majority of the work in coding "emotional" information and orchestrating the body's responses. But studies are now linking more and more areas of the brain—both the cortex and in subcortical regions—to the complex mix of perceptions, sensations and judgments we call emotion.

At the same time, brain centers once viewed as intimately involved in emotions are now known to be more marginal. The sea horse-shaped hippocampus, for example, one of several limbic regions, appears more involved in memory and other cognitive tasks than in emotion, as previously believed. Much more critical, scientists are finding, is a tiny almond called the amygdala, buried deep in the temporal lobe (see diagram).

Indeed, the fingernail-size amygdala, which communicates with many other brain areas, is increasingly being viewed as a kind of "Emotion Central." As far back as 1937, studies showed that damage to the amygdala region produced changes in emotional behavior in monkeys: They became tame and oblivious to normally frightening situations, copulated with other monkeys of the same sex and ate nearly anything they were offered. Recent work has refined this understanding—showing, for example, that amygdala nerve cells fire selectively in response to emotionally laden stimuli, and that some of these neurons are more sensitive to unfamiliar stimuli.

Quick and Dirty

According to New York University neuroscientist Joseph LeDoux, the amygdala may make the first, crude judgment of an event's emotional significance. Consider a man walking through a forest who hears what sounds like a rifle shot at close range. Scientists previously believed that sensory information traveled first to the cerebral cortex, where the sound was consciously perceived. The cortex then sent signals to subcortical areas of the brain like the amygdala, which evaluated the sound's emotional importance. These "lower" regions then sent return messages back up to the cortex and fired up the autonomic nervous system, producing the pounding heart, rapid breathing and rising blood pressure that are the familiar accompaniments of fear.

But LeDoux's research indicates that, at least for primitive emotions like fear, the brain is constructed to respond even more quickly to potentially threatening events. He and his colleagues have identified in animals an additional nerve pathway carrying impulses directly between the thalamus—an early processing station for sensory

FALSE OR GENUINE?

Anatomy of a smile

Not all smiles are the same. Psychologist Paul Ekman describes 18 different types, including the miserable smile, the false "cocktail party" smile and the smile of relief, each marked by different movements of the facial muscles. Most striking is the disparity between the "social" smile and the smile of true enjoyment, called the "Duchenne smile" after French anatomist Duchenne de Boulogne, who first described it in 1862. Smiles of real joy draw in the *Orbicularis oculi* muscle around the eyes, as well as the *Zygomaticus major* cheek muscle (see below). But when people put on a phony expression of pleasure, they smile only with their cheeks, not their eyes. Ten-month-old infants, experts find, are more apt to display a Duchenne smile when their mother approaches, while the approach of strangers often elicits "false" smiles.

ORBICULARIS OCULI MUSCLE. This muscle "does not obey the will," wrote Duchenne de Boulogne, but "is put in play only by the sweet emotions of the soul . . ."

ZYGOMATICUS MAJOR MUSCLE. Faked smiles exercise voluntary cheek muscles; eye muscles remain unsmiling.

GRIMACE & GRIN

Faces of emotion

ANXIETY. When people are anxious, cerebral blood flow—a measure of brain cell activity—increases in an area at the tips of the brain's temporal lobes just behind the eyes, according to brain scanning studies by University of Arizona psychiatrist Eric Reiman.

DISGUST. Would you stir your coffee with a new comb? Eat a sterilized cockroach? Most Americans wouldn't, though both are perfectly safe. Psychologist Paul Rozin argues that the things we find disgusting often evoke primitive beliefs about contamination.

HAPPINESS. Moments of intense happiness are not necessarily the key to an overall sense of well-being, says psychologist Ed Diener. Long-term happiness, his studies suggest, depends more on the frequency than the vividness of happy experiences.

EMBARRASSMENT. Darwin believed blushing was like the appendix, a fluke with no purpose. But Wake Forest University psychologist Mark Leary finds that turning red may serve to repair people's social image after they have appeared stupid or incompetent.

FIGURE 1

input—and the amygdala. Information sent along this "shortcut" reaches the amygdala two to three times faster than that sent up to the cortex first. Studies also demonstrate that even when the "longer" route through the cortex is destroyed, animals still are able to learn fear of sudden noises, or, in very recent work, flashing lights.

Such high-speed transmission, LeDoux contends, may allow the amygdala to make an almost instantaneous analysis of whether the sound is something to be afraid of, probably even before it is consciously heard or identified. This "quick and dirty" assessment, he speculates, is then elaborated and refined by the neocortex and other brain regions, allowing the hunter to conclude, for example, that the sound was the crack of a tree branch, not a rifle.

LeDoux's findings support the view that at least some emotional processes take place unconsciously, and that cognition and emotion—though they interact—are separate systems in the brain—both points that have been vigorously debated for decades. In addition, the studies imply that the brain is designed, quite sensibly from an evolutionary standpoint, to react more to some things—loudness, for instance, or abrupt movement—than to others.

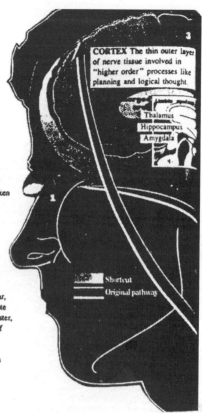

BRAIN CIRCUITS

An emotional "shortcut"

The brain appears "programmed" to size up the emotional importance of certain stimuli, such as a flash of light, much more quickly than scientists once thought. Researchers previously knew that information taken in by the senses (1) travels to the thalamus (2), an early sensory processing station, then to the cortex (3), where it is consciously taken in and relayed to subcortical areas of the brain such as the amygdala (4). These interior regions then send messages back to the cortex, and also set in motion physiological responses (5). But neuroscientist Joseph LeDoux has found an additional and more direct pathway between thalamus and amygdala that bypasses the cortex completely. In primitive emotions like fear, nerve impulses transmitted along this route reach the amygdala two to three times faster, allowing a "quick and dirty" judgment of whether the stimulus is something to be afraid of—probably even before it is consciously perceived. This assessment is then elaborated by thinking and memory.

MATT ZANG—*USN&WR*

FIGURE 2

No Fear of Mushrooms

The idea that human beings are "programmed" to be wary of particular events may help explain why some people develop irrational fears of spiders, snakes, heights or close spaces, but never of electrical outlets or daffodils. Northwestern University psychologist Susan Mineka and her coworkers have found that monkeys quickly acquire an exaggerated fear of snakes—even toy reptiles that don't move—when they watch videotapes of other monkeys reacting fearfully. But if the same monkeys watch concocted videos of monkey role models jumping in fright at mushrooms or flowers, they remain unswayed.

Twenty years ago, much was made of reports that the brain's left and right hemispheres seemed to "specialize" in different types of thinking, though media accounts of this "right brain/left brain" division were often greatly oversimplified. Now a growing body of work suggests that the two sides of the brain may play distinct emotional roles, perhaps because such a division of labor is more efficient. Neurologists have known for many years that stroke patients whose right hemispheres have been

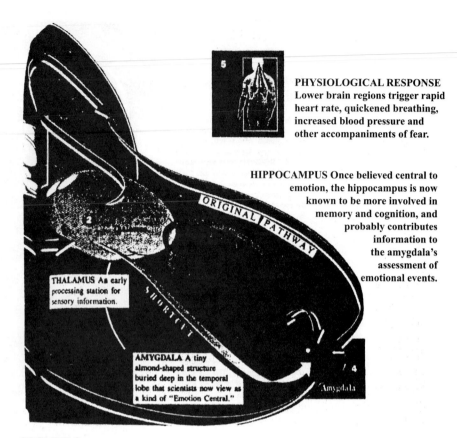

PHYSIOLOGICAL RESPONSE
Lower brain regions trigger rapid
heart rate, quickened breathing,
increased blood pressure and
other accompaniments of fear.

HIPPOCAMPUS Once believed central to
emotion, the hippocampus is now
known to be more involved in
memory and cognition, and
probably contributes
information to
the amygdala's
assessment of
emotional events.

ORIGINAL PATHWAY

SHORTCUT

THALAMUS As early
processing station for
sensory information.

AMYGDALA A tiny
almond-shaped structure
buried deep in the temporal
lobe that scientists now view as
a kind of "Emotion Central."

Amygdala

FIGURE 3

damaged have trouble both expressing emotion and perceiving the emotional signals of others. They will understand the statement, "I am angry," for example, but
fail to detect the speaker's injured tone or the angry expression on his face.

University of Florida neurologist Kenneth Heilman suggests that the right hemisphere may contain a kind of "lexicon" of emotion-laden images, which is impaired
when the hemisphere is injured. In a series of studies, Heilman and his colleagues
found that patients with right hemisphere damage had great difficulty imagining
and describing a smiling face, though they could easily describe imagined objects
such as pennies or horses. Yet such patients do retain some ability to grasp emotional concepts, the scientists have found, perhaps relying upon a combination of
logical reasoning and past experience. Told that a man "drank the water and then
saw the sign," for example, they can usually figure out that the man is anxious
about what he just drank.

The brain's right and left hemispheres may divide negative and positive emotions as well. When subjects report feeling emotions such as fear and disgust,
their right frontal lobes show increased electrical activity, according to studies by

psychologists Richard Davidson at the University of Wisconsin and Donald Tucker at the University of Oregon. Sadness seems to diminish activity in the left frontal lobe as measured by an electroencephalogram (EEG), while certain positive emotions like happiness and amusement increase it.

Right and left brain asymmetries may even prove to be a marker of differences in overall temperament. In a series of studies, Davidson and his colleagues have found that infants more prone to distress when separated from their mothers show increased activity in the right frontal lobe, as do people with a more pessimistic outlook. People who have at some point in their lives been clinically depressed show decreased left frontal-lobe activity compared with subjects who have never been depressed.

Such emotional lopsidedness, Davidson suggests, may be adaptive in a broader, evolutionary sense. Positive emotions draw people toward things that are pleasant or satisfying, engaging them with the world; negative emotions encourage withdrawal from what may be threatening or dangerous. In the hostile environment in which early man evolved, it may have been useful to have approach and avoidance unmistakably delineated in the brain.

Your face, my thane, is a book where "men may read strange matters," Lady Macbeth warns her husband in Shakespeare's great tragedy, knowing that a furrowed brow or curled lip can be a revealing barometer of emotional life. But it remained for psychologists inspired by Silvan Tomkins, to develop systematic ways to measure and compare the precisely tuned movements of more than 30 facial muscles, and to link the language of sneers, smiles and grimaces to other aspects of emotion.

Their work has challenged long-held assumptions about facial expression. It was widely believed, for example, that the way emotions are expressed by the face was learned after birth and differed from culture to culture. But in cross-cultural studies over the past two decades, psychologists Paul Ekman at the University of California at San Francisco and Carroll Izard of the University of Delaware have demonstrated that facial representations of sadness, fear, anger, disgust and other emotions are remarkably constant and recognizable around the globe.

Darwin's Delight

The social rules for displaying emotion do vary culturally. The Japanese, for example, are more likely to hold back negative expressions in public. Individuals, of course, also differ in the intensity of their emotional expressions, and to some extent in the events that trigger different emotions. But the researchers found familiar scowls and grins even in members of isolated cultures in New Guinea and Indonesia and in blind children, who can not learn them by visual imitation.

Such findings would have pleased biologist Charles Darwin, who explored the universality of emotion in his 1872 book, "The Expression of Emotions in Man and Animals" (see box on page 226). The findings are equally sweet to modem investigators who believe that humans possess innate, genetically wired templates of emotional expression and recognition, refined versions of those seen in primates and other "lower order" species.

But how does the face, with its Esperanto of feeling, fit into the larger emotional system—the rising pulse and rapid breathing of a man who has just been called a "sniveling scum bucket," for example, or the intangible experiences we label grief and joy? In an intriguing series of studies, their results still being debated, Ekman and his colleagues Robert Levenson and Wallace Friesen have shown that instructing people to produce the muscular movements of a particular emotional expression—a grimace of disgust, for example—produces changes in autonomic nervous system response, such as heart rate and skin temperature, even though the subjects are not told which emotion they are displaying. The scientists also found them these physiological patterns are, to some extent, specific for different emotional expressions, particularly negative ones such as anger, fear and disgust. The research team recently reported that distinctive heart rate and skin temperature patterns are also produced when subjects are asked to relive the memory of a particular emotional experience.

The person who communicates his feelings is, of course, only half the equation. In a complex social world, we are readers of emotion, too. Using ever more sophisticated tools, researchers are beginning to find out how the brain detects and analyzes emotional signals. Working with monkeys, for example, neuroscientist Edmund Rolls and his colleagues at Oxford University have isolated a group of nerve cells, located in part of the brain's temporal-lobe that processes visual information, that respond exclusively to faces and appear capable of recognizing individual faces as well. A second set of neurons about 2 millimeters away, apparently helps determine which emotion a face displays. Together, Rolls says, the two sets of cells allow monkeys—and probably humans as well—to determine who and what they are dealing with in the environment.

Unfamiliar Faces

Just how crucial these mechanisms are is evident in the extraordinary case of a 41-year-old brain-injured patient studied over several years by Massachusetts Institute of Technology neuroscientist Nancy Etcoff. Mr. H., who suffered damage to the temporal lobes of his brain in a car accident many years ago, has no trouble conversing. He holds a responsible job and can quickly distinguish a Mercedes from a Mazda. But he has entirely lost the ability to recognize faces—even those of the people closest to him. He asks his wife to wear a ribbon in her hair at parties, so he can tell her from the other guests. Arriving at his own house, Mr. H. will stare blankly at the two children in the driveway. "Are those your children?" Etcoff will ask him. "I guess they must be," her patient replies. "They're in my yard."

Yet Mr. H., whose condition is called prosopagnosia, still retains some ability to discern emotions, lending support to the notion that facial recognition and emotional interpretation are separate in the brain. Shown a picture of a sad face, he cannot at first name the feeling he sees. But he is able to mimic the downcast expression and in some way, Etcoff believes, this recreation of sadness on his own face "teaches" his brain, which then correctly labels the emotion in the picture. Still, such maneuvering makes any sojourn into the social world difficult. Says Etcoff: "People who can't recognize facial emotions feel like they can't read between the lines, and there's a tremendous awkwardness in relating to other people."

The snubbing of emotion in scientific theory was not confined to the study of adults. Child psychologists, too, were riveted by logical reasoning, as if infants and toddlers were, as one expert put it, "little computerized robots dealing with their environment." Even Swiss psychologist Jean Piaget—whose meticulous observations of his own children's intellectual growth serve as a primer for every student of child psychology—barely nodded at emotion, stressing instead the child's developing powers of thought and analysis. Feelings seemed irrelevant to infants, who could not even form goals or distinguish cause and effect.

Hormone of Love

The Chemistry of Romance and Nurturance

By Joannie M. Schrof

The romantic notion that love is a matter of the right chemistry may not be far off the mark. Scientists are now finding links between behavior and the brain's many chemicals, and recent animal studies of one particular hormone, oxytocin, suggest the chemical promotes the social bondings involved in choosing a mate and reproducing. Scientists speculate that the hormone may do the same for humans, fostering friendship, love and nurturance.

Oxytocin is well known for its ability to hasten childbirth and promote lactation but it is also present in areas of the brain linked to emotions and seems to influence how animals relate to one another. For example, when the hormone is given to two prairie voles, according to zoologist Sue Carter, they immediately form a monogamous bond. In the wild, the small mammals pair up only after sex, when oxytocin floods their systems. In sociable mice, adding oxytocin boosts the instinct for cuddling to a frenzied pitch.

The hormone not only seems to ensure that animals are attracted in the first place, it also appears to promote good parenting later on. Studies by Cort Pedersen and Jack Caldwell at the University of North Carolina and Gustav Jirikowski at Scripps Research Institute show that virgin female rats, normally nasty to babies, will respond to oxytocin by acting in a more motherly way. Parent rats will even mistreat their children if oxytocin is blocked.

In humans, oxytocin levels rise dramatically during sex, and scientists believe the chemical's presence may promote accompanying feelings of love or infatuation. Some researchers even suspect that oxytocin may play a part in most social behavior. "Human relations are influenced by the model of the parent-child relationship in that they include the notions of nurturing, care, help," says Pedersen. "The deficiency of a hormone tied to that parenting instinct may account for some of the anti-social behavior we think of as psychopathic."

Scientists emphasize that no hormone acts alone. Several dozen chemicals combine in intricate ways to influence emotions. "You will never find one specific hormone for one emotion," neurologist Marsel Mesulam notes. "Rather, it's the overall pattern that's important, just as in music it is the song that makes you feel happy or sad, not a particular instrument." Even so, scientists hope that understanding how oxytocin works may illuminate the most powerful of human emotions.

In the last decade, the scientific work that has reshaped the understanding of emotion has transformed the field of child psychology as well. A rapidly expanding body of work now makes it clear not only that infants have emotions, but that they are crucial from the very first moments of life. Nonverbal expressions of enjoyment, anger and other sentiments have been detected in children younger than 8 months old, and even a 10-week-old baby can distinguish his mother's smile of joy from her scowl of anger. "By nine months, the infant is an emotional being," writes Alan Sroufe, at the University of Minnesota.

It is not just that the infant is joyful upon seeing his mother's face or fearful at a loud noise. University of California at Berkeley developmental psychologist Joseph Campos and others argue that emotions are powerful tools for becoming a human being. Through them, children signal their needs and wants and are spurred to satisfy them. Feelings help forge—or sever—bonds with other people. By closely observing the emotional reactions of others—a mother's welcoming look when a stranger approaches, for example—a child also learns to size up uncertain situations, a process Campos and his colleagues call "social referencing."

Language adds sophistication and subtlety both to the expression of emotion and to children's ability to influence the feelings of others. By the age of 20 months, most children possess an emotional vocabulary, voicing in words their distress, pleasure or fatigue: In one study, each of six children said, "I love you" to a parent before his or her second birthday. By 28 months, discussions of feelings take place in a wide variety of contexts, from squabbles with siblings to pretend tea parties given for imaginary guests. And during their third year, children begin to refer to past and future states of emotion, and probe the reasons behind feelings, asking, for example, why an older brother is crying.

Jokes and Affection

Experts in child development once devoted their attention mostly to how children learned to "damp down" emotional extremes, controlling tantrums, for example. But in groundbreaking studies, Pennsylvania State University child development expert Judith Dunn has shown that children also actively use emotional expression to obtain comfort, give affection, learn social rules, make jokes, irritate siblings, form friendships and deepen intimacy in relationships.

According to new research by Dunn's group, how much time parents devote to discussing emotions with their children may influence sensitivity to the feelings of others later in life. Studies indicate, for example, an association between the frequency of mothers' exchanges about emotions with firstborn children and the friendly behavior of those children toward their infant brothers and sisters. Dunn and her colleagues have recently suggested that the frequency and content of family conversations about feelings may affect children's ability to recognize emotions in adults six years later.

Even at birth, investigators are finding, children vary in their emotional reactions to people and events, suggesting a hereditary contribution to temperament. Studies of children over a period of time by Harvard University psychologist Jerome Kagan show marked differences between those who are "inhibited"—by which Kagan means shy, quiet and socially withdrawn—and their more talkative, outgoing and sociable peers. Kagan has found that inhibited children have higher and more stable heart rates, react more to stress and may be more prone to depression and anxiety disorders later in life.

Primatologists are now finding that similar temperamental differences are present in monkeys studied in the wild, and may play a role in evolutionary adaptation. Male rhesus monkeys who are highly reacting emotionally, for example, display differences in heart rate similar to those of Kagan's socially inhibited children, according to research by Stephen Suomi and Kathlyn Rasmussen of the National Institute of Child Health and Human Development. These heart rate patterns appear to predict how male monkeys will react at puberty, when they typically emigrate from their own troop and join another. Unusually "shy" monkeys, the scientists found, tend to hang back, working their way into the new group slowly over months or years, while more aggressive monkeys tend to fight their way into the group instead. Both strategies, says Suomi, have pros and cons: "Outgoing individuals have the opportunity to get into the gene pool earlier, but they run a greater risk of getting killed. Shy ones slower to integrate, are at greater risk for starving to death, but their chances of being killed in a fight are lower."

Sadly, cancer stole the seven more books that Silvan Tomkins hoped to write. But before his death, he completed the final two volumes of "Affect/Imagery/Consciousness," the treatise he began 30 years ago. The books, one just published and the other soon to follow, make their appearance in a vastly changed climate. Emotion research is now everywhere, its importance no longer argued before indifferent auditors. Scientists, finally, are joining the poets in granting the "passions" their rightful place as "the elements of life."

Discussion Questions for Article 2

Section 8: Motivation and Emotion

Name: _____

PID: _____

Date: __ __ / __ __ / __ __ (MM/DD/YY)

CRN: _____

Recitation Day/Time: _____

Honor Code Signature: _____

1. What is prosopagnosia? Why was this condition discussed in the article?

2. The left hemisphere processes what emotions? The right hemisphere processes what emotions?

3. Why has Oxytocin been described as the "hormone of love"?

4. Although over generalized, the left brain and right brain do perform different tasks. For what reasons might this "division of labor" be beneficial?

Section 9
Personality

What is it that makes us who we are, what makes us unique? Many would not hesitate to exclaim that it is our personality that makes us unique, makes us who we are. While the definition of personality seems malleable based on the theoretical perspective used to define it, it can generally be thought of as a person's particular cognitive responses and behaviors. This idea leads us to many other questions, such as how does our personality develop and what causes it to evolve or not evolve as we age. Proposed explanations for the development and evolution of personality have ranged from levels of bodily fluids producing particular temperaments in what was known as Humoral psychology, to struggles between a person's impulsive tendencies of the id and the hyper-moral ideals of the superego (psychoanalysis), to the idea of specific genetic and psychological traits interacting with transpersonal environmental conditions. The question still remains, does any single theory, trait, or environmental condition fully account for the complex nature of human personality, or are many forces acting together to create something greater?

Is this personality construct nothing more than the additive sum of a person's genetic or biological predispositions and whatever environmental circumstances they find themselves in or are there more aspects, not so easily quantified? Perspectives arising from General Systems Theory address this question by looking at personality as its own system. As with many systems, personality is seen not only as the additive sum of its constituent parts (the biological organism and its subsequent environmental circumstances), but as a construct that is greater than the mere sum of its parts. The personality is born out of the interaction of an organism and its environment. It is the never-ending interrelationship between these constituent parts that gives rise to a person's personality and their unique sense of self. This codependency leads to something more complex than just the additive sum of its constituent parts. These never ending interactions are continually changing as the organism grows, evolves, and learns along with the fluid environment that surrounds it. Organism based (i.e. learning) and environmental changes moderate and mold the interaction between the organism and its fluid environment. These situational factors lead to new experiences and forms of interaction that over time create, maintain, and change characteristic behavioral and cognitive patterns.

In whatever method it is decided to explain the development and evolution of personality, be it a systems based, psychoanalytic, or humanistic approach, some elements remain certain. Personality is in many ways a contradicting construct: both stable and fluid. This contradiction coupled with the human desire to understand what makes them and those around them unique fuels research regarding the self, personality, and its implications.

Article 1: Effortful Control, Surgency, and Reading Skills in Middle Childhood

This article investigates the role of temperament in the development of reading skills, specifically the roles of effortful control and surgency. Effortful control is characterized as one's ability to self regulate and includes traits such as attention focusing, inhibitory control, perceptual sensitivity, and low-intensity pleasure. Surgency, on the other hand, is based on impulsivity, high-intensity pleasure, high activity level, and low levels of shyness. The authors note the modest effects of effortful control on word skills as well as the moderation of this relationship by surgency levels.

Article 2: Maslow's Puzzle: A Reconfiguration

What constitutes a creative attitude? Why are some individuals considered more creative than others and how does this creative personality develop? This article begins to look at the expression and development of a creative personality. The interaction between the individual and their environment and its role in creativity is explored through the lens of Maslow's puzzle. Throughout this article, you can indulge your creativity and contemplate how the interactions between a person and their environment work to create, maintain, and change an individual's personality, or self.

—*Nathaniel P. Van Kirk*

Effortful Control, Surgency, and Reading Skills in Middle Childhood

Kirby Deater-Deckard
Paula Y. Mullineaux
Stephen A. Petrill
Lee A. Thompson

We examined the associations between components of temperament and children's word and pseudo-word reading skills, in a school-age sample using a within-family internal-replication design. We estimated the statistical prediction of word and pseudo-word reading in separate regression equations that included the main effects of, and two-way interaction between, Surgency and Effortful Control. Children with better Effortful Control scores showed better reading skills. Surgency was unrelated to reading skills, but moderated the effect of Effortful Control. The positive association between reading skills and Effortful Control was present only for children who were low in Surgency. Thus, reading achievement in school-age children is optimized by strong Effortful Control, but these processes may be disrupted for those children who are high in Surgency.

Keywords: *Effortful Control, Reading, Surgency, Temperament*

Abbreviations

CBQ-SF	*Child Behavior Questionnaire-Short Form*
EC	*Effortful Control*
S	*Surgency*

Introduction

Successful mastery of reading is fundamental not only to the development of other cognitive skills but to educational outcomes, occupational success, and social-emotional development and well-being. Understanding how and why some children and adolescents excel while others fall behind in reading is critical to addressing ways to intervene and enhance achievement and maximize educational attainment. To this end, research is needed that examines individual differences in children's behaviors that pertain to the development of reading skills, when those skills are first being acquired and applied. In the current study of reading skills among early readers (grades 1 and 2), we studied potential additive and interactive effects of two aspects of temperament—Effortful Control (i.e., self-regulatory capacities) and Surgency (i.e., impulsive hedonic activation tendencies).

Temperament and Reading

In the developmental psychology literature, there have been many approaches to operationalizing temperament (Posner & Rothbart, 2006; Strelau, Zawadzki, & Piotrowska, 2001). These theories generally converge to define temperament as biologically influenced behaviors that vary widely across individuals, are readily observed from infancy, and are moderately stable over time and across settings.

In the current study, we have focused on two aspects of temperament that may be particularly important in children's reading skill development—Effortful Control (EC) and Surgency (S). In Rothbart's theory of temperament (Putnam & Rothbart, 2006), the EC factor represents self-regulatory capacity and includes four facets: Attention Focusing, Inhibitory Control, Low Intensity Pleasure, and Perceptual Sensitivity. The S factor represents high-energy activation and is derived from four scales: Impulsivity, High Intensity Pleasure, Activity Level, and low levels of Shyness. These dimensions of temperament are thought to represent individual differences in brain mechanisms involved in energy/activation, response to new information (specifically, tendency to approach versus a tendency to withdraw), and regulation of arousal—mechanisms that are part and parcel of successful completion of demanding tasks and, ultimately, learning and achievement (Nęcka, 2003; Posner & Rothbart, 2006).

To our knowledge, the current study is the first to examine additive and interactive statistical effects of the EC and S factors on reading skills. Some of the component behaviors within the broader EC and S factors have been implicated in prior research on reading skill development. Foundational research by Oates (1928) and Porteus (1942) pointed to the importance of considering "behavioral styles" as fundamental contributors to scholastic achievement. More recently, Martin, Olejnik, and Gaddis (1994) found that better scholastic achievement in elementary school was predicted from greater task persistence and less distractibility—behaviors that are represented within the EC construct. Other studies using different methods and measures have found similar results (for a review see Keogh, 2003).

Behaviors that are indicative of the S factor also have been implicated, although there are far fewer studies compared to the research on EC behaviors. Several studies have shown a link between poorer reading and high motor activity, and higher impulsivity has been implicated as an impediment to reasoning and cognitive performance generally (Martin et al., 1994; Schweizer, 2002).

Aim and Hypothesis

Our aim was to examine the statistical associations between the broad temperament dimensions of EC and S, and two indicators of reading skills among early readers (grades 1 and 2)—"real" word and "pseudo" word identification (i.e., "word attack"). Based on the literature described above, we anticipated finding better reading skills to be associated with better self-regulation capacity (higher EC) and fewer impulsive activation/approach behaviors (lower S). In addition to testing this hypothesis, we conducted an exploratory analysis of the interaction between EC and S as a statistical predictor of reading performance to test for non-additive effects of temperament on reading skill development. We used an internal replication design by testing for these effects in two sub-samples: the first-born twin (Sub-sample 1) and the second-born twin (Sub-sample 2) in a sample of school-age twin pairs.

Methods

Participants

The data were from the Western Reserve Reading Project. In this on-going longitudinal twin study, the children are assessed annually (see Petrill, Deater-Deckard, Thompson, DeThorne, & Schatschneider, 2006, for a detailed description of the study). The sample included 178 families with same-sex twins (61% of the pairs were females, 44% of the pairs were genetically identical) for whom we had complete data for the current study. Based on parents' reports at the beginning of the study, 7% of the families reported that one or both twins had, or might have, a learning disability. However, no children were excluded from analyses.

The children were 7.1 years old on average (SD = .88 years, from 5.3 to 8.9 years). There was a wide range of parental education that was similar for mothers and fathers: 1–2% high school or less, 39% some college, 30% bachelor's degree, 25% some post-graduate education or degree, 5% not specified. The majority was Caucasian (92%) and lived in two-parent households (6% single mothers). The total sample included 356 children in 178 families (2 children per family). For the internal replication design, we analyzed separately the 178 first-born ("sub-sample 1") and 178 second-born twins ("sub-sample 2").

Procedures

In the on-going WRRP study, we are conducting annual visits to the home to assess children's reading and cognitive skills. For the current study, we examined data from the second home visit, for which we have the most complete assessment of reading that is closest in time to the assessment of temperament. During the home visit, two testers assess each child's reading and cognitive skills using a 2.5-h assessment battery. Parents and children participated in an informed consent and assent procedure, and received honoraria for their time. All procedures were in compliance with the protocol that was approved by Institution Review Boards at the investigators' institutions.

As a separate component of the on-going longitudinal study, after this home visit parents were asked if they would be willing to complete a mailed questionnaire that included ratings of child temperament. The timing of completion of the supplemental questionnaire was not systematic, although on average these were completed 11 months after the home visit.

Measures

Reading Skills

Children's reading skills were measured using two sub-tests from the Woodcock Reading Mastery Test, WRMT-R (Woodcock, 1987). We administered the Word Identification sub-test, and also assessed pseudo-word reading using the Word Attack sub-test. Word Attack was administered only to those children who demonstrated an ability to complete at least a portion of the Word Identification subtest. All of the children in the analyses in the current study were able to complete both sub-tests.

Temperament

We used the Child Behavior Questionnaire-Short Form, CBQ-SF (Putnam & Rothbart, 2006) as a measure of temperament in middle childhood. The CBQ-SF is the most recently published instrument of child temperament. It is based on a longstanding series of studies that have established evidence for strong psychometric properties of this instrument, and for the theoretical and empirical distinctiveness of the multiple temperament dimensions that the questionnaire identifies. The measure is derived from Rothbart's theory of temperament that specifies components of behavior and affect that represent individual differences in reactivity and self-regulation.

In the current study, we focused on the Effortful Control (EC) and Surgency (S) factors in the CBQ-SF. The CBQ-SF utilizes a seven-point Likert-type scale (1 = extremely untrue of your child to 7 = extremely true of your child). The Surgency (S) scale is derived from averaging four sub-scales: Impulsivity, High-Intensity Pleasure, Activity Level, and Shyness (reversed). The Effortful Control (EC) scale is based on four sub-scales: Attentional Focusing, Inhibitory Control, Low-Intensity Pleasure, and Perceptual Sensitivity. Exploratory factor analysis yielded strong evidence of replication of the simple-structure factor solution for the CBQ-SF (Putnam & Rothbart, 2006). The loadings for S were .62–.86, and loadings for EC ranged from .67 to .80. Mothers' and fathers' scores were substantially correlated (.72 for EC, .61 for S), so parents' reports were averaged for those children who had both mothers' and fathers' reports (93 of the 178 families).

Results

Descriptive statistics are shown in Table 1. The age standard scores for Word Identification and Word Attack were above the population mean of 100, although the standard deviations were close to population average of 15. This suggests that the children were performing above-average for their age, although there was a great deal of variability within the sample. In regard to temperament scores, mothers' and fathers' reports for EC revealed moderate negative skew, with the majority of children being rated above the middle (3.5) of the seven-point scale. Surgency was more normally distributed, with the means falling close to the middle of the scale. There was ample variability in both mothers' and fathers' reports for both temperament dimensions. The distributions were very similar across the two replication sub-samples.

We also estimated associations between the four study variables (Word Attack, Word Identification, EC, and S), and two child factors: age in years and gender (coded as 1 = female and 2 = male). Word Identification standard scores were modestly higher for older children, $r(353) = -.20$, $p < .001$. Girls were higher than boys in EC, $r(353) = -.29$, $p < .001$, and lower than boys in S, $r(353) = .18$, $p < .01$. None of the other tests was significant.

To test our hypothesis and explore potential interactions between temperament dimensions, we began by estimating bivariate Pearson correlations between study variables within the two replication sub-samples (shown as the off-diagonal elements in the correlation matrix in Table 1). The pattern of covariation among the four study variables was replicated across the two sub-samples. Word Attack and Word Identification were substantially positively correlated. There was a modest

TABLE 1 Means and standard deviations with matrix of Pearson correlations: sub-sample 1 in rows and below diagonal, sub-sample 2 in columns and above diagonal, twin intra-class correlations on diagonal.

		Sub-sample 2			
		Word Attack	Word Ident.	Eff. Control	Surgency
Sub-sample 1	M (SD)	110.7 (11.2)	112.2 (12.7)	5.34 (.68)	4.43 (.90)
Word Attack	110.1 (12.1)	.58	.82	.13^{ns}	−.07^{ns}
Word Identification	112.1 (12.8)	.78	.75	.12^{ns}	−.09^{ns}
Effortful Control	5.38 (.58)	.18	.20	.60	−.27
Surgency	4.45 (.74)	−.06ns	−.04^{ns}	−.19	.09^{ns}

Note: All correlations significant at $p < .05$ (two-tailed) unless ns (non-significant). Descriptive statistics for Effortful Control and Surgency based on mothers' reports, which were not significantly different from fathers' reports. Mothers' and fathers' reports were averaged prior to estimation of correlations and for subsequent regression analyses

to moderate negative association between EC and S. We found modest positive associations between EC and the two reading scales (ranging across sub-samples and measures from .12, non-significant, to .20, $p < .05$), and negligible nonsignificant negative associations between S and the two reading scores (ranging from −.04 to −.09). Although not pertinent to the goal of the current study, for descriptive purposes we estimated twin intra-class correlations, shown in the diagonal of the correlation matrix in Table 1. Twin similarity was moderate to substantial, with the exception of negligible sibling similarity for S.

We used hierarchical regression to estimate equations predicting Word Attack and Word Identification scores. For each equation, the main effects of EC and S were included in the first step, followed by the two-way interaction between EC and S in the second step. EC and S scores were centered prior to analysis. The equations were estimated twice, once for each sub-sample (see Table 2).

We hypothesized that better reading skills would be statistically predicted by higher EC and lower S. There was partial support for this hypothesis, in that higher EC was associated significantly with better both measures of reading performance. However, the effect size was modest. Contrary to expectation, there was no evidence of an association between S and reading skills.

Exploratory analysis of the two-way interaction between EC and S revealed evidence for a negative statistical interaction for both reading outcomes that was significant in sub-sample two. Visual inspection of the interaction was conducted by creating four sub-groups of children by splitting at the means on the EC and S scores (Figure 1). The overall pattern suggested that the positive association between

TABLE 2   Hierarchical regression models: Word Attack and Word Identification.

	Word Attack	**Word Identification**
Sub-sample 1		
Model *F*(df), *p-value*	$F(3,173) = 2.34, p < .08$	$F(3,173) = 2.43, p < .08$
R^2	$R^2 = .04$	$R^2 = .04$
Betas		
Effortful Control (EC)	.16*	.20*
Surgency (S)	−.01	.01
EC × S interaction	−.09	−.03
Sub-sample 2		
F(df), *p-value*	$F(3,174) = 3.18, p < .05$	$F(3,175) = 3.08, p < .05$
R^2	$R^2 = .05$	$R^2 = .05$
Betas		
Effortful Control (EC)	.14*	.13*
Surgency (S)	−.04	−.07
EC × S interaction	−.19*	−.17*

*$p < .05$; **$p < .01$ (two-tailed)

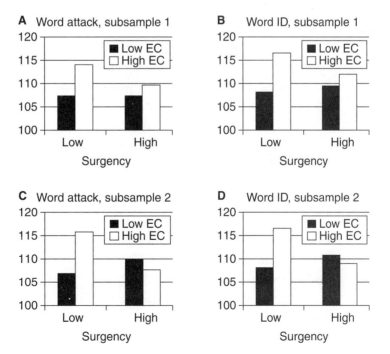

FIGURE 1   Group means for Word Attack (a, c) and Word Identification (ID, b, d) as a function of Surgency (S) and effortful control (EC) in two sub-samples. Low and High S and EC groups were created using mean splits.

EC and reading performance may only be present among children who were lower in S. This interpretation was supported by post-hoc correlational analyses. In both subsamples, EC and reading skills were correlated (.3 range, $p < .01$) for children who had S scores below the mean: sub-sample 1, $r = .29$ for Word Attack and .31 for Word Identification, $p < .01$; sub-sample 2, $r = .36$ for Word Attack and .34 for Word Identification, $p < .01$. In contrast, the correlations between EC and reading skills were modest and non-significant for those with S scores above the mean: sub-sample 1, $r = .01$ for Word Attack and .04 for Word Identification; sub-sample 2, $r = -.17$ for Word Attack and $-.14$ for Word Identification.

In supplementary analyses, we examined whether the interaction between EC and S was present for general intelligence test performance, measured as the composite sum of area scores on the Stanford-Binet. We found no evidence for this two-way interaction for general intelligence test performance in either sub-sample.

Discussion

The development of reading skills among early readers during the first half of the elementary school years appears to be optimized for children who have better self-regulation of attention, cognition and behavior—essential components of the temperament dimension of Effortful Control. In the current study the effect was modest, but it was consistent within our internal replication design, as well as replicating the literature on attention span and reading achievement in elementary school (Martin et al., 1994). This finding also is consistent with the growing literature on reading disabilities within the population of children diagnosed with attention deficit hyperactivity disorder (Spira & Fischel, 2005; Willcutt et al., 2007).

Surgency did not emerge as a statistical predictor of reading achievement. Although there is evidence in the literature that children who are highly active show poorer reading performance (Martin et al., 1994), other research suggests that the association between reading performance and impulsive hyperactivity is modest (Willcutt et al., 2007). Activity level is only one aspect of the Surgency factor, which also includes impulsivity, high-intensity pleasure and low levels of shyness. To our knowledge, ours is the first study to test directly the association between the Surgency factor and reading performance, and the results revealed essentially no association.

Although there was no main effect of Surgency, there was a significant two-way interaction between Surgency and Effortful Control scores for word and pseudo-word reading performance. The results were clear in showing that Surgency served as a moderator of the association between reading achievement and Effortful Control. One sub-group of children had higher reading scores compared to all others—those who were low in Surgency and high in Effortful Control. Post-hoc correlational analyses showed that better reading scores were associated with higher Effortful Control, but only for those children who were low in Surgency. This suggests that the processes linking Effortful Control and better reading performance may be disrupted for those children who are impulsive, overactive and sensation-seeking in their behavior.

This statistical model represents individual differences in the application of cognitive resources to the task of striving to read (and possibly even more generally as "motivation to learn"). If a child must devote considerable conscious effort to maintain motivation and control attention to perform a task, that leaves relatively little processing capacity for problem solving. Learning will take longer and be more arduous, especially if the goals and expectations surrounding a given task and its successful completion do not include some intrinsic reward for that child. On the other hand, if a child readily attends and regulates her or his attention well, and does not have competing impulses to contend with, a greater proportion of available cognitive processing capacity can be applied to task performance in a particular situation, as well as to learning in a broad sense.

To the extent that temperament also reflects a child's coping and adaptation in the face of stressors (including the demands arising from tasks in reading and other scholastic activities), these individual differences probably affect the amount and quality of learning that occurs. Cognitive growth occurs when a child is close to the limits of her current knowledge and problem solving abilities, and learning must therefore be facilitated by others such as teachers, parents, and peers (Vygotsky, 1978). Those who are more impulsive and sensation-seeking and who have a more difficult time regulating that arousal are less likely to endure the prolonged time periods required to attempt to solve problems or carry out cognitive tasks that are even only modestly stressful or aversive. This reduces the amount of time and the number of attempts such individuals will make, resulting in less optimal learning (Strelau et al., 2001).

The implication of the current findings is that the effects of effortful self-regulation and Surgency on reading achievement are underestimated in community studies, since only main effects are tested typically. Our results also suggest that intervening to reduce impulsivity, activity level and sensation seeking behaviors is just as important as improving attention regulation or behavioral persistence, when the goal is to improve reading achievement.

There are limitations to the study that should be considered. First, the effect sizes in the current study were modest, and although the pattern of findings was replicated within the sample, we have examined only a few components of a much wider array of behaviors that are related to reading achievement. Second, the CBQ-SF is not intended to be used with children who are older than 8 years of age, but nearly half of our sample was above this threshold when the CBQ-SF was completed. Although we found no evidence of differences in means, variances, or factor structures on the CBQ-SF for children who were older or younger than 8 years of age, this remains an important caveat. Third, although we examined each twin in separate sub-samples in the current study, our findings are based on a sample of twins and the findings may not generalize to non-twin siblings or to singletons. Finally, the reading and temperament data were not collected concurrently, making attenuation of effect sizes more likely. However, reading and temperament scores are moderately to substantially stable by middle childhood, so the attenuation effect probably is minimal.

Caveats aside, the results point to the value of considering individual differences in temperament when the goal is to discern ways to improve children's reading achievement. Ultimately, this kind of research can inform practitioners—especially teachers and school administrators—about the ways in which the "fit" between particular aspects of children's individual attributes and the methods of reading instruction and intervention can be ascertained and optimized. This area of inquiry also can provide information to professionals working with parents of children who show challenging behaviors that interfere with achievement and learning. Although there is no question that individual differences in temperament and reading performance are influenced by genetic factors, these attributes are very likely modifiable through systematic changes in environments (Keogh, 2003; Posner & Rothbart, 2006).

Acknowledgements

We thank the study participants and research staff, and our collaborators on the Western Reserve Reading Project—Laura DeThorne, Christopher Schatschneider, and David Vandenbergh. This study was supported by grants from NICHD (HD38075) and NICHD/OSERS (HD46167).

References

Keogh, B. K. (2003). *Temperament in the classroom: Understanding individual differences.* Baltimore, MD: Brookes.

Martin, R. P., Olejnik, S., & Gaddis, L. (1994). Is temperament an important contributor to schooling outcomes in elementary school? Modeling the effects of temperament, scholastic ability on academic achievement. In W. B. Carey & S. C. McDevitt (Eds.), *Prevention and early intervention: Individual differences as risk factors for the mental health of children* (pp. 59–68). New York: Brunner/Mazel.

Nęcka, E. (2003). Intelligence and temperament. In R. J. Sternberg, J. Lautrey, & T. I. Lubart (Eds.), *Models of intelligence: International perspectives* (pp. 293–309). Washington, DC: American Psychological Association.

Oates, D. (1928). An experimental study of temperament. *British Journal of Psychology*, 19, 1–30.

Petrill, S. A., Deater-Deckard, K., Thompson, L., DeThorne, L., & Schatschneider, C. (2006). Genetic and environmental effects of serial naming and phonological awareness on early reading outcomes. *Journal of Educational Psychology*, 98, 112–121.

Porteus, S. (1942). *Qualitative performance in the maze test*. Vineland: The Smith Printing House.

Posner, M. I., & Rothbart, M. K. (2006). *Educating the human brain*. Washington, DC: American Psychological Association.

Putnam, S., & Rothbart, M. K. (2006). Development of short and very short forms of the Children's Behavior Questionnaire. *Journal of Personality Assessment*, 87, 103–113.

Schweizer, K. (2002). Does impulsivity influence performance in reasoning? *Personality and Individual Differences*, 33, 1031–1043.

Spira, E. G., & Fischel, J. E. (2005). The impact of preschool inattention, hyperactivity, and impulsivity on social and academic development: A review. *Journal of Child Psychology and Psychiatry*, 46, 755–773.

Strelau, J., Zawadzki, B., & Piotrowska, A. (2001). Temperament and intelligence: A psychometric approach to the links between both phenomena. In J. M. Collis & S. Messick (Eds.), *Intelligence and personality: Bringing the gap in theory and measurement* (pp. 61–78). Mahwah, NJ: Erlbaum.

Vygotsky, L. S. (1978). *Mind and society: The development of higher mental processes*. Cambridge, MA: Harvard University Press.

Willcutt, E. G., Betjemann, R. S., Wadsworth, S. J., Samuelsson, S., Corley, R., DeFries, J. C., Byrne, B., Pennington, B. F., & Olson, R. K. (2007). Preschool twin study of the relation between attention-deficit/hyperactivity disorder and prereading skills. *Reading and Writing*, 20, 103–125.

Woodcock, R. (1987). *Woodcock reading mastery tests—revised*. Circle Pines, MN: American Guidance Service.

Editor's Note

K. Deater-Deckard and P. Y. Mullineaux, Psychology, Virginia Polytechnic Institute and State University, 109 Williams Hall (0436), Blacksburg, VA 24061, USA, e-mail: kirbydd@vt.edu

S. A. Petrill, Human Development and Family Science, Ohio State University, 135 Campbell Hall, 1787 Neil Avenue, Columbus, OH 43210-1295, USA

L. A. Thompson, Psychology, Case Western Reserve University, Mather Memorial Room 103, 10900 Euclid Ave., Cleveland, OH 44106, USA

Discussion Questions for Article 1

Section 9: Personality

Name: _____

PID: _____

Date: __ __ / __ __ / __ __ (MM/DD/YY)

CRN: _____

Recitation Day/Time: _____

Honor Code Signature: _____

1. Specific theories define temperament in a variety of ways; describe a general definition of temperament as proposed by this article.

2. In this article, temperament is divided into two aspects that are important when considering reading development, Effortful Control (EC) and Surgency (S). Briefly describe each aspect and how they differ.

3. Which combination (i.e. high or low) of Effortful Control and Surgency was associated with the best outcome (i.e. highest reading scores)?

4. What are some limitations of this study?

Article 2
Maslow's Puzzle: A Reconfiguration

Joseph Germana

A.H. Maslow (1963, 1993) characterized the "creative attitude" in ways such as giving up the past and future, loss of ego or self-forgetfulness, Taoistic receptivity, and innocence. He suggested that underlying these and related characteristics may be "certain prerequisites," which he offered to us as a "puzzle."

"Maslow's puzzle" may be considered in relation to what he regarded as a sine qua non of creativeness: "fusion of person and world." The greater intimacy of such a relationship means that the individual has more fully extended self into that which lies beyond self, that is, into transpersonal realms or fields. A study of such fields, based on representations of fields in general, may provide a different insight into "Maslow's puzzle" and the enhanced creativity with which it is associated.

A.H. Maslow (1963, 1993) begins his treatment of the "creative attitude" with the following profession:

> *My feeling is that the concept of creativeness and the concept of the healthy, self-actualizing, fully human person seem to be coming closer and closer together, and may perhaps turn out to be the same thing. (p. 55)*

He then concludes that creative art education or "education-through-art" may be of special importance not only to artists, but also, for "turning out better people," whom he characterizes as being comfortable with change because they are confident enough to improvise in unfamiliar situations.

Next, he lays out "a puzzle . . . suggested by the observation that the creative person, in the inspirational phase . . . lives totally immersed, fascinated and absorbed in the present with the matter-in-hand," and that "certain prerequisites of creativeness—in whatever realm—have something to do with this ability" (p. 59).

Finally, in this most insightful work, Maslow concludes that "fusion between person and his world" may be considered a sine qua non of creativeness, "better understood as a natural event. . . . an isomorphism, a molding of each to each other, a better fitting together or complementarity, a melting into one" (p. 68).

This "integration of self with nonself"—this "one," which incorporates both person and world, stands thereby as a transpersonal form of organization in which the individual participates. And the creative attitude which promotes a fuller, more intimate engagement in such transpersonal realms may be characterized as extending oneself beyond one's self on behalf of that which is greater than just oneself, alone. That form of psychbiological organization "greater" is the "one" which incorporates person and world as an emergent property based on their ongoing interrelationships.

Then, if both life and art can be seen as such transpersonal forms of psychobiological organization and so, "natural events," the humanistic value of "education-through-art" may be found in their common denominators.

Furthermore, the process of engaging the creative attitude puzzle, when taken within a different, greater framework, may offer Humanistic Psychology different expressions of the virtues—efficacies, that promote self-extension and the "courage to create" (May, 1975). If the entire span of human maturational development extends through self-actualization on and into ego transcendence, as Maslow suggested, then a reconfiguration of his puzzle—one centered around "fusion of person and world," may prove of some heuristic value. It may suggest in different ways how the creative attitude leads to lives more properly fitted, placed, shaped, adjusted, that is, in-true, and thusly, to the truer actualization of the "farther reaches of human nature."

To the extent to which the construal of something depends on the context, frame, or gestalt in which it is found (and founded), its reconfiguration may disclose new features. In this case, the matter of the puzzle is reconfigured, first, within the more inclusive context of fields in general, then, more specifically, within the psychbiological fields of life and art.

The common denominators of human life and creative art work—manifestations of human nature—are at least twofold. First, there are the most fundamental organizational features shared by all forms of holarchically organized complexity. These characteristics of holarchical organization, by being so broadly generalized, are taken as the outer frame of this study.

Then, the more specifically relevant set of denominators common to life and art lie in their special nature as *psychobiological* forms of holarchically organized complexity. At the level of psychobiological organization superior or superordinate to the person lies the transpersonal realm of the person-environment complex or field. It is at this level, which subsumes both person and environment (or world), that human life and art work are to be wholly found, set in inextricable relationship.

One meaningful response to Maslow's puzzle may be derived by regarding his creative attitude as an object placed within this twofold frame: whole psychobiological or transpersonal integration as a case of holarchical organization.

General Field Theory

This set of constructs is an adaptation of classical, general system theory as offered by von Bertalanffy (1968) and Laszlo (1972). *The adaptation specifically addresses systems which form a layered or nested hierarchy,* so that subordinate levels are subsumed or incorporated by greater, that is, superordinate forms of organization.

The distinction between "hierarchy" and "holarchy" has been well made by Volk (1995):

> *Let's keep* hierarchy *for the non-contained variety, the command pyramid of generals and troops. . . . Let the nested pattern of parts in wholes that are in turn parts of still greater wholes be called a* holarchy. *Its image is not a pyramid, but concentric spheres.* (p. 130; emphasis in the original)

Field is a unitive construct that appreciates the mutual implication of two core constructs of system theory: "emergent property" and "holarchical organization" (Germana, 2000, 2001).

Note the interrelationship between these constructs. A property may be said to be "emergent" when its special organization incorporates the contributions and constraints of its constituents and thereby "transcends and includes" them (cf. Wilber, 1996). The emergent property represents a form of organization that is "other than" and, with equal step, "greater than" the mere sum of its parts.

Finally, if the system view is most thoroughgoing, by taking the constituents themselves as emergent properties, as in the case of holarchically organized complexities, then this field theory may be seen as a derivation of system theory.

In these ways, the core construct of "organized complexity" may be likened to a seed crystal. A seed crystal is a most elementary structure which when dropped into a supersaturated solution forms a complete new crystal. As the original building block, the seed crystal *has all the facets of the new crystal.* By analogy, when the "seed crystal" of "organized complexity" is "dropped" into the "supersaturated" solution of a world view, the universe is seen as a

> *dynamic web of interrelated events . . . (consisting of) networks within networks. At each scale, under closer scrutiny, the nodes of the network reveal themselves as smaller networks. . . . There are only networks within other networks. (Capra, 1997, pp. 35–39)*

Finding networks within networks, multilayered systems within systems, or fields within fields—each subordinate case actualized under superordinate auspices precipitates a world view of matrices within matrices. Such a general field theory would have certain implications or corollaries that could provide a most fundamental or ultimate apologia for a transpersonal psychology.

Any field, so conceived, would include in its complete array of responsibilities those concerning the value of its correspondences with the greater matrix within which it is found and founded, along with those specifically directed toward itself. So situated, the field would be required, by natural law, to extend itself beyond itself on behalf of that which is greater than just itself, alone. When applied to a personal field, this set of responsibilities could be phrased: extending oneself beyond one's self on behalf of that which is greater than just oneself, alone, that is, on behalf of the transpersonal matrix or field in whose actualization the person participates.

The Transpersonal Fields of Life and Art

The whole psychophysiological field of the person is subsumed along with environmental variables by the still greater psychobiological, transpersonal matrix within and through which human life and art emerge (Germana, 1996). The defining feature of this ecological level is its incorporation of organism (person) along with "other members of its species, creatures of other types, and physicochemical factors of the abiotic environment" (Jessop, 1970, p. 115). Jessop goes on to state that these relationships are *reciprocal* and operate *at all levels of biological organization.*

According to the general field theory, as outlined, the person would be directed by two primary sets of responsibilities, roughly comparable to Andras Angyal's (1941) "autonomy/homonomy."

On the one hand, there would be all those special functions through which any biological complexity maintains and promotes itself. These would include all activities that Laszlo (1972) described as "adaptive self-stabilization" and "adaptive self-organization"—(psycho-)biological organization homeostatically regulating, reorganizing, and developing. Taken collectively, they seem to constitute what Wilber (1996) calls "agency."

A complementary set of responsibilities would be to transcend self on behalf of the relationships with other participants of their matrix. This set seems to correspond well with the contributions Wilber (1996) describes as "communion." In the special case of the human being, these responsibilities are transpersonal.

When both sets are taken in their conjunction, they form overall "agency-in-communion" (Wilber, 2000).

When all these "within, between and among" responsibilities are so collectively considered, that is, as forming a comprehensive set of functional interrelationships, and when they are regarded teleologically, then one might ask toward what state, condition, or quality is any (psycho-)biological field striving in the course of life? Perhaps manifesting all of its resilience, what is it trying to establish, maintain, and develop—actualize, for itself vis-a-vis its correspondence with its matrix?

If there be one embracing principle guiding lifestyle, is it the inherent tendency to become wholly in-true—coherent, itself as well as congruent in relation to its matrix? Such a principle would subsume attempts to self-stabilize and organize, to effectively govern its constituents, and to contribute well to that which is greater than itself. Such "agency-in-communion" would find life in search of whole-truth.

The Creative Attitude in Life and Art

According to Stephen Nachmanovitch (1990), "There is something biological about art" (p. 176), which he explains in the following way: "Creativity, like life, is a recursive process, involving interactive, interlooping circuits of control and nourishment between organism and environment" (p. 186).

When life and art are so compared—as emergent properties based on the ongoing reciprocal determination between person and world, then occasions of enhanced "fusion" may be recognized as entirely natural. Indeed, Rollo May (1975) has observed that such "encounters" or "engagements" are mainly distinguished on the basis of their "intensity."

> *World is interrelated with the person at every moment. A continuous dialectical process goes on between world and self, self and world; one implies the other, and neither can be understood if we omit the other. (May, 1975, p. 50)*

The essence of Maslow's creative attitude is that its primary orientation is transpersonal investment, encouraging fusion of person and world. Therefore, the primary regard of the attitude is the whole set of interrelationships in which the person is participating. In this sense, one might say that fusion of person and world comes about when consciousness becomes more unitive or transpersonal, or that the person is manifesting a transpersonal actualizing attitude.

Such an attitude is not just a matter of the person becoming less bound or attached to ego, past, expectations, "shoulds, oughts and other pictures-in-the-head," but rather, *entirely less partial*—the ego and its contents being one set of participants along with the particulars of the world. The person is thereby disposed to form a fuller, more intimate relationship with world.

A person more earnestly in search of whole-truth would be advancing toward the farther reaches of human nature. And, "education-in-art" would be "education-in-life."

References

Angyal, A. (1941). *Foundations for a science of personality.* New York: Viking.

Capra, F. (1997). *The web of life.* New York: Anchor.

Germana, J. (1996). A transactional analysis of biobehavioral systems. *Integrative Physiological and Behavioral Science, 30,* 138–150.

Germana, J. (2000). The whole and main ideas of systems science: An essay in systems philosophy. *Systems Research and Behavioral Science, 17,* 311–313.

Germana, J. (2001). Emergent properties: A fundamental postulate of classical systems theory in schematic representation. *Systems Research and Behavioral Science, 18,* 565–567.

Jessop, N. M. (1970). *Biosphere: A study of life.* Englewood Cliffs, NJ: Prentice-Hall.

Laszlo, E. (1972). *Introduction to a systems philosophy.* New York: Gordon and Breach.

Maslow, A. H. (1993). *The farther reaches of human nature.* New York: Penguin-Arkana. (Original work published 1963)

May, R. (1975). *The courage to create.* New York: W.W. Norton.

Nachmanovitch, 5. (1990). *Free play: Improvisation in life and art.* New York: Tarcher/Putnam.

Volk, T. (1995). *Metapatterns across space, time and mind.* New York: Columbia University Press.

von Bertalanffy, L. (1968). *General system theory.* New York: George Braziller.

Wilber, K. (1996). *A brief history of everything.* Boston: Shambala.

Wilber, K. (2000). *A theory of everything.* Boston: Shambala.

Author Note

Joseph Germana received his PhD in psychophysiology from Rutgers University (1965). For the last 40+ years, he has held a full-time teaching position at Virginia Tech. He has published in the fields of experimental and theoretical psychophysiology, systems theory, art and criticism, as well as a book of satires on experimental psychology. For the last 10 years, his teaching interests have returned to their origin: personality, psychology of self, psychology and creative art, humanistic and transpersonal psychologies. His paintings have been widely exhibited.

Editor's Note

Correspondence should be addressed to Joseph Germana, Department of Psychology, 117 Williams Hall, Virginia Tech, Blacksburg, VA 24061.

Discussion Questions for Article 2

Section 9: Personality

Name: _____

PID: _____

Date: __ __ / __ __ / __ __ (MM/DD/YY)

CRN: _____

Recitation Day/Time: _____

Honor Code Signature: _____

1. According to this article, what is creativity?

2. What is the essence of Maslow's creative attitude?

3. According to Rollo May, why is it necessary to understand both "the self and the world" in order to understand either one?

4. How are creativity and life alike?

Section 10
Therapies and Treatment

In many cases, one's interest in psychology is linked to an ultimate desire to work in a clinical setting, providing therapy for individuals with psychological disorders. This introductory psychology class may even be your first step toward a career in psychotherapy. But how does one go about providing psychotherapy? There are as many answers to this question as there are various schools of psychotherapy. Each school has its own explanation of how disorders develop (called etiology) and how to treat the client's particular needs. The psychodynamic therapies are a modern interpretation of the work of Sigmund Freud, who proposed that psychological problems stem from subconscious conflicts largely arising from childhood and sexuality. Freudian psychoanalysis seeks to resolve a client's subconscious conflicts by exploring them in the clinical setting.

Humanistic approaches, which are sometimes called client-centered, owe much to the work of psychologist Carl Rogers. Humanistic approaches are based on his theory that a client who is having psychological difficulties is out of touch with his or her inherent drive towards fulfillment, known as the actualizing tendency. Rogerian therapy defines the role of the therapist as one of providing a safe environment for the client to explore their barriers to fulfillment and experiencing growth; to create this environment, the therapist must display empathy, congruency, and unconditional positive regard for the client. A slight tweak on this theory is seen in Motivational Interviewing, which is often used in treatment for substance users.

Behavioral therapy is largely based on the reinforcement principles you have studied previously during the learning section; behavioral therapy often includes educational and skills training components. Cognitive therapy seeks to help clients by examining the links between their patterns of thinking and emotional responses. Cognitive behavioral therapy emerged, as the name suggests, from both of these therapies as a treatment developed by Aaron Beck specifically for sufferers of depression. Cognitive behavioral therapy has been widened and shown to be effective in treating a multitude of mental disorders, ranging from insomnia to schizophrenia.

Many therapists and training programs for clinical psychologists are beginning to use empirically-supported treatments (also called evidence-based treatment). Empirically-supported treatments are those that have been shown, by research, to be effective for people with the same disorder or diagnosis. Comparing results across studies can give valuable information about the efficacy of certain treatments; indeed, we would rarely consider a single study to be sufficient for empirical support. Another way of testing treatments is by adapting them to a new population and diagnosis and testing their effectiveness. As you read these articles, note how the authors evaluate the efficacy of the treatments examined. How would you rate these interventions?

Article 1: Social Skills Development in Children with Autism Spectrum Disorders: A Review of the Intervention Research

Social skills training groups for children with autism spectrum disorders seek to address the difficulties in social interactions that these children often face. This article is a meta-analysis review comparing results from 14 studies that assessed the efficacy of such social skills groups in children with autism spectrum disorders. Results from these studies were mixed, suggesting further research is needed. Specifically, the authors outline a rigorous process that involves manualized treatments and randomized clinical trials. This process makes it possible to develop a protocol that could be considered empirically supported by the American Psychological Association.

Article 2: The Marijuana Check-up: Promoting Change in Ambivalent Marijuana Users

The researchers in the second article adapted a program that has been moderately successful with alcohol users, the Drinker's Check-up, for a new population, marijuana users. The intervention is specifically designed to address some of the known barriers to treatment for substance users. It targets individuals who are *not* motivated to change their behavior, and it is very brief, requiring only a single ninety-minute session with a therapist. The authors note that individuals in the personalized feedback intervention reported fewer days of use per week and fewer dependence symptoms at a 12-month follow-up when compared with an educational control group.

—*Neville Galloway-Williams*

Social Skills Development in Children with Autism Spectrum Disorders: A Review of the Intervention Research

Susan Williams White
Kathleen Keonig
Lawrence Scahill

Social reciprocity deficits are a core feature of the autism spectrum disorders (ASD). This review summarizes the state of research in group-based social skills training programs for school-age children and adolescents with ASD. All published studies of group social skills interventions between 1985 and 2006 were reviewed, as well as dissertations examining group-based social skills intervention programs. To assess the state of the science, a template developed by an NIMH work group was applied to 14 identified studies. Based on this review, the empirical support for this approach is incomplete, but promising intervention strategies were identified. Recommendations for the design of future treatment trials to guide clinical practice are offered.

Keywords: Autism, Asperger's Disorder, Social skills training

Introduction

Profound deficit in social reciprocity skills is the core, underlying feature of the autism spectrum disorders (ASD), which include autistic disorder, Aspergers disorder, and Pervasive Developmental Disorder—Not Otherwise Specified (PDD-NOS). Socialization deficits are a major source of impairment regardless of cognitive or language ability for individuals with ASD (Carter, Davis, Klin, & Volkmar, 2005). Furthermore, social skill deficits do not remit with development. Indeed, impairment and distress may increase as children approach adolescence because the social milieu becomes more complex and the child becomes more aware of their social disability (Schopler & Mesibov, 1983; Tantam, 2003).

Individuals with ASD suffer direct and indirect consequences related to social interaction deficits. Youth with ASD often report a desire for more peer social interaction, and may also express poor social support and more loneliness than their typically developing peers (Bauminger & Kasari, 2000). Ironically, when integrated with typically developing peers in mainstream classrooms, children and adolescents with ASD may be at increased risk for peer rejection and social isolation (Chamberlain, 2001). There is also evidence that social skill deficits in youth with ASD contribute to academic and occupational underachievement (Howlin & Goode, 1998). Finally, social skill deficits may presage mood and anxiety problems later in development (Myles, 2003; Myles, Bock, & Simpson, 2001; Tantam, 2003).

The social impairments in individuals with ASD are diverse and involve speech, linguistic conventions and interpersonal interaction. Frequently identified problem areas include impairments in social pragmatics (e.g., turn-taking in conversation and the ability to take the listener's perspective), poor speech prosody (e.g., typical rising and falling of voice pitch and inflection that aids verbal communication), a tendency to dwell on certain topics, difficulty understanding and expressing emotions, and difficulty interpreting nonliteral language such as sarcasm and metaphor (Krasny, Williams, Provencal, & Ozonoff, 2003; Kerbel & Grunwell, 1998; Shaked & Yirmiya, 2003; Tager-Flusberg, 2003). Interventions based on principles of applied behavior analysis have been shown to improve functional communication skills in children with ASD and decrease problematic behaviors such as aggression (Hanley, Iwata, & Thompson, 2001; Lovaas, 1987), but therapeutic interventions targeting social deficits have not achieved the same level of attention (Bailey, 2001). Indeed, social deficits in this population remain a major treatment challenge (Weiss & Harris, 2001).

For a sizeable proportion of individuals with ASD, the social deficits are not explained by lack of social interest. Lack of social skills and an ability to determine when to use such skills also contribute to the overall disability (Mesibov, 1984;

Bauminger, 2003). Given that children with ASD fail to acquire appropriate social skills and may lack opportunities for positive peer interactions, explicit training in a group format is a rational intervention. Moreover, given the increased recognition of ASD in children with average cognitive ability (Croen, Grether, J.K., Hoogstrate, J., & Selvin, 2002) and the emphasis on the inclusion of students with special needs in regular education classrooms (Williams, Johnson, & Sukhodolsky, 2005), schools and clinicians can expect to be increasingly called upon to enhance the social deficits of school-age children and adolescents with ASD.

Social skills training (SST) is one type of child-specific intervention (McConnell, 2002). This intervention involves teaching specific skills (e.g., maintaining eye contact, initiating conversation) through behavioral and social learning techniques (Cooper, Griffith, & Filer, 1999). SST has been reported to be an effective component of treatment regimens for many childhood disorders including childhood social phobia (Spence, Donovan, & Brechman-Toussaint, 2000) and specific learning disabilities (Forness & Kavale, 1999). Group-based SST is an appealing intervention approach for use with children with ASD because it provides the opportunity to practice newly learned skills in a relatively naturalistic format that may promote interaction with other children (Barry et al., 2003). The goal of this review is to provide guidance on the logical 'next steps' in research on group-based SST for ASD in service of the broader goal of establishing efficacy and promoting dissemination of effective interventions for ASD. The review is organized according to the following aims: (1) to summarize the state of empirical research on group-based SST for ASD; (2) to identify limitations within this body of research in order to inform future treatment trials; and (3) to identify promising outcome measures and techniques that could inform the enterprise of manual development.

Methods

Search Strategies

This review was based on a systematic search of published research and unpublished dissertation studies available through August 2006. The *Psych-Info* and *Medline* online databases were searched concurrently for entries containing any combination of the terms: (1) *autism* or *asperger*; (2) either *social* or *socialization*, and (3) *treatment*, *intervention*, or *training*. Abstracts of identified articles were then screened for three inclusion criteria: (a) an explicitly identified, direct SST intervention was implemented; (b) a group format was employed; (c) and the target population was school-age children or adolescents diagnosed with ASD, including autism, Asperger's Disorder, or PDD-NOS. Thus, studies of groups comprised of adults or preschoolers with ASD or children with developmental disorders not on the autism spectrum, were excluded from this review. Similarly, studies describing interventions delivered in a one-on-one format were excluded, as were studies of interventions not delivered to children with ASD (e.g., parent or peer training only). To ensure full inclusion of relevant studies, references of the articles identified through this process were reviewed to identify "ancestor" studies.

Criteria for Evaluation

An empirically supported treatment (EST) is one that has been identified as having a rigorous line of research, usually in the form of randomized clinical trials (RCTs), supporting its utility as a treatment for a particular disorder (American Psychological Association Division 12 Task Force on Promotion and Dissemination of Psychological Procedures, 1995). Empirical support for efficacy can be established through well-designed group experiments or several (>9) single case experiments. In addition, the experiments must be conducted with treatment *manuals* and the patient samples must be *clearly defined*. Establishing a psychosocial intervention as an EST clearly requires much more than preliminary evidence. The role of systematic reviews is to evaluate the state of the art and identify progress and gaps in the field.

Following a systematic assessment of the field of psychosocial intervention in ASD more broadly, an NIMH working group recommended a stepwise approach to the development, testing, and dissemination of psychosocial interventions (Smith, Scahill, Dawson et al., 2006). This starts with technique development, which may be validated by single subject design. The next step might be a case series in which a set of techniques could be examined in a pilot study. Following this pilot phase, a promising set of techniques can be assembled into a manual. A useful, though only rarely accomplished step in ASD research, is pilot testing of the manual across sites. Multi-site pilot testing of a treatment manual demonstrates that the intervention is acceptable to the patient population, can be implemented uniformly by different therapists, and provides preliminary data on efficacy. Next, RCTs are conducted to test the efficacy of the intervention under controlled conditions. The distinct advantage to multisite trials in the conduct of RCTs is their ability to show exportability of the intervention and to accrue a sufficient sample size in a timely manner. To demonstrate effectiveness, the last step is to implement the intervention in community settings (e.g., clinics, schools).

Using the template presented by Smith et al. (2006), the literature on SST was evaluated to summarize the state of the art in and to guide the next round of treatment trials. After summarizing the studies' inclusion/exclusion criteria and outcome measurement procedures used, the studies are reviewed according to the phases of research development outlined by Smith and colleagues (2006): (1) Phase I: Formulation and systematic examination of intervention techniques;

(2) Phase II: Manual development; (3) Phase III: RCT; and (4) Phase IV: Community effectiveness studies. The review also identifies specific treatment strategies that appear promising.

Results

The initial literature search resulted in over 200 citations. Ten of the studies met the stated inclusion criteria (direct SST intervention delivered in group format to school-age youth with ASD), three of which were unpublished dissertations. Many of the unselected studies from the initial pool involved samples outside the targeted age range (e.g., preschoolers) or without clear ASD diagnoses. The second phase, in which identified study's references were searched, resulted in four additional published articles for a total of 14 empirical studies of group-based SST programs for children and adolescents diagnosed with ASD. Table 1 summarizes the study designs and how well each study fulfilled specific criteria necessary for replication, including detailed subject characterization, use of an explicitly identified treatment manual, and use of a control group. Table 2 summarizes the outcomes of the 14 studies.

TABLE 1 Studies of group-based social skills training programs for children with ASD.

Author	N	Age range	Characteristics*			Design/Sample
			A	B	C	
Mesibov (1984)	15	14–35	No	No	No	Pre-post
Williams (1989)	10	9–15	No	No	No	Pre-post
Ozonoff & Miller (1995)	9	7–13	Yes	No	Yes	Controlled
Marriage et al. (1995)	8	8–12	No	No	No	Pre-post
Cotter (1997)	6	7–13	Yes	No	No	Single-subject
Mishna & Muskat (1998)	6	10–13	No	No	No	Pre-post
Barnhill et al. (2002)	8	12–17	No	Yes	No	Pre-post
Barry et al. (2003)	4	6–9	Yes	No	No	Pre-post
Yang et al. (2003)	6	7–9	No	Yes	Yes	Single subject
Provencal (2003)[a]	20	12–16	Yes	No	Yes	Controlled
Webb et al. (2004)	10	12–17	Yes	Yes	No	Pre-post
Trimarchi (2004)[a]	11	8–12	Yes	Yes	Yes	Controlled
Solomon et al. (2004)	18	8–12	Yes	No	Yes	Controlled
Carter et al. (2004)	10	8–15	No	No	No	Pre-post

Study Characteristics: A, Sample described in terms of age, diagnoses, ascertainment source(s), functional level and identified inclusion criteria; B, Explicitly identified use of a treatment manual; C, Study employed a control group
[a] Dissertation study

TABLE 2   Outcome measures used and findings

Author	Type of outcome measure[a]						Findings
	Direct	Parent	Other	Self	Observ	Accept	
Mesibov (1984)	–	x	–	x	x	–	No quantitative data. Anecdotal reports indicated that participants received positive peer social experience in group
Williams (1989)	–	–	x	–	–	–	Only significant improvement from baseline to endpoint (4 years) was in peer relations [school staff report]
Ozonoff & Miller (1995)	x	x	x	–	–	–	No change in SSRS over time or between groups. Theory of mind skills improved with SST, relative to controls (ES = 1.6)
Marriage et al. (1995)	–	x	–	–	–	–	Parent reported children's social skills showed negligible pre/post change
Cotter (1997)	–	x	x	–	x	–	Significant improvement (P < .05) on parent-report SSRS. No significant improvement in observed behaviors or teacher ratings
Mishna & Muskat (1998)	–	–	–	–	–	p,c	No quantitative data; 5 of 6 boys participated in post-group interview. All stated that they enjoyed group and felt safe
Barnhill et al. (2002)	x	–	–	–	–	p,c	Five of Seven assessed subjects improved scores on DANVA2; no statistically significant improvement
Barry et al. (2003)		x	–	x	x	–	Improvements in greeting and play skills [direct observations]. No change in SSRS (pretest = 75.7, posttest = 77.5)
Yang et al. (2003)	–	–	–	–	x	–	Improvement in frequency of positive social behavior for SST group. Group effect size: .02–.21; Control effect size: .01–.04
Provencal (2003)[b]	x	x	x	x	–	p	Large effect-symptom reduction: ADOS[η_p^2 = .21], medium effectsocial skills: SSRS[η_p^2 = .08], small effect-knowledge of friendship: Friendship interview[η_p^2 = .05]
Webb et al. (2004)	x	x	–	–	x	p,c	No improvement in social competence [parent-report SSRS] Knowledge of social skills improved: pre-, M = 2.4, post-, M = 8.2

(Continued)

TABLE 2 Outcome measures used and findings (cont.)

Author	Type of outcome measure[a]						Findings
	Direct	Parent	Other	Self	Observ	Accept	
Trimarchi (2004)[b]	–	x	x	–	–	p,c	No differences in parent/teacher-report symptom severity. Parents reported at least minimal improvement on (90%) targeted skills
Solomon et al. (2004)	x	x	–	–	–	–	Significant improvement in facial recognition on DANVA2 ($F = 12.51$, $P = .003$) & problem solving ($F = 4.44$, $P < .05$)
Carter et al. (2004)	–	–	–	–	–	p,c	No quantitative data. Qualitative data indicated fair participant and parent satisfaction

[a] *Type of social functioning outcome measure:* Direct, direct testing or assessment of child's skills or knowledge; Parent, parent-report measure; Other, other-report (e.g., teacher); Self, self-rating; Observ, coded behavioral observations; Accept, parent (p) or child (c) ratings of acceptability, or satisfaction with group
Note: x = measure used; – = measure not used

Study Samples

The most commonly reported inclusion criteria across the 14 studies were ASD diagnosis and age range. All of the reviewed studies specified an autism spectrum disorder as one of the inclusion criteria for group participants. In one study, educational eligibility for an ASD program fulfilled this criterion (Webb et al., 2004). In most, a clinical diagnosis was indicated. Only three studies (Cotter, 1997; Provencal, 2003; Solomon, Goodlin-Jones, & Anders, 2004), however, specified use of widely used and standardized diagnostic tools for ASD that are considered reliable and valid (i.e., Autism Diagnostic Interview-Revised: ADI-R; Lord et al., 1994; Autism Diagnostic Observation Schedule: ADOS; Lord et al., 2000) to confirm diagnoses. It should be noted, however, that some of the studies were published prior to the publication of these diagnostic tools. Some studies used additional entry criteria based on dimensional cutoffs (e.g., minimum standard scores on language or intellectual ability measures). Other studies required placement in a mainstream classroom. Collectively, participants in these studies ranged in age from 6 years to 35 years, with some studies accepting a wide age range (e.g., Mesibov, 1984: ages 14–35). Of note, although this review is focused on SST for minors, the Mesibov (1984) study was included because its participants comprised both adolescents and adults.

Subjects were drawn from multiple sources, including research databases (e.g., Barry et al., 2003), schools (e.g., Webb et al., 2004), parent support groups (e.g., Carter et al., 2004), and local autism societies (e.g., Ozonoff & Miller, 1995).

Some studies specifically mentioned that subjects were selected based on a desire for more social interaction (Barry et al., 2003). Inclusion criteria were sometimes ambiguous, referring to "level of commitment" and "appropriateness of participation" (Barnhill et al., 2002; p. 113) or "features of Asperger" and "average cognitive reasoning" (Mishna & Muskat, 1998; p. 103), or not reporting any inclusion criteria beyond the ASD diagnosis (Yang et al., 2003).

Outcome Measurement

A variety of outcome measures were employed in these 14 studies, including parent-report measures of social skills, teacher reports, child self-reports of knowledge of social skills, and direct behavioral observations (Table 2). The most frequently used parent-report quantitative measure of social skills was the Social Skills Rating System (SSRS; Gresham & Elliott, 1990). The SSRS was developed to help screen for social behavior difficulties in typically developing children. Five studies reported using the SSRS as an outcome measure (Cotter, 1997; Barry et al., 2003; Ozonoff & Miller, 1995; Provencal, 2003; Webb et al., 2004). Provencal (2003) also used the adolescent self-rating form of the SSRS and teachers were occasionally used as reporters (Cotter, 1997; Yang et al., 2003).

Child self-report was used in some of the studies. Barry et al. (2003) evaluated children's self-reported feelings of loneliness (Asher & Wheeler, 1985), and Solomon et al. (2004) included self-reported depressive symptoms in the children. Webb et al. (2004) used a paper and pencil measure concerning knowledge of social skills. Some studies used formal assessment instruments that specifically addressed the skills targeted in the intervention. For instance, Barnhill and colleagues (2002) employed the Diagnostic Analysis of Nonverbal Accuracy 2 (DANVA2; Nowicki, 1997), as did Solomon et al. (2004). This measure assesses nonverbal communication skills including emotion recognition through facial expressions and tone of voice. Ozonoff and Miller (1995) used several theory of mind tasks in addition to the SSRS. Theory of mind tasks were included to assess social cognition abilities, such as false beliefs and second-order attributions. These measures were apparently selected because the intervention focused on teaching theory of mind skills and perspective taking. Feasibility and acceptability of the interventions were assessed in two studies (Trimarchi, 2004; Webb et al., 2004), with parent and child-report surveys of satisfaction with the group experience.

Four studies reported direct observational assessments. Barry et al. (2003) assessed the presence or absence of specific skills during 5-minute play sessions with typical peers. Yang et al. (2003) had teachers do event recording of socially appropriate behaviors (e.g., playing with classmates). Mesibov (1984) rated socially appropriate behaviors, such as number of questions asked, during role-plays with a confederate. Cotter (1997) used an observational coding system to record behaviors during videotaped dyadic play assessment sessions with a peer. A strength of the Cotter study was that the coders were blind to the hypothesis of the study. In the Yang et al. (2003) study, teachers were aware of the program but did not know when the intervention was implemented. Barry et al. (2003) used student raters who were not blind to the treatment goals or study hypotheses; the Mesibov (1984) study did not specify who conducted the observations.

Qualitative and observational data from these studies generally indicate beneficial effects. For instance, Barnhill et al. (2002) reported that, at the endpoint of the intervention, all of the parents wanted their children to continue in the group. Mishna and Muskat (1998) reported that subjects enjoyed being in the group. Evidence for the efficacy of these interventions as measured by quantitative skill-based measures, on the other hand, is inconsistent. Some studies showed no improvement (Ozonoff & Miller, 1995; Webb et al., 2004) and others reported small to moderate improvements (Cotter, 1997; Provencal, 2003). Change was infrequently observed on parent-reported skill-based measures of children's behavior in naturalistic settings, despite generally high levels of satisfaction with the groups and reported gains in knowledge. Another consideration in synthesizing the findings is the possibility of differential improvement in various skills. For instance, Barry et al. (2003) found that play skills and greeting skills (based on coded observations) improved when they were specifically taught. Despite specific instruction, however, improvement in conversation skills showed smaller effects. This difference in improvement across skills may indicate that some skills are more amenable for teaching using scripts and concrete rules, while perhaps 'higher level' skills (e.g., maintaining a conversation) require different teaching approaches (Barry et al., 2003).

Of the studies employing quantitative data analysis, many did not report effect sizes or data with which to compute effect sizes, making comparison across studies and intervention approaches difficult. Ozonoff and Miller (1995) found that performance on theory of mind tasks improved substantially, reporting an effect size for a group difference (treatment versus control) of 1.6. Unfortunately, this degree of improvement was not realized in actual social skill use as measured by the SSRS (Ozonoff & Miller, 1995). The intervention conducted by Solomon and colleagues (2004) also targeted theory of mind, along with emotion recognition/understanding and executive functioning. They reported statistically significant improvements in the treatment group in facial expression recognition and problem solving, but did not include measures of day-to-day social functioning, other than parent logs of problem behavior (Solomon et al., 2004).

Webb et al. (2004) targeted five core social skills in their SCORE Skills Strategy Program. Results indicated that participants increased their knowledge of the targeted social skills and demonstrated improved proficiency in four of the five skills, as measured by non-blinded behavior ratings. However, similar to Ozonoff and Miller (1995) and Solomon et al. (2004), parent reported SSRS showed no significant improvement, indicating that parental perceptions of social competence did not change. The Cotter (1997) study reported statistically significant improvements in parent reported SSRS scores for their six participants; however, inadequate data was provided with which to calculate effect size. Provencal (2003), calculating effects sizes based on the strength of association between the intervention and the outcome measures, reported a fairly large effect for the ADOS (.21) as well as on the SSRS (.19).

Phase I: Technique Refinement

As discussed by Smith et al. (in press), the goal of this first phase is to refine treatment strategies and test the efficacy of these techniques. This may be accomplished through single-case studies. In the single-case design, data are collected continuously through direct observation, in order to evaluate the change in a specific behavior following the implementation of the intervention under study. This can also be accomplished via between-group studies, though the single-subject design is more sensitive to detecting effects of specific techniques.

Using single-subject methodology, Yang et al. (2003) assessed their SST program with an AB design. The baseline was established by repeated measures in the week prior to intervention. Once the baseline was established, the SST program was initiated. Four children received the training program and two were in the education control condition. Based on the report of teachers who were unaware of when the intervention began, the frequency of positive social behaviors increased for those in SST, compared to students in the control condition (Yang et al., 2003). Cotter (1997) employed a single-subject, repeated-measures design with six children. Six pre-identified target behaviors were coded during repeated, eight-minute dyadic play sessions with typically developing peers. Raters were blind to the study hypothesis, child identity, and assessment session. This study showed the children did not improve significantly in naturalistic interactions with peers, although they did demonstrate improved use of targeted social skills within adult directed activities in the training setting. The other studies in Table 1 used a pre-post design or comparison of SST to a control condition, but no studies used random assignment. As shown in Table 1, sample sizes were small. The largest sample included 10 in the experimental group and 10 in the control group (Provencal, 2003).

Phase II: Manual Development

Treatment manuals, which assemble and organize intervention procedures, are necessary prerequisites for conducting and replicating clinical trials. Although treatment manuals do not guarantee uniform delivery of the intervention, standardization of the intervention cannot be assured without them (Smith et al., 2006). Most of the studies in this review did not use a treatment manual. Two of the studies (Trimarchi, 2004; Yang et al., 2003) used published manuals developed specifically for use with children with ASD. Two studies adapted treatment manuals from other populations such as children with learning disabilities (Barnhill et al., 2002; Webb et al., 2004). Several studies (Barry et al., 2003; Cotter, 1997; Mesibov, 1984; Ozonoff & Miller, 1995; Provencal, 2003; Williams, 1989) provided detailed descriptions of specific activities, while others did not (Marriage et al., 1995; Mishna & Muskat, 1998). The absence of a clear description of the full curriculum or the group activities used in the program renders replication in a clinical trial or practice impossible.

Phase III: Randomized Clinical Trials

After initial feasibility studies demonstrate that an intervention manual can be delivered as planned and is acceptable to clinicians and subjects, the manual is ready for a RCT to evaluate efficacy (Smith et al., 2006). Of the 14 studies reviewed, five included a comparison group and none of these used random assignment to condition. Provencal (2003) assigned the first 10 adolescents enrolled in the study to the experimental group and the next 10 to the control group. Yang et al. (2003) reported that subjects were divided into two trials based on cognitive ability, one with mental retardation and the other with high functioning autism. Within each trial, one child was in the control condition but treatment assignment procedures were not described. In the Ozonoff et al. (1995) trial, placement of the five subjects in the treatment group was determined by subject availability. The four control subjects were not able to attend the weekly sessions at the set time. Trimarchi (2004) and colleagues attempted to conduct a randomized study. Unfortunately, most of the subjects randomized to the wait-list control withdrew. In response to this attrition, the investigator recruited additional control subjects from other sources (e.g., local support groups), which clearly undermines cross-group comparisons. The withdrawal of subjects in the wait-list control group raises questions about this approach in an RCT. If wait-list control is used, specific steps may be required to guard against attrition.

Phase IV: Effectiveness Studies

Once an intervention demonstrates efficacy via a largescale RCT, effectiveness studies show if similar outcomes can be achieved in settings other than specialized research centers (Smith et al., 2006). Community-based effectiveness studies, in which the intervention is delivered by practitioners in "real world" settings represent an important step in dissemination. These studies test whether an intervention can achieve similar results when delivered by clinicians in non-research settings. The interventions described in this review took place in a variety of settings including schools (Williams, 1989; Yang et al., 2003), public community agencies available for research (Webb et al., 2004), private practice clinics (Trimarchi, 2004), university classrooms (Barnhill et al., 2002), university-based specialty treatment clinics (Barry et al., 2003), and university-based research clinics (Mesibov, 1984; Provencal, 2003; Cotter, 1997). In some studies, it was unclear where the intervention took place (Marriage et al., 1995; Mesibov, 1984; Mishna & Muskat, 1998; Ozonoff & Miller, 1995).

Several of the studies implemented intervention programs developed by the authors (e.g., Yang et al., 2003) but this was not always the case. For example, Webb and colleagues (2004) evaluated the SCORE Skills Strategy Program (Vernon, Schumaker, & Deshler, 2001) in children with ASD. This program had been developed and tested in children with learning disabilities. Trimarchi (2004) evaluated a curriculum developed for youth with ASD and related conditions, SST for Children and Adolescents with Asperger Syndrome and Social-Communication Problems (Baker, 2003). None of the studies in this review can be described as an effectiveness trial.

Promising Treatment Strategies

Specific treatment components that comprise SST interventions for children with ASD have not been systematically evaluated. However, several intervention strategies show promise. Frequently cited intervention strategies implemented in the reviewed studies are included in Table 3. These strategies may be considered to be promising, or meriting further investigation, based on theoretical and logical links to characteristics of youth with ASD (e.g., framing complex social conventions as rules that can be learned, to build on proclivities for structure) as well as the preliminary efficacy data presented in these studies.

In addition to the studies reviewed here, other researchers have proposed strategies used in a variety of contexts (e.g., single subject studies), which may be beneficial in group-delivered social skills instruction for individuals with ASD (Brent, Rios, Happe, & Charman, 2004; Krasny et al., 2003; Weiss & Harris, 2001). Techniques based on Pivotal Response Training (Koegel, Koegel, & Brookman, 2005), for example, can be incorporated into group-based programs (e.g., child choice of activities). Conducting a functional analysis of interfering behaviors to identify maintaining factors, an approach often used in applied behavior analysis, can also be applied in a group teaching format. These strategies may be helpful when integrated into group-based SST programs for children with ASD, but they require further empirical investigation in this context.

TABLE 3   Promising teaching strategies for social skills training in ASD.

Goal	Strategies
Increase social motivation	Foster self-awareness and self-esteem
	Develop nurturing, fun environment
	Intersperse new skills with previously mastered skills
	Start with simple, easily learned skills (errorless teaching)
Increase social initiations	Make social rules clear and concrete (e.g., stay one arm's length from other person)
	Model age-appropriate initiation strategies
	Use natural reinforcers for social initiations (e.g., follow child's conversation lead/interest)
	Teach simple social 'scripts' for common situations
Improve appropriate social responding	Teach social response scripts
	Reinforce response attempts
	Use modeling and role-play to teach skills
Reduce interfering behaviors	Make teaching structured & predictable
	Differentially reinforce positive behaviors
	Keep behavior charts (e.g., checkmarks or stars) for positive behavior
	Review socially appropriate and inappropriate behaviors of the participants as a group, via video or audiotape segments
Promote skill generalization	Orchestrate peer involvement (e.g., prompting & initiating social interactions, physical proximity)
	Use multiple trainers & individuals with which to practice skills
	Involve parents in training
	Provide opportunities to practice skills in safe, natural settings (e.g., field trips)
	Use time between session to practice skills (e.g., via 'homework')

Discussion

This comprehensive review had two goals: (1) to summarize the state of the research on group-based SST programs for youth with ASD, and (2) to provide recommendations for how to proceed in the scientific advancement and evaluation of this type of intervention. With regard to the first goal, it appears that considerable progress has been made on the first two phases of treatment research development: technique identification and manual development. Many of the studies demonstrated that targeted skills can be improved in youth with ASD. However, this improvement may be confined to those skills that are directly and explicitly taught. Further, there is evidence that skills may be displayed in laboratory/clinic settings, but not necessarily applied in the child's daily life at school or home. Generalization and flexible skill use in natural environments continues to be a challenge, based on parent reported social competency.

Several promising intervention strategies were identified. By and large, these strategies were developed based on knowledge of the literature, including characteristic learning styles and specific deficits associated with ASD, as well as knowledge of the individual participants in the groups. With some exceptions (e.g., Ozonoff & Miller, 1995), few of the intervention programs included in this review were based on a defined theoretical conceptualization of ASD. Some investigators adapted general theoretical approaches (e.g., social learning theory; Cotter, 1997) for the intervention. It is clear that further refinement and evaluation of the strategies is needed. Future studies will also need to compare the relative impact of these strategies and develop treatment manuals that operationalize how to most effectively implement them.

With regard to the second goal, this review identified several methodological weaknesses in group-based SST trials for children with ASD. Major weaknesses include inadequate measurement of social skills and deficits associated with ASD, small and poorly characterized samples, and minimal examination of the degree to which learned skills generalize. Several investigators have cited the need for reliable and socially valid outcome measures that are sensitive to change in treatment studies with this population (Krasny et al., 2003; Ozonoff & Miller, 1995; Scahill & Lord, 2004; Wolery & Garfinkle, 2002). Such measures should not only assess whether a child learned a specific skill in the context of treatment, but also the degree to which the child then actually uses and adapts new skills in natural environments (e.g., at school). At minimum, this calls for ratings from multiple informants. This review shows that there is little consensus on outcome measures for SST.

This lack of consensus may reflect the simple fact that appropriate measures are not available. For instance, the Social Skills Rating System (SSRS; Gresham & Elliott, 1990) is a commonly used measure of actual skill use. However, most studies that used the SSRS did not show change with treatment. This could be due to small sample sizes, the use of an ineffective treatment, or perhaps this measure is not appropriate for assessing the impact of such interventions in children with ASD. The SSRS measures broad-based behaviors associated with developing social skills but does not assess the nuances of behavior associated with social reciprocity that are lacking in children with autism. Indeed, the SSRS was created to assess change in typically developing children with disruptive behavior problems, not children with ASD (Gresham & Elliott, 1990). Other measures (e.g., Social Responsiveness Scale; Constantino, Przybeck, Friesen, & Todd, 2000; Social Competence Inventory; Rydell, Hagekull, & Bohlin, 1997), which are more relevant to ASD and may be sensitive to change with treatment, could be useful but have not been employed thus far.

Several studies used coded behavioral observations as an outcome measure. This approach, though appealing because of its reduced risk of reporter-bias, is vulnerable to problems such as faulty recording equipment and uncertain stability of the observed behavior even in the absence of treatment (Scahill & Lord, 2004). In addition, in a large trial, direct observational measurement would be time-consuming and expensive. Another approach to obtaining data across settings is the use of multiple informants (e.g., parent, teacher, and child). Teachers may be particularly informative because they can provide behavioral ratings that are blind to the intervention, at least when the intervention is not delivered at school. Child self-reports may be useful in gathering data on closely related outcomes such as severity of anxiety or depression (Stallings & March, 1995). Future studies should also consider the use of blinded, independent evaluators. In most of the studies reviewed here, the principal investigator or group leader was responsible for administering and scoring outcome measures, introducing undue potential bias. At present, there are no clinician ratings of social skills for youth with ASD. In the absence of such measures, global measures such as the clinical global improvement (CGI) score could be used. Future studies should include examination of outcome measures as well as measurement strategies such as using multiple informants and independent evaluators.

Equally as important as sensitive and valid outcome measures is subject characterization, including documentation of diagnosis and intellectual and adaptive functioning (Scahill & Lord, 2004). Subject characterization provides essential information on who was in the trial and indicates for whom the treatment is relevant. Adequate subject characterization is also essential for replication. Three of the 14 studies reported using either the ADI-R or ADOS for subject selection (Cotter, 1997; Provencal, 2003; Solomon et al., 2004). Barry et al. (2003) reported use of structured play sessions and parent interviews, but did not identify the instruments used. In some studies, the diagnosis was based on parent report or school program eligibility. In evaluating the appropriateness of a given program for use with a defined group of children, consideration must be given to how the sample was ascertained. Discrepancies between clinical diagnosis of ASD and educational classification or class placement are common. Ideally, programs that are intended to be implemented in schools should include some type of school-based criteria (e.g., a special needs classification of autism). Some students have clinical ASD diagnoses, but do not have an educational classification of autism or receive school-based services (Williams, Scahill, Klin, Koenig, & Volkmar, in press). Treatment providers and clinical investigators, as well as parents, need to be aware of these discrepancies.

Another limitation in the studies included in this review is the lack of control groups with random assignment. Uncontrolled trials do not permit attribution of observed effects to the intervention (i.e., improvement may be due to the passage of time alone). Furthermore, without random assignment to groups, it is impossible to assume group equivalence. Clinical research with this population poses special challenges. Given the variability in the expression of ASD across children, investigators need to consider other variables (e.g., level of cognitive functioning) in case ascertainment and group assignment, to ensure that group assignment is balanced as well as random. A practical dilemma must be faced when making decisions of how heterogeneous a sample should be. Indeed, if inclusion criteria are too stringent, recruitment can lag and generalizability may be threatened (Scahill & Lord, 2004).

Conclusion

Despite the pervasive socialization deficits in youth with ASD and the negative impact that such deficits have on other aspects of development, we know relatively little about efficacious psychosocial intervention approaches. Unfortunately, only preliminary evidence is available regarding the efficacy of structured curricula and specific treatment strategies. Group-based SST is an under-studied, but worthy, candidate for further development and testing.

This review synthesized available research on group-based SST programs for children with ASD to establish the state of the art and to guide the next step for treatment trials. Based on this review, several recommendations are offered. First, there is a need to develop and test structured, manual-based curricula. Structured interventions are essential for replication and are amenable to evaluation of treatment fidelity. Multi-site feasibility studies demonstrating that the structured intervention can be applied uniformly across sites is another important step toward formal testing and dissemination. Second, future studies should use control groups, with random assignment whenever possible. Third, as in other fields of empirical research, social skills intervention trials in ASD should identify a primary outcome measure. However, multiple informants and the use of independent raters who are blind to treatment assignment should become the standard. Clearly, the progress of treatment research rests on the application of reliable and valid outcome measures that are practical to use and sensitive to change. The uncertain state of outcome measures in ASD suggests that new measures are needed. Alternatively, available measures may be adapted for use in the ASD population. The utility of new or adapted outcome measures should be evaluated for reliability and validity, as well as the cost and ease of interpretation.

Fourth, in order to accrue sufficient sample sizes to evaluate the impact of a treatment in a randomized study, multi-site treatment trials are needed. A mainstay in medical research, multi-site RCTs will be increasingly important to psychosocial intervention research (Lord, Wagner, & Rogers et al., 2005; Smith et al.,

2006). Indeed, the National Institute of Mental Health has issued a call for more RCTs to be conducted to test the efficacy and safety of both pharmacological and psychosocial treatments (Vitiello & Wagner, 2004). In conclusion, group-based social skill training approaches may be a useful intervention for children with ASD, based on evidence provided by several small initial efficacy studies. The field now requires the development of manual-based curricula that can be evaluated in a step-wise fashion in feasibility studies and in large-scale RCT.

Acknowledgments

The authors acknowledge support from the following grants: National Institutes of Mental Health Childhood Neuropsychiatric Disorders Training Grant at the Yale University Child Study Center [T32 #MH18268; PI: James F. Leckman, MD]; Organization for Autism Research [PI: Lawrence Scahill, MSN, PhD].

References

Asher, S. R., & Wheeler, V. A. (1985). Children's loneliness: A comparison of rejected and neglected peer status. *Journal of Consulting and Clinical Psychology*, 53, 500–505.

Bailey, K. J. (2001). Social competence of children with autism classified as best-outcome following behavior analytic treatment. Unpublished doctoral dissertation. Washington State University.

Baker, J. E. (2003). *Social skills training for children with asperger syndrome, high-functioning autism, and related social communication disorders.* Autism: Asperger Publishing Company.

*Barnhill, G. P., Cook, K. T., Tebbenhamp, K., & Myles, B. S. (2002). The effectiveness of social skills intervention targeting nonverbal communication for adolescents with asperger syndrome and related pervasive developmental delays. *Focus on Autism and Other Developmental Disabilities*, 17, 112–118.

*Barry, T. D., Klinger, L. G., Lee, J. M., Palardy, N., Gilmore, T., & Bodin, S. D. (2003). Examining the effectiveness of an outpatient clinic-based social skills group for high-functioning children with autism. *Journal of Autism and Developmental Disorders*, 33, 685–701.

Bauminger, N. (2003). Peer interaction and loneliness in high functioning children with autism. *Journal of Autism and Developmental Disorders*, 33, 489–507.

Bauminger, N., & Kasari, C. (2000). Loneliness and friendship in high-functioning children with autism. Child Development, 71, 447–456.

Brent, E., Rios, P., Happe, F., & Charman, T. (2004). Performance of children with autism spectrum disorder on advanced theory of mind tasks. *Autism*, 8, 283–299.

Carter, A. S., Davis, N. O., Klin, A., & Volkmar, F. R. (2005). Social development in autism. In F. R. Volkmar, R. Paul, A. Klin, & D. Cohen (Eds.), *Handbook of autism and pervasive developmental disorders: Vol. 1. Diagnosis, development, neurobiology, and behavior.* Hoboken, NJ: John Wiley & Sons.

*Carter, C., Meckes, L., Pritchard, L., Swensen, S., Wittman, P. P., & Velde, B. (2004). The friendship club: An after-school program for children with asperger syndrome. *Fam Community Health*, 27, 143–150.

Chamberlain, B. O. (2001). Isolation or involvement? The social networks of children with autism included in regular classes. Unpublished doctoral dissertation, University of California, Los Angeles.

Constantino, J. N., Przybeck T., Friesen, D., & Todd, R. D. (2000). Reciprocal social behavior in children with and without pervasive developmental disorders. *Journal of Behavioral Pediatrics*, 21, 2–11.

Cooper, M. J., Griffith, K. G., & Filer, J. (1999). School intervention for inclusion of students with and without disabilities. *Focus on Autism and Other Developmental Disabilities*, 14, 110–115.

*Cotter, M. W. (1997). Improving the social behavior of high functioning children with autism: A social skills support group intervention. Unpublished doctoral dissertation, University of Alabama.

Croen, L. A., Grether, J. K., Hoogstrate, J., & Selvin, S. (2002). The changing prevalence of autism in California. *Journal of Autism and Developmental Disorders*, 32, 207–215.

Forness, S., & Kavale, K. (1999). Teaching social skills in children with learning disabilities: A meta-analysis of the research. *Learning Disability Quarterly*, 19, 2–13.

Gresham, F. M., & Elliott, S. N. (1990). *Social skills rating system*. Circle Pines, MN: American Guidance Service.

Hanley, G. P., Iwata, B. A., & Thompson, R. H. (2001). Reinforcement schedule thinning following treatment with functional communication training. *Journal of Applied Behavior Analysis*, 34, 17–38.

Howlin, P., & Goode, S. (1998). Outcome in adult life for people with autism, asperger syndrome. In F. R. Volkmar (Eds.), *Autism and pervasive developmental disorders* (pp. 209–241). New York: Cambridge University Press.

Kerbel, D., & Grunwell, P. (1998). A study of idiom comprehension in children with semantic-pragmatic difficulties. Part II: Between-groups results and discussion. *International Journal of Language and Communication Disorders*, 33, 23–44.

Koegel, L. K., Koegel, R. L., & Brookman, L. I. (2005). Childinitiated interactions that are pivotal in intervention for children with autism. In E. D. Hibbs (Eds.), *Psychosocial treatments for child and adolescents disorders: Empirically based strategies for clinical practice* (2nd ed., pp. 633–657). Washington, DC: American Psychological Association.

Krasny, L., Williams, B. J., Provencal, S., & Ozonoff, S. (2003). Social skills interventions for the autism spectrum: Essential ingredients and a model curriculum. *Child & Adolescent Psychiatric Clinics of North America*, 12, 107–122.

Lord, C., Risi, S., Lambrecht, L., Cook, E. H., & Leventhal, B. L., et al. (2000). The autism diagnostic observation schedule-generic: A standard measure of social and communication deficits associated with the spectrum of autism. *Journal of Autism and Developmental Disorders*, 30, 205–223.

Lord, C., Rutter, M., & LeCouteur, A. (1994). Autism Diagnostic Interview—Revised: A revised version of a diagnostic interview for caregivers of individuals with possible pervasive developmental disorders. *Journal of Autism and Developmental Disorders*, 24, 659–685.

Lord, C., Wagner, A., Rogers, S. Szatmari P., Aman M., & Charman T., et al. (2005). Challenges in evaluating psychosocial interventions for autistic spectrum disorders. *Journal of Autism and Developmental Disorders*, 35(6), 695–708.

Lovaas, O. I. (1987). Behavioral treatment and normal educational and intellectual functioning in young autistic children. *Journal of Consulting and Clinical Psychology*, 55, 3–9.

*Marriage, K. J., Gordon, V., & Brand, L. (1995). A social skills group for boys with asperger's syndrome. *Australian and New Zealand Journal of Psychiatry*, 29, 58–62.

*Mesibov, G. B. (1984). Social skills training with verbal autistic adolescents and adults: A program model. *Journal of Autism and Developmental Disorders*, 14, 395–404.

McConnell, S. R. (2002). Interventions to facilitate social interaction for young children with Autism: Review of available research and recommendations for educational intervention and future research. *Journal of Autism and Developmental Disorders*, 32, 351–373.

*Mishna, F., & Muskat, B. (1998). Group therapy for boys with features of asperger syndrome and concurrent learning disabilities: Finding a peer group. *Journal of Child and Adolescent Group Therapy*, 8, 97–114.

Myles, B. S., Bock, S. J., & Simpson, R. L. (2001). *Asperger syndrome diagnostic scale*. Austin, TX: Pro-Ed.

Nowicki, S. (1997). *Instruction manual for the receptive tests of the diagnostic analysis of nonverbal accuracy 2 (DANVA2)*. Atlanta, GA: Peachtree.

*Ozonoff, S., & Miller, J. N. (1995). Teaching theory of mind: A new approach to social skills training for individuals with autism. *Journal of Autism and Developmental Disorders*, 25, 415–433.

*Provencal, S. L. (2003). The efficacy of a social skills training program for adolescents with autism spectrum disorders. Unpublished doctoral dissertation, University of Utah.

Rydell, A., Hagekull, B., & Bohlin, (1997). Measurement of two social competence spects in middle childhood. *Developmental Psychology*, 33, 824–833 .

Scahill, L., & Lord, C. (2004). Subject selection and characterization in clinical trials in children with autism. *CNS Spectrums*, 9, 22–32.

Schopler, E., & Mesibov, G. (1983). *Autism in adolescents and adults*. New York: Plenum Press.

Shaked, M., & Yirmiya, N. (2003). Understanding social difficulties. In M. Prior (Eds.), *Learning and behavior problems in asperger syndrome* (pp.126–147). New York: Guilford Press.

Smith, T., Scahill, L., Dawson, G., Guthrie, D., Lord, C., & Odom, S., et al. (2006). Designing research studies on psychosocial interventions in autism. *Journal of Autism and Developmental Disorders*, in press.

*Solomon, M., Goodlin-Jones, B. L., & Anders, T. F. (2004). A social adjustment enhancement intervention for high functioning autism, asperger's syndrome, and pervasive developmental disorder NOS. *Journal of Autism and Developmental Disorders*, 34, 649–668.

Spence, S. H., Donovan, C., & Brechman-Toussaint, M. (2000). The treatment of childhood social phobia: The effectiveness of a social skills training-based, cognitive-behavioural intervention, with and without parental involvement. *Journal of Child Psychology & Psychiatry*, 41, 713–726.

Stallings, P., & March, J. S. (1995). Assessment. In J. S. March (Eds.), *Anxiety disorders in children and adolescents*. New York: Guilford Press.

Tager-Flusberg, H. (2003). Effects of language and communicative deficits on learning and behavior. In M. Prior (Eds.), *Learning and behavior problems in asperger syndrome* (pp. 85–103). New York: Guilford Press.

Tantam, D. (2003). The challenge of adolescents and adults with asperger syndrome. *Child Adolescence and Psychiatric Clinics of North America, 12,* 143–163.

Task Force Promot. Dissem. Psychol. Procedures (1995). Training in and dissemination of empirically validated psychological treatments: Report and recommendations. *Clinical Psychologist, 48,* 3–23.

*Trimarchi, C. L. (2004). The implementation and evaluation of a social skills training program for children with asperger syndrome. Unpublished doctoral dissertation, University at Albany, State University of New York.

Vernon, D. S., Schumaker, J. B., & Deschler, D. D. (2001). *The SCORE skills: Social skills for cooperative groups.* Lawrence, KS: Edge Enterprises.

Vitiello, B., & Wagner, A. (2004). Government initiatives in autism clinical trials. *CNS Spectrums, 9,* 66–70.

*Webb, B. J., Miller, S. P., Pierce, T. B., Strawser, S., & Jones, W. P. (2004). Effects of social skill instruction for high functioning adolescents with autism spectrum disorders. *Focus on Autism and Other Developmental Disabilities, 19,* 53–62.

Weiss, M. J., & Harris, S. L. (2001). Teaching social skills to people with autism. *Behavior Modification, 25,* 785–802.

Williams, S. K., Johnson, C., & Sukhodolsky, D. G. (2005). The role of the school psychologist in the inclusive education of school-age children with autism spectrum disorders. *Journal of School Psychology, 43,* 117–136.

Williams, S. K., Scahill, L., Klin, A., Koenig, K., & Volkmar, F. (in press). Educational placements and service use patterns of individuals with autism spectrum disorders. *Journal of Autism and Developmental Disorders.*

*Williams, T. I. (1989). A social skills group for autistic children. *Journal of Autism and Developmental Disorders, 19,* 143–155.

Wolery, M., & Garfinkle, A. N. (2002). Measures in intervention research with young children who have autism. *Journal of Autism and Developmental Disorders, 32,* 463–478.

*Yang, N. K., Schaller, J. L., Huang, T., Wang, M. H., & Tsai, S. (2003). Enhancing appropriate social behaviors for children with autism in general education classrooms: An analysis of six cases. *Education and Training in Developmental Disabilities, 38,* 405–416.

*Included in review.

Editor's Note

S. Williams White, School of Medicine, Virginia Treatment Center for Children, Virginia Commonwealth University, 515 North 10th Street, Richmond, VA 23298, USA e-mail: swilliams25@vcu.edu

L. Scahill, Child Study Center and School of Nursing, Yale University, New Haven, CT, USA

K. Keonig, Child Study Center, Yale University, New Haven, CT, USA

Discussion Questions for Article 1

Section 10: Therapies and Treatment

Name: _____

PID: _____

Date: __ __ / __ __ / __ __ (MM/DD/YY)

CRN: _____

Recitation Day/Time: _____

Honor Code Signature: _____

1. Which disorders are included in the category of autism spectrum disorders (ASD)?

2. What are the criteria for a treatment to be considered empirically supported by the APA?

3. Of the treatment strategies identified as "promising", which do you think would be the most effective? Why?

4. Name two of the methodological problems the authors found with some of the studies examined and explain why they might inappropriately influence a study's results.

Article 2

The Marijuana Check-up: Promoting Change in Ambivalent Marijuana Users

Robert S. Stephens
Roger A. Roffman
Stephanie A. Fearer
Carl Williams
Randy S. Burke

Aims: To evaluate the efficacy of a two-session assessment and feedback intervention designed to reach and increase motivation for change in marijuana users who were experiencing negative consequences but were ambivalent about change. Design: Random assignment to one of two types of feedback conditions or a delayed feedback control (DFC) with follow-up assessments at 7 weeks, 6 months and 12 months. Setting: University of Washington research center in Seattle, Washington. Participants: A total of 188 adult male and female marijuana users who responded to advertisements. Interventions: A personalized feedback (PF) condition utilizing motivational interviewing was compared to an educational control condition labeled multi-media feedback (MMF). Measurements: Marijuana use, dependence symptoms, other associated negative consequences and motivational constructs were assessed at all time-points. Findings: PF participants reported fewer days of use per week, fewer periods of use per day and fewer dependence symptoms at 7 weeks than those in the MMF and DFC conditions. PF participants also reported fewer days of use per week compared to MMF participants at the 12-month follow-up and fewer dependence symptoms at both the 6- and 12-month follow-ups compared to MMF participants.

311

Conclusions: The PF intervention, delivered in the context of a check-up, shows potential as a way of reaching and motivating change in marijuana users with a diagnosable disorder who otherwise are not ready to approach treatment. Ways of augmenting the modest absolute levels of change are discussed.

Keywords: Cannabis, marijuana, motivational enhancement therapy, multimedia feedback, personalized feedback.

Introduction

The number of people in the United States, aged 12 years or older, who used marijuana in 2005 was estimated to be 25.4 million, making it the most commonly used illicit substance [1]. Nearly 5.1 million of these users consumed marijuana on 20 or more days in the past month and 4.1 million of them reported consequences consistent with the diagnosis of either cannabis dependence or abuse. Recent studies have demonstrated the efficacy of a variety of intervention approaches for adult marijuana users who seek treatment [2–6], but marijuana users who experience negative consequences appear to be under-represented in drug treatment. Of those who met criteria for cannabis dependence or abuse in 2003, only 9.8% reported receiving drug abuse treatment. In contrast, 23.6% of those with cocaine abuse or dependence and 13.8% of those abusing pain relievers reported receiving drug treatment [1].

The most commonly reported reasons for not seeking treatment among alcohol and drug users who acknowledged a need for treatment were: (1) not being able to afford the cost; (2) not being ready to stop using; and (3) stigma associated with receiving treatment [1]. Embarrassment, stigma and a negative attitude towards treatment were frequently endorsed in other studies of reasons for delaying seeking treatment [7,8]. Thus, brief, low-cost, low-demand interventions that reduce stigma associated with treatment and do not insist on abstinence as the only goal may be appealing, particularly for users who are in the earlier stages of change or are unsure whether they need treatment or want to quit.

In the present study, the Drinkers' Check-up (DCU) was adapted to reach marijuana users who were experiencing negative consequences but who were ambivalent about change and unlikely to approach formal treatment. The original DCU offered a brief motivational enhancement intervention designed to promote change in alcohol abusers [9]. In order to overcome stigma, the DCU was promoted as a free assessment and feedback service for drinkers who wanted to find out whether alcohol was harming them. Recruitment announcements emphasized that the DCU was confidential, not a treatment program, not intended for 'alcoholics' and that it would be 'up to the individual to decide what, if anything, to do with the feedback' [10]. In the initial session, alcohol use and risk factors for abuse and dependence were assessed. In the second session, a therapist provided normative and risk-related feedback to the participants using a motivational interviewing style [11]. DCU participants appeared similar to clients already in treatment on measures of alcohol use and related problems, but few had ever been in formal treatment. These problem drinkers reduced their alcohol intake significantly and maintained changes up to 18 months after participating in the DCU [10,12]. The DCU appeared to be a promising strategy for attracting and intervening with individuals who might not otherwise approach treatment. However, studies of the DCU have used either short-term (i.e. 6 weeks) delayed feedback control groups [12] or failed to find differences when the motivational interviewing approach was compared with a confrontational approach at a 12-month follow-up [10]. Thus, to date, there are no studies demonstrating long-term change that is clearly attributable to participation in the DCU.

Reviews of other brief, motivational interviewing interventions have found them to be efficacious for a variety of drug and non-drug behavior problems (e.g. [13,14]). Two studies of the treatment of marijuana dependence found that two-session motivational interventions were effective in reducing marijuana use and associated problems [4,6]. Like most other studies of brief treatments, these studies recruited adult marijuana users who were willing to engage in treatment with the goal of abstinence. Such individuals are more likely to make changes than the larger population of users, many of whom use at comparable rates and experience similar negative consequences. To our knowledge, the effects of brief interventions have not been tested with populations of marijuana users who are less motivated to make changes.

In the present study, a brief motivational interviewing intervention was modeled after those offered in the DCU studies and tested in the context of a Marijuana Check-up (MCU). In an initial publication from this project, analyses of baseline data showed that the MCU attracted and enrolled near-daily users of marijuana who experienced negative consequences but were highly ambivalent about making changes [15]. Two-thirds of those screened for participation were in the pre-contemplation or contemplation stage of change. Further, comparisons of those who enrolled in the MCU with a sample of marijuana-dependent users participating in a separate trial of abstinence-oriented treatment showed that MCU participants met fewer abuse and dependence criteria, reported fewer marijuana-related problems and were less ready to make changes despite similar levels of marijuana use. The findings suggested that the MCU may have a role in the continuum of care for substance abuse problems (see [16,17]) by reaching marijuana users with potentially problematic patterns of use who would not be ready to approach formal treatment.

In order to improve upon earlier tests of the DCU, the current study employed two comparison conditions. A 7-week delayed feedback control condition was similar to those used in the DCU studies. It provided a control for baseline assessment effects and allowed for an assessment of short-term efficacy of the motivational interviewing condition relative to no intervention. However, delayed intervention control groups cannot serve as comparison groups at longer-term follow-ups because those assigned to the delayed condition must receive the intervention within a reasonable period of time. Therefore, we developed an attention-placebo feedback condition that served as the comparison group at the longer-term follow-ups. It was important that this control condition fulfill MCU advertising promises regarding the availability of objective feedback about marijuana with no pressure to change, and yet be devoid of personalized normative feedback and the motivational interviewing style central to the target intervention. The result was an educational control condition that provided information about the latest research on marijuana delivered in an objective, stimulating, but largely didactic manner. It was hypothesized that the motivational interviewing intervention would promote greater reductions in marijuana use and related negative consequences relative to both control conditions by increasing readiness to change and enhancing efficacy for change.

Method

Participants

Participants were 188 marijuana-using adults who represented a subset of 587 individuals who responded to advertisements and were screened for participation (see Figure 1). Of the 587 callers, 214 (36%) met one or more exclusion criteria: less than 15 days of marijuana use out of the last 30 days ($n = 139$), action or maintenance stage of change ($n = 40$), heavy alcohol ($n = 20$) or other drug use ($n = 18$), involved in other substance abuse treatment or a self-help group ($n = 25$), had severe psychiatric difficulties ($n = 12$), legal status that might have interfered with participation ($n = 9$), planned to move out of the area within the next 12 months ($n = 8$), did not live within 60 miles of the study site ($n = 5$), living with someone already enrolled in the study ($n = 5$) and not fluent in English ($n = 1$). Self-identification in the action or maintenance stage of change was later dropped as an exclusion criterion, allowing inclusion of 17 otherwise ineligible participants. These participants were prompted to reclassify themselves in either the precontemplation, contemplation or preparation stages based on their interest in further change relative to their pattern of use over the past 30 days. See Stephens and colleagues [15] for analyses showing little, if any, impact of the earlier exclusion of action and maintenance stage participants on the overall characteristics of the sample.

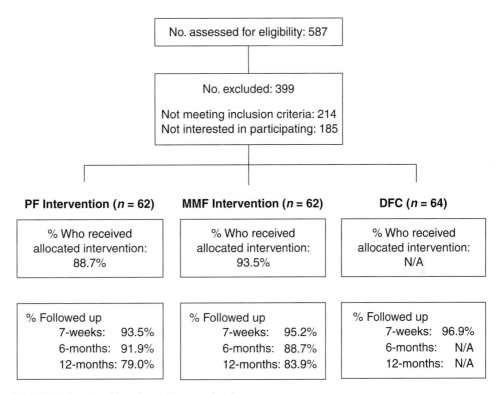

FIGURE 1   Profile of marijuana check-up.

Of the 373 eligible individuals, 185 (50%) failed to schedule or attend an initial assessment session following screening and therefore were not randomized. Eligible individuals who failed to attend the initial assessment were about 4 years younger, reported slightly fewer drinks per typical drinking day and were more likely to be in the precontemplation stage of change compared to those who agreed to participate. Otherwise, eligible enrolled participants and eligible non-enrolled participants appeared very similar demographically, particularly with regard to recent marijuana use. See Stephens *et al.* [15] for a more detailed presentation of differences between the enrolled versus non-enrolled subsamples.

Research Design

Eligible participants were assigned randomly to one of three intervention conditions: (1) personalized feedback (PF; *n* = 62); (2) multimedia feedback (MMF; *n* = 62); or (3) delayed feedback control (DFC; *n* = 64). Participants were assigned using an urn randomization program [18] to balance key variables (i.e. sex; ethnicity; white versus non-white; stage of change: precontemplation/contemplation versus preparation). Both the PF and MMF conditions consisted of a single session delivered individually approximately 1 week after the initial assessment. PF and MMF participants completed follow-up assessments 7 weeks, 6 months and 12 months after the initial assessment. DFC participants waited 7 weeks before completing a follow-up assessment and receiving the feedback intervention of their choice, but were not assessed at subsequent follow-ups.

Procedures

Recruitment for the MCU occurred in the greater Seattle, Washington area via paid newspaper and radio advertisements, public service announcements, posted flyers and outreach at community events. The MCU was advertised as an opportunity for individuals to receive objective feedback about marijuana in a non-judgmental atmosphere. Advertisements emphasized that the MCU was not treatment. Some of the advertisements indicated that individuals would be compensated for their participation. However, interested callers were told that compensation was only for completing in-person follow-up assessments and no incentives were offered for the initial assessment or the feedback sessions. Callers were also told that eligible participants would receive one of two types of feedback or wait 7 weeks before receiving the feedback type of their choice. The PF condition was described as providing feedback about one's personal marijuana use. The MMF condition was described as providing state-of-the-art, objective research findings about marijuana. Detailed presentation and results of project publicity efforts have been published and discussed elsewhere [19].

After describing the project, trained research staff conducted brief screening interviews. Responses to an algorithm placed the individual in one of the stages of change (SOC) [20]: (1) I'm basically satisfied with my use of marijuana and do not plan to change it (precontemplation); (2) I'm thinking about stopping or reducing my use of marijuana, but I don't think I'll begin doing that in the next 30 days (contemplation); (3) I think I will stop or reduce my use of marijuana sometime in the next 30 days (preparation); (4) some time within the past 6 months I stopped or reduced my level of marijuana use and I've not returned to my previous level of use (action); (5) more than 6 months ago, I stopped or reduced my level of marijuana use and I've not returned to my previous level of use (maintenance). Callers who appeared to be eligible based on the screening interviews were scheduled for initial assessment sessions. Ineligible callers were not informed of the reasons for their ineligibility and were given referrals to local treatment providers, if interested.

Initial Assessment   At the initial assessment session, trained research staff administered structured interviews and self-report questionnaires. The Psychoactive Substance Use Disorders section of the Structured Clinical Interview for DSM-IV (SCID) [21] was used to assess current diagnoses (past 90 days) of dependence and abuse for marijuana, alcohol and other substances. Participants who met

DSM-IV diagnostic criteria for dependence on alcohol or a drug other than marijuana during the past 90 days were deemed ineligible and excluded from further participation. The number of cannabis dependence symptoms (range 0–7) served as one index of problem severity.

The time-line follow-back (TLFB) interview [22] utilized calendars for the 90 days prior to the initial assessment to assess the number of days on which marijuana, alcohol and other drugs were used. The average number of days of marijuana use per week was the primary outcome variable. For each day of marijuana use, participants identified the periods of the day during which they smoked (i.e. 6 a.m.–12 p.m.; 12 p.m.–6 p.m.; 6 p.m.–12 a.m.; 12 a.m.–6 a.m.). Totaling the number of periods of use for each day (range 0–4) served as a measure of the extent of use throughout the day. Single-item questions regarding the typical quantity or intensity of marijuana use (e.g. ounces smoked per week, hours high per day, times smoked per day) and the number of standard alcohol drinks consumed per typical day were included at the end of the TLFB interview for descriptive purposes. Interviewers also conducted a detailed assessment of participants' recent in-patient, out-patient and 12-Step group treatment participation related to medical, marijuana, alcohol, other drug and psychological problems.

Participants completed several questionnaires that served as secondary outcomes and potential mediators of intervention effects. The Marijuana Problem Scale (MPS) [6] was used to measure the occurrence of 19 problems related to marijuana in the past 90 days. Counting the number of items endorsed as either minor or major problems resulted in a single index with a range of 0–19 (alpha = 0.85). Two similar questionnaires assessed the same set of 19 negative consequences resulting from alcohol (alpha = 0.82) and drug use (alpha = 0.94) in order to explore the effects of the interventions on other substance use problems.

Self-efficacy for avoiding marijuana use was assessed using a 19-item inventory of high risk situations for use previously shown to predict outcomes both before and after treatment (alpha = 0.91) [23].

The 12-item Readiness to Change Questionnaire (RTC) [24], adapted for marijuana, assessed readiness to change using three subscales of four items each: precontemplation (alpha = 0.78), contemplation (alpha = 0.84) and action (alpha = 0.87).

Other measures were created primarily to promote discussion during feedback in the PF condition. The costs and benefits scale was adapted from the outcome expectancy scale [25] and consisted of 40 items tapping expected positive and negative consequences of reducing marijuana use. The Marijuana Effects Questionnaire (MEQ) consisted of 40 items representing acute positive and negative effects of marijuana.

Follow-up Assessments   The research staff was trained carefully and monitored routinely in the standardized administration of all measures, but was aware of assigned condition. The initial battery of structured interviews and self-report instruments was repeated at each follow-up, with some self-report questionnaires dropped from the 12-month assessment. At the 7-week follow-up, the TLFB assessment was for the period since the initial assessment. At the 6-month and 12-month follow-ups the TLFB was conducted for only the past 90 days. Use indices were converted to weekly averages for comparison with initial assessment values. Participants were paid $50 for completing each follow-up assessment. Participants who were unable to attend in-person follow-ups were paid $25 for completing telephone interviews that assessed only marijuana, alcohol and other drug use and negative consequences via the MPS.

Urine Screening and Self-Report Validity   Urine specimens were collected at each assessment point and analyzed for the presence of drug metabolites via enzyme immunoassay tests. Results were compared with self-reported abstinence from marijuana for the past 2 weeks, with percentage agreement ranging from 85% to 93%. Most discrepancies occurred because participants reported marijuana use when the urine screening indicated that the participant was abstinent. Less than 4% of participants reported abstinence when their urine screens were positive. Urinalysis cannot address the validity of self-reported frequency of marijuana use, but previous trials employing collateral reports on frequency of use have supported their validity (e.g. [4]). Other drug use was detected infrequently and not analyzed.

Intervention Conditions

Personalized Feedback   The PF condition consisted of one 90-minute session in which the therapist reviewed a personal feedback report (PFR) with the participant (see Doyle et al. 2003 [26], for a detailed description and discussion of this condition). The PFR included summaries of the participant's recent marijuana use, self-reported problems, expected positive and negative effects of using, anticipated costs and benefits of reducing use and self-efficacy for avoiding use in specific situations. Feedback was presented in relation to normative data from national surveys or prior studies of marijuana users in treatment whenever such data existed. Therapists utilized motivational interviewing techniques, such as open-ended questions, reflective listening, affirmation and reframing to elicit self-motivational statements and promote motivation for change, and were trained to avoid confrontation [11]. If participants expressed interest in reducing or stopping use, therapists helped to set goals, identified behavioral strategies for change and reviewed typical high-risk situations to avoid. Therapists provided a list of drug treatment options in the community if the participant was interested.

Multi-Media Feedback   In order to be true to advertisements for the MCU (i.e. objective feedback with no pressure to change) we developed the MMF condition as a balanced presentation of the multiple points of view on the consequences associated with marijuana use, being careful to delineate reliable information from research studies. It consisted of one 90-minute individual session. Participants first watched a 25-minute documentary on recent marijuana research that included commentary by researchers on the effects of marijuana and by marijuana users on the perceived benefits of marijuana [27]. Next, therapists gave a slide presentation on topics such as how marijuana produces its effects; the health, cognitive and psychological consequences of marijuana use; and potential for dependence. Participants were invited to ask questions at any time but no feedback regarding the participant's use of marijuana was provided and therapists avoided using motivational interviewing techniques. Again, therapists were prepared to provide a list of drug treatment options if the participants inquired.

Therapist Training and Treatment Fidelity   Three masters-level therapists with previous experience in behavioral therapies conducted the feedback sessions in both intervention conditions. Therapists received approximately 20 hours of training from the supervisor (Roffman) over a 2-month period using detailed manuals that prescribed the content and technique of the feedback sessions for each condition. Therapists were assigned actual study participants only after they were judged competent in conducting the interventions via review of audiotaped therapy sessions. All feedback sessions were audiotaped and therapists participated in weekly group supervision sessions with the supervisor throughout the study. Checklists and ratings of adherence completed by therapists after sessions were reviewed during supervision.

Two independent evaluators coded 25 (i.e. 20%) randomly selected feedback sessions (12 PF, 13 MMF) for therapist adherence to protocol. The coding system [10] consisted of 10 categories of therapist behaviors that were counted for frequency of occurrence. Inter-rater correlations were greater than 0.70 for all but two categories. Inter-rater agreement was 0.28 for the confrontation category, most probably because the frequency of confrontation was very low with little variability (M = 1.20; SD = 1.36). Inter-rater agreement was also low for the direction category ($r = 0.39$), which included a number of different types of therapist behaviors (i.e. advice, command, explain rationale, modeling, review/summarize, structuring) that made rater training difficult. *t*-Tests showed that eight categories differed between the two intervention conditions. Therapists conducting the PF sessions exhibited more behaviors in the query (questions and clarifications), restructure (interpreting and reframing), teaching-personal information (personal feedback) and understanding (filling in and paraphrasing) categories, while therapists conducting the MMF sessions exhibited more behaviors in the answer (answering participant's questions), direction (advice-giving, modeling and summarizing), general talk and teaching-general information (giving general information about marijuana effects or other topics) categories. No differences were found in the supportive (empathy, reinforcement, humor) and confrontation (challenges, disagreements, sarcasm) categories. In general, these differences between conditions provide evidence of the intended differences in the intervention conditions. Although we might have expected instances of support to have been greater in the PF than MMF condition, therapists in both conditions were trained to be respectful and avoid condescending, judgemental or confrontational interactions.

Rating scales completed by participants immediately following feedback sessions showed that the therapists were generally perceived positively by participants in both conditions. Fourteen items assessing participants' perceptions of, and relationship with, their therapist did not differ between the two conditions. Participants in the PF condition were more satisfied overall with their therapists and they rated their therapists as listening more and being more likely to try to convince them to quit smoking. Two items assessing perceived helpfulness and one assessing overall satisfaction with the feedback did not differ between the two conditions.

Data Analysis

Preliminary analyses revealed no significant differences between conditions on demographic, marijuana use, problem severity or motivational measures with two exceptions. Despite including SOC as a balancing factor with two levels (precontemplation/contemplation versus preparation) in the urn randomization program, more participants assigned to the MMF condition (87%) placed themselves in the precontemplation/contemplation category compared to the PF (68%) or DFC (70%) conditions, $\chi^2 = 9.75$, $P = 0.026$). A similar pattern was found on the precontemplation subscale of the RTC. Because the SOC algorithm and the precontemplation subscale were significant predictors of outcomes at various time-points, these variables were included as covariates in all outcome analyses.

The follow-up rates at the 7-week, 6-month and 12-month assessments were 95%, 90% and 83%, respectively. Rates of attrition from follow-ups were low and did not differ significantly by condition, but preliminary analyses of all baseline demographic and drug use characteristics revealed two baseline variables that showed significant condition × follow-up completion interactions. Participants in the PF condition who did not attend the follow-up at 6 and 12 months reported fewer marijuana-related problems at baseline than those who did attend. Participants in the DFC condition who did not attend the 7-week follow-up reported more baseline marijuana dependence symptoms compared to those who did attend and participants in the PF condition who did not attend the 12-month follow-up reported fewer baseline marijuana dependence symptoms than those who did attend. Therefore, the baseline measures of marijuana-related problems and dependence symptoms were also included as covariates in all analyses, and multiple approaches to handling missing data were used to assess the robustness of findings.

A multivariate analysis of covariance (MANCOVA) approach to repeated measures was used to evaluate treatment outcome [28]. The primary outcome measure was the number of days of marijuana use per week averaged across the weeks in each assessment period. Secondary outcome measures included the number of periods of marijuana use per day of use, the number of problems related to use from the MPS and the number of SCID dependence symptoms. In each analysis, treatment condition was the between-subjects factor and the initial and follow-up assessment points formed a within-subjects factor labeled time. Outcomes at the 7-week follow-up were evaluated with 3 (treatment: PF, MMF, DFC) $\times$ 2 (time) MANCOVAs. Significant treatment $\times$ time interactions were followed by planned contrasts comparing the covariate adjusted means of the three treatment conditions at follow-up. Next, longer-term treatment outcomes were evaluated across the initial assessment, 7-week, 6-month and 12-month follow-up assessments with 2 (treatment: PF versus MMF) $\times$ 4 (time) MANCOVAs. Parallel analyses were conducted to evaluate treatment effects on alcohol and other drug use and potential mediating variables. Effect sizes are reported in terms of the partial eta-squared for results from the MANCOVAs and as Cohen's d for comparisons between adjusted means of specific treatment conditions. In the reported analyses, missing values at follow-ups were replaced with baseline values. Results were highly similar when missing data were replaced with predicted values based on all relevant information available at baseline. Results were also similar when participants with missing data points were excluded entirely. The similarity of findings across three different methods of handling missing data provides confidence that the results are not due to systematic attrition.

Results

Sample Characteristics

Table 1 presents demographic and substance use information for the 188 randomized participants. Participants were primarily male, white and averaged 32 years of age (range: 18–57). The majority of participants were employed either full-or part-time and were single. Participants used marijuana an average of almost 6 days per week during the past 90 days and most reported smoking during more than one quarterly period of the day. They estimated being high for an average of almost 6 hours on a typical day. Consistent with exclusion criteria, use of other illicit substances was infrequent and alcohol use was moderate. Participants met an average of 3.45 of the seven dependence criteria and 64% met DSM-IV criteria for cannabis dependence. An additional 29% of the sample met DSM-IV criteria for cannabis abuse. Based on the SOC algorithm, 39% of the sample were in the pre-contemplation stage, 30% were in the contemplation stage, 21% were in the preparation stage, 7% were in the action stage and 2% were in the maintenance stage based on their initial self-categorizations during screening.

TABLE 1   Demographic and drug use measures at initial assessment.

Variable	PF	MMF	DFC	Total sample
Age (in years)	31.48 (9.22)	32.48 (11.11)	31.53 (10.69)	31.83 (10.33)
Sex (male)	77.4%	69.4%	76.6%	74.5%
Race (white)	87.1%	87.1%	87.5%	87.2%
Single	73.8%	82.0%	74.6%	76.8%
Employed (full or part-time)	80.3%	62.3%	61.0%	68.0%
Age of first marijuana use	14.71 (3.81)	14.74 (3.55)	15.27 (3.08)	14.91 (3.48)
Age of first daily use	18.94 (4.35)	17.74 (3.82)	18.58 (4.20)	18.42 (4.14)
Days of marijuana use in past 90 days	74.84 (16.71)	74.84 (16.44)	76.77 (13.34)	75.49 (15.49)
Periods smoked per day	2.07 (0.71)	2.01 (.76)	2.16 (0.78)	2.08 (0.75)
Ounces per week	0.22 (0.27)	0.24 (0.31)	0.23 (0.26)	0.23 (0.28)
No. of times smoked per day	3.30 (1.56)	3.13 (1.66)	3.27 (1.77)	3.23 (1.66)
No. of hours felt high per day	6.06 (3.86)	5.42 (4.05)	5.95 (3.81)	5.81 (3.90)
No. of dependence symptoms	3.92 (1.78)	3.26 (1.93)	3.17 (1.93)	3.45 (1.90)
No. of marijuana-related problems	6.37 (3.71)	5.31 (3.53)	6.31 (4.28)	6.00 (3.87)
No. of days of alcohol use per week	2.00 (2.08)	1.38 (1.63)	1.90 (2.12)	1.76 (1.97)
No. of drinks per drinking day	2.18 (1.77)	1.98 (1.84)	2.48 (2.08)	2.21 (1.90)
No. of days of other drug use per week	0.16 (0.43)	0.13 (0.23)	0.11 (0.19)	0.13 (0.30)

$n = 188$. All values are means followed by standard deviations in parentheses unless otherwise indicated. There were no significant differences between the conditions on any of the variables. PF: personalized feedback; MMF: multi-media feedback; DFC: delayed feedback control.

Treatment Attendance

Attendance of the feedback session following initial assessment was similar in the PF (89%) and MMF (94%) conditions. Fifty-two per cent of the DFC participants failed to attend a feedback session following the delay period. Of those who did attend, 16 chose the PF condition and 15 chose the MMF condition.

Marijuana Use and Related Consequences

7-Week Outcomes   Table 2 presents adjusted means for the primary and secondary cannabis-related outcome measures × treatment condition at all assessment points. The MANCOVA performed on the days of marijuana use per week at the 7-week follow-up showed a significant effect of condition, $F_{2,181} = 3.64$, $P = 0.028$, partial eta-squared = 0.04, that was qualified by a treatment × time interaction, $F_{2,181} = 3.49$, $P = 0.033$, partial eta-squared = 0.04. The main effect of time was not significant.

TABLE 2 Adjusted means, standard errors (SE), and confidence intervals (CI) for marijuana use and related consequences assessed at initial assessment, 7 weeks, 6 months and 12 months by treatment conditions.

Measure	Assessment	PF (n = 62)			MMF (n = 62)			DFC (n = 64)		
		M	(SE)	95% CI	M	(SE)	95% CI	M	(SE)	95% CI
Days of marijuana use per week	Initial	5.76[a]	(0.15)	(5.47; 6.06)	5.79[a]	(0.15)	(5.49; 6.08)	6.06[a]	(0.15)	(5.77; 6.35)
	7-week	4.74[a]	(0.24)	(4.27; 5.22)	5.44[b]	(0.24)	(4.97; 5.92)	5.75[b]	(0.24)	(5.30; 6.21)
	6-month	4.90[a]	(0.27)	(4.37; 5.43)	5.22[a]	(0.27)	(4.79; 5.75)			
	12-month	4.65[a]	(0.28)	(4.09; 5.20)	5.58[b]	(0.28)	(5.03; 6.14)			
Periods smoked per day	Initial	2.04[a]	(0.10)	(1.86; 2.23)	2.00[a]	(0.10)	(1.81; 2.19)	2.19[a]	(0.09)	(2.01; 2.38)
	7-week	1.66[a]	(0.11)	(1.46; 1.87)	1.90[b]	(0.11)	(1.69; 2.11)	2.20[b]	(0.10)	(2.00; 2.41)
	6-month	1.84[a]	(0.11)	(1.61; 2.06)	2.02[a]	(0.11)	(1.74; 2.25)			
	12-month	1.79[a]	(0.12)	(1.56; 2.02)	1.97[a]	(0.12)	(1.74; 2.19)			
Dependence symptoms	Initial	3.76[a]	(0.19)	(3.38; 4.13)	3.51[a]	(0.19)	(3.13; 3.88)	3.09[a]	(0.19)	(2.73; 3.46)
	7-week	2.38[a]	(0.20)	(1.97; 2.78)	2.91[b]	(0.21)	(2.51; 3.32)	2.85[b]	(0.20)	(2.45; 3.24)
	6-month	2.59[a]	(0.21)	(2.17; 3.02)	3.26[b]	(0.21)	(2.84; 3.69)			
	12-month	2.43[a]	(0.18)	(2.07; 2.79)	2.88[b]	(0.18)	(2.52; 3.24)			
Number of problems	Initial	5.55[a]	(0.35)	(4.86; 6.24)	5.93[a]	(0.35)	(5.25; 6.62)	6.51[a]	(0.34)	(5.83; 7.18)
	7-week	3.70[a]	(0.41)	(2.89; 4.51)	5.03[a]	(0.41)	(4.22; 5.84)	5.01[a]	(0.40)	(4.23; 5.80)
	6-month	4.06[a]	(0.41)	(3.24; 4.88)	5.46[a]	(0.41)	(4.64; 6.27)			
	12-month	3.95[a]	(0.40)	(3.17; 4.74)	5.21[a]	(0.40)	(4.42; 5.99)			

PF = personalized feedback; MMF = multi-media feedback; DFC = delayed feedback control. Data are adjusted for initial assessment scores on the SOC algorithm, the precontemplation scale of the RTC, number of marijuana-related problems and number of marijuana dependence symptoms. Initial assessment values were substituted for missing data at follow-ups. Means (M) in the same row with different superscripts differ significantly at $P < 0.05$.

Planned contrasts showed that participants in the PF condition reported significantly fewer days of use per week than those in the MMF ($d = 0.42$) or DF ($d = 0.47$) conditions ($Ps < 0.05$), which did not differ significantly.

The MANCOVA performed on the numbers of smoking periods per day at 7 weeks showed a significant effect of condition, $F_{2,181} = 3.89$, $P = 0.022$, partial eta-squared = 0.04, that was qualified by a treatment × time effect, $F_{2,181} = 5.30$, $P = 0.006$, partial eta-squared = 0.06. PF participants reported smoking during fewer periods per day than MMF ($d = 0.42$) or DF ($d = 0.69$). On the number of dependence symptoms at 7 weeks there was a significant effect of time, $F_{1,182} = 4.08$, $P = 0.045$, partial eta-squared = 0.02, and a treatment × time effect, $F_{2,182} = 8.42$, $P = 0.000$, partial eta-squared = 0.09. PF participants reported fewer dependence symptoms relative to MMF ($d = 0.48$) or DF ($d = 0.58$) participants ($Ps < 0.05$). The MANCOVA on the number of problems related to marijuana use did not reveal any significant effects.

Longer-Term Outcomes   When 2 (treatment) × 4 (time) MANCOVAs were performed on the days of marijuana use per week across the initial, 7-week, 6-month and 12-month follow-ups for the PF and MMF conditions only, results showed a significant treatment × time interaction, $F_{3,116} = 2.72$, $P = 0.048$, partial eta-squared = 0.07 (see Table 2 and Fig. 2). The main effects of time and treatment condition were not significant. Comparisons of the PF and MMF conditions did not quite reach statis-

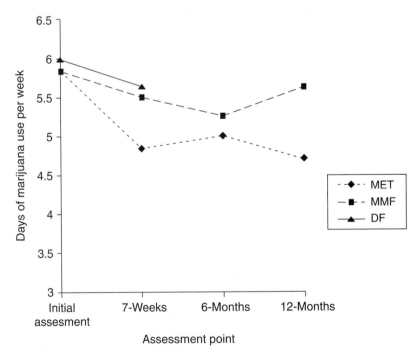

FIGURE 2 Days of marijuana use per week by treatment condition and assessment point.

tical significance at the 7-week follow-up in these analyses ($P = 0.073$; $d = 0.34$) but the effect size was similar to the previous analysis and lower power resulting from loss of DFC participants explains the differences in significance tests. Conditions did not differ at the 6-month ($P = 0.408$) follow-up, but PF participants reported significantly fewer days of marijuana use per week compared to the MMF participants at the 12-month follow-up ($P = 0.019$; $d = 0.45$).

MANCOVAs for periods of smoking per day and number of marijuana-related problems did not show any significant effects across the 12-month follow-up. On the measure of dependence symptoms there was a significant effect of time, $F_{3,117} = 4.18$, $P = 0.008$, partial, eta-squared = 0.10) and a marginally significant treatment × time interaction, $F_{3,117} = 2.64$, $P = 0.053$, partial eta-squared = 0.06). In addition to previously reported differences at 7 weeks, PF participants reported significantly fewer dependence symptoms at the 6-month ($P = 0.019$; $d = 0.45$) and 12-month ($P = 0.049$; $d = 0.37$) follow-ups compared to MMF participants.

Other Drug Abuse Treatment

Participation in other treatment for drug abuse during the 90 days before initial assessment occurred in only 1% of the sample. Rates of additional drug treatment were between 1% and 4% across the follow-up assessments with no evidence of differential treatment participation by condition. Involvement in 12-Step or other self-help groups for drug abuse was similarly low across assessment points (range 2–7%) and did not differ by condition.

Mediating Variables

We investigated whether the PF condition exerted its effects on marijuana use and dependence symptoms via changes in self-efficacy or readiness to change by repeating the MANCOVA analyses on these measures. Only a single effect of time on the action subscale of the RTC was statistically significant, $F_{1,182} = 8.44$, $P = 0.004$, partial eta-squared = 0.04. Participants indicated greater efforts at making changes at the 7-week follow-up (M = 0.06) than at initial assessment (M = –0.31). The absence of differential treatment condition effects in these analyses made further exploration of mediation inappropriate.

Alcohol and Other Drug Use

A significant effect of time on the self-reported number of problems related to alcohol was found, $F_{3,116} = 4.40$, $P = 0.006$, partial eta-squared = 0.10. The number of problems reported was reduced at 7 weeks (M = 0.98) and 6 months (M = 1.21) compared to initial assessment (M = 1.44), but not at the 12-month (M = 1.48) assessment, but there were no differential treatment effects. No effects were significant on measures of alcohol and other drug use or problems related to other drug use.

Discussion

The MCU was successful in attracting a sample of near daily adult marijuana users, the majority of whom showed little interest in reducing or quitting marijuana use in the near future. The sample was similar to those in treatment for marijuana dependence in terms of frequency of use [15] and they averaged over three dependence symptoms and six self-reported problems with marijuana use. Almost all (93%) met criteria for either cannabis dependence or abuse. The brief motivational intervention produced greater reductions in the frequency of marijuana use and dependence symptoms compared with both control conditions. Although the magnitudes of the reductions were modest, findings provide further evidence of the utility of brief interventions for drug use.

At the 7-week follow-up, participants who received PF reduced their frequency of marijuana use and the number of periods of the day during which they smoked more than those in either the delayed feedback or educational comparison conditions. The reductions in marijuana use corresponded to reductions in the number of dependence symptoms. However, the magnitude of the reduction was in the order of about 1 day less of use per week and an average of about one-half fewer periods of use per day. Given that participants were averaging 6 days of use per week and two periods of use per day at initial assessment, they remained fairly regular users who still met an average of two dependence symptoms and self-reported almost four problems related to use. More encouraging were the findings that reductions in the frequency of use and dependence symptoms were sustained throughout the 12-month follow-up period. Although reductions in use by the participants in the MMF condition had almost caught up at the 6-month follow-up, the groups had diverged again by 12 months on the measure of frequency. This pattern suggests that the effect was not transient, and was more robust for days of any use relative to intensity or duration of use per day.

Significant effects were not found on a self-reported measure of marijuana-related problems, even though there were significant reductions in dependence symptoms at all follow-ups for those in the PF condition. The meaning of this pattern is not entirely clear, but may relate to greater variability in the acknowledgement of problems or to the differences in the nature of dependence symptoms and negative consequences. Dependence symptoms were assessed by trained interviewers using a structured set of questions with guidelines for scoring the presence or absence of the symptom. In contrast, the MPS required participants to make judgements regarding the presence or absence of specific negative consequences leading to greater variability. Although the MPS has been sensitive to changes in negative consequences associated with much greater reductions in marijuana use [4,6], it may not be able to capture subtler changes. It may also be that changes in perceptions of self-control assessed by most of the dependence criteria are affected by even small reductions in use that signal a new degree of control to the user.

The effect sizes for frequency of use and dependence symptoms fell in the small to medium range (0.34–0.69). Other studies that have investigated the effectiveness of brief interventions specifically with non-treatment-seeking populations have found a similar range of effect sizes (e.g. [10,29–32]). On the other hand, the effects for problems related to use were smaller and non-significant. Thus, it is unclear whether the present findings represent clinically meaningful change. The focus of the MCU was on reaching a population of users who would not be ready to present for treatment and, indeed, they were less interested in change and perceived themselves as less impaired than those who seek treatment [15]. It does not seem appropriate to expect the same level of absolute change in this population as in treatment studies, which have found effect sizes for brief motivational treatments in the large range [6]. Any change might be considered meaningful if it occurs with a very brief intervention in a population who otherwise would not receive intervention. This may be particularly true if the MCU had been offered as part of a continuum of care in an integrated, comprehensive treatment facility where additional treatment was available to those who increased their motivation for change. It is also important to note that the initial assessment may have been reactive and promoted change in the control conditions, making the magnitude of the effect of the PF condition in this study a conservative estimate of its clinical significance. Future studies attracting non-treatment-seeking populations could include no assessment control conditions, as well as systematically manipulate the availability of additional treatment to estimate its impact more effectively.

We were unable to detect an effect of the PF intervention on changes in readiness for change or self-efficacy for avoiding use. Other studies of motivational interventions have also failed to detect changes in similar measures of mediating processes (see Burke *et al.*, 2002 [13], for review). Paper-and-pencil measures do not seem to capture whatever processes mediate the effects of these interventions. Studying therapist and client behaviors within sessions may be more likely to identify processes that explain the effects of motivational interventions (e.g. [33,34]).

Treatment fidelity and participant satisfaction results indicated that both intervention conditions were conducted as intended. In the PF condition, the motivational interviewing was delivered with a high degree of fidelity. Careful training and ongoing supervision resulted in clear differences on eight of 10 therapist behavior scales in the intended direction, and the lack of differences on one scale, confrontation, could be attributed to very low frequency of this behavior, which would have been inappropriate in either condition. PF participants rated their therapist as more likely to try to convince them to quit using relative to the MMF condition, but the absolute values of the ratings were low (M = 1.75 on a five-point scale) and probably reflected that therapists were systematically eliciting and reflecting self-motivational statements as intended, whereas this type of behavior was completely absent in the MMF condition.

The MMF condition served as a good, if imperfect, attention-placebo control that allowed for the assessment of longer term outcomes in the context of a 'check-up' study that promised participants feedback. Although the use of a video as part of the MMF intervention controlled only partially for therapist contact, the amount of time that participants were engaged was held constant. Post-intervention ratings showed that PF participants were more satisfied with their therapists, but otherwise there were few differences in perceptions of the therapists and similar ratings of the helpfulness of the feedback received. DFC participants were equally likely to choose the MMF as the PF condition following the waiting period, further attesting to its appeal and credibility. While it is possible that acknowledging perceived benefits of marijuana use in the MMF condition may have diluted any potential for producing change, there were no differences between MMF and DFC conditions at 7 weeks, suggesting that it did not hinder any natural change. Further, the PF intervention also required therapists to acknowledge and reflect positive statements about marijuana use in order to avoid resistance. All in all, it is not surprising that an educational intervention was not effective in producing change and it remains possible that other types of brief interventions may perform as well as the PF condition. However, this is one of only a few studies to show long-term change that can clearly be attributed to a brief intervention.

In summary, the results support the efficacy of a brief motivational intervention delivered in the context of a MCU. Questions remain about the magnitude and long-term meaningfulness of the change that was produced. However, at a minimum, it appears to open doors to reaching illicit drug users that do not currently exist in our treatment system and it may have a role in continuum of care models that propose that treatment start with the least intensive, effective interventions.

Acknowledgements

This research was supported by grant R01 DA09425 from the National Institute on Drug Abuse. The views expressed are those of the authors. Carl Williams is now at the University Counseling Center, University of Notre Dame; Randy S. Burke is now at the G. V. (Sonny) Montgomery Veterans Affairs Medical Center. We wish to express special thanks to Aimee Campbell and Megan Swan for their diligent and highly competent efforts in project publicity and data collection.

References

1. Substance Abuse and Mental Health Services Administration (SAMHSA). *Results from the 2005 National Survey on Drug Use and Health: National Findings*. NSDUH Series H-30; DHHS Publication no. SMA 06–4194. Rockville, MD: Office of Applied Studies. Available at: http://oas.samhsa.gov/nhsda.htm (accessed 21 September 2006).

2. Budney A. J., Moore B. A., Rocha H. L. Clinical trial of abstinence-based vouchers and cognitive-behavioral therapy for cannabis dependence. *J Consult Clin Psychol* 2006; **74**: 307–16.

3. Budney A. J., Higgins S. T., Radonovich K. J., Novy P. L. Adding voucher-based incentives to coping skills and motivational enhancement improves outcomes during treatment for marijuana dependence. *J Consult Clin Psychol* 2000; **68**: 1051–61.

4. Marijuana Treatment Project Research Group (MTPRG). Brief treatments for cannabis dependence: findings from a randomized multisite trial. *J Consult Clin Psychol* 2004; **72**: 455–66.

5. Stephens R. S., Roffman R. A., Simpson E. E. Treating adult marijuana dependence: a test of the relapse prevention model. *J Consult Clin Psychol* 1994; **62**: 92–9.

6. Stephens R. S., Roffman R. A., Curtin L. Comparison of extended versus brief treatments for marijuana use. *J Consult Clin Psychol* 2000; **68**: 898–908.

7. Cunningham J. A., Sobell L. C., Sobell M. B., Agrawal S., Toneatto T. Barriers to treatment: why alcohol and drug abusers delay or never seek treatment. *Addict Behav* 1993; **18**: 347–53.

8. Sobell L. C., Sobell M. B., Toneatto T. Recovery from alcohol problems without treatment. In: Heather N., Miller W. R., Greeley J., editors. *Self-control and the addictive behaviours*. Botany, Australia: Maxwell Macmillan Publishing; 1991, p. 198–242.

9. Miller W. R., Sovereign R. G. The Check-up: a model for early intervention in addictive behaviors. In: Loberg T., Miller W. R., Nathan P. E., Marlatt G. A., editors. *Addictive behaviors: prevention and early intervention*. Amsterdam: Swets & Zeitlinger; 1989, p. 219–31.

10. Miller W. R., Benefield G. S., Tonigan J. S. Enhancing motivation for change in problem drinking: a controlled comparison of two therapist styles. *J Consult Clin Psychol* 1993; **61**: 55–61.

11. Miller W. R., Rollnick S. *Motivational Interviewing: Preparing People to Change Addictive Behavior*, 2nd edn. New York: Guilford Press; 2002.

12. Miller W. R., Sovereign R. G., Krege B. Motivational interviewing with problem drinkers. II. The Drinker's Check-up as a preventive intervention. *Behav Psychother* 1988; **16**: 251–68.

13. Burke B. L., Arkowitz H., Dunn C. The efficacy of motivational interviewing and its adaptations: what we know so far. In: Miller W. R., Rollnick S., editors. *Motivational interviewing: preparing people to change addictive behavior*, 2nd edn. New York: Guilford Press; 2002, p. 217–50.

14. Burke B. L., Arkowitz H., Menchola M. The efficacy of motivational interviewing: a meta-analysis of controlled clinical trials. *J Consult Clin Psychol* 2003; **71**: 843–61.

15. Stephens R. S., Roffman R. A., Fearer S. A., Williams C., Picciano J. F., Burke R. S. The Marijuana Check-up: reaching users who are ambivalent about change. *Addiction* 2004; **99**: 1323–32.

16. Humphreys K., Tucker J. A. Towards more responsive and effective intervention systems for alcohol-related problems. *Addiction* 2002;97: 127–32 [Editorial].

17. Sobell M. B., Sobell L. C. Stepped care as a heuristic approach to the treatment of alcohol problems. *J Consult Clin Psychol* 2000; **68**: 573–9.

18. Stout R. L., Wirtz P. W., Carbonari J. P., Del Boca F. K. Ensuring balanced distribution of prognostic factors in treatment outcome research. *J Stud Alcohol* 1994; **12**: 70–5.

19. Campbell A. N. C., Fisher D. S., Picciano J. F., Orlando M. J., Stephens R. S., Roffman R. A. Marketing effectiveness in reaching non-treatment-seeking marijuana smokers. *J Soc Work Pract Addict* 2004; **4**: 39–59.

20. Prochaska J. O., DiClemente C. C. Stages and processes of self-change of smoking: toward an integrative model of change. *J Consult Clin Psychol* 1983; **51**: 390–5.

21. First M. B., Spitzer R. L., Gibbon M., Williams J. B. *Structured Clinical Interview for DSM-IV, Axis I Disorders—Patient Edition (SCID-I/P)*, version 2.0.New York: Biometrics Research Department, New York State Psychiatric Institute; 1996.

22. Sobell L. C., Sobell M. B. Timeline follow-back, a technique for assessing self-reported alcohol consumption. In: Litten R., Allen J., editors. *Measuring alcohol consumption*. New Jersey: The Humana Press, Inc.; 1992, p. 41–72.

23. Stephens R. S., Wertz J. S., Roffman R. A. Self-efficacy and marijuana cessation: a construct validity analysis. *J Consult Clin Psychol* 1995; **63**: 1022–31.

24. Rollnick S., Heather N., Gold R., Hall W. Development of a short 'readiness to change' questionnaire for use in brief, opportunistic interventions among excessive drinkers. *Br J Addict* 1992; **87**: 743–54.

25. Solomon K. E., Annis H. M. Development of a scale to measure outcome expectancy in alcoholics. *Cogn Ther Res* 1989; **13**: 409–21.

26. Doyle A., Swan M., Roffman R., Stephens R. The Marijuana Check-up: a brief intervention tailored for individuals in the contemplation stage. *J Soc Work Pract Addict* 2003; **3**: 53–71.

27. Bell J., producer. *Quantum—What's Your Poison—Marijuana* [videocassette]. Sydney: Australian Broadcasting Corporation; 1997.

28. O'Brien R. G., Kaiser M. K. MANOVA method for analyzing repeated measures designs: an extensive primer. *Psychol Bull* 1985; **97**: 316–33.

29. Borsari B., Carey K. B. Effects of a brief motivational intervention with college student drinkers. *J Consult Clin Psychol* 2000; **68**: 728–33.

30. Collins S. E., Carey K. B., Sliwinski M. J. Mailed personalized normative feedback as a brief intervention for at-risk college drinkers. *J Stud Alcohol* 2002; **63**: 559–67.

31. Hester R. K., Squires D. D., Delaney H. D. The Drinker's Check-up: 12-month outcomes of a controlled clinical trial of a stand-alone software program for problem drinkers. *J Subst Abuse Treat* 2005; **28**: 159–69.

32. McCambridge J., Strang J. The efficacy of single-session motivational interviewing in reducing drug consumption and perceptions of drug-related risk and harm among young people: results from a multi-site cluster randomized trial. *Addiction* 2004; **99**: 39–52.

33. Amrhein P. C., Miller W. R., Yahne C. E., Palmer M., Fulcher L. Client commitment language during motivational interviewing predicts behavior outcomes. *J Consult Clin Psychol* 2003; **71**: 862–78.

34. Moyers T., Martin T., Catley D., Harris K. J., Ahluwalia J. S. Assessing the integrity of motivational interviewing interventions: reliability of the motivational interviewing skills code. *Behav Cogn Psychother* 2003; **31**: 177–84.

Editor's Note

Roger A. Roffman, School of Social Work, University of Washington, Seattle, Washington, USA.

Correspondence to: Robert S. Stephens, Department of Psychology 0436, Virginia Tech, Blacksburg, Virginia 24061, USA. E-mail: stephens@vt.edu.

Discussion Questions for Article 2

Section 10: Therapies and Treatment

Name: _____

PID: _____

Date: __ __ / __ __ / __ __ (MM/DD/YY)

CRN: _____

Recitation Day/Time: _____

Honor Code Signature: _____

1. What are some of the barriers that prevent marijuana users from seeking treatment?

2. How does the proposed intervention address these barriers?

3. What were the three conditions to which participants were assigned? Briefly describe each.

4. Is reduction in frequency of use a better goal than total abstinence for substance users? Explain your answer.

Section 11
Abnormal Behavior

There is no strict definition of abnormal behavior. There never has been. The parameters of what defines abnormal behavior are constantly evolving. Through this evolution, we understand abnormal behavior through a flexible framework that is constantly reshaped by time and culture. For example, before Major Depression became known as a mental disorder characterized by persistent depressed mood, low self-esteem, and a loss of interest or pleasure in everyday activities in the twentieth century, it was conceptualized in a variety of different ways. More specifically, Major Depression was once labeled melancholia and was characterized as slowed circulation and depleted energy. Additionally, melancholia was thought to be a disturbance of the soul due to inner moral conflict. Although the presenting symptoms of Major Depression have not changed, the articulation of Major Depression (and all other disorders) must change in order to stay congruent with societal norms.

Up until the start of the nineteenth century, abnormal behavior was not considered a medical ailment, but rather encompassed disorders of moral. Individuals exhibiting abnormal behavior were then described as fallen characters. Abnormal behavior was also once thought to be caused by malevolent spirits, and thus religious rituals played a significant role in their treatment. As the definition of abnormal evolved throughout the nineteenth and twentieth centuries, it is now defined as behaviors atypical to a culture, and furthermore it is behavior considered to be socially unacceptable. This abnormal behavior is also characterized as maladaptive, distressing to the individual exhibiting such behavior as well as the individual's family and friends. The persistence of these abnormal behaviors gives evidence of mental illness.

Just as the definitions of abnormal behavior are quite variable, there are multiple theoretical models which attempt to explain and interpret abnormal behavior. For example, such etiological perspectives include: medical/biological, evolutionary, psychodynamic, socio-cultural, as well as cognitive and behavioral. Each model provides unique insight into the potential causes of mental disorders categorized by the DSM-IV (i.e., substance-related disorders, disorders of mood, anxiety, and personality, sexual disorders, eating disorders, and psychotic disorders). As the causes of mental disorders are many, so are the corresponding treatments. Thus, evaluating multiple perspectives helps to account for individual variability in diagnoses and therefore allows for a more comprehensive analysis of the origins of the disorder. This comprehensive analysis can provide answers to which treatment approaches might be most effective.

In a given year, an estimated 20–30% of Americans reportedly suffer from a diagnosable mental illness. Due to the pervasive nature of mental illness, there is an overwhelming need for extensive research in the field. Through research, we can continue to learn as much as possible about the behaviors in addition to what might be causing these illnesses in individuals and how they can be successfully treated. Thus, exploring all of the possible causes of a disorder as well as effective treatments will continue to be essential as the evolution of the mental health field continues.

Article 1: Fear of the Beast: A Prospective Study on the Effects of Negative Information on Childhood Fear

In the article, Muris et al. (2003) sought to extend previous research conducted in this area by Field et al. (2001) by investigating the development of childhood fears. This extension included the effects of positive and negative information on the persistent nature of the fears, as well as the generalizability of the negative information received to the appraisal of other similar stimuli (i.e., dogs and predators). Assessments measuring fear and anxiety in children between the ages of four and twelve were conducted at three time points following the child's receipt of negative or positive information about an "unknown, doglike animal, called the beast." The authors also looked at the impact of gender, age of the child, and individual differences variables to determine possible differences in the vulnerability to the impact of the negative information. Similar to what was hypothesized, the results indicate that in comparison to positive information, negative information significantly increases the levels of fear in children. Furthermore, these fears were also shown to generalize to similar stimuli. In congruence with these findings, Muris et al. suggest that adults might control children's level of fear merely by the information they present.

Article 2: Ethnic and Sex Differences in Children's Depressive Symptoms: Mediating Effects of Perceived and Actual Competence

The symptoms of depression in children vary, just as the nature of depression in pre-adolescence remains somewhat misunderstood. Building upon previous research conducted by Cole et al. (1998), the authors investigated ethnic and sex differences associated with depression among preadolescents. 630 Euro-American boys and girls and 272 African American boys and girls in grades three through five completed a battery of assessments measuring depression, academic achievement, peer acceptance, and self-perception. Kistner et al. found significant ethnicity differences in the reporting of depressive symptoms, and additionally, this difference was found to be qualified by sex. Finally, it was found that academic achievement acts as a mediator in the interaction relationship between ethnicity and sex. One possibility noted by the authors is that members of a disadvantaged group may feel distress about whether they confirm a negative academic stereotype. These results identify important variables (i.e., sex, ethnicity, and academic achievement) that can partially explain the mechanisms of preadolescent depressive symptoms.

—*Sarah Kelleher*

Article 1

Fear of the Beast: A Prospective Study on the Effects of Negative Information on Childhood Fear

Peter Muris
Denise Bodden
Harald Merckelbach
Thomas H. Ollendick
Neville King

The current study examined the effects of negative information on the enhancement of childhood fear. A large group of normal primary school children aged between 4 and 12 years (N=285) received either negative or positive information about an unknown, doglike animal, called 'the beast'. Children's fears were assessed at three points in time: before, directly after, and one week after the information about the beast was provided (i.e., pre-, post- and follow-up assessment). Results showed that type of information changed children's fear of the beast in the predicted direction with negative information increasing fear levels and positive information decreasing fear levels. This was not only the case directly after the experi¬mental manipulation but also at one week follow-up. Furthermore, fear of the beast appeared to generalize, that is, children who became more fearful of the beast after receiving negative information, also became more apprehensive of other dogs and predators.

Keywords: Fears; Children; Negative information

1. Introduction

Specific fears of the dark, animals, blood, heights and so on are common in children (e.g., Gullone, 2000; Muris & Merckelbach, 2001; Ollendick, King, & Muris, in press). Studies on childhood fears have predominantly relied on self-report instruments that list a broad range of potentially fear-provoking stimuli. A widely used instrument for this purpose is the Fear Survey Schedule for Children—Revised (FSSC-R; Ollendick, 1983). The FSSC-R requires children to indicate on three-point scales ('none', 'some', 'a lot') how much they fear specific stimuli or situations. Studies employing the FSSC-R have consistently found that the more prevalent fears of children are nearly always related to dangerous situations and physical harm. More specifically, the following rank order for common childhood fears is typically reported: (1) Not being able to breathe, (2) Being hit by a car or truck, (3) Bombing attacks, (4) Getting burned by fire, (5) Falling from a high place, (6) Burglar breaking into the house, (7) Earthquake, (8) Death, (9) Illness, and (10) Snakes (e.g., King et al., 1989; Ollendick, King, & Frary, 1989; Ollendick, Yule, & Ollier, 1991).

In relation to the origins of childhood fears, there is convincing evidence for the contribution of a genetic factor. For example, Stevenson, Batten, and Cherner (1992) conducted analyses on FSSC scores of monozygotic and dizygotic twin pairs with ages between 8 and 16 years. These authors found that a twin's level of fearfulness could be predicted from the co-twin's score. It is generally assumed that the genetic factor constitutes the biological substrate of what is typically referred to as 'neuroticism' or 'negative affectivity' (see Craske, 1997). In the clinical child psy¬chology literature, a number of individual difference variables can be found that represent this factor. Examples of such variables are *trait anxiety* which can be defined as the inclination to react anxiously to potentially anxiety-provoking stimuli (Spielberger, 1973), *anxiety sensitivity* which is viewed as the more specific tendency to react anxiously to one's own anxiety and anxiety-related sensations (Reiss, Peterson, Gursky, & McNally, 1986), and *behavioural inhibition* which is described as the propensity to be unusually shy and to react with fear and withdrawal in novel and/or unfamiliar situations (Kagan, 1997). It is generally accepted that trait anxiety, anxiety sensitivity, and behavioural inhibition contribute to the development of childhood fear and anxiety (Biederman, Rosenbaum, Chaloff, & Kagan, 1995; Eysenck, 1987; Reiss, Silverman, & Weems, 2001).

Learning experiences are also thought to be involved in the onset of childhood fears (see for a review King, Hamilton, & Ollendick, 1988). According to Rachman's (1977, 1991) three-pathways theory, there are three types of discrete learning experiences that may play a role in the acquisition of phobias: (1) aversive classical conditioning, (2) modeling (i.e., vicarious learning), and (3) negative information transmission (i.e., exposure to negative information about the feared stimulus). A number of studies have evaluated the role of the three pathways in the origins of normal childhood fears. In the first study, Ollendick and King (1991) examined to what extent Rachman's theory of fear acquisition can be applied to the top 10 intensive FSSC fears. Children who reported 'a lot' of fear to FSSC-R items such as "Not being able to breathe", "Being hit by a car or truck", and so forth, were given a short questionnaire that asked them whether they had experienced conditioning, modeling, and/or informational events related to these stimuli or situations. Ollendick and King found that a majority of the children (88.8%) attributed their fear to negative information. Modeling and conditioning events were less often mentioned by the children (56.2% and 35.7%, respectively). In an attempt to replicate these findings, Muris, Merckelbach, and Collaris (1997) had children specify their top intense fear and then asked them whether conditioning, modeling, and negative information played a role in that fear. In agreement with Ollendick and King (1991), these authors found that exposure to negative information was the most prominent pathway to fear, followed by conditioning and modeling (see also Muris, Merckelbach, Gadet, & Moulaert, 2000).

However, most research evaluating Rachman's (1977, 1991) theory of fear acquisition has been criticized because of its retrospective nature (see review by King, Gullone, & Ollendick, 1998). That is to say, fearful subjects are asked to reflect on past experiences and identify conditioning, modeling and negative information events in relation of the feared stimulus. Retrospective accounts may be fueled by the attributional style of fearful children rather than their actual experiences (e.g., Withers & Deane, 1995). Interestingly, Field, Argyrus, and Knowles (2001) recently conducted a prospective study on the role of negative information in the exacerbation of childhood fear. In two experiments, 7–9-year-old children received either negative or positive information about an unknown monster doll. Results showed that negative information significantly increased children's fear ratings, whereas after positive information fear ratings only slightly decreased. Furthermore, the fear enhancing effect of negative information was particularly strong when the information about the monster doll was directly provided by an adult person.

Field et al. (2001) point out a number of issues that are in need of future research. First, it would be worthwhile to investigate whether fear beliefs generalize to other stimuli that bear resemblance to the stimulus about which children have received negative information. Second, Field et al. employed a simple pre–post test design to examine the effects of negative information on children's fears. The persistence of verbally transmitted fears could be examined by including a follow-up assessment following children over a somewhat longer time period. Third, Field et al. only studied 7–9-year-olds, but it is important to find out whether children in other age groups are equally affected by negative information. For example, emprical studies consistently show that younger children are more susceptible to accept information provided by adults than older children (e.g., Bruck, Ceci, & Hembrooke, 1998). Finally, a consistent finding in the literature is that girls generally are more fearful than boys (Bernstein, Borchardt, & Perwien, 1996; Craske, 1997; King & Ollendick, 1989; Muris & Merckelbach, 2001). This raises the question whether girls are more susceptible to fear-provoking information than boys.

With these issues in mind, the present study extends the research of Field et al. (2001) focusing on the effects of negative information in the enhancement of childhood fear. A large group of normal primary school children aged between 4 and 12 years ($N=285$) received either negative or positive information about an unknown, doglike animal, called the beast. Children's fear of the beast was assessed at three points in time: (1) before, (2) directly after, and (3) one week after the information about the beast was provided (i.e., pre-, post-and follow-up assessment). It was hypothesized that children who receive negative information about the beast will become more fearful of this unknown animal compared to children who receive positive information about the beast. Additional research questions were: Does negative information about the beast also affect the evaluation of other dogs and predators? Are younger children and girls more susceptible to the influence of negative information than respectively older children and boys? Lastly, do individual difference variables such as trait anxiety, anxiety sensitivity, and behavioural inhibition mediate the influence of negative information?

2. Method

2.1. Participants

The sample consisted of 285 children (143 boys and 142 girls) who were recruited from three primary schools in Maastricht, The Netherlands. Informed consent was obtained from parents and children before participation in the study; approximately 50% of those invited to participate eventually did so (about 10% of the parents and children refused to participate, whereas the remaining 40% did not respond to our informed consent mailing at all). Ages of the children ranged between 4 and 12 years. Mean age of the total sample was 8.6 years (SD=2.2).

2.2. Assessment

The *Fear of the Beast Questionnaire* (FBQ) was developed for the purpose of the present study. The FBQ consisted of a picture of a dog-like animal called 'the beast'[1] which was clearly shown to the children on a large poster (1.5×1 m.) and 12 items referring to fearful feelings of the child when confronted with the beast (e.g., How do you feel about this animal? How would you feel when you had to pet this animal? How would you feel if this animal would lick you?). Each item had to be answered on a three-point scale with 1=*no fear*, 2=*some fear*, and 3=*a lot of fear*. A total 'fear of the beast' score was computed by summing scores on all items (range: 12–36).

A *modified version of the FSSC-R* (Ollendick, 1983) was used to assess children's general fear levels and fear levels to dog- and predator-like animals. The scale contained 35 items. Twenty-five items were taken from the original FSSC-R with five items representing each of the commonly found childhood fear factors: 'Fear of Failure and Criticism' (e.g., "Making mistakes"), 'Fear of the Unknown' (e.g., "Going to bed in the dark"), 'Fear of Small Animals' (e.g., "Spiders"), 'Fear of Danger and Death' (e.g., "Being hit by a car or truck"), and 'Medical Fears' (e.g., "Getting a shot from the doctor") (e.g., Gullone & King, 1992; Ollendick, 1983; Muris & Ollendick, in press). The other 10 items measured 'fear of dogs' ("Dingos", "Hyenas", "Wolves", "Pitbulls", "Dogs") and 'fear of predators' ("Tigers", "Crocodiles", "Lions", "Sharks", "Panthers"). Each item is scored on a three-point scale with 1=*no fear*, 2=*some fear*, and 3=*a lot of fear*. FSSC-R total and factor scores are obtained by summing across relevant items (ranges of respectively 25–75 and 5–15).[2]

The *trait anxiety scale of the State-Trait Anxiety Inventory for Children* (STAIC; Spielberger, 1973) contains 20 items that measure chronic symptoms of anxiety. The child is asked to rate the frequency with which (s)he experiences anxiety symptoms such as "I am scared", "I feel troubled", and "I get a funny feeling in my stomach" using 3-point scales: 1=*almost never*, 2=*sometimes*, and 3=*often*. A total trait anxiety score can be calculated by summing the ratings on all items (range: 20–60).

The *Childhood Anxiety Sensitivity Index* (CASI; Silverman, Fleisig, Rabian, & Peterson, 1991) is an 18-item self-report questionnaire for assessing the fear of anxiety symptoms in children and adolescents. Example items are "It scares me when

---

[1] The beast was a Tasmanian tiger. Post-experimental questioning revealed that none of the children had ever heard about this animal.

[2] In order to make the FBQ and modified FSSC more appropriate to the younger children in our sample, the three-point rating scales of these questionnaires were all accompanied by a visual fear scale depicting Koalas expressing various degrees of fear (no fear, some fear, a lot of fear; see Muris et al., submitted).

my heart beats fast", "It scares me when I feel nervous", and "It scares me when I feel shaky". Children have to rate on a 3-point Likert scale (1=*none*, 2=*some*, 3=*a lot*) the extent to which they believe that the experience of anxiety will have negative consequences. CASI scores range between 18 and 54, with higher scores indicating higher levels of anxiety sensitivity.

The *Behavioural Inhibition Scale* (BIS; Muris, Merckelbach, Wessel, & Van de Ven, 1999) contains eight items referring to shyness, communication, fearfulness, and smiling when meeting unfamiliar children and adults. Items (e.g., "I am shy when I have to talk to an unfamiliar child", "I feel good and I am able to laugh, when I talk to an unfamiliar adult") are rated on 4-point Likert scales with 1=*never*, 2=*sometimes*, 3=*often*, and 4=*always*. After recoding positive items, scores are summed to yield a BIS total score (range: 8–32) with higher scores reflecting higher levels of behavioural inhibition.

2.3. Procedure

The procedure somewhat differed for younger and older children. More specifically, children younger than 7 years were assessed individually in a private room at school by the experimenter. They first completed the FBQ and the modified FSSC-R. As the reading abilities of these children were insufficient, items of both scales were read aloud by the experimenter while children rated fear levels to these stimuli/situations on a visual fear scale. After the administration of the FBQ and modified FSSC-R, children received either positive or negative information about the beast. The positive information story about the beast ran as follows: "This animal, called 'the beast', was recently discovered in a rain forest in South-America by a young boy who was playing with his friends in the forest. At a certain point, the boy couldn't find his friends anymore. They were gone and he was all alone. He was lost and had no clue about where to go. He called for help but nobody could hear him. He sat down on the ground and started to cry. Suddenly, the boy felt a wet tongue licking his hands. He looked up and saw a strange animal. The animal looked at him and pushed its nose gently in his belly. The boy stood up. The animal went behind the boy and started to push its nose in the boy's back. It was as if the animal tried to show him the way. Initially, the boy didn't get it. But the animal continued to push the boy in the back. Finally, the boy understood what the animal was up to and he started to walk. The animal walked along and kept pushing the boy in the right direction. After several hours, the boy heard the voices of his friends calling for him. The animal had brought him back to his friends by pushing him with its nose. The boy gently stroke the animal and thanked it. The animal jumped up against him and licked his face. Then, the animal walked away. The boy and the animal still meet each other in the rain forest every day".

The negative information story ran as follows: "This animal, called 'the beast', was recently discovered in a rain forest in South-America. The animal appears to be very dangerous and violent as it recently attacked a young boy. The boy and his friends were playing in the rain forest. Suddenly, they heard a loud and scary sound and then saw a strange animal hiding in the bushes. Suddenly, this animal came out of the bushes towards them. The boy and his friends started to run as fast as they could but the animal was faster. The animal jumped on the boy who fell on the ground. The animal pushed its nose in the boy's belly and licked the skin with its tongue. There was blue poison on the animal's tongue and the boy felt a burning pain on his skin. The boy screamed, but the animal wasn't finished yet: it bit the boy's leg with its sharp teeth. The boy was bleeding severely. Fortunately, the police came and the animal ran off. The boy was brought to the hospital. The doctor gave the boy some medicine against the poison and operated on the boy's leg. It took quite some time before the boy recovered completely, but his skin still looks very scary". After presentation of the story, children completed the FBQ and the modified FSSC for a second time. One week later, the experimenter visited the schools again to carry out the individual follow-up assessment of FBQ and modified FSSC.

For children aged 7–12 years, the procedure was run in class sessions by the same experimenter who carried out the assessment in the younger children. Children first completed the trait anxiety scale of the STAIC, the CASI, the BIS, the FBQ, and the modified FSSC. Next, all children in one class listened either to the positive or the negative information story. Directly after the presentation of the story, children completed the FBQ and modified FSSC again. One week later, classes were revisited to obtain the follow-up assessment of FBQ and modified FSSC.

When the last class of a school was tested, the experimenter visited all classes for the last time to debrief the children and to explicitly state that the stories were just invented for the purpose of the study.

2.4. Data Analysis

The Statistical Package for Social Sciences (SPSS) was used to compute descriptive statistics and reliability coefficients. To evaluate the effects of positive and negative information on children's fear levels, a series of 2 (information type: positive story vs. negative story)×2 (gender)×3 (age group: 4–6-year-olds vs. 7–9-year-olds vs. 10–12-year-olds)×2 (occasions: pre- vs. post-assessment or pre- vs. follow-up assessment) multivariate analyses of variance (MANOVAs), with the last factor being a repeated measure were carried out. To investigate the role of individual difference variables on the influence of negative and positive information, correlations (corrected for gender and age) between STAIC, CASI, BIS, and general fearfulness as indexed by the FSSC, on the one hand, and fear of beast, dogs and other predators change scores (i.e., post minus pre, follow-up minus pre), on the other hand, were computed within each information condition.

3. Results

3.1. Reliability of Fear Measures

Table 1 presents internal consistency coefficients (Cronbach's alphas) for the various measures at pre-, post-, and follow-up assessment. As can be seen, all scales were reliable with alphas generally well above 0.70 notwithstanding the fact that most scales only contained a small number of items.

3.2. Effects of Negative and Positive Information on Children's Fear

Mean FBQ and FSSC scores of the children in both experimental conditions are displayed in Table 2. The 2 (information type)×2 (gender)×3 (age group)×2 (occa-

TABLE 1   Reliability coefficients of the FBQ and the modified FSSC-R at pre-, post-, and follow-up assessment.

	Pre	Post	Follow-up
FBQ			
Fear of the beast	0.91	0.97	0.97
FSSC-R			
Total fear score	0.89	0.92	0.91
Fear of danger and death	0.76	0.81	0.83
Fear of failure and criticism	0.66	0.73	0.74
Fear of the unknown	0.73	0.77	0.78
Fear of small animals	0.65	0.75	0.75
Medical fears	0.71	0.76	0.73
Fear of dogs	0.72	0.82	0.82
Fear of predators	0.84	0.89	0.91

Note. N=285. FBQ=Fear of the Beast Questionnaire, FSSC-R=Fear Survey Schedule for Children—Revised.

sions) MANOVA performed on pre- and post-assessment FBQ data showed that the crucial interaction of information type and occasions was significant [$F_{Hotellings}$(1, 273)=553.8, $P<0.001$, Eta^2=0.67]. That is, fear of beast scores increased in the negative information condition, but showed a clear decrease in the positive information condition. The MANOVA carried out on the pre- and follow-up FBQ data indicated that these effects of negative and positive information were still present at a one-week follow-up [$F_{Hotellings}$(1, 273)=333.1, $P<0.001$, Eta^2=0.55] (see Table 2 and Figure 1).

TABLE 2   Mean scores (standard deviations) of children in both experimental conditions at pre-, post-, and follow-up assessment.

	Negative information			Positive information			Interaction effect (condition × occasions)	
	Pre	Post	Follow-up	Pre	Post	Follow-up	Pre–post	Pre–follow-up
FBQ								
Fear of the beast	25.4	31.7	30.3	25.0	16.4	17.4	553.8*	333.1*
	(6.1)	(4.7)†	(6.1)†	(6.2)	(4.7)†	(6.0)†		
FSSC-R								
Total fear score	40.6	40.7	38.9	41.0	39.7	38.6	4.7	0.7
	(8.5)	(9.4)	(9.0)	(9.1)	(10.4)	(10.0)		
Fear of danger and death	11.0	10.9	10.3	11.1	10.5	10.3	8.1*	0.8
	(2.7)	(2.7)	(3.0)	(2.8)	(3.2)†	(3.1)		
Fear of failure and criticism	6.6	6.7	6.3	6.7	6.6	6.4	0.2	0.1
	(1.6)	(1.9)	(1.7)	(1.8)	(2.0)	(2.0)		
Fear of the unknown	7.2	7.5	7.1	7.4	7.1	6.9	9.9*	1.8
	(2.3)	(2.4)†	(2.4)	(2.3)	(2.4)†	(2.3)		
Fear of small animals	7.8	7.8	7.7	7.7	7.5	7.3	0.8	2.7
	(2.1)	(2.3)	(2.2)	(2.2)	(2.5)	(2.5)		
Medical fears	8.0	7.8	7.5	8.1	8.0	7.6	0.8	0.7
	(2.4)	(2.4)	(2.3)	(2.3)	(2.6)	(2.4)		
Fear of dogs	9.3	9.8	9.6	9.0	8.6	8.5	21.2*	16.9*
	(2.4)	(2.7)†	(2.7)	(2.3)	(2.7)†	(2.8)†		
Fear of predators	10.9	11.2	11.0	10.5	9.8	9.8	13.9*	9.2
	(2.9)	(3.0)†	(3.2)	(3.0)	(3.4)†	(3.4)†		

Note. $N=154$ for the negative information condition, $N=131$ for the positive information condition. FBQ=Fear of the Beast Questionnaire, FSSC-R=Fear Survey Schedule for Children—Revised. *$P<0.05/9$ (i.e., Bonferroni correction). †Significant change compared to pre-assessment ($P<0.05$) as tested by means of a paired follow-up $t$test within each condition.

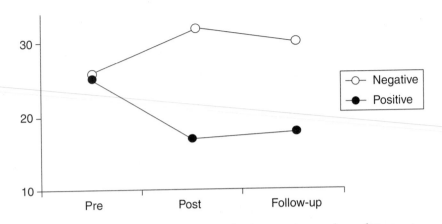

FIGURE 1 Mean FBQ scores of children in both experimental conditions at pre-, post-, and follow-up assessment. Note. FBQ=Fear of the Beast Questionnaire.

MANOVAs performed on FSSC data revealed that negative and positive information also resulted in significant changes in 'fear of dogs' and 'fear of predators' from pre- to post-assessment [$F_{Hotellings}(1, 273)=21.2$, $P<0.001$, Eta^2=0.07 and $F_{Hotellings}(1, 273)=13.9$, $P<0.001$, Eta^2=0.05, respectively] and from pre- to follow-up assessment [$F_{Hotellings}(1, 273)=9.2$, $P<0.005$, Eta^2=0.03 and $F_{Hotellings}(1, 273)=16.9$, $P<0.001$, Eta^2=0.06, respectively]. Thus, information about the beast also affected fear evaluations of dogs and other predators. That is, negative information about the beast increased children's fears of dogs and predators, while positive information decreased these fears (see Table 2 and Figures 2 and 3). Other types of fears did not show a consistent change after the information manipulation, although 'fear of danger and death' and 'fear of the unknown' significantly covaried with information type from pre- to post-assessment [$F_{Hotellings}(1, 273)=8.1$, $P<0.01$, Eta^2=0.03 and $F_{Hotellings}(1, 273)=9.9$, $P<0.005$, Eta^2=0.04, respectively].

3.3. Age and Gender and the Influence of Negative and Positive Information

Although a number of MANOVAs indicated that there were significant main effects of age group (i.e., fear levels generally decreased as children were older), no evidence was found for the notion that younger children would be more susceptible to the influence of negative/positive information: that is, none of the crucial age groupxinformation typexoccasions interactions reached significance. Although one should be cautious with making comparisons between the three age groups (as there were differences in the experimental assessment between the 4–6-year-olds and the two older age groups), these results at least suggest that younger children were not more susceptible to the effects of information than older children.

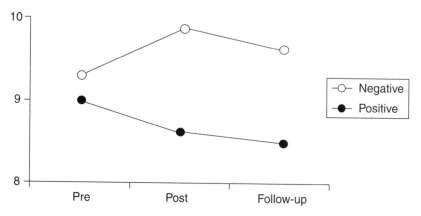

FIGURE 2 Mean FSSC-R Fear of dogs scores of children in both experimental conditions at pre-, post-, and follow-up assessment. Note. FSSC-R=Fear Survey Schedule for Children—Revised.

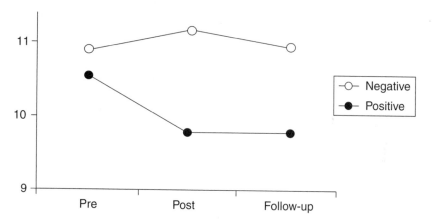

FIGURE 3 Mean FSSC-R Fear of predators scores of children in both experimental conditions at pre-, post-, and follow-up assessment. Note. FSSC-R=Fear Survey Schedule for Children—Revised.

In all MANOVAs, significant main effects of gender were found with girls consistently displaying higher fear levels than boys. However, no interaction effects of gender with information type×occasions emerged, indicating that boys and girls were equally affected by the negative and positive information about the beast.

3.4. Individual Difference Variables and the Influence of Negative and Positive Information

To examine whether individual difference variables mediate the influence of negative and positive information, correlations (corrected for age and gender) between modified FSSC-R, STAIC, CASI, and BIS scores, on the one hand, and fear of beast, dogs, and predators change scores (i.e., post minus pre and follow-up minus pre), on the other hand, were computed within each condition. As can be seen in Table 3, only 12 out of 48 correlations were found to be significant and note that these associations were all rather small (with rs between 0.19 and 0.34, all

TABLE 3   Means scores (standard deviations) and reliability coefficients for the various individual difference measures that were administered to the 8–12-year-old children in our sample, and correlations (corrected for gender and age) between these measures and FBQ/FSSC-R Fear of dogs/FSSC-R Fear of predators (change) scores calculated for both conditions separately.

	Negative information				Positive information			
	FSSC-R (pre)	STAIC	CASI	BIS	FSSC-R (pre)	STAIC	CASI	BIS
M (SD)	40.3 (8.3)	32.1 (7.5)	27.0 (5.7)	20.0 (3.8)	39.2 (8.7)	31.4 (6.6)	27.2 (6.0)	18.8 (4.2)
Cronbach's α	0.89	0.87	0.82	0.79	0.90	0.83	0.83	0.74
FBQ Fear of the beast								
Pre	0.50**	0.29*	0.37**	0.21*	0.65**	0.52**	0.50**	0.35*
Post	0.43**	0.20*	0.21*	0.18	0.26*	0.13	0.27*	0.12
Follow-up	0.44**	0.12	0.12	0.16	0.41**	0.25*	0.37**	0.25*
Change Pre-								
Post	0.19*	0.04	−0.01	0.07	−0.05	−0.13	0.06	−0.05
Change Post-								
Follow-up	0.26*	−0.03	−0.08	0.07	0.11	−0.02	0.15	0.08
FSSC-R Fear of Dogs								
Pre	0.55**	0.25*	0.32*	0.24*	0.60**	0.26*	0.37**	0.24*
Post	0.58**	0.30*	0.38**	0.28*	0.57**	0.32*	0.39**	0.22*
Follow-up	0.57**	0.30*	0.32*	0.23*	0.57**	0.33*	0.48**	0.22*
Change Pre-								
Post	0.28*	0.18	0.21*	0.15	0.16	0.20	0.16	0.04
Change Post-								
Follow-up	0.23*	0.17	0.09	0.04	0.23*	0.21*	0.34*	0.06
FSSC-R Fear of predators								
Pre	0.47**	0.24*	0.30*	0.20*	0.51**	0.22*	0.38**	0.08
Post	0.46**	0.22*	0.26*	0.21*	0.49**	0.34*	0.43**	0.09
Follow-up	0.43**	0.22*	0.26*	0.20*	0.51**	0.27*	0.42**	0.14
Change Pre-								
Post	0.13	0.04	0.01	0.06	0.13	0.31*	0.22*	0.03
Change Post-								
Follow-up	0.12	0.06	0.05	0.07	0.22*	0.16	0.22*	0.12

Note. N=110 for the negative information condition, N=92 for the positive information condition. FBQ=Fear of the Beast Questionnaire, FSSC-R=Fear Survey Schedule for Children—Revised. $P<0.05$, $P<0.05/60$ (i.e., Bonferroni correction).

Ps<0.05). In other words, individual difference variables did not have a substantial impact on the effects of negative and positive information. Interestingly, correlations between individual difference measures and fear scores at pre-assessment indicated that, already from the beginning of the experiment, general fearfulness (FSSC-R), anxiety sensitivity (CASI), and to a lesser extent, trait anxiety (STAIC), and behavioural inhibition (BIS) were significantly linked to fear of the beast, dogs, and predators. Furthermore, especially fearfulness as indexed by the modified FSSC-R appeared to be a solid predictor of fear of the beast, dogs, and predators scores throughout the entire experiment (see Table 3).

4. Discussion

The present study examined the effects of negative and positive information on children's fear evaluations of an unknown, doglike animal (i.e., the beast). Results showed that type of information changed children's fear of the beast in the predicted direction with negative information increasing fear levels and positive information decreasing fear levels, and this was not only the case directly after the experimental manipulation but also at one week follow-up. Furthermore, fear of the beast appeared to generalize, that is, children who became more fearful of the beast after receiving negative information, also became more apprehensive of other dogs and predators. These findings are consistent with and extend those of Field et al. (2001) who also showed that verbal information significantly changed children's fear beliefs.

The effects of negative and positive information were rather specific. That is, information affected children's fear evaluations of the beast, dogs, and predators, whereas fear levels in other domains remained largely unchanged. Only 'fear of danger and death' and 'fear of the unknown' to some extent covaried with information type from pre- to post-assessment, a finding which was not that surprising as the stories contained several elements that were relevant for these particular fear domains (i.e., danger, getting lost, serious injury).

Our findings suggest that it is possible to enhance children's fears by providing them with negative information about an unknown stimulus and thus support Rachman's (1977, 1991) theory that negative information promotes fear. However, in most cases, mere exposure to negative information is probably not enough to produce severe fear and avoidance behaviour. According to current conditioning models (e.g., Dadds, Davey, & Field, 2001; Davey, 1997), negative information may install expectancies about the probable outcome of a conditioning episode that can assist the learning of CS-UCS contingencies. For example, when a child already has negative information about a certain stimulus, a subsequent direct conditioning experience involving that stimulus is more likely to produce a fear reaction that is resistant to extinction (e.g., Davey, 1992).

In his hallmark book 'Fears, phobias, and rituals. Panic, anxiety, and their disorders', Marks (1987) has accumulated evidence for the existence of sensitive periods for the development of certain fears. This phenomenon probably has to do with children reaching a certain maturational stage. For example, experimental research employing the so-called visual cliff procedure has shown that fear of heights critically depends on children's locomotor development (Bertenthal, Campos, & Barrett, 1984). Similarly, fear of separation only occurs after children have developed object permanence for faces (Kagan, Kearsley, & Zelazo, 1975). Perhaps, one might have expected that, given their still limited cognitive capacities, the younger children in our sample would be more susceptible to the influence of negative and positive information, resulting in more pronounced changes of their fear levels. However, no support was found for this notion as age did not interact with the effects of information. It may well be the case, however, that the differential procedure that was used for younger and older children (i.e., individual versus classwise assessment) has obscured such age effects. A future study solely relying on individual interviews may clarify whether age indeed mediates the effects of negative and positive information on children's fears.

Consistent with previous research (e.g., Bernstein et al., 1996; Craske, 1997; Muris & Merckelbach, 2001), girls clearly displayed higher fear levels than boys. However, no evidence was found for the idea that girls were more affected by the negative information about the beast than boys. It is still unclear what the origins of this marked gender difference in fearfulness are. The most plausible explanations in the literature relate to biological (genetics and hormones) or socialization factors (i.e., greater permission for girls to exhibit and report fears than boys) (see for a comprehensive review Merckelbach & Muris, 2001).

Individual difference variables did not substantially mediate the effects of negative and positive information. Yet, it should be noted that general fearfulness, anxiety sensitivity, and to a lesser extent trait anxiety and behavioural inhibition, were already linked to fear of the beast, dogs, and other predators before the experimental manipulation, hence leaving little room for change. At the very least, this finding suggests that there is a group of anxiety-prone children who tend to make inflated fear evaluations and become easily scared of a wide range of potentially threatening stimuli (see Lonigan & Phillips, 2001).

Admittedly, the present study suffers from one important limitation in that it solely relied on children's self-report and so it is possible that the results are obscured by demand bias. However, fear ratings showed an interesting specific generalization effect, which suggests that findings were more than just a simple demand effect.

More specifically, verbal information did not only change children's fear evaluations about the beast but also affected their ratings of dogs and predators, whereas fear evaluations in other domains largely remained unchanged. Nevertheless, it would have strengthened our study if we had included a direct in vivo assessment of children's responses to a dog-like animal before and after the provision of the negative/positive information.

The present data as well as those obtained by Field et al. (2001) indicate that verbal information affects children's fear evaluations. The results suggest that adults can increase children's fears by expressing negative ideas about certain stimuli and situations as well as reduce or diminish fears in children through positive statements. Currently, we are investigating this issue more directly by examining the connection between the number of negative expressions of parents who describe a series of ambiguous situations to their children and children's level of fear to these situations. Future work should also examine whether the transmission of positive information can be exploited therapeutically. Particularly in combination with exposure exercises, careful provision of positive information could be a valuable clinical tool in correcting fear-provoking cognitions and decreasing children's level of fear overall.

References

Bernstein, G. A., Borchardt, C. M., & Perwien, A. R. (1996). Anxiety disorders in children and adolescents: A review of the past 10 years. *Journal of the American Academy of Child and Adolescent Psychiatry*, 35, 1110–1119.

Bertenthal, B. I., Campos, J. J., & Barrett, K. C. (1984). Self-produced locomotion: An organizer of emotional, cognitive, and social development in infancy. In R. Emde, & R. Harmon (Eds.), *Continuities and discontinuities in development*. New York: Plenum Press.

Biederman, J., Rosenbaum, J. F., Chaloff, J., & Kagan, J. (1995). Behavioral inhibition as a risk factor for anxiety disorders. In J. S. March (Ed.), *Anxiety disorders in children and adolescents* (pp. 61–81). New York: Guilford Press.

Bruck, M., Ceci, S. J., & Hembrooke, H. (1998). Reliability and credibility of young children's reports. *American Psychologist*, 53, 136–151.

Craske, M. G. (1997). Fear and anxiety in children and adolescents. *Bulletin of the Menninger Clinic, 61*(Suppl. A), A4–A36.

Dadds, M. R., Davey, G. C. L., & Field, A. P. (2001). Developmental aspects of conditioning processes in anxiety disorders. In M. W. Vasey, & M. R. Dadds (Eds.), *The developmental psychopathology of anxiety* (pp. 205–230). New York: Oxford University Press.

Davey, G. C. L. (1992). An expectancy model of laboratory preparedness effects. *Journal of Experimental Psychology: General*, 121, 24–40.

Davey, G. C. L. (1997). A conditioning model of phobias. In G. C. L. Davey (Ed.), *Phobias: A handbook of theory, research, and treatment*. Chichester: Wiley.

Eysenck, H. J. (1987). The role of heredity, environment, and preparedness in the genesis of neurosis. In H. J. Eysenck, & I. Martin (Eds.), *Theoretical foundations of behavior therapy*. New York: Plenum Press.

Field, A. P., Argyrus, N. G., & Knowles, K. A. (2001). Who's afraid of the big bad wolf: A prospective paradigm to test Rachman's indirect pathways in children. *Behaviour Research and Therapy*, *39*, 1259–1276.

Gullone, E. (2000). The development of normal fear. *Clinical Psychology Review*, *20*, 429–451.

Gullone, E., & King, N. J. (1992). Psychometric evaluation of a revised fear survey schedule for children and adolescents. *Journal of Child Psychology and Psychiatry*, *33*, 987–998.

Kagan, J. (1997). Temperament of the reactions to unfamiliarity. *Child Development*, *68*, 139–143.

Kagan, J., Kearsley, R. B., & Zelazo, P. R. (1975). The emergence of initial apprehension to unfamiliar peers. In M. Lewis, & L. A. Rosenblum (Eds.), *Friendship and peer relations*. New York: Wiley.

King, N. J., Gullone, E., & Ollendick, T. H. (1998). Etiology of childhood phobias: Current status of Rachman's three pathways theory. *Behaviour Research and Therapy*, *36*, 297–309.

King, N. J., Hamilton, D. I., & Ollendick, T. H. (1988). *Children's phobias: A behavioural perspective*. New York: Wiley.

King, N. J., & Ollendick, T. H. (1989). Children's anxiety and phobic disorders in school settings: Classification, assessment, and intervention issues. *Review of Educational Research*, *59*, 431–470.

King, N. J., Ollier, K., Iacuone, R., Schuster, S., Bays, K., Gullone, E., & Ollendick, T. H. (1989). Child and adolescent fears: An Australian cross-sectional study using the Revised Fear Survey Schedule for Children. *Journal of Child Psychology and Psychiatry*, *30*, 775–784.

Lonigan, C. J., & Phillips, B. M. (2001). Temperamental influences on the development of anxiety disorders. In M. W. Vasey, & M. R. Dadds (Eds.), *The developmental psychopathology of anxiety* (pp. 60–91). New York: Oxford University Press.

Marks, I. M. (1987). *Fears, phobias, and rituals. Panic, anxiety, and their disorders*. New York: Oxford University Press.

Merckelbach, H., & Muris, P. (2001). Specific phobias. In E. J. L. Griez, C. Faravelli, D. Nutt, & J. Zohar (Eds.), *Anxiety disorders: An introduction to clinical management and research* (pp. 105–135). New York: Wiley.

Muris, P., & Merckelbach, H. (2001). The etiology of childhood specific phobia: A multifactorial model. In M. W. Vasey, & M. R. Dadds (Eds.), *The developmental psychopathology of anxiety* (pp. 355–385). New York: Oxford University Press.

Muris, P., Merckelbach, H., & Collaris, R. (1997). Common childhood fears and their origins. *Behaviour Research and Therapy*, *35*, 929–937.

Muris, P., Merckelbach, H., Gadet, B., & Moulaert, V. (2000). Fears, worries, and scary dreams in 4-to 12-year-old children: Their content, developmental pattern, and origins. *Journal of Clinical Child Psychology*, *29*,43–52.

Muris, P., Merckelbach, H., Wessel, I., & Van de Ven, M. (1999). Psychopathological correlates of self-reported behavioural inhibition in normal children. *Behaviour Research and Therapy*, *37*, 575–584.

Muris, P., Meesters, C., Mayer, B., Bogie, N., Luijten, M., Geebelen, E., & Smit, C. (submitted). The Koala Fear Questionnaire: A standardized self-report scale for assessing fears and fearfulness in pre-school and primary school children.

Muris, P., & Ollendick, T. H. (in press). The assessment of contemporary fears in adolescents using a modified version of the Fear Survey Schedule for Children—Revised. *Journal of Anxiety Disorders*.

Ollendick, T. H. (1983). Reliability and validity of the Revised Fear Survey Schedule for Children (FSSC-R). *Behaviour Research and Therapy, 21*, 685–692.

Ollendick, T. H., & King, N. J. (1991). Origins of childhood fears: An evaluation of Rachman's theory of fear acquisition. *Behaviour Research and Therapy, 29*, 117–123.

Ollendick, T. H., King, N. J., & Frary, R. B. (1989). Fears in children and adolescents: Reliability and generalizability across gender, age, and nationality. *Behaviour Research and Therapy, 27*,19–26.

Ollendick, T. H., King, N. J., & Muris, P. (in press). Fears and phobias in children: Phenomenology, epidemiology, and etiology. *Child Psychology & Psychiatry Review*.

Ollendick, T. H., Yule, W., & Ollier, K. (1991). Fears in British children and their relationship to manifest anxiety and depression. *Journal of Child Psychology and Psychiatry, 32*, 321–331.

Rachman, S. J. (1977). The conditioning theory of fear acquisition: A critical examination. *Behaviour Research and Therapy, 15*, 375–387.

Rachman, S. J. (1991). Neoconditioning and the classical theory of fear acquisition. *Clinical Psychology Review, 11*, 155–173.

Reiss, S., Peterson, R. A., Gursky, D. M., & McNally, R. J. (1986). Anxiety sensitivity, anxiety frequency, and the prediction of fearfulness. *Behaviour Research and Therapy, 24*,1–8.

Reiss, S., Silverman, W. K., & Weems, C. F. (2001). Anxiety sensitivity. In M. W. Vasey, & M. R. Dadds (Eds.), *The developmental psychopathology of anxiety* (pp. 92–111). New York: Oxford University Press.

Silverman, W. K., Fleisig, W., Rabian, B., & Peterson, R. A. (1991). Childhood anxiety sensitivity index. *Journal of Clinical Child Psychology, 20*, 162–168.

Spielberger, C. D. (1973). *Manual for the State-Trait Anxiety Inventory for children*. Palo Alto, CA: Consulting Psychologists Press.

Stevenson, J., Batten, N., & Cherner, M. (1992). Fears and fearfulness in children and adolescents: A genetic analysis of twin data. *Journal of Child Psychology and Psychiatry, 33*, 977–985.

Withers, R. D., & Deane, F. P. (1995). Origins of common fears: Effects on severity, anxiety responses and memories of onset. *Behaviour Research and Therapy, 33*, 903–915.

Editor's Note

Perter Muris, Corresponding author. Tel.: +31-43-388-1264; fax: +31-43-367-0968.
E-mail address: *p.muris@dep.unimaas.nl* (*P. Muris*).

Discussion Questions for Article 1

Section 11: Abnormal Behavior

Name: _____

PID: _____

Date: __ __ / __ __ / __ __ (MM/DD/YY)

CRN: _____

Recitation Day/Time: _____

Honor Code Signature: _____

1. What did Muris et al. report were common childhood fears? Do any of those seem surprising to you?

2. What individual difference variables did the authors say represent the genetic factor constituting 'neuroticism' or 'negative affectivity' and likely contribute to the development of childhood fear and anxiety?

3. Summarize and discuss the main findings of the study. What are some implications of these findings?

4. What were some of your childhood fears? Can you pinpoint the origin of those fears?

Article 2

Ethnic and Sex Differences in Children's Depressive Symptoms: Mediating Effects of Perceived and Actual Competence

Janet A. Kistner
Corinne F. David
Bradley A. White

Examined ethnic and sex differences in depressive symptoms, along with hypothesized mediators of those differences (academic achievement, peer acceptance), for a sample of African American (n = 272) and Euro-American (n = 630) children in Grades 3 to 5. Group comparisons revealed a significant Ethnicity × Sex interaction in depressive symptoms. African American boys reported more depressive symptoms than Euro-American boys, whereas African American and Euro-American girls reported comparable levels of depressive symptoms. Sex differences in depressive symptoms differed by ethnicity: Boys were more depressed than girls in the African American group whereas girls were more depressed than boys in the Euro-American group. The Ethnicity × Sex interaction was mediated by academic achievement, but not peer acceptance. These findings have implications for understanding the mechanisms underlying depressive symptoms in preadolescence and for developing interventions to prevent depression.

Although depressive symptoms and disorders are found in all cultures (Weissman et al., 1997), ethnic differences in prevalence and correlates of depression have been noted (Carr, Gilroy, & Sherman, 1996; Culbertson, 1997; Hayward, Gotlib, Schraedley, & Litt, 1999; Leutwyler, 1997; Siegel, Yancey, Aneshensel, & Schuler, 1999; Wrobel & Lachar, 1995). Continued examination of the nature and causes of ethnic differences in depression is important to understand how various internal and external mechanisms may differentially give rise to the emergence of depressive symptoms across ethnic groups. Additionally, such research is necessary to the design of culturally sensitive assessment and intervention strategies.

The majority of studies examining ethnic differences in depression have focused on the functioning of adolescents and adults, whereas children have received relatively less attention. This imbalance in our knowledge is understandable given the relatively low prevalence of clinically diagnosed depression prior to adolescence (i.e., estimated to be less than 3%; Speier, Sherak, Hirsch, & Cantwell, 1995) compared to a much higher prevalence by mid-adolescence (i.e., 15% to 20% of adolescents have experienced one or more depressive episodes; Birmaher, Ryan, Williamson, Brent, & Kaufman, 1996). However, the alarmingly high prevalence of depression in adolescence coupled with evidence that age of first depressive episode is decreasing (Lewinsohn, Rohde, Seeley, & Fischer, 1993; Reich et al., 1987) underscores the importance of investigating factors associated with depression in preadolescents.

The few studies that have investigated ethnic differences in depressive symptoms of preadolescents focus on comparisons of African Americans and Euro-Americans (Cole, Martin, Peeke, Henderson, & Harwell, 1998; Doerfler, Felner, Rowlison, Raley, & Evans, 1988; Helsel & Matson, 1984; Reynolds & Graves, 1989; Treadwell, Flannery-Schroeder, & Kendall, 1995), and results have been inconsistent. Differences in measures, sample sizes, and characteristics of participants, particularly with respect to the range of ages included, probably contributed to the disparate findings. Cole and colleagues addressed some of these variations and limitations of previous work. For instance, they analyzed data of preadolescents (i.e., children in Grades 3 to 5) separately and included sufficiently large numbers of African American and Euro-American children to provide a sensitive test of ethnic differences. They found that, on average, African American children were more depressed than Euro-American children.

This study attempted to replicate the findings of Cole et al. (1998) of ethnic differences in preadolescents' self-reported depressive symptoms and extend this research in two ways. First, we investigated multiple factors that may potentially mediate ethnic differences in depressive symptoms. Second, we assessed sex differences to determine the generality of ethnic differences in depressive symptoms (i.e., are ethnic group differences characteristic of both boys and girls?) and to examine moderating effects of ethnicity on sex differences in preadolescents' depressive symptoms (i.e., does the pattern of sex differences differ between African American and Euro-American children?).

Mediators of Ethnic Differences in Depressive Symptoms

The competency-based model of childhood depression (Cole, 1990, 1991) guided our selection of potential mediators of ethnic differences in depressive symptoms. According to this model, children with competence deficits receive negative feedback from others. Repeated exposure to negative feedback in multiple domains, in turn, inhibits the emergence and differentiation of positive self-schemata, thus increasing children's risk for developing depressive symptoms. We examined the mediating role of two competence domains that preadolescents view as important and ones in which they receive feedback from others about their level of functioning: academic competence and peer acceptance. In the late elementary school years, children regularly receive direct and indirect feedback about their level of academic proficiency. Deficits in this domain have been shown to be associated with elevated levels of depressive symptoms (see Weisz, Rudolph, Granger, & Sweeney, 1992). Peer acceptance is also of importance to preadolescents and a domain in which they receive overt and subtle feedback from their peers (Harter, 1985). Social acceptance plays a central role in theories of depression (e.g., Coyne, 1976). Consistent with these theories, depression is higher among children with problematic peer relationships compared to children who are accepted by peers (for reviews, see Hartup, 1983; Weisz et al., 1992).

We hypothesized that ethnic differences in depressive symptoms may derive from ethnic differences in competence in one or both of these domains. Regarding the academic domain, there is considerable evidence that African American children experience more academic achievement difficulties than Euro-American children (e.g., Hedges & Nowell, 1999; Mickelson, 1990). As for the social domain, a number of studies of children's peer relationships have found that being an ethnic minority in a classroom is associated with lower peer acceptance (e.g., Graham & Cohen, 1997; Kistner, Metzler, Gatlin, & Risi, 1993). Interestingly, Cole et al. (1998) examined peer acceptance as a mediator of their finding of ethnic differences in depression. African American and Euro-American children in their sample were equally accepted by peers, thus peer acceptance did not explain the elevated depressive symptoms of the African American children in their study. This study provides an opportunity to replicate these findings, as well as to examine the mediating role of academic achievement.

Sex Differences in Depressive Symptoms Among Preadolescents

Beginning in adolescence and continuing until old age, girls and women are as much as twice as likely to be diagnosed depressed (Birmaher et al., 1996) and experience substantially more depressive symptoms than boys and men (Nolen-Hoeksema & Girgus, 1994). Prior to adolescence, studies are almost evenly divided between those that find no sex differences in diagnosed depression or depressive symptoms (e.g., Angold, Erklani, Loeber, & Costello, 1996; Speier et al., 1995) and those that find that symptoms and diagnoses of depression are more elevated in boys than girls (e.g., Anderson, Williams, McGee, & Silva, 1987; Kashani, Cantwell, Shekim, & Reid, 1982; Rutter, 1986). In contrast to the large body of research that attempts to explain elevated depressive symptoms among adolescent and adult females (Nolen-Hoeksema & Girgus, 1994; Peterson, Sarigiani, & Kennedy, 1991), little attention has focused on why boys may report more depressive symptoms than girls prior to adolescence. Furthermore, it remains to be examined why some studies find preadolescent sex differences in depressive symptoms whereas others do not.

Just as academic achievement problems were hypothesized to account for ethnic differences in depression, they may also contribute to sex differences in depression in preadolescence. In the elementary-school years, boys tend to have lower academic achievement and more school-related problems than girls (e.g., Dweck & Goetz, 1977; Fagot, 1981). This gap may contribute to elevated depressive symptoms among boys. Interestingly, the gap between boys and girls in measures of school achievement is greater among African American children than it is among Euro-American children (Garibaldi, 1992; Winfield & Lee, 1990), with African American boys having substantially more problems in the academic domain than African American girls and Euro-American boys and girls. These findings suggest that ethnicity may interact with sex to predict depressive symptoms in preadolescence.

Summary

Symptoms of depression were assessed for a large, community sample of African American and Euro-American children in Grades 3 through 5. The following predictions were tested: (a) African American children report more depressive symptoms than Euro-American children; (b) ethnic differences are moderated by sex, such that ethnic differences are larger among boys than girls; (c) sex differences are moderated by ethnicity, such that sex differences (i.e., boys more depressed than girls) are larger among African Americans than Euro-Americans; (d) academic achievement mediates ethnic and sex differences in children's depressive symptoms; and (e) peer acceptance mediates ethnic differences in children's depressive symptoms. To test these hypotheses, objective indexes of children's academic achievement (i.e., standardized test scores) and peer acceptance (i.e., sociometric ratings) were obtained. Also, children's perceptions of their competence in these two domains were assessed and tested as possible mediators of depressive symptoms. The mediating role of perceived competence is important to consider because prior research indicates that children's perceptions are only moderately associated with objective measures of competence (Harter, 1985). Such perceptions are likely to reflect internalization of negative feedback and thus are expected to contribute to depressive symptoms, even when they are at odds with objective indicators of competence.

Method

Participants

Participants were recruited from third-, fourth-, and fifth-grade classrooms of nine elementary schools in a small metropolitan area in northern Florida. Only the data of Euro-American (68%) and African American (29%) participants were examined in this study because of the small number of students from other ethnic groups (2% Hispanic, 1% other ethnic groups). The percentage of Euro-American children in classrooms in the final sample ranged from 12% to 91%, with a median of 76%. Parental signed informed consent was obtained from 59% of the eligible pool; consent rates were comparable across ethnic and sex groups (range of 57.7% to 59.7% across the four groups). Previous research has indicated that child samples requiring parental participation may not be representative, particularly when minority status or social functioning is pertinent to the research questions (La Greca & Silverman, 1993). Parental consent for child participation could in theory be similarly biased. To assess for bias due to differing response rates, we divided the sample into those from classrooms above or below the median response rate and compared these groups on all measures; no significant differences were found (all p values > .10). Also, results were unchanged when analyses were limited to participants from classrooms with response rates above 60%.

Due to repeated absences, invalid response profiles, or reluctance to participate, eight children for whom parental consent had been obtained were dropped from the sample. The final sample was composed of 291 Euro-American boys, 339 Euro-American girls, 126 African American boys, and 146 African American girls, ranging in age from 8 to 14 years. The average age of participants was 9.6 years (SD = 1.1); mean ages for ethnic and sex groups were 9.95 years (SD = 1.10) for African American boys, 9.72 years (SD = 1.09) for African American girls, 9.61 years (SD = 1.06) for Euro-American boys, and 9.59 years (SD = 1.00) for Euro-American girls. A

2 (ethnicity) × 2 (sex) analysis of variance (ANOVA) revealed significant ethnic and sex differences in age (African Americans and boys were older). Achievement scores, taken from children's academic files, were unavailable for 79 children (25 Euro-American boys, 17 Euro-American girls, 17 African American boys, and 20 African American girls). These children were retained in the sample and included in analyses that did not involve achievement scores.[1]

The percentage of children who qualified for free and reduced lunches at each of the schools in this sample was used to provide some information about the socioeconomic status (SES) of the sample; this percentage ranged from 20.6% to 89.6% across schools. A median split was used to classify schools as lower or upper SES. Ethnicity was associated with school SES, $\chi^2(1, N = 902) = 51.80$, $p < .01$; African American participants were more likely to attend lower SES schools (65%) than were Euro-American participants (39%). SES was included as a variable in data analyses to control for this association.

Measures

CDI (Kovacs, 1985)   The Children's Depression Inventory (CDI) is a 27-item self-report measure of depressive symptoms for children under age 13. Kovacs (1985) reported adequate internal consistency and retest reliability for the scale. Evidence for the validity of this measure is well documented (e.g., Kazdin, Esveldt-Dawson, Unis, & Rancurello, 1983; Kovacs, 1985; Saylor, Finch, Spirito, & Bennett, 1984). Cole et al. (1998) found this measure to be equally reliable and valid for Euro-American and African American children. Internal consistency of the CDI for this sample was .87; alpha coefficients were comparable for our ethnic and sex groups (range of .85 to .89 across the four groups). The possible range of CDI scores is 0 to 54; the range of scores obtained for this sample was 0 to 45.

Academic Achievement   Children's scores from the Comprehensive Test of Basic Skills (CTBS; CTB/McGraw-Hill, 1977) were taken from their school records from the same year for which the other data for the study were collected. The CTBS is a group-administered, norm-referenced achievement test that is administered annually to all children in the school district from which the sample was drawn. This test is comprised of 11 subtests. In this study, a total composite score was used to

---

[1]African American children and children in lower SES schools were more likely to have missing achievement scores. Participants with missing achievement scores had higher CDI scores, lower peer acceptance, and more negative perceptions of their social and academic competence compared to other participants. Because of these differences, we analyzed the data both with and without this subgroup; results were the same, so we report analyses with all participants included.

index children's achievement. Norms for the CTBS were based on a large, ethnically diverse sample randomly selected from U.S. school districts stratified by size, socioeconomic level, and geographic region. Evidence supporting the reliability and validity of the CTBS is reported in the manual (CTB/McGraw-Hill, 1977) as well as in numerous other publications (e.g., Gross, 1982; Klein, 1980). For this sample, percentile scores ranged from 1 to 99.

Peer Acceptance   Participants were provided a class roster of all of their classmates and asked to rate on a 5-point rating scale, ranging from 1 (*do not like at all*) to 5 (*like very much*), how much they liked each classmate. Across all classes, a mean of 13.46 (*SD* = 3.64) children rated each child. Ratings were summed and averaged to form a measure of peer acceptance. The possible range of scores was 1 to 5; the range of scores obtained for this sample was 1.2 to 5. Peer ratings have been shown to be reliable and valid indexes of children's social competence (see Hartup, 1983, for a review).

SPPC (Harter, 1985)   Children's perceptions of their competence were assessed with the Self-Perception Profile for Children (SPPC), a 36-item self-report measure with six subscales. Five subscales assess children's perceptions of competence in specific domains (scholastic, social, athletic, physical appearance, behavioral conduct), and one assesses global self-worth. Each item presents children with two descriptive statements regarding their competence (e.g., *some kids are popular with others their age* but *other kids are not very popular*). Children decide which of the two statements is most like them, and then, for that statement, rate whether it is *really true* or just *sort of true* for them, resulting in a possible range of 1 to 4 (higher scores reflect more positive perceptions of competence). Evidence for test–retest reliability and criterion validity of this measure is well documented (e.g., Cole, 1991; Harter, 1985). Harter reported internal consistencies that ranged from .75 to .82 across subscales. The range of internal consistencies obtained for this sample was comparable (range of .71 to .78 for the subscales, with a mean of .74).

Only two SPPC subscales were of interest in this study based on the availability of complementary objective criteria. The scholastic competence subscale was used to index children's perceptions of their academic competence, and the social acceptance subscale composed our measure of perceived peer acceptance. The possible range of scores for each of the perceived competence measures was 1 to 4; the obtained range for this sample for both subscales was 1 to 4. For the full sample, internal consistency was .72 for the scholastic competence subscale and .71 for the social acceptance subscale. Internal consistencies for the scholastic competence subscale were somewhat higher for Euro-American children (.73 for boys, .77 for girls) than African American children (.63 for boys, .67 for girls). Similarly, internal consistencies for the social acceptance subscale were higher for the Euro-American group (.75 for boys and .73 for girls) than the African American group (.58 for boys and .65 for girls).[2]

Procedure

Data for this study were collected as part of a larger research project. Measures for the study were obtained during two 60-min data collection sessions, typically in the school lunchroom or resource center. Children who did not return consent forms remained in their classroom with their teachers. Research assistants presented instructions to small groups (i.e., 6 to 8 students) that consisted of students from different classrooms and grades to reduce the possibility that participants would compare or share answers. Participants were then allowed to complete the measures at their own pace. Participants were encouraged to respond to all items, and they were individually queried about any omitted items. Research assistants provided individual assistance to participants who required additional help (e.g., reading the questionnaires or understanding the directions). When participants completed the assessment battery, they were provided with distracter tasks, such as crossword puzzles and word-finds, to work on until the end of the data collection session. Based on our observations and feedback solicited from teachers, no negative effects associated with data collection were noted.

Results

Overview and Preliminary Analyses

Means and standard deviations for all measures are presented in Table 1. A 2 (ethnicity: African American vs. Euro-American) $\times$ 2 (sex) $\times$ 2 (SES: lower vs. upper SES) ANOVA was used to test hypotheses. Prior to conducting this analysis, the data were screened for skew and kurtosis and found to be within acceptable limits. Because of ethnic and sex differences in age, preliminary analyses were conducted to examine the effects of age on CDI scores. Age was uncorrelated with CDI

---

[2]Unexpected ethnicity and sex differences in internal consistencies for the scholastic and social SPPC subscales were followed up with factor analyses (principal components, varimax rotation) to examine the factor structure of these measures for our four groups. Single-factor solutions were obtained for Euro-American boys and girls for both subscales: two-factor solutions (with comparable factor loadings of items on each factor) were obtained for African American boys and girls for both subscales. We used these results to form two additional measures of perceived competence. Data were reanalyzed using these revised measures of perceived competence; results were comparable to those obtained when the full subscale was included.

TABLE 1   Mean and standard deviation CDI scores, achievement test scores, peer acceptance ratings, and perceived competence of African American and Euro-American boys and girls.

| | Euro-American | | | | African American | | | | | |
| | Boys[b] | | Girls[c] | | Boys[d] | | Girls[e] | | Total[a] | |
Variable	M	SD	M	SD	M	SD	M	SD	M	SD
CDI	8.82	7.34	10.10	8.34	12.62	8.69	10.10	7.57	10.05	8.03
Achievement scores[f]	66.72	26.52	66.44	24.91	36.49	27.89	47.83	26.56	59.80	28.44
Peer ratings	2.91	.74	3.10	.58	2.99	.77	3.19	.75	3.04	.70
Perceived competence										
Academic	3.08	.63	2.95	.69	2.86	.64	3.03	.65	2.99	.66
Social	2.96	.73	2.89	.63	2.90	.64	2.96	.70	2.92	.70

Note: CDI = Children's Depression Inventory.
[a]$n = 902$. [b]$n = 291$. [c]$n = 339$. [d]$n = 126$. [e]$n = 146$. [f]Achievement tests scores (national percentiles) were available for 266 Euro-American boys, 323 Euro-American girls, 109 African American boys, and 126 African American girls.

scores and did not interact with ethnicity or sex to predict CDI scores so it was not included in further analyses.

Relations Among Measures

Intercorrelations among measures are presented in Table 2. Children's perceptions of competence in the academic and social domains as assessed by the SPPC were significantly negatively correlated with CDI scores for all groups, as were peer acceptance ratings and academic achievement test scores. According to tests of differences between independent correlations, the magnitude of correlations did not significantly differ across ethnic and sex groups.

Depressive Symptoms: Ethnic and Sex Differences

Results of a 2 (ethnicity) $\times$ 2 (sex) $\times$ 2 (SES) ANOVA applied to children's CDI scores revealed a main effect of sex, $F(1, 899) = 10.74$, $p < .01$, as well as a significant Ethnicity $\times$ Sex interaction, $F(1, 899) = 10.79$, $p < .01$. The main effect of sex was not significant, $F(1, 899) < 1$, $p > .10$. Neither the main effect of SES nor the interaction of SES with other independent variables was significant (all Fs < 1, ps $> .10$).

Tests of the simple main effect of ethnicity indicated that CDI scores of Euro-American and African American children significantly differed for boys. $F(1, 415)$

TABLE 2   Correlations of age, depressive symptoms, academic achievement, peer acceptance, and self-perceptions of academic and social competence.

Variable	1	2	3	4	5
1. Age					
2. CDI	−.01				
3. Achievement scores	−.13*	−.30*			
4. Peer ratings	−.03	−.19*	.16*		
5. Perceived academic comp.	−.03	−.45*	.35*	.13*	
6. Perceived peer acceptance	.05	−.49*	.10*	.19*	.47*

Note: CDI = Children's Depression Inventory, $n = 824$ for correlations with achievement scores; $n = 902$ for all other correlations.
*$p < .05$.

= 20.03, $p < .01$, but not girls, $F(1, 483) < 1$, $p > .10$. African American boys reported significantly more depressive symptoms ($M = 12.62$, $SD = 8.69$) than Euro-American boys ($M = 8.82$, $SD = 7.34$); depressive symptoms of Euro-American ($M = 10.10$, $SD = 8.34$) and African American girls ($M = 10.10$, $SD = 7.57$) did not significantly differ from each other. To determine whether sex differences in depressive symptoms differed across our two ethnic groups, we tested for simple main effects of sex within the African American and Euro-American groups. As predicted, African American boys reported more depressive symptoms than African American girls, $F(1, 270) = 6.80$, $p < .05$. The opposite pattern was obtained for the Euro-American group; Euro-American girls reported significantly more depressive symptoms than Euro-American boys, $F(1, 628) = 4.20$, $p < .05$.[3]

The same pattern of results was found for extreme CDI scores. Logistic regression analysis was used to test for ethnic and sex differences in CDI scores that exceeded the recommended clinical cutoff score of 19 (Kovacs, 1985). Ethnicity (Wald = 0.19, $p < .05$), sex (*Wald* = 5.45, $p < .05$), and the Ethnicity × Sex interaction (Wald = 10.71, $p < .01$) increased the odds of having CDI scores in the clinical range. Euro-American girls were almost twice as likely to have CDI scores in the clinical range as Euro-American boys (9% of girls vs. 4.8% of boys). The pattern of sex differences was reversed for African American children; 12.5% of African

[3]As the finding of elevated depressive symptoms among girls in this age group is not typically found, post hoc analyses within the Euro-American group were conducted to determine when these differences emerged. No sex differences were found among third graders. Girls had significantly higher CDI scores than boys in Grade 4 ($M = 10.56$, $SD = 8.50$ for girls, $M = 8.34$, $SD = 7.35$ for boys; $t(206) = -2.00$, $p < .05$) and a marginally significant tendency toward higher CDI scores in Grade 5 ($M = 10.35$, $SD = 9.05$ for girls, $M = 8.29$, $SD = 7.25$ for boys; $t(218) = -1.83$, $p = .06$).

American boys had CDI scores in the clinical range compared to 8.1% of African American girls.

Mediation of the Ethnicity × Sex Interaction

In accord with the recommendations of Baron and Kenny (1986), multiple regression analyses were used to test for *mediated moderation*, that is, the mechanisms to explain the significant effect of Ethnicity × Sex on CDI scores. A mediated moderation model is supported if the following four conditions are met: (a) the interaction of interest (i.e., Sex × Ethnicity) has an effect on proposed mediators (i.e., actual and perceived competence in academic achievement and peer acceptance); (b) the Sex × Ethnicity interaction has an effect on the outcome measure (i.e., CDI scores); (c) the proposed mediators have an effect on CDI scores after controlling for the Sex × Ethnicity interaction; and (d) the effect of the Sex × Ethnicity interaction on CDI scores is substantially reduced after controlling for the mediators.

Testing Condition 1: Sex × Ethnicity Effects on Proposed Mediators   To test for the first condition, a series of regression analyses were conducted in which each proposed mediator was regressed onto sex, ethnicity, and the Sex × Ethnicity interaction; results of these analyses are presented in Table 3. Only two mediators (academic achievement test scores and perceived academic competence) met the first condition (i.e., a significant effect of Sex × Ethnicity).

Testing Condition 2: Sex × Ethnicity Effects on CDI Scores   As shown in Table 4 and consistent with the ANOVA results reported in the previous section, the interaction of sex and ethnicity accounted for a significant amount of the variance in CDI scores.

Testing Conditions 3 and 4: Evidence of Mediated Moderation   Tests of the third condition (i.e., proposed mediators covary with CDI scores after controlling for the Ethnicity × Sex interaction) and fourth condition (i.e., the relation between the Sex × Ethnicity interaction to CDI scores is substantially reduced when the proposed mediators are controlled) of the mediated moderation model were conducted as part of the same regression analysis. Only the two mediators that met the first condition, academic achievement scores and perceived academic competence, were tested.

To conduct these tests, we regressed CDI scores onto sex and ethnicity in Step 1, and the Sex × Ethnicity interaction, with either academic achievement test scores or perceived academic competence, in Step 2. Table 5 shows the results of these analyses. Both achievement test scores and perceived academic competence were significantly and negatively related to CDI scores, even after controlling for sex, ethnicity, and the Sex × Ethnicity interaction, thus the third condition was met.

TABLE 3   Mediation model (test of Condition 1): Effect of the sex × ethnicity interaction on perceived academic competence and academic achievement test scores, controlling for sex and ethnicity.

Predictor	B	SE B	β	R^2
DV = Achievement Test Scores				
Step 1				.39**
Sex	3.07	1.82	.05	
Ethnicity	23.97	2.00	−.38**	
Step 2				.40**
Sex × Ethnicity	11.61	4.00	.40**	
DV = Peer Acceptance Ratings				
Step 1				.15*
Sex	.20	.05	.14**	
Ethnicity	.00	.05	.05	
Step 2				.15
Sex × Ethnicity	.00	.10	−.01	
DV = Perceived Academic Competence				
Step 1				.05
Sex	.00	.04	−.03	
Ethnicity	.00	.05	−.04	
Step 2				.11*
Sex × Ethnicity	.29	.10	.44**	
DV = Perceived Peer Acceptance				
Step 1				.03
Sex	.00	.05	−.02	
Ethnicity	.00	.05	.01	
Step 2				.05
Sex × Ethnicity	.14	.10	.20	

Note: DV = dependent variable.
*$p < .05$. **$p < .01$.

The beta weight associated with the Sex × Ethnicity interaction was substantially reduced when the mediators were in the model (−.33 and −.25 for mediators of achievement test scores and perceived academic competence, respectively) than when they were not in the model (−.48). These results show that academic achievement test scores and perceived academic competence have significant direct effects on CDI scores and that they partially mediate the Sex × Ethnicity effects on CDI scores.

TABLE 4 Mediation model (test of Condition 2): Effect of the sex × ethnicity interaction on depressive symptoms, controlling for sex and ethnicity.

Predictor	B	SE B	β	R^2
Step 1				.11*
Sex	.34	.55	.02	
Ethnicity	1.88	.61	.11*	
Step 2				.16*
Sex × Ethnicity	−3.90	1.22	−.48*	

*$p < .05$.

TABLE 5 Mediation model (tests of Conditions 3 and 4): Direct effects of academic achievement (test scores and perceived competence) and the sex × ethnicity interaction on depressive symptoms, controlling for sex and ethnicity.

Predictor	B	SE B	β	R^2
Step 1 (control variables)				.01*
Sex	.34	.55	.02	
Ethnicity	1.88	.61	.11*	
Mediator = Achievement Test Scores				
Step 2				.31*
Sex × Ethnicity	−2.76	1.15	−.33*	
Achievement Test Scores	.00	.01	−.29*	
Mediator = Perceived Academic Competence				
Step 2				.46*
Sex × Ethnicity	−2.09	1.02	−.25*	
Perceived Academic Competence	−5.33	.36	−.44*	

*$p < .05$.

Discussion

This study investigated ethnic and sex differences in depressive symptoms among preadolescents and examined mediators of these differences. Five major findings emerged: (a) African American preadolescents reported significantly more depressive symptoms than Euro-American peers; (b) the observed ethnicity difference was qualified by sex: African American boys reported more depressive symptoms than Euro-American boys, whereas African American and Euro-American girls reported comparable levels of depressive symptoms; (c) the interaction of ethnicity and sex was mediated by academic achievement, as assessed by achievement test scores and children's perceptions of their academic competence; (d) the pattern of sex differences varied by ethnicity; elevated levels of depressive symptoms of boys relative to girls were found among African American children, whereas the opposite pattern of sex differences was found for the Euro-American group; and (e) correlates of depressive symptoms were similar across ethnic and sex groups. We elaborate on these findings and their implications for research and clinical practice later.

This study replicated and extended the findings of Cole et al. (1998) by examining the moderating effect of sex on ethnic differences in depressive symptoms. African American boys reported more depressive symptoms than Euro-American boys, as well as more depressive symptoms than African American and Euro-American girls. What accounts for the elevated depressive symptoms of African American boys? Our results suggest that school-related problems, both perceived and actual, play an important role. According to Cole's (1990, 1991) competence-based theory, repeated negative feedback due to academic problems increases risk for depression. In light of evidence of lower academic performance for African American boys through adolescence (Hedges & Nowell, 1999), one would expect elevated risk for depression among African American boys to continue into adolescence; yet there is no consistent pattern of evidence of elevated depression for African American adolescents relative to Euro-American adolescents (e.g., Cole et al., 1998; Garrison, Jackson, Marsteller, McKeown, & Addy, 1990; Lubin & McCollum, 1994; Wrobel & Lachar, 1995). The importance placed on school achievement may be central to understanding why depression is elevated among African Americans (relative to Euro-American peers) in preadolescence but perhaps not in adolescence.

Steele (1992) suggested that members of disadvantaged groups for whom negative stereotypes of low academic achievement are prominent are likely to experience distress about confirming the negative stereotypes; to reduce this distress they may engage in academic disidentification (i.e., change in the relation of one's academic self-perceptions and achievement values with one's global self-esteem, going from a stronger positive association to a weaker association or complete disassociation). Academic disidentification has been found to be more prominent among African American boys relative to boys of other ethnicities and to African American girls (Osborne 1995, 1997). Disidentifying with school performance (and concomitant identification with other domains, such as social or athletic competence; Osborne, 1997) may alleviate depressive symptoms for African American boys, so that as they age into adolescents and adults they do not report or perceive as much depression. However, negative consequences, such as loss of academic motivation and a concomitant downward spiral of academic achievement (Steele & Aronson,

1995), with increased likelihood of school dropout and delinquency (Hindelang & Finn, 1973), may occur. Interventions to reduce African American boys' depressive symptoms thus should address their academic difficulties and identify ways to keep them academically engaged.

In addition to examining ethnic differences in preadolescents' depressive symptoms, this study also examined a moderating effect of ethnicity on sex differences in depressive symptoms in this age group. We predicted that sex differences in depressive symptoms (i.e., boys are more depressed than girls) would be greater among African American children relative to Euro-American children because of the greater sex gap in preadolescent academic achievement among African American children (Garibaldi, 1992; Winfield & Lee, 1990). Consistent with this prediction, elevated depressive symptoms of boys relative to girls was found for the African American participants but not the Euro-American participants. These findings suggest that variability in findings of prior research regarding sex differences in preadolescent depression may be a function of differences in ethnic composition of research samples.

Interestingly, for the Euro-American group, the opposite pattern of sex differences was found (i.e., girls reported significantly more depressive symptoms than boys). This finding appears to be at odds with prior research in which elevated depressive symptoms of girls relative to boys do not emerge until around 13 years of age (Hankin et al., 1998). However, it is important to note that prior research has not examined sex differences within ethnic groups as was done in this study. Also, in contrast to most previous studies of sex differences in preadolescents' depressive symptoms, this study was conducted with a large sample that had sufficient statistical power to detect a small effect size. Our finding of elevated depressive symptoms among Euro-American girls relative to Euro-American boys does not appear to be due to anything unusual about our sample. Mean CDI scores of our sample are slightly higher than the means of other research samples (for review, see Twenge & Nolen-Hoeksema, 2002) but they are comparable to the means reported for the standardization sample (Kovacs, 1985). Twenge and Nolen-Hoeksema found that CDI scores tend to decrease with repeated administrations; perhaps the means reported in some prior studies are lower than the means obtained in this study due to repeated testing effects. Identifying the onset of the emergence of differences may provide important information about causal mechanisms underlying depression (Hankin et al., 1998; Nolen-Hoeksema & Girgus, 1994). Our results suggest that elevated depressive symptoms of girls relative to boys occur earlier for Euro-Americans than for African Americans (i.e., by fourth grade). Recent research of ethnic differences in correlates of depression among adolescents may be helpful for understanding our findings. Pubertal status, and changes in physical appearance that accompany puberty, are associated more strongly with depressive symptoms among Euro-American girls than among girls of other ethnic groups

(Hayward et al., 1999; Siegel et al., 1999). As many of the physical changes associated with puberty among girls are evident in the late elementary school years, one might expect sex differences in depressive symptoms in this age group. To the extent that Euro-American girls are more affected by the stress of pubertal changes than African American girls, this pattern of sex difference in preadolescence would be more likely to characterize Euro-Americans than African Americans. Elevated depressive symptoms among girls may not emerge until adolescence for African American children when other types of stressors that are thought to contribute to elevated depression among women (e.g., social role conflicts, sexual harassment) become more prevalent. Our finding of elevated depressive symptoms of girls in our Euro-American group should be interpreted with caution until it is replicated. Nonetheless, our results underscore the importance of examining the moderating effects of ethnicity on sex differences in depressive symptoms during preadolescence.

In addition to providing information about ethnic and sex differences in preadolescents' depressive symptoms, this study adds to the research literature by assessing ethnic and sex differences in correlates of depressive symptoms among preadolescents. Consistent with prior research and the competency-based model of depression, children who were experiencing problems with schoolwork or difficulties getting along with peers reported more depressive symptoms than those who were doing well in these domains. The magnitude of these associations did not differ by sex or ethnicity.

As with any study, there are limitations and caveats to the conclusions that may be drawn. First, our results are based on data obtained at one point in time; thus, inferences about direction of influences among variables are speculative. Second, we assessed symptoms associated with depression; our findings may or may not generalize to clinically diagnosed depression. Also, our findings may not be specific to depressive symptoms but may apply more generally to emotional distress. Third, this study attempted to tease apart the effects of ethnicity and SES on depressive symptoms. Ethnic differences were significant after controlling for SES of schools; however, inclusion of a measure of SES based on family data would have strengthened our conclusions. Fourth, as with any null findings, lack of support for a mediating role of peer acceptance, both perceived and actual, is difficult to interpret. This finding replicates the results of Cole et al. (1998) with a similar measure of children's peer relations; however, our results may not generalize to measures of other aspects of children's social relationships (e.g., friendships). Finally, the unexpected finding of differences in internal consistencies of Euro-American and African American children's responses to two self-perception measures requires caution in interpreting ethnic differences on these measures; further study of ethnic differences in the factor structure of perceived competence is warranted.

Conclusions

The high prevalence of depression in adolescence, coupled with the decreasing age of first onset of depressive episodes, underscores the need to study depressive symptoms in preadolescents. This study replicated Cole et al.'s (1998) finding of elevated depressive symptoms among African American children relative to Euro-American children and added to our knowledge in two ways: (a) ethnic differences in depressive symptoms were found to differ by sex; elevated depression among African American children was specific to boys; and (b) academic achievement difficulties mediated ethnic and sex differences in children's depressive symptoms. These findings have implications for understanding ethnic- and sex-specific mechanisms underlying depressive symptoms, including perceived and actual academic competence, and thus for developing better targeted interventions to treat or prevent depression. The hypothesized causal directionality among these variables awaits investigation of longitudinal patterns. Also, the impact of ethnic differences in academic difficulties on other aspects of psychopathology remains an important area of further inquiry. Future research of depression in preadolescence should broaden its focus to include additional ethnic groups.

References

Anderson, J. C., Williams, S., McGee, R., & Silva, P. A. (1987). *DSM-III* disorders in preadolescent children: Prevalence in a large sample from the general population. *Archives of General Psychiatry, 44,* 69–76.

Angold, A., Erklani, A., Loeber, R., & Costello, E. J. (1996). Disappearing depression in a population sample of boys. *Journal of Emotional and Behavioral Disorders, 4,* 95–104.

Baron, R. M., & Kenny, D. A. (1986). The moderator–mediator variable distinction in social psychological research: Conceptual, strategic, and statistical considerations. *Journal of Personality and Social Psychology, 51,* 1173–1182.

Birmaher, B., Ryan, N. D., Williamson, D. E., Brent, D. A., & Kaufman, J. (1996). Childhood and adolescent depression: A review of the page 10 years: Part II. *Journal of American Academy of Child and Adolescent Psychiatry, 35,* 1575–1583.

Carr, J. G., Gilroy, F. D., & Sherman, M. F. (1996). Silencing the self and depression among women. *Psychology of Women Quarterly, 20,* 375–392.

Cole, D. A. (1990). Relation of social and academic competence to depressive symptoms in childhood. *Journal of Abnormal Psychology, 99,* 422–429.

Cole, D. A. (1991). Preliminary support for a competency-based model of depression in children. *Journal of Abnormal Psychology, 100,* 181–190.

Cole, D. A., Martin, J. M., Peeke, L., Henderson, A., & Harwell, J. (1988). Validation of depression and anxiety measures in Euro-American and African American youths: Multitrait–multimethod analyses. *Psychological Assessment, 10,* 261–276.

Coyne, J. C. (1976). Depression and the response of others. *Journal of Abnormal Psychology, 85,* 186–93

CTB/McGraw-Hill. (1977). *Comprehensive Tests of Basic Skills*. Monterey, CA.

Culbertson, F. M. (1997). Depression and gender—An international review. *American Psychologist, 53*, 25–31.

Doerfler, L., Felner, R., Rowlison, R., Raley, P., & Evans, E. (1988). Depression in children and adolescents: A comparative analysis of the utility and construct validity of two assessment measures. *Journal of Consulting and Clinical Psychology, 56*, 769–772.

Dweck, C. S., & Goetz, T. E. (1977). Attributions and learned helplessness. In J. H. Harvey, W. Ickes, & R. F. Kidd (Eds.), *New directions in attribution research* (Vol. 2, pp. 157–179). Hillsdale, NJ: Lawrence Erlbaum Associates, Inc.

Fagot, B. I. (1981). Male and female teachers: Do they treat boys and girls differently? *Sex Roles, 7*, 263–272.

Garibaldi, A. M. (1992). Educating and motivating African American males to succeed. *Journal of Nego Education, 61*, 4–11.

Garrison, C., Jackson, K., Marstellar, E., McKeown, R., & Addy, C. (1990). A longitudinal study of depressive symptomatology in young adolescents. *Journal of the American Academy of Child and Adolescent Psychiatry, 29*, 581–585.

Graham, J. A., & Cohen, R. (1997). Race and sex as factors in children's sociometric ratings and friendship choices. *Social Development, 6*, 355–372.

Gross, A. L. (1982). Predicting academic achievement over a one-year period. *Educational and Psychological Measurement, 42*, 371–375.

Hankin, B. L., Abramson, J. Y., Moffitt, T. E., Silva, P. A., McGee, R., & Angell, K. E. (1998). Development of depression from preadolescence to young adulthood: Emerging gender differences in a 10-year longitudinal study. *Journal of Abnormal Psychology, 107*, 128–140.

Harter, S. (1985). *Self-Perception Profile for Children*. Denver, CO: University of Denver.

Hartup, W. W. (1983). Peer relations. In E. M. Hetherington (Vol. Ed.), *Handbook of child psychology* (Vol. 4, pp. 103–196). New York: Wiley.

Hayward, C., Gotlib, I. H., Schraedley, P. K., & Litt, I. F. (1999). Ethnic differences in the association between pubertal status and symptoms of depression in adolescent girls. *Journal of Adolescent Health, 25*, 143–149.

Hedges, L. V., & Nowell, A. (1999). Changes in the Black–White gap in achievement test scores. *Sociology of Education, 72*, 111–135.

Helsel, W., & Matson, J. (1984). The assessment of depression in children: The internal structure of the child depression (CDI). *Behaviour Research and Therapy, 22*, 289–298.

Hindelang, M. J., & Finn, P. (1973). Causes of delinquency: A partial replication and extension. *Social Problems, 20*, 471–487.

Kashani, J. H., Cantwell, D. P., Shekim, W. O., & Reid, J. C. (1982). Major depressive disorder in children admitted to an inpatient community mental health center. *American Journal of Psychiatry, 139*, 671–672.

Kazdin, A. E., Esveldt-Dawson, K., Unis, A. S., & Rancurello, M. D. (1983). Child and parent evaluations of depression and aggression in psychiatric inpatient children. *Journal of Abnormal Child Psychology, 11*, 401–413.

Kistner, J. A., Metzler, A., Gatlin, D., & Risi, S. (1993). Classroom racial proportions and children's peer relations: Race and gender effects. *Journal of Educational Psychology, 85*, 446–452.

Klein, A. E. (1980). Redundancy in the comprehensive tests of basic skills. *Educational and Psychological Measurement, 40,* 1105–1110.

Kovacs, M. (1985). The Children's Depression Inventory. *Psychopharmacology Bulletin, 21,* 995–998.

La Greca, A. M., & Silverman, W. K. (1993). Parent reports of child behavior problems: Bias in participation. *Journal of Abnormal Child Psychology, 21,* 89–101.

Leutwyler, K. (1997). Depression's double standard: Clues emerge as to why women have higher rates of depression. *Scientific American, 272,* 23–26.

Lewinsohn, P. M., Rohde, P., Seeley, J., & Fischer, S. (1993). Age-cohort changes in the lifetime occurrence of depression and other mental disorders. *Journal of Abnormal Psychology, 102,* 110–120.

Lubin, B., & McCollum, K. (1994). Depressive mood in Black and White female adolescents. *Adolescence, 29,* 241–245.

Mickelson, R. (1990). The attitude–achievement paradox among Black adolescents. *Sociology of Education, 63,* 44–61.

Nolen-Hoeksema, S., & Girgus, J. S. (1994). The emergence of gender differences in depression in adolescence. *Psychological Bulletin, 115,* 424–443.

Osborne, J. W. (1995). Academics, self-esteem, and race: A look at the underlying assumptions of the disidentification hypothesis. *Journal of Personality and Social Psychology Bulletin, 21,* 449–455.

Osborne, J. W. (1997). Race and academic disidentification. *Journal of Educational Psychology, 89,* 728–735.

Peterson, A. C., Sarigiani, P. A., & Kennedy, R. E. (1991). Adolescent depression: Why more girls? *American Psychologist, 48,* 155–168.

Reich, T., Van Eerdewegh, P., Rice, J., Mullaney, J., Klerman, G., & Endicott, J. (1987). The family transmission of primary depressive disorder. *Journal of Psychiatric Research, 21,* 613–624.

Reynolds, W., & Graves, A. (1989). Reliability of children's reports of depressive symptomatology. *Journal of Abnormal Child Psychology, 17,* 647–655.

Rutter, M. (1986). The development of psychopathology of depression: Issues and perspectives. In M. Rutter, C. E. Izard, & P. B. Read (Eds.), *Depression in young people* (pp. 3–30). New York: Guilford.

Saylor, C. F., Finch, A. J., Spirito, A., & Bennett, B. (1984). The Children's Depression Inventory: A systematic evaluation of psychometric properties. *Journal of Consulting and Clinical Psychology, 52,* 955–967.

Siegel, J. M., Yancey, A. K., Aneshensel, C. S., & Schuler, R. (1999). Body image, perceived pubertal timing, and adolescent mental health. *Journal of Adolescent Health, 25,* 155–168.

Speier, P. L., Sherak, D. L., Hirsch, S., & Cantwell, D. P. (1995). Depression in children and adolescents. In E. E. Beckham & W. R. Leber (Eds.), *Handbook of depression* (2nd ed., pp. 467–493). New York: Guilford.

Steele, C. (1992). Race and the schooling of African American Americans. *The Atlantic Monthly, 269,* 68–78.

Steele, C., & Aronson, J. (1995). Stereotype threat and the intellectual test performance of African Americans. *Journal of Personality and Social Psychology, 69,* 797–811.

Treadwell, K. R. H., Flannery-Schroeder, E. C., & Kendall, P. C. (1995). Ethnicity and gender in relation to adaptive functioning, diagnostic status, and treatment outcome in children from an anxiety clinic. *Journal of Anxiety Disorders, 9,* 373–384.

Twenge, J. M., & Nolen-Hoeksema, S. (2002). Age, gender, race, socioeconomic status, and birth cohort differences on the children's depression inventory: A meta-analysis. *Journal of Abnormal Psychology, 111,* 578–588.

Weissman, M. M., Bland, R. C., Canino, G. J., Faravelli, C., Greenwald, S., Hwu, H. G., et al. (1997). The cross-national epidemiology of panic disorder. *Archives of General Psychiatry, 54,* 305–309.

Weisz, J. R., Rudolph, K. D., Granger, D. A., & Sweeney, L. (1992). Cognition, competence, coping in child and adolescent depression: Research finding, developmental concerns, therapeutic implications. *Development and Psychopathology, 4,* 627–653.

Winfield, L. F., & Lee, V. E. (1990). *Gender differences in reading proficiency: Are they constant across racial groups?* Baltimore, MD: The Johns Hopkins University Center for Research on Effective Schooling for Disadvantaged Students.

Wrobel, N., & Lachar, D. (1995). Racial differences in adolescent self-report: A comparative validity study using homogeneous MMPI content measures. *Psychological Assessment, 7,* 140–147.

Editor's Note

Requests for reprints should be sent to Janet Kistner, Psychology Department, Florida State University, Tallahassee, FL 32306-1270. E-mail: kistner@psy.fsu.edu

Discussion Questions for Article 2

Section 11: Abnormal Behavior

Name: _____

PID: _____

Date: __ __ / __ __ / __ __ (MM/DD/YY)

CRN: _____

Recitation Day/Time: _____

Honor Code Signature: _____

1. List three plausible reasons why you think beginning in adolescence, Euro-American girls and women are as much as twice as likely to be diagnosed with depression than Euro-American boys and men.

2. Why do you think there is a reversal of sex differences in reporting of depressive symptoms in African-American children versus Euro-American children?

3. Name the two major factors that underscore the need to study depressive symptoms in preadolescents.

4. Can you think of other possible variables that may affect preadolescent depressive symptoms? Explain your reasoning.

Section 12
Stress, Health, and Coping

Individuals face various stressors throughout their daily lives which can have wide-ranging impacts on their physical and emotional health. One of the most serious and long-lasting stressors can often occur with members of the military. For some time those who were affected by combat were labeled as "shell-shocked" however psychologists have helped diagnose these people with post-traumatic stress disorder (PTSD) which is now widely accepted as a serious form of psychological scarring. Other life-threatening events, such as natural disasters or terrorist attacks, can cause similar symptoms.

There are many other ways in which psychology has impacted the fields of health and stress. While many people endlessly seek out the newest diets and exercise programs to increase health and prolong their lives, they often overlook some of the smaller but still well established contributors to health. As the medical field has advanced, the leading cause of death in the United States changed from the early part of the twentieth century. In the most recent decade, the leading causes of death are more lifestyle and stress related such as: heart disease, cancer, stroke, and lung disease.

Psychologists have long understood the impact of stress on health, as some experts have found that 50 to 70 percent of all physical illness is related in some way to stress (Frese, 1985). Mental well-being can positively impact health while negatively well-being can influence health-reducing behaviors such as substance abuse. Small activities, such as meditation or simple relaxation, can have enormous benefits both physically and mentally. In addition to activities which correspond with health, active and passive coping techniques have been examined in relation to health.

Psychologists have also examined practical applications of health and stress, such as their application to athletic and job performance. Stress from work, such as low job control, work overload, or even poor communication can impact not only performance, but health as well. While this is true, some findings indicate that certain types of stress, and in certain occasions, can boost performance. Not enough stress and the individual has low arousal which reduces performance; too much stress and the overload negatively affects performance. This might explain why athletes may rise to the occasion and employees may reach peak productivity when the happy medium is met. These examples are just a few of the ways psychologists can help us understand how to increase health and decrease harmful stress.

Article 1: Hurricane Katrina: Experiences of Psychologists and Implications for Future Disaster Response

Hurricane Katrina was a devastating event for all those involved, and those in the region have still not fully recovered. The first article in this section delves into the experience of a clinical psychologist in the field aiding those in need following hurricane Katrina. It chronicles his multiple visits to the affected area and explains how psychologists and other mental health professionals have aided those affected by Katrina. Dr. Jones describes his role following the hurricane as well as how psychologists and other mental health professionals were deployed, analyzed psychological effects, and ultimately helped comfort those who in the area of the hurricane. In addition, suggestions regarding future disaster relief efforts are made, highlighting the importance of continued research on the field.

Article 2: Forgiveness, Health, and Well-Being: A Review of Evidence for Emotional Versus Decisional Forgiveness, Dispositional Forgiveness, and Reduced Unforgiveness

Forgiveness is not likely to be a topic commonly associated with overall health and health-related behaviors; however the second article addresses this relationship. The article explains the distinction between different types of forgiveness as well as a broad overview of their relationships to health, brain physiology, and medical interventions. Conceptual distinctions are made between two main types of forgiveness (emotional and decisional) as well as between forgiveness (state) and forgivingness (trait). Recommendations are given for the study of forgivingness in medical field including awareness by patients and practitioners.

—*Greg Longo*

Hurricane Katrina: Experiences of Psychologists and Implications for Future Disaster Response

Russell T. Jones
Christopher S. Immel
Rachel M. Moore
James M. Hadder

The landfall of Hurricane Katrina marked not only one of the most significant and destructive natural disasters for the United States in recent history, but also a new benchmark in challenges faced by psychologists providing services. The authors explain their roles following the hurricane, describing not only local activities for recovery but efforts conducted in the Gulf Coast as well. Experiences and perceptions of the first author, who was deployed to the Gulf Coast on numerous occasions, are highlighted. In addition, psychological assessments were carried out with a small number of displaced Katrina survivors who were relocated to the authors' local community. The authors document many of the challenges faced by psychologists and other mental health workers during relief efforts in the Gulf Coast, concluding with a set of recommendations for future disaster-relief initiatives regarding such issues as ways in which psychologists can participate in disaster-relief efforts, challenges faced when implementing interventions, cultural competency, community preparedness, and scientific research.

Keywords: trauma, disaster, Katrina, cultural competence

Hurricane Katrina developed in the Atlantic Ocean as a hurricane on August 23, 2005 (National Weather Service, 2005). On August 25, the storm traveled over the Florida peninsula and, on August 29, made landfall near New Orleans, Louisiana. Before, during, and immediately following the storm, relief efforts were carried out by several local, state, and national government agencies, as well as numerous relief organizations. However, it quickly became apparent that these agencies were sorely lacking in light of the immensity of the many challenges presented by the storm and its aftermath. Although psychologists were only a small part of the relief efforts following Hurricane Katrina, their clinical, research, and applied skill sets have contributed significantly to the ongoing recovery efforts in the Gulf Coast.

Our Roles

Over the past 23 years, the Stress and Coping Lab at Virginia Tech (and more recently the Recovery Efforts After Child Trauma [REACT] team) has responded to and examined the impact of both technological and natural disasters. Experiences with a variety of natural disasters, including hurricanes, wildfires, and upwards of 200 residential fires across five states, have afforded the lab a solid theoretical and empirical knowledge base. Insights gained from these endeavors have guided much of our thinking and actions during the acute and long-term phases of the hurricane's aftermath.

Throughout the recovery efforts of Hurricane Katrina, we took on many roles, including consulting with local, state, and national government agencies, advising the White House, and training crisis workers and counselors in the areas of disaster mental health and cultural competence. Several of these recent efforts were made possible through membership in the Disaster Technical Assistance Cadre (DTAC) sponsored by the Substance Abuse Mental Health Services Administration (SAMHSA, a division of the U.S. Department of Health and Human Services). A brief overview of deployments to the Gulf Coast and related cities follows.

During the initial two deployments of the first author (2 and 6 weeks posthurricane) to Baton Rouge, Louisiana, and Jackson, Mississippi, the primary role of two teams of mental health workers was to assist state emergency directors in the coordination of the mental health response to Hurricane Katrina. One of the first steps in gaining an understanding of the storm's devastation was an automobile and walking tour of New Orleans. Another important function of the teams was attendance at numerous meetings with a variety of mental and physical health professionals and military personnel at temporary disaster shelters, centers, and military command posts. Conferences with representatives from numerous organizations, including the Federal Emergency Management Agency (FEMA), the American Red Cross (ARC), and the Centers for Disease Control and Prevention

(CDCP), were essential to the coordination of multiple efforts. The ultimate goal of these meetings was to establish and, at times, strengthen working relationships with national, state, and local officials.

Formal and informal interviews with children, parents, and other adults affected by the storm were also undertaken. While serving as team leader during the second deployment, the primary task of the first author was the organization and coordination of the day-to-day activities of team members (consisting of eight mental health professionals). Overseeing their safety, along with their mental and physical health, was an essential role. Two additional tasks that ranked high on the priority list were grant writing and advocating for training in cultural competence and disaster behavioral health.

In light of his background as a clinical psychologist and trauma researcher, the first author was asked to make formal recommendations to determine the extent of exposure and potential psychosocial consequences of the storm on children and adolescents. A primary goal of this endeavor was to inform mental health workers of appropriate screening, assessment, and intervention strategies. Another key concern was the racial, cultural, and ethnic diversity of storm survivors. Specifically, the team provided insight into methods for becoming culturally and ethnically sensitive when approaching, interacting, screening, assessing, and treating those in need of assistance. The implications of these factors for all phases of the recovery process for both survivors and mental health professionals were enormous.

The first author made two later trips (8 and 9 weeks post-hurricane) to Jackson, Mississippi, and Atlanta, Georgia, for the purpose of participating in two workshops sponsored by the U.S. Department of Education. In his role as a DTAC consultant, clinical psychologist, and disaster expert, the first author shared his experiences from the Gulf Coast. In addition, he also had opportunities to inform teachers, school administrators, mental health professionals, and community leaders about the knowledge base describing children and adolescents' responses to disasters, as well as empirically supported and empirically informed interventions. He is currently serving as a member of an advisory committee for the U.S. Department of Education.

In December 2005, the first author was asked to assist First Lady Laura Bush by briefing and preparing her for a meeting with a group of children and their parents at an event in Metairie, Louisiana. He was invited to accompany her to this event to discuss issues related to loss, coping, and recovery. Since that time, he has met with a member of Mrs. Bush's staff at her office in the White House to discuss issues related to children affected by the storm, as well as trauma-related initiatives of our team. Providing updates on continuous initiatives with children of the Gulf Coast is an ongoing activity. This exemplifies how we as psychologists are able to apply our knowledge, expertise, and skills to real-world problems.

Three subsequent deployments (January–March 2006) targeted the topic of cultural competence and disaster behavioral health. The mobilization of staff to disaster areas to attend to the emotional needs of survivors defines disaster mental health operations (SAMHSA, 2006). Consistent with both DTAC teams' recommendations to provide training in cultural competence to state and local professionals and paraprofessionals, innovative steps were initiated to achieve this goal. The first stage in this process was to carry out focus groups with approximately 100 crisis counselors to ascertain the needs of storm survivors and levels of proficiency in the domains of disaster mental health and cultural competence.

In March 2006, the Louisiana Department of Mental Health charged four professionals in disaster behavioral mental health and cultural competency with the task of developing and implementing a training curriculum to enhance the skills of crisis workers in delivering effective, culturally and linguistically appropriate strategies and interventions. A primary goal of this effort was to address the unique mental health needs of the storm survivors. Team members included Barbara J. Bazron, Russell T. Jones, Mareasa Isaacs, and Kermit A. Crawford. As an initial step in developing the curriculum, nine focus groups were conducted to gather specific information from crisis workers while providing services to survivors of the storm. Five specific objectives of the focus groups were to (a) determine the extent to which survivors had received services and showed progress toward recovery; (b) identify the most significant concerns facing survivors, including children and the elderly; (c) determine the type of assistance needed by trainees to enhance their ability to provide culturally and linguistically competent disaster behavioral health care services; (d) determine the demographics and cultural strengths of respondents; and (e) determine the extent to which crisis workers have been able to provide disaster behavioral health services within the context of the cultures of those people being served. During the analyses captured via the Focus Group Session Questionnaire and notes obtained by facilitators, each of the four facilitators carried out a manual content analysis. They identified common and divergent themes, which are summarized below.

Information regarding training needs, format, and focus provided a clear framework for developing a curriculum and carrying out training. Participants overwhelmingly requested development of a curriculum and training to provide concrete, practical tools and strategies to enhance cultural sensitivity during disaster relief. Consequently, team members developed a training manual that addressed issues raised during the focus groups. Two-day seminars were carried out in Baton Rouge and New Orleans, Louisiana, in August 2006. (More information on this training and copies of the manual can be obtained on request from the first author.)

Katrina-Related Efforts in the Local Community

In addition to trips to the Gulf Coast, in September 2005, the Virginia Tech REACT team was invited to perform psychological and needs-based assessments with storm survivors by the local ARC chapter and the director of an evacuation shelter. In addition, a description of services within the local community was provided. Following a brief social interaction with survivors, an assessment area was created where families could voluntarily participate in individual interviews to objectively determine levels of distress. Instruments for children and adolescents included the Hurricane Assessment and Referral Tool for Children and Adolescents, developed by the National Child Traumatic Stress Network (NCTSN, 2005), the Child Reaction to Traumatic Stress Scale–Revised (Jones, Fletcher, & Ribbe, 2002), and the Posttraumatic Stress Disorder/Acute Stress Disorder module of the Anxiety Disorder Interview Schedule for *DSM–IV* (Albano & Silverman, 1996). For adults, the team administered the Impact of Events Scale (Horowitz, Wilner, & Alvarez, 1979) and the Posttraumatic Stress Disorder/Acute Stress Disorder module of the Anxiety Disorder Interview Schedule for *DSM–IV* (Di Nardo, Brown, & Barlow, 1994). We provided individuals with immediate feedback and, when appropriate, referrals to the REACT Clinic and other local agencies.

Longitudinal Assessment of Psychological Functioning

The REACT team established a partnership with the Hurricane Katrina Community Advisory Group (spearheaded by Ronald Kessler at Harvard University) in November 2005. Its purpose was to carry out a series of studies assessing the short- and long-term mental health impact of the storm on adults. The team employed a random digit dialing method between January and March 2006 to collect data from 1,043 English-speaking storm survivors (ages 18+). By using both random digit dialing and ARC frames of hurricane survivors, the researchers were able to access households on file prior to the storm as well as households applying for ARC assistance after the storm. For residents who evacuated to various parts of the country, simply dialing their cell phone numbers enabled contact with them.

Comparisons of prestorm levels of functioning with poststorm functioning were made possible through a previous survey carried out by Kessler and colleagues (2004). Primary findings suggested elevated levels of both posttraumatic symptoms and depression. In addition, levels of suicidality were lower than hypothesized (Kessler, Galea, Jones, & Parker, 2006). Interpretation of these findings and further data collection are presently ongoing.

Lessons Learned and Recommendations

Getting into the Field

Steps to Rapid Deployment   One of several ways to facilitate rapid deployment to disaster sites is through the DTAC program. The first author felt that his level of preparedness was greatly enhanced by a 3-day workshop held in May 2005 in

Bethesda, Maryland. This training (the Cadre of Consultants Initiative Orientation) was developed in the fall of 2004 with the goal of ensuring that needs related to disaster preparedness, as well as response and recovery, would be successfully met in crisis situations.

Training was carried out by staff at SAMHSA, as well as individuals from partner groups, including the NCTSN and the National Center for Posttraumatic Stress Disorder. Experts in the areas of all-hazards disaster planning and response, substance abuse, psychosocial impact, and the SAMHSA grant programs participated.

One of several problems witnessed by the first author during his deployments was a lack of coordination and structure amid the influx of psychologists deployed to various disaster areas of the Gulf Coast. This lack of organization and structure appeared to compromise the effectiveness of psychologists responding to the disaster. Future coordination efforts may consist of simply having organizations such as the ARC or FEMA encourage psychologists to contact whichever agency is responsible for deploying psychologists. This would allow the agencies to first assess whether the psychologists' presence was needed, and then direct them to areas where they would be of greatest service. In addition, longer deployments might well facilitate the continuity and completion of various initiatives. It may prove beneficial for psychologists to have a preassembled kit including necessary instruments, contact numbers, office supplies, recording devices, and other such materials. Logistical concerns are of the utmost importance in disaster areas, and the need to coordinate and partner with local agencies and gatekeepers should be an important component of any deployment effort. When such planning does not take place, problems are likely to arise. For example, FEMA was criticized for taking motel rooms from families and giving them to personnel deployed to the area (Hsu, 2005).

Similarly, if existing agencies are not made aware of deployments in advance, it may be difficult to use consultants' expertise in a timely and balanced fashion. This problem was noted shortly following the 9/11 terrorist attacks, when large numbers of psychologists were deployed to New York City. Unfortunately, the skills and expertise of this group were not capitalized on; directly following the event, survivors were more concerned with immediate needs, including food, housing, medical treatment, and restoration of infrastructure, than with issues related to mental health treatment (Seely, 2003). In summary, psychologists need to coordinate their deployment with existing agencies and community representatives prior to entering the disaster area.

Licensure   An important consideration for mental health workers responding to disasters is licensure qualifications. Most mental health workers are licensed by a state government or board and not at a national level. Immediately following Hurricane Katrina, the legislature of the State of Louisiana waived licensure and certification requirements on a temporary basis to allow mental health workers to provide primary care to storm survivors. However, this information was not made widely available; as a result, some psychologists were turned away and not allowed to practice in the disaster area (American Psychological Association, 2005a). Psychologists displaced by the storm who desired to provide services in a new state needed to obtain a temporary license or an exemption from licensure rules. However, the rules for obtaining temporary licensure or being relicensed vary by state. In the future, psychologists should familiarize themselves with an affected state's board of psychology for licensure information to determine what is necessary to achieve adequate licensure when working in a disaster area. We also recommend that directors of mental health organizations seek immediate, temporary licensures for their providers to allow a smooth and efficient ingress of psychologists participating in disaster-relief efforts.

Impact on Independent Practice   Following the storms, many psychologists in the affected area found themselves struggling to rebuild their communities and support those in need of services. Many were forced to not only deal with personal issues of safety and recovery, but also difficult business decisions in an environment marked by uncertainty. In the future, according to the American Psychological Association (APA), when clinicians are able to access their offices, they should quickly assess the damage and losses, review insurance policies, and talk to an insurance representative immediately to begin the claims process (APA, 2005b). In addition, it is important for clinicians in private practice to review their business plans to determine whether goals, services, clientele, referral sources, and communication with these sources are viable, given the disaster's impact. After the initial assessment of the damages, they should consider the following options: close, sell, relocate, or reopen the practice.

For psychologists desiring to practice provisionally in a disaster area, temporarily closing one's own practice to assist with recovery may significantly affect their functioning. It is important to determine whether one's services are essential and to assess the effects of potential disruptions to treatment of one's current clients. With all variables considered, we recommend that psychologists perform a cost–benefit analysis of temporarily closing their practice before making a final decision. Psychologists wishing to provide assistance to disaster-stricken areas should have a contingency plan established so as to not jeopardize their clients' well-being or their practice's economic welfare. It is important to generate referral options for clients, especially if the clinician plans to be away for an extended time. In addition, alternative treatment options, such as telephone or online therapy services, should be provided to clients if applicable.

Travel Expenses   A very practical concern for psychologists considering assisting in crisis situations such as Hurricane Katrina is the cost. The cost of travel to disaster areas depends on the deploying organization. For example, members of the

SAMHSA DTAC team who traveled to and from the Gulf Coast were reimbursed by SAMHSA. However, unlike SAMHSA, many other volunteer organizations may be unable to reimburse one's travel-related expenses. We advocate full-time disaster-relief positions and stipends for psychologists and other mental health workers associated with such organizations as FEMA, ARC, and the APA Disaster Response Network.

Communication Systems   An additional recommendation for psychologists in the field includes developing more sophisticated and effective communication systems (i.e., cell phones, landlines, and two-way radios) for consultants, providers, and volunteers. The hurricane significantly impaired the functionality of both cell phones and landlines in many communities. Psychologists who intend to work in disaster areas should stay informed about the latest communication systems employed in such areas. By building relationships and working with local fire departments and rescue services prior to disasters, psychologists can become familiar with the use of such technologies.

Issues Related to Safety, General Well-Being, and Vicarious Traumatization

A major concern for psychologists and other mental health professionals deployed to disaster sites is personal safety. It is important for psychologists to be aware of health concerns and dangers in disaster areas. These include the presence of environmental toxins and other health hazards that may later lead to disease and illness. One need only recall first responders' unfortunate bouts with physical problems following 9/11 to note these dangers. Physical examinations and tetanus shots prior to traveling to disaster sites are highly recommended. During exit procedures, screenings for personal distress and organizational debriefings are also recommended.

Another problem likely to be encountered by psychologists is the potential psychological impact of working with those suffering from trauma, referred to as *vicarious traumatization*, *compassion fatigue*, or more simply *burnout*. Madrid and Schacher (2006) described vicarious traumatization as emotional or psychological reactions triggered by the experiences of empathetic engagement with clients who are survivors of trauma. This reaction is often considered an inescapable aspect of trauma work and can lead to depression, anxiety, substance abuse, maladaptive coping, and neglect of self-care in health care professionals. Findings suggest that the prophylactic use of self-care techniques is often neglected until serious signs of stress develop. To combat this trend, we encourage psychologists working in disaster areas to periodically engage in techniques designed to lower stress while deployed in the field. When feasible, it also may be advisable to have psychologists in disaster areas undergo brief psychological screenings and assessments at various intervals to formally evaluate them for any signs of vicarious traumatization.

Issues Related to Intervention

Psychologists and other mental health professionals should be aware of the empirical literature documenting risk and protective factors of those affected by disaster. Knowledge of such factors will afford a comprehensive evaluation of each, as well as the provision of screening, assessment, and intervention strategies targeting them. Parelkar, Jones, and Ollendick (2006) discussed the presence of protective factors shown to lessen negative reactions to disasters, which include availability of social support, coping strategies (i.e., active, avoidance, religious), and cultural strengths (i.e., beliefs, identity, traditions). A protective factor that may be of particular relevance for those in the Gulf Coast is religious coping styles, as African Americans have reported higher church attendance, more reading of religious materials, and greater pursuit of spiritual comfort through religion than Caucasians (R. J. Taylor, Chatters, Jayakody, & Levin, 1996). Following a traumatic event, the use of spiritually based coping has been found to be inversely related to levels of distress in African American children and adolescents (Parelkar et al., 2006).

Awareness of the timing of intervention is also of extreme relevance. For example, decisions as to when interventions should actually be carried out with survivors should be based on empirically driven data rather than one's passion, zeal, or desire to help those in great need. Current science suggests that early interventions may do more harm than good, because they may prevent individuals from recovering more naturally; most individuals will recover without intervention (Litz, Gray, Bryant, & Adler, 2002). Whereas treatments such as debriefing are discouraged because of a lack of empirical support, we advocate evidenced-informed and evidenced-based cognitive–behavioral interventions.

Although the clinical literature regarding treatment of traumatized children describes a wide variety of interventions, including crisis initiatives, psychoanalytic techniques, creative arts, play therapy, eye movement desensitization and reprocessing, and pharmacotherapy (Cohen, Mannarino, & Rogal, 2001), there appears to be no clear consensus about an effective treatment of posttraumatic stress disorder with this population. Variants of cognitive–behavioral therapy, which combines information about expected reactions (psychoeducation) to stress and trauma, relaxation training, coaching on coping strategies, and direct exposure to traumatic studies, have been used in the few studies described below that address traumatic stress, posttraumatic stress disorder, and trauma symptoms.

In similar trauma research, Cohen and colleagues reported significant improvements for a trauma-focused cognitive–behavioral therapy (TF-CBT) treatment as compared with child-centered therapy for 8- to 14-year-old children (Cohen,

Deblinger, Mannarino, & Steer, 2004). This TF-CBT approach specifically targeted posttraumatic stress disorder symptoms with the following components: training in coping skills and expressing feelings; identifying thoughts, feelings, and behaviors; gradual exposure to the trauma by creating a trauma narrative (writing and illustrating their personal story); parent–child sessions; psychoeducation; and parental management skills. Such an approach, which combines adult posttraumatic stress disorder treatment and treatment strategies for child anxiety, is receiving growing support as a treatment for child abuse trauma. Overall, however, given the high prevalence of child trauma, the treatment efficacy literature for posttraumatic stress disorder, including trauma following natural disaster, is in its infancy (T. L. Taylor & Chemtob, 2004). In the absence of a convincing body of empirical literature showing superior efficacy of a specific treatment modality, clinicians working with child survivors of Hurricane Katrina and other natural disasters must adapt treatment models such as those described by Cohen and colleagues (2004) or base treatment decisions on empirical evidence combined with more subjective criteria (e.g., what they are most comfortable using, what has worked best in their own experience, etc.; Cohen et al., 2001).

Stein and colleagues (2003) evaluated the effectiveness of a school-based intervention to reduce the symptoms of posttraumatic stress disorder, anxiety, and depression related to exposure to violence. The intervention was a 10-session cognitive–behavioral therapy group called the Cognitive–Behavioral Intervention for Trauma in Schools (CBITS), which was designed for use in inner-city schools and mental health clinics with a multicultural population. The CBITS intervention incorporates cognitive–behavioral skills in a group format, using a mixture of didactic presentation, age-appropriate examples and games to solidify concepts, as well as individual exertion on worksheets during and between sessions. The CBITS approach was reported to significantly reduce self-reported symptoms of posttraumatic stress disorder and depression at a 3-month follow-up when compared with a delayed intervention comparison group.

Finally, the Stress and Coping Lab of Virginia Tech employs an evidence-informed treatment strategy aimed at ameliorating the adverse effects of disaster exposure and posttraumatic stress disorder. This treatment, which employs a cognitive–behavioral approach, uses such components as deep muscle relaxation, diaphragmatic breathing, rehearsal plus evacuation skills (Jones & Randall, 1994), grief counseling, and tools for strengthening social support. Given that resource loss increases psychological distress posttrauma (Hobfoll, 1998), an additional aim of this intervention strategy is to put disaster survivors in contact with local recovery community organizations to facilitate the replacement of important documents and possessions. By combining therapeutic efforts with the means to replace disaster survivors' physical belongings, our treatment strategy helps to put these individuals on the path to recovery (Jones, Hadder, Moore, Immel, & Sirbu, 2006).

Cultural Sensitivity for Psychologists Working in Disaster Relief

Cultural sensitivity was (and remains) particularly important in the Gulf Coast, as upwards of 67% of the impacted communities were predominantly African American (U.S. Census Bureau, 2000). In addition, data released by the U.S. Census Bureau (2006) showed that nearly 1 in 10 Louisiana residents fled the state following the hurricane season of 2005. Louisiana's population decreased from approximately 4,068,028 from January through August 2005 to approximately 3,688,996 from September through December 2005, as estimated by the bureau. This is a loss of 379,032 residents, or 9.32% of the state's population, following the 2005 hurricane season and highlights the fluctuation of different groups of people.

Furthermore, some hurricane-affected parishes lost huge numbers of residents, whereas others withstood significant increases as displaced hurricane survivors relocated throughout the state. For example, in one extreme population loss, the coastal Louisiana parish of St. Bernard (southeast of New Orleans) saw 94.8% of its population leave and not return by January 1, 2006. St. Bernard's population fell from 64,576 on July 1, 2005, to 3,361 6 months later, a loss of nearly 61,215 residents. In addition, detailed data from the U.S. Census Bureau (2006) showed that the number of people per household statewide in Louisiana increased, as families moved in together and neighbors accommodated one another. The average household size in Louisiana grew from 2.47 to 2.55 people per household, whereas the total number of households decreased from 1,645,112 to 1,448,443, a loss of nearly 12% of the state's households. In addition, the percentage of Louisiana residents who moved in the past year rose from 15.2% prior to the hurricanes of 2005 to 17.8% following the disaster. Data indicate that people moved regardless of race, income, family size, and economics. The U.S. Census Bureau has noted that this relocation effort may be the largest postdisaster migration in U.S. history, given that it involved individuals across all social divides and groupings. This vast shift in population demographics represents a significant challenge to psychologists in developing and maintaining culturally competent practices.

In addition to training in the basics of disaster preparedness, response, and recovery, it is essential that consultants be trained in cultural competence. Cultural competence may best be described by three characteristics: obtaining knowledge about specific people and groups of people; integrating and transforming this knowledge into specific standards, policies, practices, and attitudes; and using these tools to increase the quality of services and produce better outcomes (Davis, 1997). During countless interactions with African American survivors shortly after the first author's initial visit to the Gulf Coast and his most recent visit in March 2007, they raised many concerns regarding linguistics, issues of trust, access to resources, and cultural differences. A detailed discussion of each of these issues and strategies to deal with them is discussed in a recent book chapter (see Jones, Hadder,

Carvajal, Chapman, & Alexander, 2006). Simply put, it is essential to have psychometrically sound and culturally sensitive screening and assessment instruments. The endorsement of intervention strategies should be based on empirical findings stemming from the information gleaned during the screening and assessment phases with people of color and other diverse groups. Unfortunately, to our knowledge, few if any validated cultural competence instruments exist. Our lab is presently initiating efforts to produce such instruments.

Members of ethnic minority and marginalized groups are more likely to accept assistance from individuals with whom they have formed meaningful relationships prior to the disaster (Jones, Hadder, Carvajal, et al., 2006). Thus, psychologists will benefit from partnering with established community organizations within a disaster area, in that aligning with trusted organizations can increase the extent to which psychologists are viewed by all ethnic group members as a viable source of assistance following a disaster. In addition, targeting diversity among group members in the planning of disaster mental health services can likewise increase the trust with which diverse ethnic groups view psychologists. Psychologists need to think outside the box. Partnering with agencies and organizations such as the National Association of Black Psychologists, the National Association of Latino Psychologists, the National Association of Black Social Workers, the National Medical Association, the National Black Nurses Association, and members of the Congressional Black Caucus, may well provide the necessary expansive knowledge base to build a greater capacity to assist the underserved. Finally, collaborating with community agencies allows psychologists to obtain valuable information on the most effective ways to reach out to minority group members in a disaster area, as well as providing an accurate assessment of these groups' primary needs (Jones & Hadder, 2006).

Community Preparedness: Transitioning Into the Community

From our combined experiences with the REACT team, as well as numerous trips to the Gulf Coast, we strongly advocate for a paradigm shift from existing approaches to disaster preparedness. Rather than adopting traditional approaches where reliance on state and national resources is advocated, or where focus is aimed at personal actions in the acute phase of disaster situations, we argue strongly for a community-based approach that draws on resources and strengths of the community prior to, during, and after traumatic events.

In our collective experience, we have noted that during the acute phase of a disaster, survivors are more likely to receive help from others than during later phases of the recovery effort. In war, it is often said that "there is no color distinction in fox holes," and in fact, distinctions and differences are minimized and similarities are magnified, leading to joint efforts to produce mutual survival. However, at later phases during the recovery process, individuals appear more selective in whom they are willing to turn to for help. More often than not, survivors will call on those with whom they have established relationships prior to the event. Relatives, friends, churches, and community agencies are more likely to be called on than "outsiders." Hence, the need to build relief capacity by establishing relationships with individuals and groups within the community is essential to the well-being of residents. Our REACT program, which is based on the Child Development Community Policing Program (CDCP; Murphy, Rosenheck, Berkowitz, & Marans, 2005) at the Yale Child Study Center, advocates such community-based intervention approaches. The CDCP was originally designed to train police officers in developmentally appropriate ways to interact with the children they encounter on domestic violence calls, coordinate with on-call clinicians, and lessen the negative effects of the traumatic events that these children experience. REACT, which implements a component of the CDCP model whereby firefighters are encouraged to call clinicians to the scene of residential fires, represents one such pre-existing community-based program that survivors are likely to call on during the acute as well as long-term phases following individual and large-scale disasters.

We recommend that psychologists accomplish this by making themselves aware of what organizations are most important within a particular community (i.e., local government, volunteer groups, religious organizations, etc.) and contacting representatives from these organizations for advice on how to proceed within that community. The pursuit of such culturally competent practices can allow for the smoother and more efficient deployment of psychologists within a disaster area.

Scientific Research

Our final set of recommendations deals with the all-important area of research. One of the most important contributions that the social sciences have to offer disaster-relief efforts is our science. When the first author left his initial deployment to the Gulf Coast, he had the following thought: "To achieve success with this daunting effort it will take our best science and utmost sensitivity." The following recommendations, based on our scientific knowledge, were developed by a group of national and international experts in disaster mental health at a consensus conference titled "Mental Health and Mass Violence." This meeting convened several weeks after the attacks of September 11, 2001. The following recommendations emerged: (a) Research and program evaluation are critically important to mental health disaster response; (b) the scientific community has an obligation to examine the relative effectiveness of interventions; (c) a national strategy should be developed and implemented to ensure systematic data collection, evaluation, and research during and after mass violence and disasters; (d) if optimal forms of intervention are unknown, there is an ethical duty to perform sound research to improve all aspects of intervention; (e) systematic evaluation activities should be conducted with mental health professionals; (f) a standard taxonomy should be developed in research; (g) a push to inform the broader research community of the importance of conducting research on disasters is required; and (h) early interventions should be founded in empirically informed and evidence-based practices, and an ethical duty exists to discourage the use of ineffective or unsafe techniques (Friedman, 2006). Although some progress on several of these recommendations has been made because of the joint efforts of a number of federal agencies (e.g., National Institute of Mental Health, SAMHSA, CDCP, Department of Defense, and the Department of Veterans Affairs), there still remains much to be done.

In conclusion, we strongly advocate for greater attention to the area of disaster behavioral health. Given the events of the past 2 years, the predictions for natural and technological disasters, as well as the threat level for acts of terrorism, this need is obvious. Although our work has been challenging, time consuming, and at moments, seemingly overwhelming, it has also been highly stimulating and rewarding. Such challenges provide a real opportunity to apply our science to the real-world problems of our times. Truly, the harvest is ripe and the need for laborers is plentiful.

References

Albano, A. M., & Silverman, W. K. (1996). *Anxiety Disorders Interview Schedule for DSM–IV: Clinical manual.* New York: Psychological Corporation.

American Psychological Association. (2005a, September 20). *After Katrina: Are you dealing with reimbursement and licensure challenges?* Retrieved September 7, 2006, from http://www.apapractice.org/apo/katrina/after_katrina.html

American Psychological Association. (2005b, October 27). *Making business decisions following a disaster.* Retrieved September 7, 2006, from http://www.apapractice.org/apo/disaster_network/katrina/after_katrina.html#

Cohen, J. A., Deblinger, E., Mannarino, A. P., & Steer, R. A. (2004). A multisite, randomized controlled trial for children with sexual abuse-related PTSD symptoms. *Journal of the American Academy of Child and Adolescent Psychiatry, 43,* 393–492.

Cohen, J. A., Mannarino, A. P., & Rogal, S. (2001). Treatment practices for childhood posttraumatic stress disorder. *Child Abuse and Neglect, 25,* 123–135.

Davis, K. (1997). *Exploring the intersection between cultural competency and managed behavioral health care policy: Implications for state and county mental health agencies.* Alexandria, VA: National Technical Assistance Center for State Mental Health Planning.

Di Nardo, P. A., Brown, T. A., & Barlow, D. H. (1994). *Anxiety Disorders Interview Schedule for DSM–IV: Lifetime version (ADIS-IV-L).* San Antonio, TX: Psychological Corporation.

Friedman, M. J. (2006). Disaster mental health research: Challenges for the future. In F. Norris, S. Galea, M. Friedman, & P. Watson (Eds.), *Research methods for studying mental health after disasters and terrorism* (pp. 265–277). New York: Guilford Press.

Hobfoll, S. E. (1998). *Stress, culture, and community.* New York: Plenum Press.

Horowitz, M. J., Wilner, N., & Alvarez, W. (1979). Impact of Events Scale: A measure of subjective stress. *Psychosomatic Medicine, 41,* 209–218.

Hsu, S. S. (2005, November 16). *FEMA tells 150,000 in hotels to exit in 15 days.* Retrieved September 7, 2006, from http://www.washingtonpost.com/wp-dyn/content/article/2005/11/15/AR2005111501704.html

Jones, R. T., Fletcher, K., & Ribbe, D. R. (2002). *Child's Reaction to Traumatic Events Scale— Revised (CRTES–R): A self-report traumatic stress measure.* Unpublished manuscript, Virginia Polytechnic Institute and State University.

Jones, R. T., & Hadder, J. M. (2006). *Culturally competent disaster services and research.* Module created for the National Child Traumatic Stress Network: Terrorism and Disaster Center, University of Oklahoma Health Sciences Center, Oklahoma City.

Jones, R. T., Hadder, J. M., Carvajal, F., Chapman, S., & Alexander, A. (2006). Conducting research in diverse, minority, and marginalized communities. In F. Norris, S. Galea, M. Friedman, & P. Watson (Eds.). *Research methods for studying mental health after disasters and terrorism* (pp. 289–303). New York: Guilford Press.

Jones, R. T., Hadder, J. M., Moore, R. M., Immel, C. S., & Sirbu, C. (2006). *REACT: The development and implementation of a community-based program designed to assist children following residential fire.* Manuscript in preparation.

Jones, R. T., & Randall, J. (1994). Rehearsal-plus: Coping with fire emergencies and reducing fire-related fears. *Fire Technology, 30,* 432–444.

Kessler, R. C., Berglund, P., Chiu, W. T., Demler, O., Heeringa, S., Hiripi, E., et al. (2004). The U.S. National Comorbidity Survey replication (NCS-R): Design and field procedures. *International Journal of Methods in Psychiatric Research, 13,* 69–92.

Kessler, R. C., Galea, S., Jones, R. T., & Parker, H. A. (2006). Mental illness and suicidality after Hurricane Katrina. *Bulletin of the World Health Organization.* Article ID: 06–033019, 1–21.

Litz, B., Gray, M., Bryant, R., & Adler, A. (2002). Early interventions for trauma: Current status and future directions. *Clinical Psychology: Science and Practice, 9,* 112–134.

Madrid, P., & Schacher, S. J. (2006). A critical concern: Pediatrician self-care after disasters. *Pediatrics, 117,* 454–457.

Murphy, R. A., Rosenheck, R. A., Berkowitz, S. A., & Marans, S. R. (2005). Acute service delivery in a police-mental health program for children exposed to violence and trauma. *Psychiatric Quarterly, 76,* 107–121.

National Child Traumatic Stress Network Screener. (2005, September). *Hurricane assessment and referral tool for children and adolescents.* Retrieved September 15, 2005, from http://www.nctsnet.org/nctsn_assets/pdfs/intervention_manules/referaltool.pdf

National Weather Service. (2005). *Hurricane Katrina advisory archive.* Retrieved September 12, 2006, from http://www.nhc.noaa.gov/archive/2005/KATRINA.shtml

Parelkar, M., Jones, R. T., & Ollendick, T. O. (2006). *The role of self-worth, social support, and family religious environment in children and adolescents' religious coping following residential fires.* Manuscript in preparation.

Seely, K. (2003, March). *Psychotherapy of trauma and the trauma of psychotherapy: Talking to therapists following 9–11.* Working Paper Series, Center on Organizational Innovation, Columbia University. Retrieved September 7, 2006, from http://www.coi.columbia.edu/pdf/seeley_pot.pdf

Stein, B. D., Jaycox, L. H., Kataoka, S. H., Wong, M., Tu, W., Elliott, M. N., et al. (2003). A mental health intervention for schoolchildren exposed to violence: A randomized controlled trial. *Journal of the American Medical Association, 290,* 603–611.

Substance Abuse Mental Health Services Administration. (2006). *SAMHSA's National Mental Health Information Center.* Retrieved September 10, 2006, from http://mentalhealth. samhsa.gov/

Taylor, R. J., Chatters, L. M., Jayakody, R., & Levin, J. S. (1996). Black and White differences in religious participation: A multi-sample comparison. *Journal for the Scientific Study of Religion, 35,* 403–410.

Taylor, T. L., & Chemtob, C. M. (2004). Efficacy of treatment for child and adolescent traumatic stress. *Archives of Pediatric Adolescent Medicine, 158,* 786–791.

U.S. Census Bureau. (2000). *Profile of general demographic characteristics: 2000.* Retrieved September 10, 2006, from http://censtats.census.gov/data/LA/1602255000.pdf

U.S. Census Bureau. (2006). *The U.S. Census Bureau released two special data products for the Gulf Coast area affected by Hurricanes Katrina and Rita.* Retrieved January 22, 2006, from http://ask.census.gov/cgi-bin/askcensus.cfg/php/enduser/std_adp/php?p_faqid=1083

Editor's Note

This article was submitted in response to an open call for submissions about psychologists responding to Hurricane Katrina. The collection of 16 articles presents psychologists' professional and personal responses to the extraordinary impact of this disaster. These psychologists describe a variety of roles, actions, involvement, psychological preparation, and reactions involved in the disaster and the months following. These lessons from Katrina can help the psychology profession better prepare to serve the public and its colleagues.—MCR

Russell T. Jones received his PhD in clinical psychology from Pennsylvania State University. He is a professor of clinical psychology at Virginia Polytechnic Institute and State University. His areas of research include disaster-related stress and coping. He is also the founder and director of the Recovery Effort After Child Trauma (REACT) Clinic.

Christopher S. Immel received his BA in psychology from the University of Northern Colorado. He is a graduate student in the clinical psychology doctoral program at Virginia Polytechnic Institute and State University. His areas of research include physical health outcomes for survivors of disaster as well as screening and assessment of mental health posttrauma. He serves as a reviewer for the Association for Psychological Science Student Caucus's Student Research Award competition.

Rachel M. Moore received her BA in psychology from Case Western Reserve University. She is a graduate student in the clinical psychology doctoral program at Virginia Polytechnic Institute and State University. Her research interests include coping following trauma and health outcomes of chronically ill children. She is a member of the APA's Division 54, Society of Pediatric Psychology.

James M. Hadder received his BS from Virginia Polytechnic Institute and State University. He is a graduate student in the clinical psychology doctoral program at Virginia Polytechnic Institute and State University. His research interests include the assessment and treatment of individuals experiencing natural and humanmade disasters, determining the validity of parental reports on traumatized children, and the effects of trauma on preexisting psychopathology.

Correspondence concerning this article should be addressed to Russell T. Jones, 137 Williams Hall, Department of Psychology, Virginia Tech, Blacksburg, VA 24061. E-mail: rtjones@vt.edu

Discussion Questions for Article 1

Section 12: Stress, Health and Coping

Name: _____

PID: _____

Date: __ __ / __ __ / __ __ (MM/DD/YY)

CRN: _____

Recitation Day/Time: _____

Honor Code Signature: _____

1. Describe several barriers faced by mental health professionals reacting to those in need.

2. Describe some of the main types of interventions mentioned in the article.

3. How should psychologists account for cultural diversity in disaster relief?

4. How were you impacted by Katrina, be it through video footage, personal experience, or second-hand knowledge?

Forgiveness, Health, and Well-Being: A Review of Evidence for Emotional Versus Decisional Forgiveness, Dispositional Forgivingness, and Reduced Unforgiveness

Everett L. Worthington Jr
Charlotte Van Oyen Witvliet
Pietro Pietrini
Andrea J. Miller

The extant data linking forgiveness to health and well-being point to the role of emotional forgiveness, particularly when it becomes a pattern in dispositional forgivingness. Both are important antagonists to the negative affect of unforgiveness and agonists for positive affect. One key distinction emerging in the literature is between decisional and emotional forgiveness. Decisional forgiveness is a behavioral intention to resist an unforgiving stance and to respond differently toward a transgressor. Emotional forgiveness is the replacement of negative unforgiving emotions with positive other-oriented emotions. Emotional forgiveness involves psychophysiological changes, and it has more direct health and well-being consequences. While some benefits of forgiveness and forgivingness emerge merely because they reduce unforgiveness, some benefits appear to be more forgiveness specific. We review research on peripheral and central nervous system correlates of forgiveness, as well as existing interventions to promote forgiveness within divergent health settings. Finally, we propose a research agenda.

Keywords: Forgiveness, Health, Cancer, Cardiovascular, Intervention, Peripheral nervous system, Central nervous system, Stress, Coping

Introduction

Recent reviews of literature pertaining to forgiveness and health have argued that (a) forgiveness is an emotion-focused coping process that can promote health (Worthington 2006; Worthington and Scherer 2004); (b) forgiveness might have its major impact on health through reducing unforgiveness rather than creating positive emotional experiences (Harris and Thoresen 2005); (c) forgiveness, especially when undertaken for altruistic motives, can affect both physical and mental health (Witvliet and McCullough 2007; Worthington et al. 2005); and (d) forgiveness interventions are appropriate for but infrequently used in medical settings (Harris and Thoresen 2006). Previous reviews have been based on relatively few studies, whereas the present review capitalizes on the recent virtual agreement by researchers on what forgiveness is (see Worthington 2005a), incorporates more empirical studies than did the previous reviews, and sets a research agenda based on both theory and research.

Definitions of Forgiveness

For years, definitional disagreements permeated the field of forgiveness studies. Many electronic bytes were occupied in proposing and justifying definitions (see Enright and Fitzgibbons 2000; McCullough et al. 2000). However, by 2005, the definitional controversies had quietly subsided, with broad consensus on what forgiveness is not, and much agreement on what it is. Forgiveness is not excusing, exonerating, justifying, condoning, pardoning, or reconciling. Depending on the context, intrapsychic processes may be both necessary and sufficient for forgiveness, although a complex interpersonal process may surround forgiveness experiences (Worthington 2005a). Forgiveness is broadly understood as a process of decreasing inter-related negative resentment-based emotions, motivations, and cognition (Worthington 2005b). This composite is referred to as unforgiveness with the content of the *primary* negative experiences (i.e., cognition, emotion, motivation, or behavior) still under debate (Worthington 2006). Mullet et al. (2005) identified two types of personal dispositions toward unforgiveness—grudge-holding and vengeful orientation. Some researchers have argued that forgiveness also involved enhanced positive experience (Fincham et al. 2005). Worthington (2005b) proposed that most researchers who studied transgressions by strangers or people in non-continuing relationships defined full forgiveness as simply reducing unforgiveness, and researchers who studied continuing relationships defined full forgiveness as decreasing and eventually eliminating unforgiveness by replacing the negative with positive and eventually building to a net positive forgiveness experience. He suggested that forgiveness was of two types: a decision to control one's behaviors (i.e., *decisional forgiveness*) and a multifaceted *emotional forgiveness* that involved changed cognition, emotion, and motivation.

The common denominators in definitions seem to be the following. First, unforgiveness involves ruminations that may be begrudging, vengeful, hostile, bitter, resentful, angry, fearful of future harm, and depressed. Second, unforgiveness is hypothesized to be directly related to the amount of remaining injustice being experienced (called the *injustice gap*, by Exline et al. 2003). Third, forgiveness involves reducing unforgiveness. Fourth, forgiveness is a process rather than an event. There is less agreement about the sequence, mechanisms, key components, and the *sine qua non* changes in the process. Fifth, the internal experience of forgiveness can be distinguished from its interpersonal context. As Baumeister et al. (1998) observed in grudge-theory, a person could internally forgive and not express it or could express forgiveness but not experience it internally. Sixth, forgiveness of strangers or people with whom one does not want nor expect continuing contact is fundamentally different from forgiving a loved one. Seventh, making a decision to change one's behavior could be a sincere and permanent form of forgiving, and yet that decision must be differentiated from emotionally forgiving. Decisional and emotional forgiveness are different processes, likely with different sequelae. Decisional forgiveness, while it might reduce hostility does not necessarily reduce stress responses. Thus, it is probably related to reconciliatory processes and through improved relationships, indirectly to health. Emotional forgiveness is likely more related to health sequelae because of its strong connection to overcoming negative affect and stress reactions by cultivating positive affect. Eighth, most would agree that (a) decisional forgiveness has the potential to lead to changes in emotion and eventually behavior whereas (b) emotional forgiveness, by definition, involves changes in emotion, motivation, cognition, and eventually behavior.

Many acts reduce unforgiveness and are thus often confused with forgiveness (Worthington 2001). As a stark example, successful vengeance will eliminate unforgiveness, but no one would confuse it with forgiveness. Other examples of unforgiveness-reducing alternatives to forgiveness include (1) seeing justice done (including civil justice, criminal justice, restorative justice), (2) shadenfreude, (3) letting go and moving on, (4) excusing an offense, (5) justifying an offense, (6) condoning an offense, (7) forbearing, (8) turning the issue over to God because one does not believe oneself capable of judging, or (9) turning the issue over to God in hopes of divine retribution. All of those reduce unforgiveness, thus usually contributing to positive health outcomes (Harris and Thoresen 2005). However, none is forgiveness.

Forgiveness, Forgivingness, and Health

Forgivingness is seen as a disposition, while forgiveness is seen as being related to a state response (Mullet et al. 2005). Forgivingness—and more rarely forgiveness—has been found to be related to health. Toussaint et al. (2001) conducted a telephone survey with a national probability sample of 1,423 respondents (young, ages 18–44, $n = 737$; middle-aged, ages 45–64, $n = 410$; and old, ages 65 and older, $n = 276$). Self-rated health was related to forgivingness of self in young and middle aged participants and to forgivingness of others in older adults. Typically, forgivingness takes years before it has discernible effects on physical health. This is reasonable when seen in the context that stress-related disorders often do not develop until chronic stress has taken a physical toll on one's body. If unforgiveness is interpersonally stressful (see Worthington 2006, for a stress-and-coping theory of forgiveness), then it should be expected that self-rated health is related to habitually forgiving others only for people who have practiced it for many years. In the methodology of the cross-sectional phone survey, it was not possible for Toussaint et al. to determine how long people considered themselves to be dispositionally forgiving.

Forgivingness of the self was related to physical health only for young and middle aged respondents—not for elderly respondents. Forgiveness of the self involves quite different psychological processes than does forgiveness of others (see Hall and Fincham 2005). In many ways, forgiveness of self is more related to being an offender than a victim of injustice. Namely, people struggle with self-condemnation because they believe they have done wrong (to self or others) and they feel guilt and shame, which are stressful. Forgiveness of self has been related to the adjustment of women with breast cancer (Glinder and Compas 1999; Romero et al. 2006) as well as college students (Macaskill et al. 2000). The mechanism by which forgiveness of self affects health, however, is likely to have features distinct from forgiveness of others. We hypothesize that self-condemnation may impair self-care, produce depression and anxiety, and demotivate coping. That might result in more immediately apparent negative health consequences than would forgiveness of others, which probably exerts most of its influence by being a coping mechanism for the chronic stress of unforgiveness (McEwen 2002).

Lawler-Row and Piferi (2006) provided some insight into why forgivingness of others might be related to health in a study of 425 participants aged 50 to 95 years. They found that a forgiving personality was related to stress, subjective well-being, psychological well-being, and depression. High and low forgivingness conditions differed on four potential mediators—healthy behaviors, social support, religious well-being, and existential well-being. Furthermore, high and low forgivingness conditions also differed on several indices of successful aging—autonomy, environmental mastery, positive relations with others, purpose in life, personal growth, and self-acceptance. Mediational analyses were conducted to determine mediators between forgivingness and health. The connection between forgivingness and depression was mediated by healthy behaviors, social support, and existential and religious well-being. Forgivingness and stress were mediated by sex, age, healthy behaviors, existential and religious well-being. Forgivingness and subjective well-being were mediated by sex, age, healthy behaviors, social support, and existential and religious well-being. Forgivingness and psychological well-being were partially mediated by age, healthy behaviors, social support and existential well-being.

The empirical literature on forgivingness and health is growing. At present, it appears that a variety of mechanisms operate and support the forgivingness-health relationships in different ways at different stages of life. However, these are survey data for which major criteria of health are self-reports. A need remains for prospective studies documenting the incidence of disease in people exhibiting self- and other-forgivingness. Some of the self-report measures created for the purpose of a survey were short and had no data supporting their estimated reliability or validity. Lawler-Row and Piferi (2006) used measures with psychometric support to establish the relationships. However, there is also a need to examine the mechanisms of influence using procedures to assess central and peripheral nervous system processes when people do and do not forgive.

Forgiveness in Relation to Brain Physiology and Functioning and Health

The development of more and more sophisticated methodologies for the functional exploration of the brain has made it possible to investigate the molecular correlates of cognitive, emotional, and behavioral functioning in the living human brain with no harm for the subjects. Several studies using electroencephalographic techniques or functional brain imaging tools, including positron emission tomography and functional magnetic resonance imaging, have been successfully used to investigate the neural bases of the decisional and emotional components involved in the modulation of behavior, in moral evaluation as well as in adopting forgivingness strategies.

Functional Magnetic Resonance Imaging and Positron Emission Tomography Studies

As one basis for distinguishing decisional and emotional forgiveness, Worthington (2006) referenced a highly visible and often cited study of moral dilemmas. Greene et al. (2001) studied two similar moral dilemmas. In the trolley dilemma, the participant imagines himself or herself to be standing on a footbridge overlooking trolley tracks and must decide whether to pull a switch to prevent the trolley from killing five strangers. By throwing the switch, that diversion will kill one stranger. About 90 percent of the people chose to divert the trolley and kill one person. In the footbridge dilemma, the runaway trolley can only be diverted (thus saving the five) by pushing a stranger from the footbridge to his death. About 10 percent of the participants were willing to push the stranger. Why the difference? Greene et al. (2001) suggested, "Some moral dilemmas (those relevant to the footbridge dilemma) engage emotional processing to a greater extent than others (those relatively similar to the trolley dilemmas), and these differences in emotional engagement affect people's judgments" (p. 2106). In Greene et al.'s experiment, people ($N = 9$) were in functional magnetic resonance imaging units as they were presented with these two dilemmas. As they contemplated the unfolding story, brain activity was the same in both scenarios until, in the footbridge problem, the experimenter posed the possibility of pushing the person to his death. Suddenly, activity in the brain areas associated with rational thought declined and activity in the emotional areas increased.

In a follow-up experiment, they found that people who went against the "natural" tide had longer decision times than those who went with the tide. In the trolley dilemma, those who sided with the 10% (do not throw the switch) delayed their choice. In the footbridge dilemma, those who sided with the 10% (push the person) delayed their choice. The researchers suggested that the delay occurred because cognition was needed to overcome the "natural" tendency. On the surface, these findings may seem remote from forgiveness processes. However, just as there is a distinction between decisional and emotional decision making, there may be a similar distinction between decisional and emotional forgiveness and processes.

In a more direct study of forgiveness, Farrow et al. (2001) used functional magnetic resonance imaging to determine the brain structures that were active in making judgments about what one might, or might not, forgive (called *forgivability* judgments), what one might or might not empathize with, and what judgments one might make in social situations. Participants ($N = 10$; 7 males, 3 females) were subjected to a number of decision-making choices while being monitored in a functional magnetic resonance imaging unit. Among the many findings, Farrow et al. reported that the judgments about whether an act was forgivable and how empathic it was involved a different portion of the cortex than judgments about fairness. Presumably, to forgive one must consider the other person, which stimulates empathy. To judge whether a decision is fair, though, does not necessarily bring in the human element and promote prosocial emotions. The left frontotemporal region was most associated with both forgivability and empathy. The implications of Farrow et al. for understanding forgiveness is that when one imagines a scenario involving judgments of fairness—as one might do in thinking about the injustice gap (as it affects oneself or others)—and one empathizes or forgives, different regions of the brain are activated.

In additional studies, Farrow and Woodruff (2005) reported that they used the regions associated with forgivability judgments as a map to indicate whether forgiveness might be occurring. Using a pre- and post-test design, they gave 13 patients who were diagnosed with post-traumatic stress disorder 10 weekly 1-hour sessions of forgiveness-oriented cognitive-behavior therapy. Relative to pretest patterns, post-test patterns showed evidence of increased forgivability judgments and empathy. Also, 14 patients with schizophrenia increased their forgivability judgments relative to healthy controls.

Using positron emission tomography to measure regional cerebral blood flow, Pietrini et al. (2000) studied the neural correlates of anger and aggression in 15 healthy young people (8 men, 7 women). People were instructed to imagine four scenarios involving themselves, their mother, and two men in an elevator. In one scenario, which represented the baseline non-emotional condition, the participant simply looked around while riding in the elevator. In the other three emotionally-laden scenarios, the two men assaulted the participant's mother while the participant (a) watched, unable to help; (b) tried to intervene but was restrained by one man while the other continued the assault; or (c) attacked the two men with a sincere intent to injure or kill them. A 9-point Likert-type scale (1 = *extremely so* to 9 = *not at all*), revealed that participants experienced greater anger, frustration, and anxiety during the aggressive scenarios as compared to the neutral baseline condition. Of note, participants reported much greater anger and frustration when they could not intervene (conditions "a" and "b" above) than when they were free to carry out their aggressive response (scenario "c").

In their functional analysis of reaction to aggressive behavior, Pietrini et al. (2000) found that when people were asked to imagine vividly angry situations—regardless of which of the three aggressive scenarios described above—they had higher activity within limbic system structures such as the anterior cingulate cortex and functional reduction in the activity of the orbitofrontal cortex, as compared to the baseline neutral condition. The medial orbitofrontal cortex is considered to be the limbic portion of the frontal association cortex. It is intimately connected with the amygdala and the limbic system, and it plays an important role in integrating emotional and motivational processes. Thus, one implication might be that negative emotion acts antagonistically toward reasoning. This suggests that reasoning is disrupted by anger and that imaginally rehearsing angry and aggressive mental scenarios (i.e., ruminating angrily) could (a) catapult one into negative emotive responding and (b) shut down rational approach and calm emotions.

Imagery as well as verbal rumination might stimulate similar effects. For example, Blair et al. (1999) found increased orbitofrontal activation when healthy males viewed pictures of angry faces. They interpreted this activation as an attempt to control a socially inappropriate behavioral response elicited by the angry faces.

Taken together, the results of these studies along with the clinical observation that traumatic or degenerative lesions of the prefrontal cortex lead to disinhibition of behavior including poor control of aggression, may indicate that a functional suppression of the orbitofrontal cortex is needed in order to enact a socially unacceptable behavior. In this regard, it is interesting to note that in the sample studied by Pietrini et al. (2000) the reduction in neural activity during the aggressive scenarios as compared to the neutral baseline condition was significantly greater in females than in males. This may suggest that a greater suppression of orbitofrontal inhibitory control is needed in females to express a violent behavior—even at an imaginal level—and is consistent with the finding that females inhibit violence more than males (Pietrini et al. 1998). With respect to males, females also showed a much greater activation of the anterior cingulate cortex during the aggressive scenarios as compared to the neutral baseline (Pietrini et al. 2000).

Adopting a similar visual imagery paradigm in conjunction with functional magnetic resonance imaging, Pietrini's group has begun to investigate the brain correlates associated with the imaginal evocation of forgiveness and unforgiveness in response to hurtful events. Ten young healthy participants (5 females and 5 males) underwent functional magnetic resonance imaging while they were asked to evoke a series of specific imaginal scenarios that comprised a hurtful event. Then they were randomly instructed to forgive or not. Imagery ability, behavioral and emotional responses were measured using the procedure described in the aggressive behavior study (Pietrini et al. 2000). Imaginal evocation of emotionally relevant hurtful events followed by forgiving and not forgiving was associated in each participant with modulation of brain areas implicated in visual/semantic representation and imagery, and with activation of more anterior areas, such as ventromedial and prefrontal cortex, amygdala, anterior cingulate and striatum, that are involved in the regulation of emotional responses, moral judgment, perception and modulation of physical and moral pain, reward and decision making processes (Pietrini et al. 2004). It is worthy to note that during the hurtful condition females showed a greater activation in the anterior cingulate cortex than did males, consistent with the positron emission tomography findings from the aggression study. Given that the anterior cingulate cortex has been shown to respond to physical and moral pain (Eisenberger et al. 2003; Rainville et al. 1997), these findings suggest that morally hurtful events likely elicit a stronger response in the areas of the brain that process the affective valence of painful stimuli in females than in males. The anterior cingulate cortex was strongly engaged when subjects granted forgiveness; furthermore, the degree of neural activation was correlated with the individual's capability to grant forgiveness. Because neural activity in the anterior cingulate cortex is modulated by pain-killing drugs but also by hypnosis and placebo

(Casey et al. 2000; Lieberman et al. 2004; Rainville et al. 1997), the authors propose that forgivingness may represent a natural "self-aid medication mechanism" that was selected through evolution for people to overcome distressful situations much before pharmacological agents or therapeutic interventions became available (Pietrini et al. 2004). As discussed below, chronic stressful situations involve damaging processes—stress hormone secretion, neuronal loss and so on—for brain function and structure as well as for the whole organism (Pietrini and Guazzelli 1997). Therefore a mechanism that enables the individual to rapidly overcome such a situation confers a strong advantage for well-being and survival.

Electroencephalographic Studies

EEG studies have shown that experiencing state anger has been associated with relative left-frontal activity compared to right-frontal activity. Harmon-Jones et al. (2004) noted how left-frontal cortical activity has been repeatedly shown to be associated with approach motivation, emotion, and behavior identified with the Behavioral Approach System (Gray 1994). Right cortical activity has been repeatedly shown to be associated with withdrawal motivation, emotion, and behavior (Coan et al. 2001), associated with the Behavior Inhibition System (Gray 1994). Harmon-Jones et al. (2003) showed that in anger provocation, people experienced high left-frontal cortical activity, especially when they were able to move toward the source of anger in order to try to resolve the anger-producing situation. If people did not anticipate having the chance to resolve the situation, they did not show an increase in left-frontal activity. Left-frontal activity is more associated with approaching a person and working things out when one is angry instead of simply stewing in resentment.

Harmon-Jones et al. (2004) sought to determine whether sympathy, which has been shown to reduce aggressive motivations, would also reduce relative left-frontal cortical activity relative to right-frontal activity. They suggested that if such a finding were to occur, it would suggest that the increase in relative left-frontal activity that has been observed after arousal to anger would be due more to approach motivations than other processes. College students (53 women, 26 men) participated in their electroencephalograph study in which sympathy was manipulated. A manipulation in which participants received insults was associated with increased left-frontal activity and decreased right-frontal activity. Notably, for participants who had high levels of sympathy, the electroencephalograph effect was eliminated. Sympathy acted in opposition to anger arousal in decreasing brain activity in the left-frontal cortex. This sympathy manipulation finding echoed previous research (Coan et al. 2001). Harmon-Jones et al. (2003) showed that manipulating (a) coping capability and (b) the experience of a positive other-oriented emotion both affected brain activity that was associated with unforgiveness, anger, and hostility.

Taken together, work from the labs of Farrow, Pietrini, and Harmon-Jones underscore how brain regions and functions are affected by decisional and affective processes in ways that are consistent with the differentiation of decisional and emotional forgiveness. Results also suggest that emotional forgiveness may happen through a mechanism of emotional replacement of negative with positive, other-oriented emotions.

Forgiveness in Relation to Peripheral Physiology and Health

To the extent that forgiveness buffers against illness or promotes health, this may be due to the emotional-replacement functions of forgiveness (see Worthington 2006, for a summary of evidence supporting that mechanism). Forgiveness may serve both as an antidote to the health-eroding processes of stress, hostility, and rumination, and as an agonist for the health-promoting processes of positive other-oriented emotion. Below, we review findings on forgiveness and peripheral physiology, with a focus on the emotional processes potentially related to forgiveness and physical health.

Forgiving Others

In a psychophysiology study, Witvliet et al. (2001) measured continuous facial electromyograph, heart rate, blood pressure, and skin conductance as 71 college students each adopted two states of unforgiveness versus two states of emotional forgiveness toward a particular real-life offender. The two unforgiving conditions were (a) rumination about the transgression and (b) nursing a grudge toward the offender. The two forgiving conditions were (a) cultivating empathic perspective taking toward the offender and (b) forgiving the offender by finding a way to genuinely wish him or her well while releasing hurt and angry emotions. This last condition is an emotional forgiveness condition. Witvliet et al. used a within-subjects design so that each participant imagined all four types of imagery multiple times using counterbalanced orders. Physiological reactivity during each imagery trial and recovery patterns during the subsequent relaxation period were assessed and compared to that same trial's pretrial baseline data. This approach highlighted the impact of each imagery condition on the physiological measures, as well as how those response patterns recovered after imagery.

As predicted, unforgiving imagery evoked higher arousal and more negative emotion ratings compared to forgiving imagery. Consistent with the high arousal ratings, unforgiving imagery was associated with higher levels of tonic eye muscle tension (orbicularis oculi electromyograph) during imagery, and higher heart rate and skin conductance level scores (indicating sympathetic nervous system activation) both during imagery and recovery. Consistent with the negative valence of unforgiving imagery (versus the positive valence of forgiving imagery), participants showed more brow muscle tension (corrugator electromyograph) during imagery and recovery periods. Systolic blood pressure (during the middle of imagery), diastolic blood pressure, and mean arterial pressure—indicating arousal and negative valence—were all higher during unforgiving versus forgiving imagery. Participants reported significantly higher joy, pleasant relaxation, empathy, and perceived control in the forgiveness conditions, but higher sadness, anger, and fear during the unforgiveness conditions. These data patterns were substantially replicated in a subsequent study of the associations of justice and forgiveness with effects on continuous measures of physiological functioning (Witvliet et al., in press).

These findings resonate with the work of Lawler et al. (2003, 2005) and Toussaint and Williams (2003), who used combined between and within subjects designs and interview-based psychophysiology paradigms. Although these researchers did not explicitly study emotional forgiveness per se, Lawler in particular has framed her group's findings in terms of a forgiving change of heart (Lawler et al. 2003). They found cardiovascular benefits of both trait and state forgiving in college students ($N = 108$; 44 males, 64 females). Higher trait forgivingness was associated with lower systolic, diastolic, and mean arterial pressure. Lower state unforgivingness and higher state forgiveness for both a parent and a peer/partner were associated with lower systolic, diastolic, and mean arterial pressure, heart rate, and rate pressure product (rate pressure product is the systolic blood pressure times heart rate divided by 100, and is an indicator of myocardial oxygen demand and stress). In response to an interview about a salient memory of conflict with a parent or primary caregiver, Lawler et al. (2003) also found that high trait forgivers showed the least reactivity and best recovery patterns for systolic, diastolic, and mean arterial pressure and rate pressure product, and forehead electromyograph, whereas low trait forgivers in unforgiving states showed the highest levels of cardiovascular reactivity and poorest recovery patterns.

In follow-up research with a community sample of 27–72 year olds ($N = 81$), Lawler et al. (2005) found that trait forgivingness was associated with lower levels of rate pressure product reactivity—but not mean arterial pressure—in the first part of an interview. Using path analyses, they found that trait forgivingness predicted state forgiveness. Higher state forgiveness and lower hostility predicted lower stress levels, which in turn predicted lower self-reported illness. Lawler et al. (2005) found that reduced negative affect was the strongest mediator between forgiveness and physical health symptoms. That suggested the importance of emotional forgiveness in reducing unforgiveness. Other variables—spirituality, social skills, and lower stress—mediated the forgiveness-health relationship, too.

In their interview study, Toussaint and Williams (2003) measured blood pressure in a diverse sample of 100 midwestern community residents, with 25 in each cell: 2 [socioeconomic status (high, low)] × 2 [race (Black, White)]. Men and women were almost evenly divided across cells. Across participants, higher levels of total forgiveness (i.e., forgiveness of others and self, and feeling forgiven by God) were associated with lower resting diastolic blood pressure. Among white participants of high socioeconomic status, total forgiveness and forgiveness of self were associated with lower resting diastolic blood pressure. Among black participants with low socioeconomic status, forgiveness of others was associated with lower resting diastolic blood pressure, and forgiveness of others, total forgiveness, and perceived divine forgiveness were associated with lower resting cortisol levels.

Together, this combined set of findings on peripheral physiology suggests that chronic unforgiving responses could contribute to adverse health by perpetuating stress beyond the duration of the original stressor, heightening cardiovascular reactivity during recall, imagery, and conversations about the hurt, and impairing cardiovascular recovery even when people try to focus on something else. By contrast, forgiving responses may buffer health both by quelling these unforgiving responses and by nurturing positive emotional responses in their place.

Additional research points to the importance of experiencing other-oriented positive emotions for emotional forgiveness to occur. Huang and Enright (2000) compared the effects of forgiving out of moral love versus cultural obligation in 22 matched pairs of male and female Taiwanese community members. We see aspects of the moral love condition as more akin to emotional forgiveness. When interviewed about a typical day, the groups did not differ in their blood pressure. When interviewed about a past experience with conflict, the groups did not differ on self-reported anger. However, those who forgave out of obligation-oriented versus moral-love motives cast down their eyes and showed more masking smiles. The authors interpreted those behaviors as signs of hidden anger. These facial patterns are also consistent with the idea that the obligatory forgivers might have been suppressing negative emotion, which we consider to be akin to decisional, rather than emotional forgiveness. In line with this view, the obligatory forgivers had significantly higher blood pressure values than did the moral love forgivers on three of twelve blood pressure comparisons. Obligation forgivers had higher raw systolic blood pressure at the beginning of the interview, and higher raw systolic blood pressure and diastolic blood pressure one minute into the interview. This study suggests that motivations emphasizing love differ from motivations that emphasize obligation in terms of affective expression and cardiovascular responding.

Receiving Forgiveness

Whereas most forgiveness research has addressed the granting of forgiveness, one study examined the effects of forgiveness on those who receive it (Witvliet et al. 2002). They used a within-subjects psychophysiology study with college students ($N = 40$; 20 females, 20 males) who reflected on and imagined a particular transgression they had committed against someone. Part of this study compared imagery of (a) receiving an unforgiving response from one's victim, with imagery of (b) receiving forgiveness and (c) experiencing reconciliation. Forgiveness and reconciliation imagery each prompted improvements in basic emotions (e.g., sadness, anger) and moral emotions (e.g., guilt, shame, gratitude, hope), with reductions in negative emotions and increases in positive emotions. Receiving forgiveness and reconciliation each also prompted less furrowing of the brow muscle (*corrugator* electromyograph) associated with negative emotion, and more electromyograph activity at the *zygomatic* muscle, indicative of smiling. Autonomic nervous system measures were largely unaffected by imagery, although skin conductance data suggested greater emotional engagement or stress when transgressors imagined reconciling with their victims. Apparently, while reconciliation is often valued, contemplating making a reconciliative gesture can provoke stress reactions.

Summary

The study of forgiveness in the psychophysiology laboratory has its limits. To generalize to real life, studies must employ tasks that mirror daily life, aggregate repeated measures across tasks, and measure physiology before, during, and after the conditions of interest (Schwartz et al. 2003). Forgiveness studies with designs close to these ideals show cardiovascular reactivity patterns that reliably distinguish unforgiving responses toward others (as a state or trait) as generating more reactivity and prolonged activation than do forgiving responses toward others (and also link facial electromyograph patterns with the negative, aroused emotion of unforgiveness). Exploratory studies that seek to correlate single resting physiology measures with forgiving personality variables do not show these patterns (Seybold et al. 2001). Nevertheless, it is important to keep in mind that it is sustained elevations in blood pressure that predict end-organ damage, and the impact of brief peaks in blood pressure, such as those measured in the forgiveness studies, is unclear (see Schwartz et al. 2003). Hence, the extant data speak only to immediate short-term patterns. As we interpret the autonomic and cardiovascular effects, it is also important to keep in mind that they may reflect not only heightened sympathetic nervous system arousal, but also impaired parasympathetically mediated responding.

Forgiveness has been shown to be beneficial in reducing victims' unforgiveness, which is associated with prolonged physiological activation, and is theorized to have more cardiovascular health implications than short-term stress reactivity (Brosschot and Thayer 2003). Forgiveness research suggests it also promotes positive and prosocial emotions for victims (e.g., Witvliet et al. 2001) and offenders (Witvliet et al. 2002), calming physiological indicators of negative and aroused emotion. To the extent that forgiveness may eclipse or reduce anger, sympathetic nervous system activation may be mitigated (McCraty et al. 1995). To the degree that forgiveness involves positive and calm emotion, the parasympathetic nervous system may exert better control (see McCraty et al. 1995).

Forgiveness and Other Mechanisms Not Reviewed

In the present limited review, we cannot consider all of the evidence for mechanisms relating forgivingness and health. For example, Worthington (2006) reviewed at length evidence from evolutionary psychology, the biochemistry of aggression, the relaxation response, emotional expression (i.e., Pennebaker's writing intervention; see McCullough et al. 2006), positive emotions (e.g., love, gratitude, etc.), and Fredrickson's (1998) Broaden and Build Model of Positive Emotions. Several other recent chapters include extensive reviews that address important mechanisms to consider. Witvliet and McCullough (2007) proposed the importance of emotion-regulation pathways for linking forgiveness and health. They address forgiveness as an antagonist to post-offense responses that have destructive effects (e.g., stress, hostility, rumination, and suppression), and forgiveness as an agonist for positive reappraisal and positive emotions. Marques and Sternberg (2007) extensively document biological features of positive emotions and their interfaces with health, and Koenig (2007) highlights the pathways by which expressions of altruistic responses can be linked with health.

Previous reviews have paid little attention to forgiveness interventions in medical settings, although Harris and Thoresen (2006) called for such attention. Until the last couple of years, few juried studies were available. In the following section, we summarize the research on applications of a forgiveness intervention to producing changes in health status.

Forgiveness Interventions in Medical Settings

Based on the preliminary evidence that forgiveness may affect health, teaching forgiveness in medical settings is gaining limited acceptance as a treatment goal (Harris and Thoresen 2006). Yet, forgiveness interventions are still implemented infrequently in medical settings. We explore here the medical conditions for which forgiveness interventions could benefit patients and their loved ones.

Medical Family Therapy

Forgiveness interventions may help families who are dealing with illness of a family member. McDaniel et al. (1999) identified emotional themes in families dealing with the impact of physical illness. One emotional theme identified was guilt versus forgiveness. For example, individuals may ask what they did to deserve the illness or have guilt regarding their illness, child's illness, or parent's illness. Such emotional themes can apply to a variety of illness experiences, whether acute or anticipated, and across the lifespan (McDaniel et al. 1999). Interventions for families dealing with illness and related guilt and forgiveness themes may benefit from including forgiveness of others and of the self.

Cardiovascular Health

Individuals at risk for coronary disease, recurrent coronary disease, and high blood pressure may benefit from forgiveness interventions. This is suggested by stress-and-coping theory (Worthington 2006) but also by the research on peripheral physiology and forgiveness reviewed above. Interventions have considered forgiveness within a treatment protocol. Friedman's Recurrent Coronary Prevention Project (RCPP; Friedman et al. 1986) involved a five-year, clinical trial of a group therapy intervention aimed at reducing the recurrence rate of post-coronary participants by reducing levels of hostility in individuals at risk for coronary problems in patients who had recovered from myocardial infarction. According to Kaplan (1992), forgiveness was an important antidote to hostility in this efficacious intervention. In a post-intervention assessment, patients indicated that learning "how to cultivate the forgiving heart" (p. 6) was one of the keys to reducing their hostility.

Waltman (2003) examined a ten-week forgiveness intervention with male patients who had coronary artery disease. No differences were found between the groups from the pre- to post-test. However, after a 10-week follow-up, a difference emerged. Participants in the forgiveness group experienced reduced anger-induced myocardial perfusion defects.

Chronic Pain

Because chronic pain can be complicated by anger and resentment (Greenwood et al. 2003), forgiveness interventions may be beneficial. Carson et al. (2005) examined individuals suffering from chronic low back pain and found that anger, affective pain and sensory pain were all lower for those who were more forgiving. State anger mediated the relationship between forgiveness and sensory pain. However, state anger did not mediate the relationship between forgiveness and affective pain. In addition, Rippentrop et al. (2005) demonstrated that pain patients with higher levels of forgiveness reported experiencing less daily pain interference and less intense pain.

Substance Use

For participants with substance dependence, Lin et al. (2004) examined the effect of either 12 weeks of forgiveness therapy or individual therapy. Individuals who participated in forgiveness therapy experienced a decrease in their vulnerability to use drugs at post-test and four-month follow-up. Individual therapy specifically focused on drug vulnerabilities, whereas forgiveness therapy did not. However, it was the participants in the forgiveness therapy group who decreased their drug vulnerabilities.

In the foregoing areas, forgiveness might be important because it affects the patient's stress response. However, there are medical problems that are not mediated by stress response. Stress shows up within the family support system, or in coping with the disease, and thus can affect physical and mental health outcomes. We illustrate that process with two examples.

Traumatic Brain Injuries

Individuals with traumatic brain injury may blame others (Smith 1989). Many individuals with traumatic brain injury were injured by others (Gisi and D'Amato 2000), and accidents leading to the injury frequently involved carelessness (e.g., running stop signs), lack of responsibility (e.g., hit and run), or alcohol (Gisi and D'Amato 2000). Anger and resentment can result in non-compliance with medical protocol (Smith 1989). Major transgressions might also occur after the injury. Caretakers or spouses might abandon or demean patients. Furthermore, brain injured patients might say hurtful things, express uncontrolled rage, or simply be a source of resentment from causing caretaker burden. To the extent that forgiveness addresses these issues, such interventions may be of benefit.

Cancer

Individuals faced with terminal cancer have been studied in forgiveness interventions. So far, this research has typically been reported in unpublished dissertations (Bennett 1998; Hansen 2002; Phillips 1999; Stone 2001). Philips (1999) identified themes that emerged from two open-ended interviews with five participants diagnosed with cancer. Participants expressed a need for (a) letting go of longstanding patterns of thoughts, feelings, and behaviors that blocked spiritual growth and (b) opening and healing through practicing forgiveness, trust, acceptance, and spirituality. Hansen (2002) reported a dissertation on a forgiveness intervention with participants diagnosed with terminal cancer. Participants expressed emotional pain due to unresolved conflicts or past emotional injuries. They participated either in a four-week forgiveness therapy or supportive therapy wait-list control group (Hansen 2002). From pre- to post-test, the forgiveness group had higher gains in forgiveness, hope, and quality of life, and higher reductions in anger than did the control group.

Published studies of forgiveness in cancer patients include case studies (Mauldin and Andersen 1998) and an uncontrolled study (Phillips and Osborne 1989). Phillips and Osborne provided six sessions of group-based forgiveness therapy to cancer patients. The sessions focused on the relief and dissipation of negative feelings and the resolution of painful psychological issues associated with cancer. The group leader-authors reported that the process of forgiving involved a struggle with guilt, blame, and revenge and growth in the understanding of the reciprocal nature of relationships.

Medical Errors

Forgiveness training could help physicians, patients, and family members in dealing with medical errors (Gerber 1990). Of note, the current culture of medical settings is not set up to encourage forgiveness. For instance, many physicians involved in medical mistakes are informed not to communicate with the patient or patient's family, which makes it difficult for anyone to begin to forgive (Berlinger and Wu 2005). Yet, forgiveness issues still exist for physicians even if they are not allowed to communicate with families (see Gerber 1990). For example, one physician stated that at times physicians need self-forgiveness, which was described as freedom from guilt and self-hatred over mistakes (Berlinger and Wu 2005). Thus, although none have been investigated empirically, self-forgiveness interventions could help physicians deal with medical mistakes.

Patients and family members could also benefit from forgiveness interventions regarding medical errors. Clearly, redress for mistakes should not be circumvented by participating in a forgiveness intervention, but after mediated resolution or litigation, family members might still need to deal with unforgiveness of physicians, lawyers, judges, juries, and third party payers.

Research Agenda and Conclusion

We suggest a brief research agenda that derives from the foregoing review of (a) whether forgiveness affects health, (b) how it might do so, and (c) how interventions might be crafted.

Refining Knowledge about Forgiveness in Relationship to Health

As outlined in this research review, much is known while much remains unknown about the forgiveness-health relationship. We suggest the importance of further research on these issues. (a) Given that forgiveness and other coping strategies may reduce unforgiveness, how does forgiveness compare to those strategies in terms of making a positive difference in health that goes beyond merely reducing unforgiveness? (b) How does the relationship between forgiveness and health change across the lifespan? Does forgiveness work through different mechanisms, as we have suggested, for the younger than for the older person? (c) What negative health effects might be associated with different approaches to forgiveness, understandings of forgiveness, features of transgressions, contexts, and timelines? It is important for forgivers not to endanger themselves or others by forgoing justice or by reconciling when instrumental behavior is needed to rectify a problem. Are there also negative health effects that directly follow forgiving? (d) What is the nature of the role of forgiveness in coping with disease? Forgiveness might play a palliative role in coping with gastrointestinal, cardiovascular, and stress-related disorders. However, in cancer control, for instance, forgiving might affect cancer risk directly by affecting glutamate and thus the N-methyl-D-asparate receptor, which affects free radical concentration, which in turn might affect cancer risk (McEwen 2002). Forgiveness might contribute to the healing or treatment of cancer only indirectly through relationships or social support, or by helping people be more at peace with their ailments, or contributing to fewer mental health consequences and more positive mental health consequences.

Mechanisms by Which Forgiveness May Affect Health

Future research should more specifically address these questions. (a) To what degree is the stress-and-coping model an adequate explanation of the direct versus indirect effects of forgiveness on health? (b) What are the roles of positive emotions such as forgiveness in stress, coping, and health research (Fredrickson 1998)? (c) To what extent might emotional forgiveness relate to meaning- and problem-focused coping (Park and Folkman 1997)? (d) Under what conditions are decisional and emotional forgiveness independent and under what conditions are they interrelated? (e) What are the physiological and behavioral mechanisms by which decisional and emotional forgiveness have different health-related effects? (f) Who tends to experience decisional versus emotional forgiveness, under what circumstances, and with what effects on physical health?

Forgiveness Intervention Research

(a) Controlled clinical trials of forgiveness interventions are in short supply in health settings. A variety of interventions should be tested with different health disorders. Furthermore, eventually, different interventions need to be compared within the treatment of a given disease. (b) Trait by state forgiveness treatment studies are needed. Perhaps those high in trait forgivingness will forgive *naturally*, and they may have ceiling effects on forgiveness intervention benefits. Better candidates for interventions might be those who are lower in trait forgivingness, who potentially have much more to gain.

With each successive review of the literature, the evidence for connections between forgiveness and health mounts. Mechanisms of influence seem highly related to decreasing the effects of the stress response, but indirect mechanisms, such as affecting the social support network, also exist. At present, interventions to promote forgiveness have been applied to a variety of conditions. The time is ripe for controlled clinical trials of tailored interventions to promote forgiveness in patients and caregivers.

References

Baumeister, R. F., Exline, J. J., & Sommer, K. L. (1998). The victim role, grudge theory, and two dimensions of forgiveness. In E. L. Worthington Jr. (Ed.), *Dimensions of forgiveness: Psychological research & theological perspectives* (pp. 79–104). Philadelphia: Templeton Foundation Press.

Bennett, M. L. (1998). A study of the relationship of prayer between family caregiver and cancer patient in easing caregiver burden. *Dissertation Abstracts International: Section B: The Sciences and Engineering, 59*(1-B), 169.

Berlinger, N., & Wu, A. W. (2005). Subtracting insult from injury: Addressing cultural expectations in the disclosure of medical error. *Journal of Medical Ethics, 31*, 106–108.

Blair, R. J. R., Morris, J. S., Frith, C. D., Perett, D. I., & Dolan, R. J. (1999). Dissociable neural responses to facial expressions of sadness and anger. *Brain, 122*, 883–893.

Brosschot, J. F., & Thayer, J. F. (2003). Heart rate response is longer after negative emotions than after positive emotions. *International Journal of Psychophysiology, 50*, 181–187.

Carson, J. W., Keefe, F. J., Goli, V., Fras, A. M., Lynch, T. R., Thorp, S. R., & Buechler, J. L. (2005). Forgiveness and chronic low back pain: A preliminary study examining the relationship of forgiveness to pain, anger, and psychological distress. *Journal of Pain, 6*, 84–91.

Casey, K. L., Svensson, P., Morrow, T. J., Raz, J., Jone, C., & Minoshima, S. (2000). Selective opiate modulation of nociceptive processing in the human brain. *Journal of Neurophysiology, 84*, 525–533.

Coan, J. A., Allen, J. J. B., & Harmon-Jones, E. (2001). Voluntary facial expression and hemispheric asymmetry over the frontal cortex. *Psychophysiology, 38*, 912–925.

Eisenberger, N. I., Lieberman, M. D., & Williams, K. D. (2003). Does rejection hurt? An fMRI study of social exclusion. *Science, 302*, 290–292.

Enright, R. D., & Fitzgibbons, R. P. (2000). *Helping clients forgive: An empirical guide for resolving anger and restoring hope.* Washington, DC: American Psychological Association.

Exline, J. J., Worthington, E. L. Jr., Hill, P., & McCullough, M. E. (2003). Forgiveness and justice: A research agenda for social and personality psychology. *Personality and Social Psychology Review, 7*, 337–348.

Farrow, T. F. D., & Woodruff, P. W. R. (2005). Neuroimaging of forgivability. In E. L. Worthington Jr. (Ed.), *Handbook of forgiveness* (pp. 259–272). New York: Brunner-Routledge.

Farrow, T. F. D., Zheng, Y., Wilkinson, I. D., Spence, S. A., Deakin, J. F. W., Tarrier, N., Griffiths, P. D., & Woodruff, P. W. R. (2001). Investigating the functional anatomy of empathy and forgiveness. *Neuroreport: An International Journal for the Rapid Communication of Research in Neuroscience, 12*, 2433–2438.

Fincham, F. D., Hall, J. H., & Beach, S. R. H. (2005). Til lack of forgiveness doth us part: Forgiveness and marriage. In E. L. Worthington Jr. (Ed.), *Handbook of forgiveness* (pp. 207–225). New York: Brunner-Routledge.

Fredrickson, B. L. (1998). What good are positive emotions? *Review of General Psychology, 2*, 300–319.

Friedman, M., Thoresen, C. E., Gill, J. J., Ulmer, D., Powell, L. H., Price, V. A., Brown, B., Thompson, L., Rabin, D. D., Breall, W. S., Bourg, E., Levy, R., & Dixon, T. (1986). Alterations of Type A behavior and its effects on cardiac recurrent in postmyocardial infraction patients: Summary results of the coronary prevention recurrence project. *American Heart Journal, 112*, 653–665.

Gerber, L. E. (1990). Transformations of self-understanding in surgeons whose medical treatment efforts were not successful. *American Journal of Psychotherapy, 44*, 75–84.

Gisi, T. M., & D'Amato, C. (2000). What factors should be considered in rehabilitation: Are anger, social desirability, and forgiveness related in adults with traumatic brain injuries? *International Journal of Neuroscience, 105*, 121–133.

Glinder, J. G., & Compas, B. E. (1999). Self-blame attributions in women with newly diagnosed breast cancer: A prospective study of psychological adjustment. *Health Psychology, 18*, 475–481.

Gray, J. A. (1994). Personality dimensions and emotion systems. In P. Ekman & R. J. Davidson (Eds.), *The nature of emotion: Fundamental questions* (pp. 329–331). New York: Oxford University Press.

Greene, J. D., Sommerville, R. B., Nystrom, L. E., Darley, J. M., & Cohen, J. D. (2001). An fMRI investigation of emotional engagement in moral judgment. *Science, 293*, 2105–2108.

Greenwood, K. A., Thurston, R., Rumble, M., Waters, S. J., & Keefe, F. J. (2003). Anger and persistent pain: Current status and future directions. *Pain, 103*, 1–5.

Hall, J. H., & Fincham, F. D. (2005). Self-forgiveness: The stepchild of forgiveness research. *Journal of Social and Clinical Psychology, 24,* 621–637.

Hansen, M. J. (2002). Forgiveness as an educational intervention goal for persons at the end of life. *Dissertation Abstracts International, 63*(1224), 4A.

Harmon-Jones, E., Sigelman, J. D., Bohlig, A., & Harmon-Jones, C. (2003). Anger, coping, and frontal cortical activity: The effect of coping potential on anger-induced left frontal activity. *Cognition and Emotion, 17,* 1–24.

Harmon-Jones, E., Vaughn-Scott, K., Mohr, S., Sigelman, J., & Harmon-Jones, C. (2004). The effect of manipulated sympathy and anger on left and right frontal cortical activity. *Emotion, 4,* 95–101.

Harris, A. H. S., & Thoresen, C. E. (2005). Forgiveness, unforgiveness, health, and disease. In E. L. Worthington Jr. (Ed.), *Handbook of forgiveness* (pp. 321–333). New York: Brunner-Routledge.

Harris, A. H. S., & Thoresen, C. E. (2006). Extending the influence of positive psychology interventions into health care settings: Lessons from self-efficacy and forgiveness. *Journal of Positive Psychology, 1,* 27–36.

Huang, S-T. T., & Enright, R. D. (2000). Forgiveness and anger-related emotions in Taiwan: Implications for therapy. *Psychotherapy, 37,* 71–79.

Kaplan, B. H. (1992). Social health and the forgiving heart: The Type B story. *Journal of Behavioral Medicine, 15,* 3–14.

Koenig, H. (2007). Altruistic love and physical health. In S. G. Post (Ed.), *Altruism and health: Perspectives from empirical research* (pp. 422–441). Oxford: Oxford University Press.

Lawler, K. A., Younger, J. W., Piferi, R. L., Billington, E., Jobe, R., Edmondson, K., & Jones, W. H. (2003). A change of heart: Cardiovascular correlates of forgiveness in response to interpersonal conflict. *Journal of Behavioral Medicine, 26,* 373–393.

Lawler, K. A., Younger, J. W., Piferi, R. L., Jobe, R. L., Edmondson, K. A., & Jones, W. H. (2005). The unique effects of forgiveness on health: An exploration of pathways. *Journal of Behavioral Medicine, 28,* 157–167.

Lawler-Row, K. A., & Piferi, R. L. (2006). The forgiving personality: Describing a life well lived? *Personality and Individual Differences, 41,* 1009–1020.

Lieberman, M. D., Jarcho, J. M., Berman, S., Naliboff, B. D., Suyenobu, B. Y., Mandelkern, M., & Mayer, E. A. (2004). The neural correlates of placebo effects: A disruption account. *Neuroimage, 22,* 447–445.

Lin, W., Mack, D., Enright, R. D., Krahn, D., & Baskin, T. W. (2004). Effects of forgiveness therapy on anger, mood, and vulnerability to substance use among inpatient substance-dependent clients. *Journal of Consulting and Clinical Psychology, 72,* 1114–1121.

Marques, A. H., & Sternberg, E. M. (2007). The biology of positive emotions and health. In S. G. Post (Ed.), *Altruism and health: Perspectives from empirical research* (pp. 149–188). Oxford: Oxford University Press.

Mauldin, G. R., & Anderson, W. T. (1998). Forgiveness as an intervention in contextual family therapy: Two case examples. *TCA Journal, 26,* 123–132.

McCraty, R., Atkinson, M., Riller, W. A., Rein, G., & Watkins, A. D. (1995). The effects of emotion on short-term power spectrum analysis of heart rate variability. *American Journal of Cardiology, 76,* 1089–1093.

McCullough, M. E., Pargament, K. I., & Thoresen, C. E. (Eds.). (2000). *Forgiveness: Theory, research and practice*. New York: Guilford Press.

McCullough, M. E., Root, L. M., & Cohen, A. D. (2006). Writing about the benefits of an interpersonal transgression facilitates forgiveness. *Journal of Consulting and Clinical Psychology, 74*, 887–897.

McDaniel, S. H., Hepworth, J., & Doherty, W. J. (1999). The shared emotional themes of illness. *Journal of Family Psychotherapy, 10*, 1–8.

McEwen, B. S. (2002). *The end of stress as we know it*. Washington D.C.: Joseph Henry Press.

Mullet, E., Neto, F., & Riviere, S. (2005). Personality and its effects on resentment, revenge, and forgiveness and on self-forgiveness. In E. L. Worthington Jr. (Ed.), *Handbook of forgiveness* (pp. 159–182). New York: Brunner-Routledge.

Park, C. L., & Folkman, S. (1997). Meaning in the context of stress and coping. *Review of General Psychology, 1*, 115–144.

Phillips, C. F. (1999). The lived experience of spirituality and healing among persons with life-threatening cancer: Making it real. *Dissertation Abstracts International, 59*(4370), 12A.

Phillips, L. J., & Osborne, J. W. (1989). Cancer patients' experiences of forgiveness therapy. *Canadian Journal of Counseling, 23*, 236–251.

Pietrini, P., & Guazzelli, M. (1997). Life events in the course of chronic diseases: A psychological myth or a psycho-neurobiochemical loop? *Clinical and Experimental Rheumatology, 15*, 125–128.

Pietrini, P., Guazzelli, M., & Grafman, J. (1998). Gender differences in brain activation during aggressive imageries. *International Journal of Psychophysiology, 30*(1–2), 33.

Pietrini, P., Guazzelli, M., Basso, G., Jaffe, K., & Grafman, J. (2000). Neural correlates of imaginal aggressive behavior assessed by positron emission tomography in healthy subjects. *American Journal of Psychiatry, 157*, 1772–1781.

Pietrini, P., Ricciardi, E., Gentili, C., Vanello, N., Sani, L., & Guazzelli, M. (2004). How the brain responds to hurtful events: neural activity elicited by aggressive versus forgiving behavior in humans. *International Journal of Psychophysiology, 54*(1–2), 26.

Rainville, P., Duncan, G. H., Price, D. D., Carrier, B., & Bushnell, M. C. (1997). Pain affect encoded in human anterior cingulate but not somatosensory cortex. *Science, 277*, 968–971.

Rippentrop, A. E., Altmaier, E. M., Chen, J. J., Found, E. M., & Keffala, V. J. (2005). The relationship between religion/spirituality and physical health, mental health, and pain in a chronic pain population. *Pain, 116*, 311–321.

Romero, C., Friedman, L. C., Kalidas, M., Elledge, R., Chang, J., & Liscum, K. R. (2006). Self-forgiveness, spirituality, and psychological adjustment in women with breast cancer. *Journal of Behavioral Medicine, 29*, 29–36.

Schwartz, A. R., Gerin, W., Davidson, K. W., Pickering, T. G., Brosschot, J. F., Thayer, J. F., Christenfeld, N., & Linden, W. (2003). Toward a causal model of cardiovascular responses to stress and the development of cardiovascular disease. *Psychosomatic Medicine, 65*, 22–35.

Seybold, K. S., Hill, P. C., Neumann, J. K., & Chi, D. S. (2001). Physiological and psychological correlates of forgiveness. *Journal of Psychology and Christianity, 20*, 250–259.

Smith, R. S. (1989). Psychological trauma following automobile accidents: A review of literature. *American Journal of Forensic Psychology, 7*, 5–20.

Stone, B. E. (2001). Cancer as initiation: Surviving the fire. *Dissertation Abstracts International: Section B: The Sciences and Engineering, 62*(1-B), 593.

Toussaint, L. L., & Williams, D. R. (October, 2003). Physiological correlates of forgiveness: Findings from a racially and socioeconomically diverse sample of community residents. Presented at A Campaign for Forgiveness Research Conference, Atlanta, GA.

Toussaint, L. L., Williams, D. R., Musick, M. A., & Everson, S. A. (2001). Forgiveness and health: Age differences in a U.S. probability sample. *Journal of Adult Development, 8*, 249–257.

Waltman, M. A. (2003). The psychological and physiological effects of forgiveness education in male patients with coronary artery disease. *Dissertation Abstracts International, 63*(3971), 8–B.

Witvliet, C. V. O. (2001). Forgiveness and health: Review and reflections on a matter of faith, feelings, and physiology. *Journal of Psychology and Theology, 29*, 212–224.

Witvliet, C. V. O., Ludwig, T. E., & Vander Laan, K. (2001). Granting forgiveness or harboring grudges: Implications for emotion, physiology, and health. *Psychological Science, 12*, 117–123.

Witvliet, C. V. O., Ludwig, T. E., & Bauer, D. (2002). Please forgive me: Transgressors' emotions and physiology during imagery of seeking forgiveness and victim responses. *Journal of Psychology and Christianity, 21*, 219–233.

Witvliet, C. V. O., & McCullough, M. E. (2007). Forgiveness and health: A review and theoretical exploration of emotion pathways. In S.G. Post (Ed.), *Altruism and health: Perspectives from empirical research* (pp. 259–276). Oxford: Oxford University Press.

Witvliet, C. V. O., Worthington, E. L., Jr., Root, L. M., Sato, A. F., Ludwig, T. E., & Exline, J. J. (in press). Retributive justice, restorative justice, and forgiveness: An experimental psychophysiology analysis. *Journal of Experimental Social Psychology*, in press.

Worthington, E. L. Jr. (2001). Unforgiveness, forgiveness, and reconciliation in societies. In R. G. Helmick & R. L. Petersen (Eds.), *Forgiveness and reconciliation: Religion, public policy, and conflict transformation* (pp. 161–182). Philadelphia: Templeton Foundation Press.

Worthington, E. L. Jr. (Ed.). (2005a). *Handbook of forgiveness*. New York: Brunner-Routledge.

Worthington, E. L. Jr. (2005b). More questions about forgiveness: Research agenda for 2005–2015. In E. L. Worthington Jr. (Ed.), *Handbook of forgiveness* (pp. 557–574). New York: Brunner-Routledge.

Worthington, E. L. Jr. (2006). *Forgiveness and reconciliation: Theory and application*. New York: Brunner-Routledge.

Worthington, E. L. Jr., & Scherer, M. (2004). Forgiveness is an emotion-focused coping strategy that can reduce health risks and promote health resilience: Theory, review, and hypotheses. *Psychology and Health, 19*, 385–405.

Worthington, E. L. Jr., Witvliet, C. V. O., Lerner, A. J., & Scherer, M. (2005). Forgiveness in medical practice and research. *EXPLORE: The Journal of Science and Healing, 1*, 169–176.

Editor's Note

The first author gratefully acknowledges support for the present project by the Fetzer Institute, grant # 2254.01 and the General Clinical Research Center at Virginia Commonwealth University, NIH 5M01 RR000065–410535. For the second author, this manuscript contributes to an interdisciplinary project on The Pursuit of Happiness established by the Center for the Study of Law and Religion at Emory University and the John Templeton Foundation.

E. L. Worthington Jr, A. J. Miller, Virginia Commonwealth University, 806 West Franklin, Box 842018, Richmond, VA 23284-2018, USA
e-mail: eworth@vcu.edu

C. V. O. Witvliet, Hope College, Holland, MI, USA

P. Pietrini, University of Pisa Medical School, Pisa, Italy

Discussion Questions for Article 2

Section 12: Stress, Health and Coping

Name: _____

PID: _____

Date: __ __ / __ __ / __ __ (MM/DD/YY)

CRN: _____

Recitation Day/Time: _____

Honor Code Signature: _____

1. Explain the difference between forgiveness and forgivingness.

2. Explain the difference between emotional forgiveness and decisional forgiveness.

3. Can you think of a time when you were either forgiving or unforgiving and how it affected your stress levels?

4. What brain region(s) were most associated with forgiveness and empathy?

Section 13
Social Psychology

W hat is one way to influence how to sell products or persuade voters to vote for either Barack Obama or John McCain? Social psychology is one of the most fascinating and fast growing fields in the area of psychology. It has contributed significantly to the understanding of the world around us. In a field that was once ruled by behaviorists and cognitive psychologists, social psychology emerged to fill in the gaps untouched by these areas and gave us a different viewpoint on the behaviors of individuals. Not only does it have relevance in our field, social psychology has also been utilized in a variety of other disciplines as well, such as business, marketing, communications, and politics. As the world changes, so does the field of social psychology as more social phenomena are being discovered and examined by social psychologists each day.

One tenet of social psychology is that people's behaviors are influenced by the situation. All too often, people underestimate the power of the situation when trying to explain why people behave the way they do. As seen in Phillip Zimbardo's infamous prison study, the "guards" and the "prisoners" became so involved in the situation that their behaviors actually resembled those of real guards and prison inmates. Another tenet of social psychology is conformity to the majority group. Whether it's a conscious or unconscious behavior, it is possible for each person at some point in his or her life to sacrifice his or her independent nature to seem similar to the majority. Solomon Asch demonstrated this phenomenon when he had confederates give wrong answers to a perceptual task to see if the research participants would act alone and go with the non-ambiguous right answer or blend in with the group and give the wrong answer. As you can guess, some of the participants conformed to the group.

A final tenet of social psychology is that it can explain the social processes that influence a person's performance and behavior. Claude Steele found minorities' performance in a task could be hampered by the salience of a negative stereotype associated with that ethnic group during the task. This process Steele refers to as stereotype threat. Finally, through understanding cultural norms and stereotypes, we can understand the interactive behaviors of others in our own and other societies. Social psychology is full of classic studies that can explain behavior in a variety of situations. As the field of social psychology continually progresses, more knowledge is being accumulated about the social processes that influence our behavior. In the present section, the articles cover classic studies emphasizing the social psychology tenets discussed above. As you read the following articles, keep in mind the factors of the situation that come into play as the research participants are forced to make difficult decisions. Will they act alone and stand up for their beliefs, or will they give in to the social pressure?

Article 1: Behavioral Study of Obedience

Looking back on the history of this world, we see people brutally hurt and killed by what appears to be normal people. What was once thought to be due to individual personality flaws was later observed by Milgram as obedience. Noting the obedient behaviors of German soldiers killing innocent bystanders during World War 2, Milgram constructed an experiment to examine if naïve subjects would continue to be obedient while administering what they believed to be extremely painful shocks to another subject (who was in fact a confederate). As Milgram watched many subjects experience emotional distress during the study, the results he obtained shocked his colleagues and assistants alike. He found that 65% of the research participants were willing to give the maximum shock value, which was underestimated by everyone surveyed. Milgram's study provides evidence that the engrained nature to be obedient can overpower one's moral character. Additionally, his study shows that before we judge a person by their actions we must take into account the power of the situation a person is facing.

Article 2: Effects of Confederate and Subject Gender on Conformity in a Color Classification Task

Whether it's a fashion trend or an unwanted judgment, we, as human beings, feel the need to fit in and belong. Therefore, we tend to conform to the majority group in order to be seen in a favorable light, in other words so we can be accepted. The social phenomenon of conformity was introduced by Asch in the 1950's, in which he showed how participants' objective judgments could be influenced by confederates. Since Asch's (1951, 1956) conformity studies, recent conformity studies (Perrin and Spencer, 1981 & Lalancette and Standing, 1990) have failed to replicate the conformity effect observed by Asch. In the article, Collins, Sano, and Malik investigate whether conformity still exists, and if so, whether a gender difference is present. Using a modified Asch (1956) paradigm, they showed conformity is indeed a social phenomenon apparent in the today's culture. They also found that females conformed more than males and attribute this gender difference in conformity to female emotional sensitivity.

—*Christopher O. Downing, Jr.*

Article 1

Behavioral Study of Obedience

Stanley Milgram

This chapter describes a procedure for the study of destructive obedience in the laboratory. It consists of ordering a naive S to administer increasingly more severe punishment to a victim in the context of a learning experiment. Punishment is administered by means of a shock generator with thirty graded switches ranging from Slight Shock to Danger: Severe Shock. The victim is a confederate of the E. The primary dependent variable is the maximum shock the S is willing to administer before he refuses to continue further. Twenty-six Ss obeyed the experimental commands fully, and administered the highest shock on the generator. Fourteen Ss broke off the experiment at some point after the victim protested and refused to provide further answers. The procedure created extreme levels of nervous tension in some Ss. Profuse sweating, trembling and stuttering were typical expressions of this emotional disturbance. One unexpected sign of tension—yet to be explained—was the regular occurrence of nervous laughter, which in some Ss developed into uncontrollable seizures. The variety of interesting behavioral dynamics observed in the experiment, the reality of the situation for the S and the possibility of parametric variation within the framework of the procedure, point to the fruitfulness of further study.

Obedience is as basic an element in the structure of social life as one can point to. Some system of authority is a requirement of all communal living, and it is only the man dwelling in isolation who is not forced to respond, through defiance or submission, to the commands of others. Obedience, as a determinant of behavior, is of particular relevance to our time. It has been reliably established that from 1933–1945 millions of innocent persons were systematically slaughtered on command. Gas chambers were built, death camps were guarded, daily quotas of corpses were produced with the same efficiency as the manufacture of appliances. These inhumane policies may have originated in the mind of a single person, hut they could only be carried out on a massive scale if a very large number of persons obeyed orders.

Obedience is the psychological mechanism that links individual action to political purpose. It is the dispositional cement that binds men to systems of authority. Facts of recent history and observation in daily life suggest that for many persons obedience may be a deeply ingrained behavior tendency, indeed, a prepotent impulse overriding training in ethics, sympathy, and moral conduct. C. P. Snow (1961) points to its importance when he writes:

> When you think of the long and gloomy history of man, you will find more hideous crimes have been committed in the name of obedience than have ever been committed in the name of rebellion. If you doubt that, read William Shirer's "Rise and Fall of the Third Reich." The German Officer Corps were brought up in the most rigorous code of obedience . . . in the name of obedience they were party to, and assisted in, the most wicked large scale actions in the history of the world [p. 24].

While the particular form of obedience dealt with in the present study has its antecedents in these episodes, it must not be thought all obedience entails acts of aggression against others. Obedience serves numerous productive functions. Indeed, the very life of society is predicated on its existence. Obedience may be ennobling and educative and refer to acts of charity and kindness, as well as to destruction.

General Procedure

A procedure was devised which seems useful as a tool for studying obedience (Milgram, 1961). It consists of ordering a naive subject to administer electric shock to a victim. A simulated shock generator is used, with 30 clearly marked voltage levels that range from 15 to 450 volts. The instrument bears verbal designations that range from Slight Shock to Danger: Severe Shock. The responses of the victim, who is a trained confederate of the experimenter, are standardized. The orders to administer shocks arc given to the naive subject in the context of a "learning experiment" ostensibly set up to study the effects of punishment on memory. As the experiment proceeds the naive subject is commanded to administer increasingly more intense shocks to the victim, even to the point of reaching the level marked Danger: Severe Shock. Internal resistances become stronger, and at a certain point the subject refuses to go on with the experiment. Behavior prior to this rupture is considered "obedience," in that the subject complies with the commands of the experimenter. The point of rupture is the act of disobedience. A quantitative value is assigned to the subject's performance based on the maximum intensity shock he is willing to administer before he refuses to participate further. Thus for any particular subject and for any particular experimental condition the degree of obedience may be specified with a numerical value. The crux of the study is to systematically vary the factors believed to alter the degree of obedience to the experimental commands.

The technique allows important variables to be manipulated at several points in the experiment. One may vary aspects of the source of command, content and form of command, instrumentalities for its execution, target object, general social setting, etc. The problem, therefore, is not one of designing increasingly more numerous experimental conditions, but of selecting those that best illuminate *the process* of obedience from the sociopsychological standpoint.

Related Studies

The inquiry bears an important relation to philosophic analyses of obedience and authority (Arendt, 1958; Friedrich, 1958; Weber, 1947), an early experimental study of obedience by Frank (1944), studies in "authoritarianism" (Adorno, Frenkel-Brunswik, Levinson, and Sanford, 1950; Rokeach, 1961), and a recent series of analytic and empirical studies in social power (Cartwright, 1959). It owes much to the long concern with *suggestion* in social psychology, both in its normal forms (e.g., Binet, 1900) and in its clinical manifestations (Charcot, 1881). But it derives, in the first instance, from direct observation of a social fact; the individual who is commanded by a legitimate authority ordinarily obeys. Obedience comes easily and often. It is a ubiquitous and indispensable feature of social life.

Method

Subjects

The subjects were 40 males between the ages of 20 and 50, drawn from New Haven and the surrounding communities. Subjects were obtained by a newspaper advertisement and direct mail solicitation. Those who responded to the appeal believed they were to participate in a study of memory and learning at Yale University. A wide range of occupations is represented in the sample. Typical subjects were postal clerks, high school teachers, salesmen, engineers, and laborers. Subjects ranged in educational level from one who had not finished elementary school, to those who had doctorate and other professional degrees. They were paid $4.50 for their participation in the experiment. However, subjects were told that payment was simply for coming to the laboratory, and that the money was theirs no matter what

TABLE 1 Distribution of age and occupational types in the experiment.

Occupations	20–29 years n	30–39 years n	40–50 years n	Percentage of total (occupations)
Workers, skilled and unskilled	4	5	6	37.5
Sales, business, and white-collar	3	6	7	40.0
Professional	1	5	3	22.5
Percentage of total	20	40	40	

Note: Total $N = 40$.

happened after they arrived. Table 1 shows the proportion of age and occupational types assigned to the experimental condition.

Personnel and Locale

The experiment was conducted on the grounds of Yale University in the elegant interaction laboratory. (This detail is relevant to the perceived legitimacy of the experiment. In further variations, the experiment was dissociated from the university, with consequences for performance.) The role of experimenter was played by a 31-year-old high school teacher of biology. His manner was impassive, and his appearance somewhat stern throughout the experiment. He was dressed in a gray technician's coat. The victim was played by a 47-year-old accountant, trained for the role; he was of Irish-American stock, whom most observers found mild-mannered and likable.

Procedure

One naive subject and one victim (an accomplice) performed in each experiment. A pretext had to be devised that would justify the administration of electric shock by the naive subject. This was effectively accomplished by the cover story. After a general introduction on the presumed relation between punishment and learning, subjects were told:

> But actually, we know very little about the effect of punishment on learning, because almost no truly scientific studies have been made of it in human beings.
>
> For instance, we don't know how much punishment is best for learning—and we don't know how much difference it makes as to who is giving the punishment, whether an adult learns best from a younger or an older person than himself—or many things of that sort.
>
> So in this study we are bringing together a number of adults of different occupations and ages. And we're asking some of them to be teachers and some of them to be learners.

We want to find out just what effect different people have on each other as teachers and learners, and also what effect punishment will have on learning in this situation.

Therefore, I'm going to ask one of you to be the teacher here tonight and the other one to be the learner.

Does either of you have a preference?

Subjects then drew slips of paper from a hat to determine who would be the teacher and who would be the learner in the experiment. The drawing was rigged so that the naive subject was always the teacher and the accomplice always the learner. (Both slips contained the word "Teacher.") Immediately after the drawing the teacher and learner were taken to an adjacent room and the learner was strapped into an "electric chair" apparatus.

The experimenter explained that the straps were to prevent excessive movement while the learner was being shocked. The effect was to make it impossible for him to escape from the situation. An electrode was attached to the learner's wrist, and electrode paste was applied "to avoid blisters and burns." Subjects were told that the electrode was attached to the shock generator in the adjoining room.

In order to improve credibility the experimenter declared, in response to a question by the learner: "Although the shocks can be extremely painful, they cause no permanent tissue damage."

Learning Task   The lesson administered by the subject was a paired-associate learning task. The subject read a series of word pairs to the learner, and then read the first word of the pair along with four terms. The learner was to indicate which of the four terms had originally been paired with the first word. He communicated his answer by pressing one of four switches in front of him, which in turn lit up one of four numbered quadrants in an answer-box located atop the shock generator.

Shock Generator   The instrument panel consists of 30 lever switches set in a horizontal line. Each switch is clearly labeled with a voltage designation that ranges from 15 to 450 volts. There is a 15-volt-increment from one switch to the next going from left to right. In addition, the following verbal designations are clearly indicated for groups of four switches going from left to right: Slight Shock, Moderate Shock, Strong Shock, Very Strong Shock, Intense Shock, Extreme Intensity Shock, Danger: Severe Shock. (Two switches after this last designation are simply marked XXX.)

Upon depressing a switch: a pilot light corresponding to each switch is illuminated in bright red; an electric buzzing is heard; an electric blue light, labeled "voltage energizer," flashes; the dial on the voltage meter swings to the right; various relay clicks are sounded.

The upper left-hand corner of the generator is labeled Shock Generator. Type ZLB, Dyson Instrument Company, Waltham, Mass. Output 15 Volts 450 Volts.

Details of the instrument were carefully handled to insure an appearance of authenticity. The panel was engraved by precision industrial engravers, and all components were of high quality. No subject in the experiment suspected that the instrument was merely a simulated shock generator.

Sample Shock   Each naive subject is given a sample shock on the shock generator, prior to beginning his run as teacher. This shock is always 45 volts, and is applied by pressing the third switch of the generator. The shock is applied to the wrist of the naive subject and has its source in a 45-volt battery wired into the generator. This further convinces the subject of the authenticity of the generator.[1]

Shock Instructions   The subject is told to administer a shock to the learner each time he gives a wrong response. Moreover—and this is the key command—the subject is instructed to "move one lever higher on the shock generator each time the learner flashes a wrong answer." He is also instructed to announce the voltage level before administering a shock. This serves to continually remind subjects of the increasing intensity of shocks administered to the learner.

Preliminary and Regular Run   Pretests revealed that the procedure of reading words and administering shocks requires some practice before it can be handled smoothly. Therefore, immediately preceding the regular run, the teacher is given a preliminary series of 10 words to read to the learner. There are 3 neutral words in the practice series (i.e., words that the learner answers correctly), so that shocks are administered for 7 of the words, with the maximum shock at 105 volts (moderate shock). Almost all subjects master the procedure by the time the preliminary run is over.

Subjects are then presented with a second list, and are told that the procedure is the same as for the first list; the experimenter adds, however:

> When you get to the bottom of the list, repeat it over again, and continue
> giving shocks, until the learner has learned all the pairs correctly.

The experimenter instructs the subject to

> start from 15 volts and increase the shock level one step each time the
> learner gives a wrong answer.

Feedback from the Victim   In all conditions the learner gives a predetermined set of responses to the word pair test, based on a schedule of approximately three wrong answers to one correct answer. In the present experimental condition no vocal response or other sign of protest is heard from the learner until Shock Level 300 is reached. When the 300-volt shock is administered, the learner pounds on the wall of the room in which he is bound to the electric chair. The pounding can be heard by the subject. From this point on, the learner's answers no longer appear on the four-way panel.

At this juncture, subjects ordinarily turn to the experimenter for guidance. The experimenter instructs the subject to treat the absence of a response as a wrong answer, and to shock the subject according to the usual schedule. He advises the subjects to allow 5–10 seconds before considering no response as a wrong answer, and to increase the shock level one step each time the learner fails to respond correctly. The learner's pounding is repeated after the 315-volt shock is administered; afterwards he is not heard from, nor do his answers reappear on the four-way signal box.

Experimenter Feedback   At various points in the experiment the subject may turn to the experimenter for advice on whether he should continue to administer shocks. Or he may indicate that he does not wish to go on. It was important to standardize the experimenter's responses to these inquiries and reactions.

If the subject indicated his unwillingness to go on, the experimenter responded with a sequence of "prods," using as many as necessary to bring the subject into line.

Prod 1: Please continue. Or Please go on.

Prod 2: The experiment requires that you continue.

Prod 3: It is absolutely essential that you continue.

Prod 4: You have no other choice. You must go on.

The prods were always made in sequence: Only if Prod 1 had been unsuccessful, could Prod 2 be used. If the subject refused to obey the experimenter after Prod 4, the experiment was terminated. The experimenter's tone of voice was at all times firm, but not impolite. The sequence was begun anew on each occasion that the subject balked or showed reluctance to follow orders.

Special Prods   If the subject asked if the learner was liable to suffer permanent physical injury, the experimenter said:

Although the shocks may be painful, there is no permanent tissue damage, so please go on. [Followed by Prods 2, 3, and 4 if necessary.]

If the subject said that the learner did not want to go on, the experimenter replied:

Whether the learner likes it or not, you must go on until he has learned all the word pairs correctly. So please go on. [Followed by Prods 2, 3, and 4 if necessary.]

Dependent Measures

The primary dependent measure for any subject is the maximum shock he administers before he refuses to go any further. In principle this may vary from 0 (for a subject who refuses to administer even the first shock) to 30 (for a subject who administers the highest shock on the generator). A subject who breaks off the experiment at any point prior to administering the thirtieth shock level is termed a *defiant* subject. One who complies with experimental commands fully, and proceeds to administer all shock levels commanded, is termed an *obedient* subject.

Further Records   With few exceptions, experimental sessions were recorded on magnetic tape. Occasional photographs were taken through one-way mirrors. Notes were kept on any unusual behavior occurring during the course of the experiments. On occasion, additional observers were directed to write objective descriptions of the subjects' behavior. The latency and duration of shocks were measured by accurate timing devices.

Interview and Dehoax   Following the experiment, subjects were interviewed, open-ended questions, projective measures, and attitude scales were employed. After the interview, procedures were undertaken to assure that the subject would leave the laboratory in a state of well being. A friendly reconciliation was arranged between the subject and the victim, and an effort was made to reduce any tensions that arose as a result of the experiment.

Results

Preliminary Notions

Before giving an account of the experimental results, it is instructive to consider how persons predict others will perform when commanded to administer powerful shocks to another person. Fourteen Yale seniors, all psychology majors, were provided with a detailed description of the experimental situation. They were asked to reflect carefully on it, and to predict the behavior of 100 hypothetical subjects. More specifically, they were instructed to plot the distribution of obedience of "100 Americans of diverse occupations, and ranging in age from 20 to 50 years," who were placed in the experimental situation.

There was considerable agreement among the respondents on the expected behavior of hypothetical subjects. All respondents predicted that only an insignificant minority would go through to the end of the shock series. (The estimates ranged from 0 to 3 percent: i.e., the most "pessimistic" member of the class predicted that of 100 persons, 3 would continue through to the most potent shock available on the shock generator 150 volts.) The class mean was 1.2 percent. The question was also posed informally to colleagues of the author, and the most general feeling was that few if any subjects would go beyond the designation Very Strong Shock.

Result of Experiment I

Subjects Accept Situation   With few exceptions subjects were convinced of the reality of the experimental situation, that they were administering shocks to another person, and the most potent shocks were extremely painful. In the post-experimental interview subjects were asked: "How painful to the learner were the last few shocks that you administered to him?" Subjects were instructed to indicate their answers on a printed 14-point scale ranging from "Not at all painful" to "Extremely painful." The modal response was 14 (Extremely painful) with the mean at 13.42.

Signs of Extreme Tension   Many subjects showed signs of nervousness in the experimental situation, and especially upon administering the more powerful shocks. In a large number of cases the degree of tension reached extremes that are rarely seen in sociopsychological laboratory studies. Subjects were observed to sweat, tremble, stutter, bite their lips, groan, and dig their fingernails into their flesh. These were characteristic rather than exceptional responses to the experiment.

One sign of tension was the regular occurrence of nervous laughing fits. Fourteen of the 40 subjects showed definite signs of nervous laughter and smiling. The laughter seemed entirely out of place, even bizarre. Full-blown, uncontrollable seizures were observed for 3 subjects. On one occasion we observed a seizure so violently convulsive that it was necessary to call a halt to the experiment. The subject, a 46-year-old encyclopedia salesman, was seriously embarrassed by his untoward and uncontrollable behavior. In the post-experimental interviews subjects took pains to point out that they were not sadistic types, and that the laughter did not mean they enjoyed shocking the victim.

Distribution of Scores   It had been conjectured that persons would not, in general, agree to administer shocks beyond the level designated as Very Strong Shock. The distribution of maximum shocks for this experiment is shown in Table 2. The obtained distribution of scores deviates radically from the prediction.

Upon command of the experimenter, each of the 40 subjects went beyond the expected breakoff point. No subject stopped prior to administering Shock Level 20. (At this level—300 volts—the victim kicks on the wall and no longer provides answers to the teacher's multiple-choice questions.)

Of the 40 subjects, 5 refused to obey the experimental commands beyond the 300-volt level. Four more subjects administered one further shock, and then refused to go on. Two broke off at the 330-volt level, and 1 each at 345, 360, and 375 volts. Thus a total of 14 subjects defied the experimenter. It is instructive to reprint their remarks at the point of defiance, as transcribed from the tape recordings:

> *[0124] I think he's trying to communicate, he's knocking . . . Well it's not fair to shock the guy . . . these are terrific volts. I don't think this is very humane . . .*
> *Oh, I can't go on with this; no, this isn't right. It's a hell of an experiment. The*

TABLE 2   Distribution of breakoff points.

Verbal designation and voltage indication	Number of subjects for whom this was maximum shock
Slight shock	
15	0
30	0
45	0
60	0
Moderate shock	
75	0
90	0
105	0
120	0
Strong shock	
135	0
150	0
165	0
180	0
Very strong shock	
195	0
210	0
225	0
240	0
Intense shock	
255	0
270	0
285	0
300	5
Extreme intensity shock	
315	4
330	2
345	1
360	1
Danger: severe shock	
375	1
390	0
405	0
420	0
XXX	
435	0
450	26

guy is suffering in there. No, I don't want to go on. This is crazy. [Subject refused to administer more shocks.]

[0123] He's banging in there. I'm gonna chicken out. I'd like to continue, but I can't do that to a man . . . I'm sorry I can't do that to a man. I'll hurt his heart. You take your check . . . No really, I couldn't do it.

These subjects were frequently in a highly agitated and even angered state. Sometimes, verbal protest was at a minimum, and the subject simply got up from his chair in front of the shock generator, and indicated that he wished to leave the laboratory.

Of the 40 subjects, 26 obeyed the orders of the experimenter to the end, proceeding to punish the victim until they reached the most potent shock available on the shock generator. At that point, the experimenter called a halt to the session. (The maximum shock is labeled 450 volts, and is two steps beyond the designation: Danger: Severe Shock.) Although obedient subjects continued to administer shocks, they often did so under extreme stress. Some expressed reluctance to administer shocks beyond the 300-volt level, and displayed fears similar to those who defied the experimenter; yet they obeyed.

After the maximum shocks had been delivered, and the experimenter called a halt to the proceedings, many obedient subjects heaved sighs of relief, mopped their brows, rubbed their fingers over their eyes, or nervously fumbled cigarettes. Some shook their heads, apparently in regret. Some subjects had remained calm throughout the experiment, and displayed only minimal signs of tension from beginning to end.

Discussion

The experiment yielded two findings that were surprising. The first finding concerns the sheer strength of obedient tendencies manifested in this situation. Subjects have learned from childhood that it is a fundamental breach of moral conduct to hurt another person against his will. Yet, 26 subjects abandon this tenet in following the instructions of an authority who has no special powers to enforce his commands. To disobey would bring no material loss to the subject; no punishment would ensue. It is clear from the remarks and outward behavior of many participants that in punishing the victim they are often acting against their own values. Subjects often expressed deep disapproval of shocking a man in the face of his objections, and others denounced it as stupid and senseless. Yet the majority complied with the experimental commands. This outcome was surprising from two perspectives: first, from the standpoint of predictions made in the questionnaire described earlier. (Here, however, it is possible that the remoteness of the respondents from the actual situation, and the difficulty of conveying to them the concrete details of the experiment, could account for the serious underestimation of obedience.)

But the results were also unexpected to persons who observed the experiment in progress, through one-way mirrors. Observers often uttered expressions of disbelief upon seeing a subject administer more powerful shocks to the victim. These persons had a full acquaintance with the details of the situation, and yet systematically underestimated the amount of obedience that subjects would display.

The second unanticipated effect was the extraordinary tension generated by the procedures. One might suppose that a subject would simply break off or continue as his conscience dictated. Yet, this is very far from what happened. There were striking reactions of tension and emotional strain. One observer related:

> I observed a mature and initially poised businessman enter the laboratory smiling and confident. Within 20 minutes he was reduced to a twitching, stuttering wreck, who was rapidly approaching a point of nervous collapse. He constantly pulled on his earlobe, and twisted his hands. At one point he pushed his fist into his forehead and muttered: "Oh God, let's stop it." And yet he continued to respond to every word of the experimenter, and obeyed to the end.

Any understanding of the phenomenon of obedience must rest on an analysis of the particular conditions in which it occurs. The following features of the experiment go some distance in explaining the high amount of obedience observed in the situation.

1. The experiment is sponsored by and takes place on the grounds of an institution of unimpeachable reputation, Yale University. It may be reasonably presumed that the personnel are competent and reputable. The importance of this background authority is now being studied by conducting a series of experiments outside of New Haven, and without any visible ties to the university.

2. The experiment is, on the face of it, designed to attain a worthy purpose—advancement of knowledge about learning and memory. Obedience occurs not as an end in itself, but as an instrumental element in a situation that the subject construes as significant, and meaningful. He may not be able to see its full significance, but he may properly assume that the experimenter does.

3. The subject perceives that the victim has voluntarily submitted to the authority system of the experimenter. He is not (at first) an unwilling captive impressed for involuntary service. He has taken the trouble to come to the laboratory presumably to aid the experimental research. That he later becomes an involuntary subject does not alter the fact that, initially, he consented to participate without qualification. Thus he has in some degree incurred an obligation toward the experimenter.

4. The subject, too, has entered the experiment voluntarily, and perceives himself under obligation to aid the experimenter. He has made a commitment, and to disrupt the experiment is a repudiation of this initial promise of aid.

5. Certain features of the procedure strengthen the subject's sense of obligation to the experimenter. For one, he has been paid for coming to the laboratory. In part this is canceled out by the experimenter's statement that:

   Of course, as in all experiments, the money is yours simply for coming to the laboratory. From this point on, no matter what happens, the money is yours.[2]

6. From the subject's standpoint, the fact that he is the teacher and the other man the learner is purely a chance consequence (it is determined by drawing lots) and he, the subject, ran the same risk as the other man in being assigned the role of learner. Since the assignment of positions in the experiment was achieved by fair means, the learner is deprived of any basis of complaint on this count. (A similar situation obtains in Army units, in which—in the absence of volunteers— a particularly dangerous mission may be assigned by drawing lots, and the unlucky soldier is expected to bear his misfortune with sportsmanship.)

7. There is, at best, ambiguity with regard to the prerogatives of a psychologist and the corresponding rights of his subject. There is a vagueness of expectation concerning what a psychologist may require of his subject, and when he is overstepping acceptable limits. Moreover, the experiment occurs in a closed setting, and thus provides no opportunity for the subject to remove these ambiguities by discussion with others. There are few standards that seem directly applicable to the situation, which is a novel one for most subjects.

8. The subjects are assured that the shocks administered to the subject are "painful but not dangerous." Thus they assume that the discomfort caused the victim is momentary, while the scientific gains resulting from the experiment are enduring.

9. Through Shock Level 20 the victim continues to provide answers on the signal box. The subject may construe this as a sign that the victim is still willing to "play the game." It is only after Shock Level 20 that the victim repudiates the rules completely, refusing to answer further.

   These features help to explain the high amount of obedience obtained in this experiment. Many of the arguments raised need not remain matters of speculation, but can be reduced to testable propositions to be confirmed or disproved by further experiments.[3]

   The following features of the experiment concern the nature of the conflict which the subject faces.

10. The subject is placed in a position in which he must respond to the competing demands of two persons: the experimenter and the victim. The conflict must be resolved by meeting the demands of one or the other; satisfaction of the victim and the experimenter are mutually exclusive. Moreover, the resolution must take the form of a highly visible action, that of continuing to shock

the victim or breaking off the experiment. Thus the subject is forced into a public conflict that docs not permit any completely satisfactory solution.

11. While the demands of the experimenter carry the weight of scientific authority, the demands of the victim spring from his personal experience of pain and suffering. The two claims need not be regarded as equally pressing and legitimate. The experimenter seeks an abstract scientific datum; the victim cries out for relief from physical suffering caused by the subject's actions.

12. The experiment gives the subject little time for reflection. The conflict comes on rapidly. It is only minutes after the subject has been seated before the shock generator that the victim begins his protests. Moreover, the subject perceives that he has gone through but two-thirds of the shock levels at the time the subject's first protests are heard. Thus he understands that the conflict will have a persistent aspect to it, and may well become more intense as increasingly more powerful shocks are required. The rapidity with which the conflict descends on the subject, and his realization that it is predictably recurrent may well be sources of tension to him.

13. At a more general level, the conflict stems from the opposition of two deeply ingrained behavior dispositions: first, the disposition not to harm other people, and second, the tendency to obey those whom we perceive to be legitimate authorities.

Notes

1. A related technique, making use of a shock generator, was reported by Buss (1961) for the study of aggression in the laboratory. Despite the considerable similarity of technical detail in the experimental procedures, each investigator proceeded in ignorance of the other's work. Milgram provided plans and photographs of his shock generator, experimental procedure, and first results in a report to the National Science Foundation in January 1961. This report received only limited circulation. Buss reported his procedure six months later, but to a wider audience. Subsequently, technical information and reports were exchanged. The present article was first received in the editor's office on December 27, 1961; it was resubmitted with deletions on July 27, 1962.

2. Forty-three subjects, undergraduates at Yale University, were run in the experiment without payment. The results are very similar to those obtained with paid subjects.

3. A series of recently completed experiments employing the obedience paradigm is reported in Milgram (1965).

References

Full bibliographic references available from your instructor.

Discussion Questions for Article 1

Section 13: Social Psychology

Name: _____

PID: _____

Date: __ __ / __ __ / __ __ (MM/DD/YY)

CRN: _____

Recitation Day/Time: _____

Honor Code Signature: _____

1. What steps did Milgram take to ensure the authenticity of the situation to the research participant?

2. Several of the participants were found to be laughing. Why did the researchers say this happened? Why do you think this happened? What did the experimenters do to ameliorate any negative effects the study may have had on the participants?

3. Did the results from the experiment turn out as the experimenter's colleagues and students predicted? Explain.

4. If Milgram's Obedience Study was conducted in today's culture, do you think the results would be the same or differ? Explain.

Effects of Confederate and Subject Gender on Conformity in a Color Classification Task

Charles A. Collin
Fred Di Sano
Rajesh Malik

Thirty-four college students were asked to classify ambiguous colors (e.g., blue-green) into their components (e.g., blue or green). They did this first while alone and later with confederates who opposed their previous answers. It was found that most subjects conformed to some degree, with results matching those of classic conformity studies. An ANOVA indicated that female subjects conformed more than males, but that there were no differences based on the gender of the confederates. An interpretation based on superior female emotional sensitivity is offered as an alternative to past explanations of this recurring gender difference.

Ever since Asch's (1951, 1956) classic conformity studies, gender differences in social influenceability have been a topic of interest. A great deal of early literature seems to support a higher level of conformity in females (see Sistrunk & McDavid, (1971) for an extensive list). There are exceptions, however. Crutchfield (1955) found that college-aged women conformed more than college-aged men, but that older women (in their 40's) conformed less than men in that same age group.

More recent findings have also been contradictory. Three literature reviews (Cooper 1979; Eagly, 1978; Maccoby & Jacklin, 1974) demonstrated, through the voting method, that there was little evidence for gender differences in conformity. However, a meta-analysis by Eagly and Carli (1981) found evidence that women did conform more than men in most experimental situations.

A variety of explanations have been offered for these alleged gender differences. Early researchers concentrated on sex-roles, hypothesizing that it was the social expectation for females to be more submissive which led to greater conformity in women (Kretch, Crutchfield, & Ballachey, 1962; Worchel & Cooper, 1976). However, Eagly and Chrvala (1986) concluded that more recent findings have undermined the validity of this hypothesis.

Eagly and Chrvala (1986) studied the aspects of gender roles which affect conformity. They suggested that one possible interpretation of gender differences in conformity research is that they were due to implicit status cues, one of which is gender. Individuals believed to be of higher status by group members are expected to lead the group and to be more competent (Darley & Fazio, 1980). The results of the Eagly and Chrvala (1986) study showed that older females conformed more than older males when subjects surveyed each other's answers or when they rated each other on likeability, but that there were no gender differences in younger subjects. "Any status interpretation of these findings must include the assumption that the status-lowering effects of younger age took precedence over the status-lowering effects of female sex (Eagly & Chrvala 1986, p. 215)." This assumption remains untested and, as such, Eagly and Chrvala's (1986) findings provide only qualified support for their hypothesis.

Many researchers have suggested that higher female conformity may be explained by the fact that most studies employed male-biased stimuli (Sistrunk & McDavid 1971). These authors found that in situations with female-oriented stimuli, males conformed more, and vice versa. However, Eagly and Carli (1981) did not find evidence for an over-representation of male-biased stimuli in their review of past conformity literature.

While many previous studies have produced conflicting findings, many recent ones have failed to find any conformity. Perrin and Spencer (1981) found only one incidence of conformity in 396 trials in a replication of Asch's (1951) experiment. Also, Lalancette and Standing (1990), in a similar experiment, failed to find significant levels of conformity. This led them to speculate that the failure of many replications in social psychology is due to an inherent historicity of the effects they measure. Perrin and Spencer (1981) speculate that the Asch effect may have been a product of the more authority-oriented culture of 1950's America.

Replication failures may also be due to inadequate methodology employed in the original conformity studies. While a large number of different paradigms have been used to study conformity, each has been found to be flawed methodologically in some way. One strong criticism of the classic Asch (1951, 1956) studies is that they lack external validity. The paradigm involved objective truths and falsehoods (line lengths) to which a majority of confederates tries to convert a minority of subjects. However, in everyday social situations, the topics to which individuals are asked to conform are not highly objective perceptual stimuli like those of Asch, rather they are subjective (e.g., religious or political beliefs).

Some studies have attempted to generate more externally valid results by focusing on more naturalistic settings (for instance, allowing subjects to attempt to persuade one another in non-structured conversations; e.g., Eagly & Chrvala, 1986). These often compromise internal validity. Tanford and Penrod (1984) note that despite the subjectivity of this task, it usually leads to increased spontaneous discussion and arguing among subjects. As a result, there exists the possibility that responses of neutrality as well as increased communication among subjects may produce more variability in the results.

The type of stimuli used in many conformity experiments also bears examination. Although Eagly and Carli (1981) dismissed this as a possible explanation to account for overall gender differences in conformity research, the findings of Sistrunk and McDavid (1971) still remain a valid caveat for experimenters in this field.

Taking all the above into consideration, it seems that a modified Asch (1951, 1956) paradigm using the classification of ambiguous colors (e.g., blue-green) into their components (e.g., blue or green) as the task would provide an improved means of measuring conformity with a balance of internal and external validity. Such a paradigm would not involve objective stimuli, since subjects are not objectively wrong if they choose to call a particular shade "blue" instead of "green". Also, such a paradigm does not involve a significant amount of interaction between subjects, thus eliminating a number of confounds (Tanford & Penrod, 1984). A color classification task can be considered relatively free of gender bias as it involves a stimulus which is neither visuospatial nor verbal in nature (Lips & Colwill, 1978; Maccoby & Jacklin, 1974), and should not favor one gender over the other.

The literature on gender differences in conformity research is vast, but much of the data is actually incidental to the main findings of the studies which report them (Deaux, 1984). Therefore, it seems fitting to study gender differences in detail as a primary interest of a research project. The tendency to dismiss non-significant results may have culminated in an inaccurate overall picture of gender differences in conformity. Unfortunately, research which hypothesizes no differences between genders in social influenceability is rare (Eagly & Carli, 1981). The present study was designed to fill this gap by hypothesizing that there would be no gender differences in conformity with regard to subjects; nor would the gender of confederates affect subjects' responses. Furthermore, in keeping with recent research (Lalancette & Standing 1990; Perrin & Spencer, 1981), it was hypothesized that levels of conformity would be small or non-existent.

Method

Subjects

Subjects were 18 male and 16 female junior college students who participated voluntarily. The mean age of subjects was 18.26 ± 1.35 years.

Apparatus and Materials

The Ishihara Test For Colour Blindness was used to pretest subjects for defective color vision according to standard procedure as recommended by Ishihara (1973). The stimuli for the experiment proper were slides made from pictures of selected color caps taken from the Farnsworth-Munsel 100 Hue Test against a black background. Color caps for critical trials (used to elicit conforming responses) were chosen to be ambiguous by selecting caps which were in the middle range of the angstrom levels between the standard limits of two colors. Caps for neutral trials (used to alleviate subjects' suspicion of the unanimous group) were chosen because they were deemed to be considerably less ambiguous, and would be largely agreed upon by subjects as to their classification. For these trials, caps with angstrom values just outside the limits of standard colors were selected.

Procedure

The experiment involved a 2 × 2 design incorporating gender of subjects and gender of confederates as between-subjects variables. Therefore, there were four cells: 1) male subjects/male confederates (n = 10); 2) female subjects/ male confederates (n = 8); 3) male subjects/female confederates (n = 8); 4) female subjects/female confederates (n = 8). All subjects participated in two conditions: one in which they were alone and one in the presence of three confederates. The mean ages of male and female confederates were 21 and 22 years respectively. Subjects were assigned to various cells based on their availability for testing at particular times.

In the alone condition, subjects were asked to sit in front of the projection surface and were read the following instructions:

> I will be presenting you with 10 slides. In the centre of each slide is a colored circle. Before projecting each slide, I will say the names of two colors. After each slide is shown for six seconds, I will say the names of the two colors again. You are then to tell me which of the color names presented best describes the color of the circle.

In the confederate condition, the experimental procedure was the same except that, when the subject entered the room, the middle two of four seats were already occupied by confederates. Once the subject was seated, the third confederate entered and sat in the remaining seat pretending to be a subject arriving late. The participants were then read the instructions presented above with the following addition: "Please answer from (left to right/right to left)." The bracketed option was read in such a way that the subject would be the last to respond.

The experiment then proceeded as stated in the instructions. Each slide was presented for six seconds, after which the slide projector was advanced to the next slide while the researcher stated the names of the two color options for that trial. There were 10 slides, six of which constituted critical trials (trials numbered 3, 4, 6, 8, 9, and 10). In the six critical trials, the confederates responded unanimously against the subjects' previous responses in the alone condition. However, in the four neutral trials (numbered 1, 2, 5, and 7), confederates responded unanimously in agreement with subjects' previous responses in the alone condition. Note that this distribution of critical and neutral trials is similar to Asch's (1956).

All subjects completed the alone condition first and were asked to return in a week's time to participate in the confederate condition. Subjects' responses in the confederate condition were compared to their responses in the alone condition to determine how many times they had conformed. A subject was considered to have conformed once if his/her response on a critical trial in the confederate condition differed from his/her response in the alone condition for the same trial.

Results

Table 1 shows the mean percentage of conforming responses and standard deviations for each cell. The overall mean percentage of conforming responses was 33.7% ± 7%. Levels of conformity exhibited by individual subjects ranged from 0% to 50%. Almost all subjects (97%) conformed to some degree, with only one failing to conform throughout. These data do not agree with the hypothesis that the general trend towards absence of conformity in the literature would manifest itself in this study.

A two-way ANOVA for independent measures showed a significant effect of subject gender, $F(1,30) = 8.38$, $p = .008$, with females showing more conformity than males. This, again, did not agree with the hypothesis which predicted that there would be no differences between genders' levels of conformity. There was no significant effect of confederate gender, $F(1,30) = < 1$, and no interaction between the two factors, $F(1,30) = < 1$. Though these latter two results seem to support

TABLE 1   Mean percentages of conforming responses and standard deviations for all cells.

	Confederate Gender	
Subject Gender	Male	Female
Male	26.7 ± 13.9 (n = 10)	29.2 ± 11.6 (n = 18)
Female	37.5 ± 11.6 (n = 8)	41.6 ± 9.1 (n = 8)

the hypotheses of the study to some degree, they cannot be said to do so in light of the significant subject gender effect, as well as the unexpectedly high level of conformity.

To assess whether the ambiguity of the stimuli presented showed the desired pattern (i.e., critical trials being ambiguous and neutral trials being nonambiguous), a chi-square goodness-of-fit test was performed for each trial in the alone condition. A significant chi-square test would indicate a preference for one color over the other in a given trial. Such a preference would indicate nonambiguity of the stimulus in that trial. On the other hand, a nonsignificant result would indicate no preference for either color in a particular trial and therefore would be regarded as ambiguous. The results are shown in Table 2.

Calculated values in the table were not consistently in accordance with the anticipated pattern. Trials 3, 4, 6, and 10 (critical trials) showed significant differences, and trials 1 and 7 (neutral trials) showed non-significant differences. Only trials 2, 5, 8, and 9 showed the expected pattern. It is doubtful, however, that these inconsistent results confounded the primary findings of this study. This is because a chi-square test designed to examine the distribution of conforming responses across the critical trials yielded nonsignificant results, X^2 (5, n = 68) = 6.65, p < 05. In other words, the distribution of the total number of conforming responses across trials was not uneven, thus greatly diminishing concerns over the appropriateness of stimulus selection.

Finally, to determine whether subjects' responses were consistent across conditions (i.e. from alone to confederate) in the neutral trials, the number of changing responses in these trials was examined. The mean percentage of responses from neutral trials which changed across conditions was 9.56% ± 6.52. This is much smaller than the percentage of changing responses in the critical trials (33.7% ± 7%), showing that subjects' responses remain consistent across neutral trials when there is no pressure to conform.

TABLE 2   Summary data for the alone condition.

Trial	Color Choices	Trial Type[a]	Cap #[b]	X^2 For Choices
1	Purple/Blue	N	57	1.47
2	Blue/Green	N	43	17.00**
3	Orange/Brown	C	11	9.94**
4	Red/Purple	C	80	9.94**
5	Yellow/Green	N	22	9.94**
6	Brown/Orange	C	13	5.88*
7	Purple/Red	N	83	3.76
8	Blue/Purple	C	64	2.88
9	Orange/Red	C	5	0.24
10	Green/Blue	C	48	11.53**

*< .05; **p < .01 (df =1)
[a]N = neutral trial, C = critical.
[b]Cap numbers taken from Farnsworth-Munsel 100 Hue Test.

Discussion

The results of this study do not agree with the hypothesis that small amounts of conformity would be found. Rather, observed levels of conformity were remarkably similar to those found in classic social influence experiments (Asch, 1951, 1956). It seems that even under the more ecologically valid conditions of this experiment, the Asch effect holds. The findings conflict with those of modern studies such as Lalancette and Standing (1990) and Perrin and Spencer (1981). Since this study was done in a similar cultural environment to these studies, it challenges the notion that the Asch effect is a historically transient phenomenon.

Overall, the levels of conformity found in the present study greatly resemble those found by Asch (1951) when he used a paradigm involving three confederates and one subject. The mean conformity level in that study was approximately 32%, remarkably close to the level of conformity found in the present experiment (33.7%). The levels found here also agree with those predicted by Tanford and Penrod's (1984) social influence model (SIM). This is a sophisticated mathematical model which attempts to predict the amount of conformity which will be found in social influence studies based on the number of influence targets (subjects) and the number of influence sources (confederates). With three confederates and one subject, the model predicts that approximately 31% of responses will be conforming ones. This is strikingly close to the findings of the present research.

The reasons for the discrepant levels of conformity between this study and others (Lalancette & Standing, 1990; Perrin & Spencer, 1981) are not clear. It is possible that the subjective nature of the task utilized here (i.e. color classification) may account for these discrepancies. This is the only significant conceptual difference between this study and Asch's (1951), as well as the replications discussed above. It can be argued that the processes involved in a subject's decision to conform are different for both objective and subjective stimuli. When faced with an objective task (e.g., line comparison), a subject is more certain of the accuracy of his/her judgment and is in a better position to resist group pressure than when confronted with a subjective task (e.g., color classification) in which the accuracy of one's judgment cannot be as certain. To date, no study has compared the cognitive processes underlying conformity in objective and subjective stimulus conditions. Future studies would do well to provide such comparisons.

With regard to gender differences, the only significant effect was that of subject gender. Female subjects conformed more than male subjects. This supports a large body of research noted in Sistrunk and McDavid (1974) and in Eagly and Carli's (1981) meta-analysis. It seems that, overall, females have a consistent tendency to conform more than males. This obviously does not agree with our hypothesis that there would be no subject-gender effects.

Explanations for the gender differences in this study are difficult to formulate. One possible explanation may be extrapolated from the work of Hall (1978). She noted that females are more effective at perceiving other's emotional states (i.e. they are more emotionally sensitive than males). If so, it is possible that females simply intercept more of the social pressure put out by the confederates in such an experimental setting. Thus, it is not a lower threshold for pressure, but a greater tendency to perceive it, which is responsible for higher female conformity.

The fact that the confederate gender and interaction (subject gender × confederate gender) effects were non-significant in the present study does not adversely affect this hypothesis as there is no evidence to suggest that females would be more sensitive to the emotions of one gender over the other (Hall, 1978). Nor is there any reason to believe that one gender would put out more powerful emotional signals than the other (Hall, 1978).

A lack of confederate gender and interaction (subject gender × confederate gender) effects, would also seem to cast doubt on Eagly and Chrvala's (1986) status interpretation of gender differences in conformity. If their interpretation were accurate, then one would expect that male confederates (with higher status) would elicit more conformity than female confederates (with less status). Similarly, male subjects would exhibit less conformity than female subjects because of their higher status.

Our results also challenge the gender role interpretation of sex differences in conformity. Unless one assumes that males exhibit different conformity-eliciting behaviors with male subjects as opposed to female subjects, the pattern of results should be similar to those expected for Eagly and Chrvala (1986). That is, the male subjects/male confederates cell should have equal conformity to the female subjects/female confederates cell, with the female subjects/male confederates cell showing the highest conformity and the male subjects/female confederates cell showing the least. This was not the case.

Finally, a methodological note should be mentioned. The pattern of responses in the alone condition was not as anticipated. Subjects were expected to select the two response options (i.e. color names) with equal frequency in the critical trials, while having a preference for a particular response in the neutral trials. As Table 2 shows, this was not the case. Instead, four critical trials showed a bias towards particular responses and two neutral trials showed a lack of preference. These findings indicate a possible confound with respect to color selection. For instance if a blue/green stimulus is discernably closer to blue than to green, then this would elicit more responses of "blue" than "green". In such trials, one might anticipate less conformity than in trials where the stimulus color was more ambiguous. The even distribution of conforming responses across critical trials alleviates most of the concerns over the inconsistent color-option selections of the subjects in this study. However, future researchers wishing to adopt this paradigm should undertake extensive pretesting to ensure color ambiguity and thus avoid concerns surrounding this issue.

In conclusion, it seems that the Asch effect can still be obtained under present social conditions if one uses a paradigm involving subjective stimuli. It seems that in present-day western society, people are no longer willing to conform to groups on matters of objective truth (Lalancette & Standing, 1990; Perrin & Spencer, 1981), however, they are still susceptible to social pressure involving matters of opinion. Secondly, we have also found that higher levels of conformity in females can still be observed. Rather than interpreting these in terms of traditional sex role theories, we have attempted to explain them using an alternative approach based on greater emotional sensitivity in females.

References

Asch, S. E. (1951). Effects of group pressure upon the modification and distortion of judgements. In H. Guetzkow (Ed.) *Groups, Leadership and Men.* Pittsburgh: Carnegie.

Asch. S. E. (1956). Studies of independence and conformity: a minority of one against a unanimous majority. *Psychological Monographs,* 70, (9), (whole no. 416).

Cooper, H. M. (1979). Statistically combining independent studies: Meta-analysis of sex differences in conformity research. *Journal of Personality and Social Psychology,* 37, 131–146.

Crutchfield, R. S. (1955). Conformity and character. *American Psychologist,* 10, 191–198.

Darley, J. M., & Fazio, R. H. (1980). Expectancy confirmation processes arising in the social interaction sequence. *American Psychologist, 35*, 867–881.

Deaux, K. (1984). From individual differences to social categories: Analysis of a decade's research on gender. *American Psychologist, 39*, 105–116.

Eagly, A. H. (1978). Sex differences in influenceability. *Psychological Bulletin, 85*, 86–116.

Eagly, A. H., & Carli, L. L. (1981). Sex of researchers and sex-typed communications as determinants of sex differences in influenceability: A meta-analysis of social influence studies. *Psychological Bulletin, 90*, (1), 1–20.

Eagly, A. H., & Chrvala, C. (1986). Sex differences in conformity: Status and gender role interpretations. *Psychology of Women Quarterly, 10*, 203–220.

Hall, J. A. (1978). Gender effects in decoding nonverbal cues. *Psychological Bulletin, 85*, (4), 845–857.

Ishihara, S. (1973). *Ishihara's tests for Colour-Blindness.* Tokyo: Kanehara Shuppan.

Kretch, D., Crutchfield, R. S., & Ballachey, E. L. (1962). *Individual in Society: A Textbook of Social Psychology.* New York: McGraw-Hill.

Lalancette, M. F., & Standing, L. (1990). Asch fails again. *Social Behavior and Personality, 18*, (1), 7–12.

Lips, H. M., & Colwill, N. L. (1978). *Psychology of Sex Differences.* Eaglewood Cliffs, N.J.: Prentice-Hall.

Maccoby, E. E., & Jacklin, C. N. (1974). *The Psychology of Sex Differences.* Palo Alto, CA.: Stanford University Press.

Perrin, S., & Spencer, C. (1981). Independence or conformity in the Asch experiment as a reflection of cultural and situational factors. *British Journal of Social Psychology, 20*, 205–209.

Sistrunk, F., & McDavid, J. W. (1971). Sex variable in conformity behaviour. *Journal of Personality and Social Psychology, 17*, 200–207.

Tanford, S., & Penrod, S. (1984). Social Influence Model: A formal integration of research on majority and minority influence processes. *Psychological Bulletin, 95*, (2), 189–225.

Worchel, S., & Cooper, J. (1976). *Understanding Social Psychology.* Homewood, IL.: Dorsey Press.

Editor's Note

Please address correspondence and reprint requests to: Rajesh Malik, Department of Psychology, Concordia University, 7141 Sherbrooke Street West, Montreal, QC Canada H4B 1R6.

Discussion Questions for Article 2

Section 13: Social Psychology

Name: _____

PID: _____

Date: __ __ / __ __ / __ __ (MM/DD/YY)

CRN: _____

Recitation Day/Time: _____

Honor Code Signature: _____

1. What were some of the methodology flaws of the past studies? And, how did Collin, Sano, and Malik account for these flaws?

2. What are the explanations offered for the gender differences found in various conformity studies?

3. What are some flaws of the present study?

4. Describe a situation in which you conformed to a group of people against your better judgment.

Section 14
Applied Psychology

By this point in the semester, you have been introduced to a variety of important concepts and theories in the field of psychology. It will be difficult for you to forget the ideas behind Harlow's study of love in infant monkeys, Skinner's article on teaching animals, or Milgram's study of obedience. However, it may very well be the case that some of you pragmatically-oriented students are now wondering, "where is the real-world application?" In other words, many students are now looking for ways to "take psychology to work." Therein lies the basis for applied psychology, a branch of the field that attempts to bridge the gap between theory and solution.

Applied psychologists are often referred to as scientist-practitioners. These psychologists test hypotheses with the appropriate research methods, and then apply their findings outside of the laboratory to help people increase performance, save money, and live better lives. In applied psychology, we see the demonstrable relevance of many principle topics discussed in this course. For example, industrial/organizational psychologists look at the results of motivation and emotion research in the process of promoting worker efficacy and job satisfaction. Psychometricians utilize personality theories in order to develop various measurement instruments which can aid in the scientific selection and assessment of employees. Sports psychologists have developed injury prevention programs for athletes based on the health and stress literature. Finally, human factors psychologists, some of who work for NASA, make use of cognition and memory research when reinforcing the interactions between people and equipment.

465

The American Psychological Association has previously developed a task force to demonstrate the value of psychology in our everyday lives. It is in the realm of applied psychology that their goal is fulfilled. Borrowing a phrase from eminent psychologist Philip Zimbardo, through applied psychology we are effectively able to "give psychology away to the public."

Article 1: Social Influence Principles: Fueling Participation in Occupational Safety

Few would deny the importance of occupational safety programs. Empirically-based interventions have demonstrated reductions in both employee injury rates and company costs. The implementation and "selling" of such programs, however, tends to be derided. As an example, think about the most recent job that you held. At some point during your orientation, you were undoubtedly introduced to a set of workplace safety policies. Unfortunately, because of factors such as approaching deadlines and management pressure for product output, it may have seemed that these policies were forced upon the employees. This would certainly affect your motivation to strive for an injury-free workplace. In this article, Dr. Geller addresses these concerns by outlining several social influence principles that bolster employee buy-in for occupational safety through the development of interdependent relationships.

Article 2: Pygmalion Goes to Boot Camp: Expectancy, Leadership, and Trainee Performance

Applied psychology involves utilizing theories and findings from other realms of psychology in order to solve real-world problems. The Pygmalion effect, a concept originally established in social and educational psychology, occurs when certain people perform better than others simply because they are expected to do so. The Pygmalion effect was once thought to be an occurrence only affecting child performance. In this article, the authors investigate the application of this phenomenon to the adult workplace (specifically, a military training base). They found that those instructors believed to be high on command potential (despite each individual being given a random group) scored higher on trainee performance and trainee attitudes at the end of the intensive course.

—*Mark D. Scott*

Article 1

Social Influence Principles: Fueling Participation in Occupational Safety

E. Scott Geller

Participation in occupational safety is facilitated or inhibited by the various social relationships in a work culture. The challenge of developing the interdependent relationships needed to achieve an injury-free workplace is dependent on the social influence of certain principles. These principles are: 1. People try to be consistent in thought and deed. 2. People reciprocate to return a favor. 3. People participate with people they like. 4. People follow the crowd. 5. The power of authority. 6. The value of scarcity. 7. Novelty attracts attention. Achieving an injury-free workplace requires a transformation from dependency and independency to interdependency. It is not enough for workers to rely on their company to keep them safe solely through engineering intervention, nor is it sufficient for employees to only count on their own individual effort to keep them injury-free. Rather, people need others to remove environmental hazards and provide corrective feedback at-risk behavior.

People are social animals. Social relationships define who we are, how we feel and how to get what we want. We participate with and for other people on a daily basis. Often, our motivation to participate comes from others, whether we are working alone or on a team. Participation in occupational safety is facilitated or inhibited by the various social relationships in a work culture. The challenge of developing the interdependent relationships needed to achieve an injury-free workplace is dependent on the social influence principles described here.

These principles can be used to analyze the interpersonal factors that hinder optimal involvement in safety and to decide which can be changed to fuel more participation. Whereas the 10 research-based principles to sustain participation in a safety improvement process are derived essentially from cognitive science [Geller(d)], these guidelines are gleaned from social science. These sets are very different, yet they are interdependent and mutually supportive. The powerful principle of consistency, which research suggests is generally the most popular and clearly relevant to increasing participation, is described first [Geller(b)].

Principle 1: We Try to Be Consistent in Thought and Deed

Simply put, when people make a choice, take a stand or develop an attitude, they encounter personal and social pressures to perform consistently with their commitment. This pressure comes from three basic sources:

1. Society values consistency within people.

2. Consistent conduct is beneficial to daily existence.

3. A consistent orientation allows for shortcuts in information processing and decision making [Cialdini(a)].

When people show inconsistencies between their promises and their behaviors, they may be labeled "flighty," "confused," "scatterbrained," "neurotic" or "two-faced"—designations that most people seek to avoid. This principle also accounts for people's resistance to change, and explains why a change in behavior often leads to a corresponding change in attitude, and vice versa.

Public, Active and Voluntary Commitment

When people sign their name to a petition or pledge card, they are making a commitment to behave in a certain way. Later, they behave in this manner to be consistent with their commitment. The consistency principle has been applied to increase various safety-related behaviors (Geller and Lehman). For example, after discussion about a particular work procedure, the audience might be asked to make a commitment to perform the desired behavior. But what kind of commitment should be requested? Commitments are most influential when they are public, active and perceived as voluntary and, thus, not coerced [Cialdini(a)]. Also, it is better to have people sign their name to a card, petition or public declaration display than to merely raise their hands. People are more likely to live up to what they write down. Of course, those pledging to follow a certain work practice must believe they made the commitment voluntarily.

Start Small and Build

To be consistent, a person who follows a small request is likely to comply with a larger related request made later. Thus, after agreeing to serve on a safety steering committee, an individual is likely more willing to give a presentation at a safety meeting. Researchers call this the "foot-in-the-door" technique and have found it to be successful in boosting product sales, monetary contributions to charities and blood donations [Freedman and Fraser; Cialdini(a); Geller(c)]. However, this technique only works to increase safe behaviors when people comply with the initial small request. If a person says "no" to the first request, this individual will find it easier to refuse a second, more important request. In this case, the consistency principle is working against the requestor.

Commitments are most influential when they are public, active and perceived as voluntary and, thus, not coerced.

Which First: Attitude or Behavior?

Because of the consistency principle, it does not matter whether attitude or behavior changes first. The issue is whether a technique is available to influence one or the other. In fact, one could argue that internal (attitudinal) dimensions are intertwined throughout a successful technique that targets behavior. For example, an effective pledge-card procedure requires that people believe (internally) their commitment was voluntary. Following successive compliance with escalating demands, internal commitment is developed, until eventually an "attitude" results.

Furthermore, the concept of self-persuasion requires that people develop an internal justification for the behavior they are asked to perform [Aronson; Geller(d)]. People attempt to keep their internal person state (like attitude) and external participation (or behavior) consistent. Thus, whether attitude or behavior is influenced first, the other will likely follow if the individual does not feel coerced.

Principle 2: People Reciprocate to Return a Favor

Have you ever felt uncomfortable after someone did you a favor—or turned down a favor because you didn't want to feel obligated to return it? This is the reciprocity principle in action: When a person receives a favor, s/he feels obligated to return it. Research has shown that the favor might actually be returned to someone other than the original source (Berkowitz and Daniels). In safety management, this means that safety leaders should look for opportunities to go out of their way for other's safety. When individuals actively care for someone else's safety, they set the tone for reciprocity—they increase the likelihood that the recipients of the caring will actively care for the safety of someone else.

How people react after receiving gratitude for their good deeds can either stifle or mobilize reciprocity. After one person thanks another for participating in a safety process, a common response is, "No problem" or "It was really nothing." This trivializes the participation and inhibits reciprocity. A better reply is, "You're welcome, but you'd do the same for me." This activates the reciprocity principle in a way that is perceived as genuine and valid.

Gifts Aren't Free

Has someone ever influenced you to listen to a sales pitch after giving you a free gift? Have you ever felt obligated to contribute to a charity after receiving individualized address labels and a stamped envelope for your check? Purchased a certain food in a supermarket after eating a free sample? Felt obliged to purchase a commodity after using it for a 10-day "free" trial period? If you answered "yes" to any of these questions, you likely have been influenced by the reciprocity principle. Many marketing and sales-promotion efforts count on this free-sample approach to influence purchasing behavior.

In one experiment, 84 percent of those individuals who found a dime in the coin-return slot of a public phone (placed there by researchers) helped a research accomplice pick up papers he dropped in the subject's vicinity. In contrast, only four percent of those who did not find a dime helped the accomplice. Similarly, students given a cookie while studying at a university library were more likely than those not given one to agree to help another student (a research accomplice) by participating in a psychology experiment (Isen and Levin).

Does this justify the distribution of free safety gifts, such as pens, T-shirts, caps, cups and similar trinkets? To some extent, but the amount of reciprocity activated depends on the recipient's perceptions. How special is the gift? Was it given to a select group or to everyone? Does the gift or its delivery represent significant sacrifice in money, time or effort? Can it be purchased elsewhere or does an imprinted slogan make it special? The more special the gift—as perceived by the recipient—the more reciprocity activated. Furthermore, the way a safety gift is presented can make a great difference. Labels and slogans linked with the gift can influence the quantity and quality of reciprocity activated. If the gift is presented to represent the participation expected from an "elite" group, a special type of reciprocity is energized. Recipients tell themselves they are considered safety leaders and need to justify this label by continuing their extra participation for the safety of others.

Door-in-the-Face: Start Big and Retreat

Suppose the plant safety director asks you to chair the safety steering committee for the next two years. Let's assume you perceive this request as outrageous, given your other assignments and the fact you have never even served on such a committee. You reply, "Thanks for asking, but no." The safety director says he understands, then asks whether you would be willing to serve on the committee. According to social psychology research, because the safety director "backed down" from his initial request, you will feel subtle pressure to make a similar concession—to reciprocate—and agree to the less-demanding request [Cialdini(a)].

Cialdini, et al were among the first to demonstrate the power of this "door-in-the-face" technique. Posing as representatives of the "County Youth Counseling Program,"

FIGURE 1 Seven principles of social dynamics.

Seven Principles of Social Dynamics

Consistency
We resist change.
We act ourselves into certain thinking and vice versa.
We honor public, active and voluntary commitment.

Reciprocity
We return favors.
We are more likely to comply after retreating.

Ingratiation
We are attracted to similarities.
We like those who praise us and cooperate.
We actively care for people we like.

Conformity
We follow those who are similar and credible.
We model most in unfamiliar situations.

Authority
We follow authority blindly and mindlessly.
We follow those with credibility.

Scarcity
We react to protect our individuality.
We value rare opportunities.
We are motivated to avoid loss.

Novelty
We habituate to the routine.
We are attentive and attracted to the unique.

they approached college students walking on campus and asked them to chaperon (unpaid) a group of juvenile delinquents on a day trip to the zoo. When this was the first and only request, only 17 percent of the students approached volunteered.

However, three times more students volunteered when the researchers first asked for a much larger favor. Specifically, they asked whether the students would be willing to counsel juvenile delinquents for two hours a week over a two-year period. Everyone refused this request, but half of them agreed to serve as unpaid chaperons for the zoo trip. Apparently, the researchers' willingness to retreat from their initial request influenced several students to reciprocate and comply with a smaller request (Cialdini, et al).

Principle 3: We Participate with People We Like

To whom do you feel most obligated after someone does you a good turn—a person you like or one you dislike? To whom are you more likely to give safety-related feedback—a team of workers you like or a team you dislike? The answers are obvious and reflect the basic liking rule. Because of this principle, it is critical to increase and sustain interpersonal liking when cultivating an actively caring work culture. Social psychologists have demonstrated three basic ways to establish a context of interpersonal liking, with each approach suggesting several specific strategies [Cialdini(a); (b)].

Emphasize Similarities

We like people who are like us. Through initial informal conversation and astute observation, people find commonalities with other people they want to influence. They might learn another person enjoys the same hobbies or recreational activities; has a parallel educational background or employment history; or has comparable opinions about current news stories, corporate issues or politics. People can forge a liking bond with others by discussing topics that accentuate interpersonal similarities. This principle comes into play when people modify their attire to be more acceptable to various audiences, such as dressing "up" or "down" to appear more like the group. Likewise, when an individual mentions acquaintances whom the other person knows and respects, s/he is showing the kind of similarity that can increase liking.

Give Praise

Genuine one-to-one praise, recognition and rewarding feedback help increase an individual's competence and self-efficacy [Geller(a); (d); Allen(a); Daniels]. Praising someone's performance also increases liking—in both directions. The person rewarded likes the other person more, while the person giving praise increases appreciation for the person who performed the commendable behavior. This exchange enhances feelings of mutual respect and gratitude. Then, through the power of the reciprocity principle, one interaction of genuine behavior-based praise will lead to more interpersonal recognition.

Promote Cooperation

Social psychologists have tracked increases in interpersonal liking when individuals transition from competitive to cooperative situations [Aronson and Patnoe; Cialdini(b)]. People experience this change many times, from competitive participation in athletic contests to teamwork on community projects, and from competitive versus cooperative interaction on work assignments. The greater the perception of interdependency toward achievement of a common goal, the greater the interpersonal liking. This connects with the need to promote a sense of belonging and interdependency throughout a work culture—a key to attaining and sustaining an injury-free workplace [Geller(b); (f)].

Principle 4: We Follow the Crowd

This is the principle of consensus or conformity [Asch(b)]. Examples of conformity are observed every day—from the types of clothes people wear to their style of communication. Producers of comedy shows use canned laughter to cause more audience laughter. Advertisers sell their wares by showing celebrities using their products. Long lines help night clubs, movie theaters and restaurants attract customers. Thus, the role of conformity in influencing participation cannot be overlooked. Research has shown that greater pressure to conform occurs when the consensus group is larger [Asch(a); (c)] and when group members are seen as relatively experienced (Allison; Cialdini and Trost). Two other factors—similarity and familiarity—also affect conformity.

Experienced employees should feel especially responsible to demonstrate safe work practices when new employees are present.

Similarity

The impact of similarity on conformity was dramatically shown when researchers went door-to-door to request charity donations and displayed a list of other contributors. Researchers varied this list from home-to-home and found that the longer list influenced more donations, verifying the effect of group size on conformity. In addition, when the donor list contained the names of those living in the same neighborhood, the size of the donations increased significantly, demonstrating the role of similarity in increasing the power of the conformity principle [Cialdini(b)].

Familiarity

When are people most likely to use the consensus principle? People are most likely to look to the behavior of others as a guide for their own behavior when in an unfamiliar situation [Allen(b); Baron, et al]. Therefore, experienced employees should feel especially responsible to demonstrate safe work practices when new employees are present. Similarly, supervisors should provide new hires opportunities to work with experienced, safety-minded employees. When these experienced employees have credible authority, the next social influence principle adds to the beneficial impact.

Principle 5: The Power of Authority

From childhood, people learn to appreciate and follow legitimate authority—they proceed from "mother knows best" to "boss knows best" (Milgram). This gives individuals an excuse to escape taking personal responsibility for their actions. In other words, if someone with authority asks employees to take a risk, they are often willing to comply because if something goes wrong, it will not be their fault—they can blame the person who told them to take the risk. It is easy to see how this relates to workplace safety. Safety leaders need to be aware of the power of authority and must encourage people to resist the temptation to follow orders blindly and mindlessly.

Conformity and Authority

Authority and social conformity go hand-in-hand to affect participation in safety-related activities. The statement, "I was just following orders" reflects obedience to authority, while "everyone else does it" reflects conformity or peer pressure. SH&E professionals must realize the powerful impact of both factors and plan interventions to overcome their potential negative influence. Note that a person who deviates from the norm and sets a safe example can decrease undesirable conformity and mindless obedience to authority [Asch(b); Allen and Levine; Morris and Miller].

The Credible Authority

Given the impact of authority on participation, safety leaders must use this principle to their advantage. That is, safety leaders need to become legitimate authority figures who set safe examples [Geller(e)]. Here, the focus is a related—and crucial—factor: credibility.

What can leaders do to demand legitimate authority? Most obviously, they should post their diplomas, certificates or awards in appropriate locations (e.g., an office wall) to show relevant experience and credentials. This does not come across as boasting; rather it is a subtle way to let others know one's specialties and skills.

People can also establish their domains of profound knowledge and competence through informal conversation. The talented communicator will reveal his/her credentials as a natural part of casual social exchange, without seeming to brag. It is best to offer such indirect and informal statements of expertise early in the "game." The sooner people establish themselves as credible authorities, the sooner they can reap the benefits of this social influence principle.

Principle 6: The Value of Scarcity

Ever gone out of your way to purchase front-row tickets to a sporting event or concert? Jammed into a department store to get a "limited-time" bargain? Participated at an auction where one-of-a-kind items were displayed and sold to the highest bidder? Each of the situations implied by these questions illustrates how the value of something increases with perceived scarcity.

Reacting to Show Individuality

When individuality or perceived personal control is made scarce through top-down control, some people will exhibit contrary behavior in an attempt to assert their freedom. Social psychologists refer to this phenomenon as psychological reactance (Brehm), while behavior analysts call it countercontrol (Skinner). Regardless of its name, the results can be devastating to participation.

The author once met a person who wore safety frames—not safety glasses, only safety frames (he had removed the lenses). When a supervisor walked up the aisle, the employee would look right at him and wave. His coworkers lauded him for thumbing his nose at the system.

In this facility, employees perceived safety as a top-down mandate that restricted individual freedom. This worker increased his status in that culture by pushing against the system and demonstrating his independence. Thus, the command-and-control approach to occupational safety can make personal freedom seem scarce and hinder participation. When people perceive the system as restrictive, they may attempt to beat it. This principle indicates that true commitment and long-term participation cannot be dictated [Geller(d)].

The Special Opportunity

So what is the relevance of the scarcity principle in getting more people involved in a safety process? First, it suggests that the distinct features of a safety process should be emphasized. How is a particular approach to injury prevention better than the rest? How is it leading-edge? When people believe they have a rare opportunity to test a new approach to occupational safety, their motivation is enhanced by the scarcity principle.

For example, organizational leaders may wish to test a particular behavior-based approach to safety, yet are not ready to apply the process companywide. Under these circumstances, the typical recommendation is to conduct a pilot program with a select group of employees (preferably a group with an above-average injury rate).

How can the scarcity principle be applied to motivate participation at a test site? Tell the group the truth. Explain that they have been selected to serve as the example for the rest of the company, that they have an unparalleled opportunity to demonstrate innovative ways to keep people safe. And, tell them they must act fast, because this "window of opportunity" is only open for so long. This latter point uses the scarcity principle in another way. It is not that the program is unique (or scarce), but that the opportunity to participate has limited duration.

The command-and-control approach to safety can make personal freedom seem scarce and hinder participation, as employees try to "beat the system."

Similarly, it can be beneficial to tell workshop audiences that their best opportunity to implement principles and procedures learned at a professional development conference is now—while the material is fresh and their organizations expect them to share and apply what they learned. As time passes, opportunities to use new information fade, because employees' self-efficacy can diminish over time (Bandura). Furthermore, over time, management's expectancy and obligation to consider a change will get buried by the familiar routine.

The Fear of Losing

The latter application of the scarcity principle focuses on what could be lost by failure to take advantage of a one-of-a-kind opportunity. Social psychologists have shown that people are especially motivated to avoid a loss [Cialdini(b)]. When the need to act immediately to avoid a loss is evident, people are roused to mindful action. The power of this principle to motivate participation in safety-related activities can be seen when the potential loss is obvious (e.g., in personal-injury testimony) and when self-efficacy and response-efficacy are activated [Geller(b); (d)]. Under these conditions, the scarcity principle provokes desired behavior (Hale and Dillard; Witte and Allen).

Principle 7: Novelty Attracts Attention

Defining novelty as "a change in stimulus conditions from previous experience," behavioral scientists have demonstrated that novelty is rewarding—even to rodents (Bevins, et al 114; Bevins). Everyone has experienced this effect. Much like the influence of scarcity, the novelty principle is based on the finding that people are attentive and attracted to the quality of uniqueness. In this case, however, uniqueness means new or different rather than scarce or rare.

Interpersonal Relationships

Social psychologists have examined this principle with regard to interpersonal attraction and interrelationships (Baxter; Montgomery). More specifically, the novelty principle is reflected in people's desire for excitement and surprise in their interpersonal experiences. The appeal of newness and unpredictability facilitates the beginning of a relationship, while the lack of it can be the key factor in the breakup of a relationship.

The impact of this principle on participation in safety is analogous to its influence on relationships. The uniqueness of a new approach to injury prevention promotes initial involvement; over time, however, the same routine can seem dull and uninspiring—prompting a decline in participation quantity and/or quality, particularly when participants do not experience consequences that support or verify their safety-related activities.

Intervention Implications

What can be done to overcome the loss of novelty and consequential participation? Most people have experienced the rise and fall of personal excitement with various fluctuations in novelty. Some have learned the value of incorporating the unexpected into a relationship. And everyone has seen the benefit of varying a work routine. In addition, most people have observed the power of adding relevant rewarding consequences to an everyday situation.

So, the recommended intervention approach is simple in principle, if not in practice: Find ways to add rewarding performance-relevant consequences for individuals and groups, and vary aspects of a particular safety process [Daniels; Geller(a); (g)].

Actually, changing the features of a safety process is essential for continuous improvement—and a mechanism for doing so should be established from the start. This usually requires the ongoing involvement of a safety steering committee that solicits and reviews employee suggestions for program refinement, decides which suggestions to implement, then monitors their impact on the organization's overall injury-prevention process. Thus, the appropriate action of this committee not only supports the vision of "never-ending improvement," but also maintains a degree of novelty in safety-related activities.

Activator Salience

Safety signs, slogans and exhortations precede opportunities to perform certain safe or risky behaviors. As such, they attempt to activate desired performance among the workforce. Various aspects of these "activators" affect the degree to which they influence behavior [Geller(c)]. One critical determinant of activator impact—activator salience—relates directly to this discussion.

The influence of an activator varies directly with its noticeability—that is, more unique or novel activators are more noticeable. It is natural for activators such as sign messages to lose their impact over time; this process is called habituation and is considered by some psychologists to be the simplest form of learning (Chance). In other words, through habituation, people learn not to respond to an event that occurs repeatedly.

Employees are more likely to notice and follow a safety activator—such as a safety sign—when it varies periodically according to their input.

When an activator changes, it becomes more conspicuous. Various techniques can be employed to change the message on safety signs. Some have removable slats on which different messages can be placed. Others allow for the interchange of letters to allow maximum flexibility in a word display. Computer-generated signs offer an infinite number of options. Some facilities have video screens throughout that can broadcast various safety messages into breakrooms, lunchrooms, visitor's lounges and hallways.

The need to maintain novelty in these activators implies another important role for a safety steering committee. This group should collect suggestions from the workforce for changing safety activators and manage their recurring modification. This not only increases activator salience—through novelty—it also facilitates compliance with the safety message—through ownership. In other words, employees are more likely to notice and follow a safety activator when it varies periodically according to their input.

Conclusion

Achieving an injury-free workplace requires a transformation from dependency and independency to interdependency. It is not enough for workers to rely on their company to keep them safe solely through engineering intervention, nor is it sufficient for employees to only count on their own individual effort to keep them injury-free.

Rather, people need others to remove environmental hazards and provide corrective feedback on at-risk behavior. Such interdependency requires interpersonal interaction. The social dynamics of the situation determine whether such exchanges are likely to occur and whether their impact will be beneficial or detrimental to safety.

An organization's social dynamics both reflect and influence its culture. That is, certain aspects of a work setting affect social dynamics that in turn, alter the culture. The seven social influence principles described reveal basic social dynamics that can inhibit or facilitate participation for occupational safety.

People's desire to be consistent influences resistance to change. But when they choose to change even a little, the consistency principle can facilitate more commitment and more beneficial change. With this principle in effect, small increases in participation can result in supportive attitude change, followed by more participation and more desired attitude change.

When people actively care for others they activate three principles of social influence that foster more caring. Specifically, when employees go beyond the call of duty for a coworker's safety, they increase interpersonal liking (ingratiation principle) and induce a sense of obligation in that person to return the favor (reciprocity principle). They also set an example that spreads more caring behavior throughout the workplace (conformity principle).

The principle of authority illustrates that people may follow orders blindly and mindlessly. This becomes a barrier to occupational safety when a manager or supervisor asks a worker to perform an at-risk behavior.

On the other hand, those who are in positions of authority can have the opposite effect. In fact, their positive role-modeling and support of interdependency and actively caring are key to achieving an injury-free workplace.

Safety leaders realize the importance of increasing interpersonal liking throughout a workforce, and they understand the critical functions of praise, cooperation and perceived similarities in achieving this. They use behavior-based recognition to 1) support other people's participation in safety; 2) increase others' appreciation and respect for them; and 3) increase their own admiration for those whom they recognize.

Employee involvement is much more likely with top-down support of safety processes that are developed, owned and continuously improved by employee teams.

The principle of scarcity explains why some employees actively resist complying with top-down safety rules, regulations and a quick-fix safety program. In some command-and-control work cultures, noncompliance or nonparticipation reflects a personal statement of "freedom."

Employee involvement is much more likely with top-down support of safety processes that are developed, owned and continuously improved by employee teams which understand the rationale and relevancy of the principles behind them.

Highlighting the uncommon and rare aspects of a safety process uses the scarcity principle to fuel participation. Involvement in a new safety effort can be provoked by explaining how the "window of opportunity" for implementation is short and by specifying what can be lost if substantial participation is not forthcoming.

Finally, the novelty principle explains why safety messages lose their impact over time and why participation wanes when safety becomes repetitive. The inattention and disinterest that accompany the mundane occupational safety message and routine result from habituation.

To overcome this, safety activators and procedures should be intermittently modified or refined based on employee input, and supported with relevant consequences. When an employee safety team monitors and manages these ongoing changes, the entire process is fueled by another social dynamic—interpersonal ownership.

Discussion Questions for Article 1

Section 14: Applied Psychology

Name: _____

PID: _____

Date: __ __ / __ __ / __ __ (MM/DD/YY)

CRN: _____

Recitation Day/Time: _____

Honor Code Signature: _____

1. How could the social influence principles outlined in this article fuel participation in other company policies outside the realm of occupational safety?

2. Compare and contrast the "foot-in-the-door" technique and the "door-in-the-face" technique.

3. What must an authority figure establish if they are to utilize their position of authority effectively?

4. In your life which social influence principle do you believe has the most effect on your behavior? Does this change depending on the situation you find yourself in?

Pygmalion Goes to Boot Camp: Expectancy, Leadership, and Trainee Performance

Dov Eden

Abraham B. Shani

The Pygmalion effect, that is, enhanced learning caused by high teacher expectancy, has been studied almost exclusively in the classroom. To test its applicability to adult trainees and to examine the effects of expectancy on instructor leadership, a field experiment was conducted at a military training base. One-hundred and five trainees in a 15-week combat command course were matched on aptitude and randomly assigned to high, regular, and unspecified instructor-expectancy conditions. The Pygmalion hypothesis that instructor expectancy influences trainee performance was confirmed. Trainees of whom instructors had been induced to expect better performance scored significantly higher on objective achievement tests, exhibited more positive attitudes, and perceived more positive leadership behavior. Instructor expectancy, the manipulated independent variable, explained 73% of the variance in performance, 66% in attitudes, and 28% in leadership. The causal interplay between expectancy, leadership, and performance, and the notion of applying the Pygmalion effect by deliberately raising supervisors' expectations through "expectancy training" are discussed.

Possibilities for practical application of the Pygmalion effect, originally attempted experimentally in the classroom by Rosenthal and Jacobson (1968), titillate the imagination. Raising instructor's expectations may be an inexpensive, feasible way to increase training effectiveness. The pervasive influence of interpersonal expectancies on behavior, that is, self-fulfilling prophecy, has been comprehensively reviewed by Jones (1977). It is surprising that investigation of the Pygmalion effect has been confined almost exclusively to the elementary school classroom. Livingston (1969) discussed implications of Pygmalion for management but presented no new empirical evidence. The present study avoided several methodological flaws of previous Pygmalion research, extended the investigation of the effect into early adulthood and to a military training base, and measured the impact of superiors' expectations on attitudes, as well as on performance. In addition, measures of instructor leadership were included in order to shed new light on a potential intervening mechanism by which expectancy might affect subordinate performance.

Many Pygmalion experiments have employed very weak, ill-timed, and unvalidated expectancy manipulations. Weak manipulation is exemplified by the original Rosenthal and Jacobson (1968) study in which teachers were given lists of pupils, designating 20% as late bloomers purportedly on the basis of test results but who actually had been selected at random. During subsequent debriefing, most teachers said they paid little attention to their lists. The 16 teachers recalled the names of only 18 of the 72 children designated as special and falsely identified 18 control-group children as having been listed. This might explain why Rosenthal and Jacobson's analysis revealed the effect only among primary-grade pupils. Similarly José and Cody (1971) found in their post-experimental questionnaire that 11 of the 18 teachers denied expecting more as a result of the manipulation.

Induction of expectations may be weakened by poor timing. During classroom interaction teachers surely develop natural expectations concerning their pupils. Many manipulations have probably failed to induce the intended expectations because they were implemented only after natural, experience-based expectations had crystallized in the teachers' minds. Even after only a few days of classroom exposure, any teacher is likely to have pupils "pegged," and such natural expectations can only be overcome by a strong, credible manipulation. For example, Kester and Letchworth (1972) induced expectations after a week of teacher acquaintance with pupils, and Zanna, Sheras, Cooper, and Shaw (1975) staged their manipulation after 7 working days of a 7-week summer enrichment program. Neither produced a Pygmalion effect. Strength and timing of expectancy manipulation appear crucial to producing performance results. It is astonishing that so few investigators have even bothered measuring whether their experimental manipulation induced the intended expectations. Some of the difficulties plaguing past Pygmalion research can be overcome easily by replication using a strong expectancy induction, timing the induction prior to any acquaintance between the instructors and their trainees, and including a manipulation check.

Researchers have been lax in exploring the Pygmalion effect among adults. This may be due to the pervasive influence of the original Rosenthal and Jacobson (1968) report, in which they concluded that "all lines of evidence tend to suggest that it is younger children who are the more susceptible to various forms of influence processes" (p. 69). The "for kids only" label has largely persisted. One of our objectives was to demonstrate the Pygmalion effect among young adults to establish its potential as a researchable and applicable topic for industrial and organizational psychology. We hypothesized that elevated instructor expectations enhance learning performance, that is, the Pygmalion effect.

Although Pygmalion research has focused on learning performance, the attitudinal effects of instructor expectancy should also be of interest. Weinstein and Middlestadt (1979) have pointed out that in much of the classroom expectancy research, performance has been the only learner variable measured; attitudes have been ignored. It is likely that any positive effect of expectancy on performance would be mirrored in increased motivation and satisfaction. The second hypothesis therefore was that high instructor expectations produce more positive attitudes among trainees.

The heart of the Pygmalion question is the behavioral mechanism through which teacher expectancy influences pupils. Several empirical studies have found mediating teacher behaviors that seem similar to leadership behaviors identified in research on superior–subordinate relationships. Teachers favor pupils from whom they expect more by giving them more visual attention (Rothbart, Dalfen, & Barrett, 1971); by expressing more satisfaction, encouragement, and praise (Meichenbaum, Bowers, & Ross, 1969); by giving more extreme levels of both rewards and punishment (Lanzetta & Hannah, 1969); by calling on them and praising them more frequently (Rubovits & Maehr, 1973); and by communicating with them more, in a more positive, accepting, and supportive manner (Kester & Letchworth, 1972). Note the similarity of many of these previously observed teacher behaviors in the classroom to leadership behaviors typically measured by organizational psychologists using the Ohio State University (Fleishman, Harris, Burtt, 1955) and Michigan (Bowers & Seashore, 1966) approaches. Dawson, Messé, and Phillips (1972) have applied leadership factors to college instructors' teaching behavior. They varied Initiating Structure and Consideration and found that both factors influenced student learning, showing the feasibility of experimentally investigating instruction style with leadership concepts. We analyzed leadership as a dependent variable influenced by expectancy.

By positing instructor leadership to be a medium by which expectancies might manifest themselves in interpersonal interaction, we sought to integrate research on Pygmalion and leadership. We hypothesized that inducing higher performance expectations influences instructors' leadership behavior in ways likely to fulfill their prophecy. Instructors' leadership behavior toward trainees expected to perform well should be characterized by greater orientation both toward the trainee as a person and toward task performance.

Method

Trainees were assigned to three expectancy conditions in an "after only" randomized block experimental design (Campbell & Stanley, 1966). They were blocked by general aptitude as measured by a standard army battery. Instructor effects were controlled since a third of each instructor's trainees were in each condition. We induced in each instructor different levels of expectancy with regard to different trainees' "command potential." Trainees' learning performance, attitudes, and their perceptions of instructor leadership were measured at the end of the course.

Subjects

The sample included 105 soldiers, all men, in a combat command course in the Israeli Defense Forces. They were selected into the course on the basis of ability and motivation, and all had at least 11 years of schooling. Instructors were four experienced training officers. Each commanded a group of about 30 trainees. The instructors were subordinate to a course commander who reported to the base commander. This intensive course involved an average of 16 hours of instructor–trainee contact daily for 15 weeks.

Measures

Learning performance in four content areas was measured objectively by paper-and-pencil multiple-choice examinations and by performance tests administered by a commander who was not the trainee's instructor and was uninformed of the experiment. The tests assessed theoretical knowledge of combat tactics, topography, standard operating procedures, and such practical skills as navigation and accuracy of weapon firing. These subjects were taught throughout the course, and grades were summarized at the end of the course. Scores on the four examinations tended to be strongly correlated. The correlations ranged between .52 and .82, and averaged .68. Therefore, the four examination scores were averaged to form a single overall measure of performance (Cronbach's coefficient $\alpha = .89$).

The *attitudinal* effects of expectancy induction were assessed by three items concerning how much the trainee desired to go on to the next course, the extent to which he would recommend the course to his friends, and overall satisfaction with the course ($\alpha = .84$).

Instructor leadership as perceived by the trainees was measured by 10 of the original 13 5-point Likert-type questionnaire items developed by Bowers and Seashore (1966) to assess four factors of leadership. These items had been translated into Hebrew in previous research (Eden & Leviatan, 1975). The four factors are Support, Goal Emphasis, Work Facilitation, and Interaction Facilitation. In addition, nine other items were included in an attempt to capture specific leadership behaviors that might be aroused in the instructors by the induction of high expectations and that in turn might facilitate trainee performance. These items asked the trainee to rate the extent to which his instructor encouraged successful performance, kept his promises, praised good work, showed expertise in the material taught, explained the material in a clear and interesting manner, overcame disciplinary problems without difficulty, aroused trust, and displayed trust and confidence in the trainee. An attempt to construct scales of the Bowers and Seashore leadership factors was unsuccessful, since not all of the original items had been used, the internal consistency reliability coefficients were substantially lower than those reported by Taylor and Bowers (1972), and the correlations among the factors were of a magnitude similar to their reliabilities, indicating low discriminant validity. The mean interitem correlation was .41. A factor analysis of all 19 items yielded three factors. However, the rotated loadings revealed that many of the items loaded high on more than one factor. Furthermore, the first factor accounted for 82% of the variance in the items accounted for by the factors. To avoid the redundancy of analyzing the individual items in light of their high shared variance, we combined the responses to all 19 leadership items into a single reliable measure (α = .93). Caution is urged in the interpretation of the results obtained with this measure. Whereas the measure may reflect actual leadership behavior on the part of the instructor, it may be only an indicator of nonveridical trainee *perceptions* of the instructors' behavior. This does not trivialize the measure; Stayrook, Corno, and Winne (1978) found that student perceptions of teacher behavior influenced achievement beyond observed objective teacher behavior. The fact that the items were all highly intercorrelated blurs the conceptual meaning of the scale and might mean that it merely measures trainee *satisfaction* with instructor. Whether the leadership scale measures actual or perceived leadership, or only satisfaction with same, we regard it as an indirect indication of differential treatment of trainees by instructors resulting from the expectancy induction.

Although the construction of multiple-item measures reduced the number of dependent variables to only three, correlation between dependent variables can still be a concern. Indeed, across all 105 trainees performance correlated .79 with attitudes, and .53 with leadership; leadership and attitudes correlated .55. However, these correlations reflect the impact of the expectancy manipulation on the dependent variables and should be regarded as spuriously high. Computed separately within each of the three expectancy conditions, the respective correlations were .20, .22, and .25 for high expectancy trainees; .43, .36, and .27 for the unknowns; and .34, .10, and .22 for the regulars. Thus, though not totally unassociated, the dependent variables are not so highly correlated as to preclude analyzing them separately.

Expectancy Induction

Four days before the trainees arrived at the training base, prior to any acquaintance between instructors and trainees, we induced differential expectations by assembling the instructors[1] and telling them the following (mis)information:

> The army is undertaking a large-scale project to evaluate training methods. We will be studying this course and collecting information of various types. We have accumulated considerable data on the trainees, including psychological test scores, sociometric data from the previous course, and ratings by previous commanders. Based on this information we have predicted the command potential (CP) of each soldier. Experience with other classes has shown that course grades predict trainee CP in 95% of the cases. On the basis of these data we have classified your trainees into 3 groups: high, regular, and unknown CP, the latter due to insufficient information. These three CP groups were divided equally among the four classes. Here is a list of your trainees indicating their CP. You will copy each trainee's CP into his personal record. You are requested to learn your trainees' names and their predicted CP by the beginning of the course. Please copy the names and predictions into the records now. Any questions?

The unknown category was used for two reasons. First, we wanted to investigate an undefined category to see how the instructors would react to it. Previous Pygmalion research has used two categories. We assumed that the high trainees would be regarded as higher than the regulars and that the unknowns would be regarded as intermediate. Second, we aimed to increase our credibility by "admitting" that we did not know how to classify every trainee. The induction was convincing and self-renewing every time the instructor opened the record. To ascertain whether the induction "took," instructors rated their trainees' CP on a 9-point scale 1 week after the course began. The induction did influence mean CP ratings as intended (6.83, 5.31, and 4.29 for high, unknown, and regular CP induction, respectively, $F(2, 102) = 25.03$, $p < .01$).

We took the following steps to ensure ethical treatment of our subjects: (a) We consulted with other psychologists familiar with this situation. (b) The course commander, who was informed of the experiment, got true data about all trainees. (c) We secured the base commander's commitment to interview personally every

---

[1]Actually each group of trainees was commanded by an instructor and an assistant instructor, both of whom were officers. The expectancies of all eight (four instructors and four assistants) were manipulated in the same manner in this session. Each trainee subsequently assessed the leadership behaviors of both his instructor and his assistant instructor. Since the results were very similar for both, to save space we present the data for the four instructors' leadership only.

soldier who failed the course at any stage and to investigate the circumstances with the course commander and class instructor in order to ascertain that the failure in no way resulted from the expectancy induction. (d) As an exception, the base commander agreed that grades and instructor evaluations in this course would not determine these trainees' admission to the next course for which they were slated. (e) We abstained from negative expectancy induction, for example, categorizing some trainees as having low CP, and used instead the weaker high, regular, and unknown categories. We compensated for this restricted range of the expectancy induction by strengthening its credibility. After the course we debriefed the instructors. The expectancy induction was so effective that it was difficult to convince the instructors that it had been random. To make the experiment a more enriching experience for them and for future trainees, we made them aware of the influence of their expectations on trainee achievements.

Results

To test the hypotheses, trainee performance, trainee attitudes, and instructor leadership were analyzed as dependent variables by comparing their means for each level of instructor expectancy. Table 1 shows these means. The mean levels of all three dependent variables significantly diminish from high to unknown to regular

TABLE 1 Effects of expectancy on performance, attitudes, and leadership.

| | Instructor expectancy | | | | |
Variable	High ($n = 36$)	Unknown ($n = 32$)	Regular ($n = 37$)	F	eta^2
Trainee performance					
M	79.98	72.43	65.18	132.04*	.73
SD	3.16	3.63	4.40		
Trainee attitudes					
M	4.55	3.76	3.11	101.57*	.66
SD	.43	.42	.44		
Instructor leadership					
M	3.97	3.57	3.23	19.76*	.28
SD	.41	.51	.57		

Note. Since all three overall *F* tests were significant, the Duncan procedure was used for the multiple-range test of the differences between all three possible pairs of means in each row. All pairs so tested differed significantly beyond the .01 level.
* p < .01.

expectancy. All three pairs of means tested in each row differ significantly beyond the .01 level using Duncan's multiple-range test. The eta^2 coefficients in the last column show that the differences are not only significant but also substantial. The expectancy induction explains 73% of the variance in performance, 66% in attitudes, and 28% in leadership.

Discussion

The results strongly support the hypotheses. Trainees whose instructors were led to expect more did indeed learn more. We produced the Pygmalion effect among *adult* trainees. The age barrier in Pygmalion research having thus been broken, further replication is now needed to determine whether or not the present results generalize to other settings and to other interpersonal relationships of interest to organizational psychologists. For example, we would predict that the performance of civilian production workers would improve if their immediate supervisors expected more of them.

Trainees of whom more was expected responded with more favorable attitudes toward the course. This attitudinal gap between the experimental groups implies that those trainees who fared well in the present course, due in large measure to high expectancy on the part of their instructors, are destined to begin the next course with more enthusiasm than their control comrades. Thus, the Pygmalion effect may constitute a self-perpetuating, as well as a self-fulfilling prophecy.

Boosting expectations among superiors evoked more positive perceptions of leadership behavior on the part of supposedly high-potential subordinates. If these reported perceptions reflect actual instructor behavior, then leadership may be a means by which superiors unwittingly fulfill their own prophecies. This finding implies a fresh view of leadership as a dependent variable. Lowin and Craig (1968) reported a laboratory experiment replicating Farris's (1966) survey results showing that subordinate performance influences superiors' leadership. They explained the effects of performance on leadership in terms of superiors' affective response to subordinate performance. The present experiment shows that superiors' *expectancy* regarding performance, rather than actual performance, may influence their leadership. Future research should investigate how affective and cognitive factors interact to shape a manager's leadership behavior, and how leadership behavior typically responds to variation in performance. At any rate, the Pygmalion paradigm is appropriate for researching the mutual effects of leadership and performance on each other, since it leaves both variables free to vary. Due to the conceptual ambiguity of the leadership scale used in the present experiment, future research should employ measures more unequivocally interpretable as indicators of superiors' leadership *behavior.*

Trainees in all three expectancy conditions were mixed together in each instructor's group. How could different trainees in the same group systematically perceive the same instructor differently? One possibility is that outside the classroom in private, one-on-one counseling sessions, each instructor treated different trainees differently, in accordance with his prior expectations. A second possibility is that instructors treated trainees differently in class sessions. Perhaps instructors naturally lavish more attention on students for whom they harbor more positive expectations. Thus, instructors, and probably other kinds of superiors as well, may be better leaders vis-à-vis some of their subordinates than others. In nonexperimental situations natural expectations probably favor subordinates known for high past performance, relegating ordinary subordinates to mediocre leadership. Viewed as a scarce resource, leadership may be suboptimally allocated due to interpersonal expectancy effects.

If experimentally induced expectations unwittingly influence managers to improve subordinate performance, what might awareness of expectations do? "Expectancy training" might give supervisors a means of consciously utilizing their anticipations by bringing them under rational control and of purposively molding their own behavior in ways that enhance their subordinates' performance. The practical application proposed is that the Pygmalion effect be deliberately harnessed to improve subordinate performance. The spontaneity born of unawareness may be an indispensable ingredient in the Pygmalion potion. But George Bernard Shaw's gentleman knew what he was doing. Perhaps there would be more ladies if more gentlemen tried earnestly to treat more Liza Doolittles as ladies. The sarcastic adage that managers get the subordinates they deserve might be restated more constructively in Pygmalion terms: Managers get the performance they expect.

References

Bowers, D. G., & Seashore, S. E. Predicting organizational effectiveness with a four-factor theory of leadership. *Administrative Science Quarterly*, 1966, *11*, 238–263.

Campbell, D. T., & Stanley, J. C. *Experimental and quasi-experimental designs for research.* Chicago: Rand McNally, 1966.

Dawson, J. E., Messé, L. A., & Phillips, J. L. Effect of instructor-leader behavior on student performance. *Journal of Applied Psychology*, 1972, *56*, 369–376.

Eden, D., & Leviatan, U. Implicit leadership theory as a determinant of the factor structure underlying supervisory behavior scales. *Journal of Applied Psychology*, 1975, *60*, 736–741.

Farris, G. F. *A causal analysis of scientific performance.* Unpublished doctoral dissertation, University of Michigan, 1966.

Fleishman, E. A., Harris, E. F., & Burtt, H. E. *Leadership and supervision in industry.* Columbus: Ohio State University Press, 1955.

Jones, R. A. *Self-fulfilling prophecies: Social, psychological, and physiological effects of expectancies.* Hillsdale, N.J.: Erlbaum, 1977.

José, J., & Cody, J. J. Teacher–pupil interaction as it relates to attempted changes in teacher expectancy of academic ability and achievement. *American Educational Research Journal,* 1971, *8,* 39–49.

Kester, S. W., & Letchworth, G. A. Communication of teacher expectations and their effects on achievement and attitudes of secondary school students. *Journal of Educational Research,* 1972, *66,* 51–55.

Lanzetta, J., & Hannah, T. Reinforcing behavior of naive trainers. *Journal of Personality and Social Psychology,* 1969, *11,* 245–252.

Livingston, J. S. Pygmalion in management. *Harvard Business Review,* 1969, *47,* 81–89.

Lowin, A., & Craig, J. R. The influence of level of performance on managerial style: An experimental object-lesson in the ambiguity of correlational data. *Organizational Behavior and Human Performance,* 1968, *3,* 440–458.

Meichenbaum, D. H., Bowers, K. S., & Ross, R. R. A behavioral analysis of teacher expectancy effect. *Journal of Personality and Social Psychology,* 1969, *13,* 306–316.

Rosenthal, R. A., & Jacobson, L. *Pygmalion in the classroom: Teacher expectation and pupils' intellectual development.* New York: Holt, Rinehart & Winston, 1968.

Rothbart, M., Dalfen, S., & Barrett, R. Effects of teacher's expectancy on student–teacher interaction. *Journal of Educational Psychology,* 1971, *62,* 49–54.

Rubovits, P. C., & Maehr, M. L. Pygmalion black and white. *Journal of Personality and Social Psychology,* 1973, *25,* 210–218.

Stayrook, N. G., Corno, L., & Winne, P. H. Path analysis relating student perceptions of teacher behavior to student achievement. *Journal of Teacher Education,* 1978, *29,* 51–56.

Taylor, J. C., & Bowers, D. G. *The survey of organizations: A machine scored standardized questionnaire instrument.* Ann Arbor, Mich: Institute for Social Research, 1972.

Weinstein, R. S., & Middlestadt, S. E. Student perceptions of teacher interactions with male high and low achievers. *Journal of Educational Psychology,* 1979, *71,* 421–431.

Zanna, M. P., Sheras, P. L., Cooper, J., & Shaw, C. Pygmalion and Galatea: The interactive effect of teacher and student expectancies. *Journal of Experimental Social Psychology,* 1975, *11,* 279–287.

Editor's Note

The second author conducted the manipulation and collected the data as part of his master's thesis at Tel Aviv University under the supervision of the first author. A briefer version of this report bearing the same title was presented at the meeting of the American Psychological Association, New York, September 1979. The Israel Institute of Business Research provided partial support for this study.

Requests for reprints should be sent to Dov Eden, Faculty of Management, Tel Aviv University, Ramat Aviv, Tel Aviv, 69978, Israel.

Discussion Questions for Article 2

Section 14: Applied Psychology

Name: _____

PID: _____

Date: __ __ / __ __ / __ __ (MM/DD/YY)

CRN: _____

Recitation Day/Time: _____

Honor Code Signature: _____

1. Briefly describe the Pygmalion effect.

2. Have you ever personally observed the Pygmalion effect in either the classroom or workplace? If so, please describe the occurrence.

3. Do you think that the results of this study would generalize to additional, non-military workplaces? If so, please provide an example.

4. Outline some of the flaws of previous research involving the Pygmalion effect.